MONASTIC WISDOM SERIES: NUMBER ONE

Thomas Merton

Cassian and the Fathers

Initiation into the Monastic Tradition

MONASTIC WISDOM SERIES

Patrick Hart, OCSO, General Editor

Advisory Board

Michael Casey, OCSO

Lawrence S. Cunningham

Bonnie Thurston

Terrence Kardong, OSB

Kathleen Norris

Miriam Pollard, OCSO

MONASTIC WISDOM SERIES: NUMBER ONE

Cassian and the Fathers
Initiation into the Monastic Tradition

by

Thomas Merton

Edited with an Introduction by
Patrick F. O'Connell

Foreword by
Patrick Hart, OCSO

Preface by
Columba Stewart, OSB

CISTERCIAN PUBLICATIONS
Kalamazoo, Michigan

for now
MW
271.0092
McC

Cistercian Publications
Editorial Offices
The Institute of Cistercian Studies
Western Michigan University
Kalamazoo, Michigan 49008-5415
cistpub@wmich.edu

*The work of Cistercian Publications is made possible in part by support from
Western Michigan University to The Institute of Cistercian Studies.*

Library of Congress Cataloging-in-Publication Data

Merton, Thomas, 1915–1968.
  Cassian and the Fathers : initiation into the monastic tradition /
by Thomas Merton ; edited with an introduction by Patrick F.
O'Connell ; foreword by Patrick Hart; preface by Columba Stewart.
    p. cm. — (Monastic wisdom series ; no. 1)
  Includes bibliographical references and index.
  ISBN-13: 978-0-87907-100-4 (alk. paper)
  ISBN-10: 0-87907-100-1 (alk. paper)
  ISBN-13: 978-0-87907-001-4 (pbk. : alk. paper)
  ISBN-10: 0-87907-001-3 (pbk. : alk. paper)
    1. Cassian, John, ca. 360–ca. 435. 2. Desert Fathers. 3. Monastic
and religious life—History—Early church, ca. 30–600. I. O'Connell,
Patrick F. II. Title. III. Series.

BR1720.C3M47 2005
271'.0092—dc22

2004026195

Printed in the United States of America

For
Patrick Hart, ocso
Abba and *Senior*
to the Worldwide Community
of Merton Scholars and Readers
with Respect, Gratitude and Love
on the Occasion
of his Golden Jubilee
of Monastic Profession
(1954–2004)

TABLE OF CONTENTS

FOREWORD

Thomas Merton's *Cassian and the Fathers* is a singularly appropriate volume with which to launch this new Monastic Wisdom Series, following on the heels of the "alliance" recently formed between Cistercian Publications of Western Michigan University at Kalamazoo, Michigan, and Liturgical Press of St. John's Abbey, Collegeville, Minnesota. It is especially fitting, of course, because John Cassian is universally recognized as one of the great sources of monastic wisdom for all ages.

As Master of Novices, Merton began giving conferences or weekly talks in the mid-fifties to the young monks at Gethsemani on Cassian and the other monastic fathers such as Pachomius and Evagrius, as well as Anthony, Basil, and the Gregorys. He would later take up the *Rule* of St. Benedict, which he considered a necessary preparation for the twelfth-century appearance and rapid expansion of the Cistercians and the subsequent reform efforts of Armand Jean le Bouthillier de Rancé of La Grande Trappe in the seventeenth century, which in some ways pointed back to Cassian and the desert tradition.

In the mid-sixties the U.S. Region of Cistercian Superiors began discussing the possibility of establishing Cistercian Publications as a source for ongoing renewal following Vatican Two with its emphasis on returning to the sources. The idea was to make available the important twelfth-century literature in accurate English translations, especially the writings of the Cistercian "evangelists": Bernard of Clairvaux, William of St.-Thierry, Aelred of Rievaulx, and Guerric of Igny. Not surprisingly, the Superiors of the U.S. Region looked to Thomas Merton as an ideal editor for the two series of books: Cistercian Fathers and the Cistercian Studies.

However, Merton had just recently (August 20, 1965) resigned as Novice Master at Gethsemani, having been given permission to live as a hermit on the property at Gethsemani. Since he was only beginning this experiment in solitude, his Abbot (James Fox) in view of his solitary aspirations felt strongly that this administrative work would be counter-productive, as did Merton himself.

At the same time Thomas Merton, or Father Louis as he was known in the monastic world, very generously offered Cistercian Publications a manuscript, *The Climate of Monastic Prayer,* which was to become Volume One in the Cistercian Studies Series. Later it would be published as *Contemplative Prayer,* and has continued to be a popular best-seller. This is another good reason to see Merton's earlier work on Cassian appear under such favorable conditions.

We are indebted to Patrick F. O'Connell, for taking on the enormous task of editing this important work to inaugurate the new Monastic Wisdom Series. With his background in historical theology, he is eminently qualified to update Merton's earlier bibliography on the more recent contemporary scholarship that has transpired during the past fifty years. His indispensable introduction situates *Cassian and the Fathers* very well in its historical context, and is essential reading for another Merton volume projected for this series, on Pre-Benedictine Monasticism, which is currently being prepared by O'Connell for publication.

Patrick Hart, ocso
Abbey of Gethsemani

PREFACE

In Thomas Merton a rare combination of skills came together in one monastic vocation. Merton possessed a deep awareness of the human aptitude for contemplation. He had a deep veneration for traditional wisdom. He had an insatiable curiosity and the knowledge of languages needed to pursue his interest. Merton's intellect, fired by his contemplative heart, led him much more deeply into monastic literature than is typical for a monk or nun, and particularly for one of his time and place. The tradition he presented in these conferences was most unfamiliar in the 1950s. The barrier had been language: the current of thought that ran from Hellenistic philosophy to Clement, Origen, and Evagrius Ponticus was Greek. John Cassian brought much of it into the Latin world, but understanding Cassian requires going back to his formation in Greek-speaking circles of late fourth-century Egyptian monasticism.

Thomas Merton discovered John Cassian early in his monastic life. In the novitiate he had been given Cassian's works as his book for Lenten reading. In the early 1950s he wrote, "Through Cassian I am getting back to everything." Merton's immersion in Cassian gave him the footing he needed to move back into Evagrius' thought and forward into later Byzantine mysticism, especially of the Hesychast movement and its Russian descendants. His study of Meister Eckhart, so fruitful for dialogue with the Zen Buddhist Roshi Suzuki, and his confidence in approaching Sufi mysticism surely came from his knowledge of the remarkable monastic mystical tradition brought by Cassian to Saint Benedict and Saint Gregory the Great.

In his pilgrimage to Cassian's Greek monastic sources, Merton was innovating. The Greek tradition had little direct

impact on the medieval monasticism that modern Benedictines
and Cistercians regarded as normative. Many key texts that had
been translated in the fourth and fifth centuries, particularly
those by Origen and Evagrius, had been lost during centuries of
misunderstanding and misinterpretation. The humanism that
reemphasized knowledge of Greek in the fifteenth century was
not principally a monastic movement, nor did it lead even among
monastic scholars to a revival of practical interest in the Greek
roots of Latin monasticism. Merton was, then, among the first
American Cistercians or Benedictines to connect his own monastic experience to the recovery and reappraisal of the eastern
tradition by European scholars such as the Jesuit Irénée Hausherr.
Hausherr and other contributors to the massive French *Dictionnaire de Spiritualité* and the series *Sources chrétiennes* made possible for western monks and nuns the *retour aux sources* that
would be the hallmark of Vatican II's call for the renewal of religious life. Merton had the prescience even before the Council to
reclaim the eastern tradition that, married with the genius of
Augustine, formed the great Latin mystics from Gregory the
Great onward. Merton knew that the work of John Cassian was
Latin monasticism's door into the Greek mystical tradition.
Cassian had adapted the theology of Evagrius Ponticus to the
needs of nascent Latin monasticism in southern Gaul of the early
fifth century. Both Cassian and Evagrius used Origen's thought
to articulate their experience of the asceticism and prayer they
had found among the Egyptian desert monks of the late fourth
century.

It is hard for us now to imagine how meager the resources
for the study of early monasticism would have been in a place
like the Gethsemani of the 1950s (or any Benedictine monastery
of the same period). Language was one obstacle; ignorance was
another. Teaching about prayer ("meditation") was influenced
more by Carmelites and Jesuits than by monastic sources. Cassian
was available in English only in an expurgated Victorian-era
translation. Jean Leclercq's now classic *The Love of Learning and
the Desire for God*, first published after Merton had already concluded the courses of lectures contained in this book, was revo-
lutionary in evoking a monastic spirituality shaped by Scripture,

the liturgy, and the Fathers and typified by regular *lectio divina* of fundamental texts. As beautiful as it was, Leclercq's portrait must have seemed far removed from the devotional piety and intellectualized meditation that had become the mainstay of preconciliar monastic practice. American Benedictines, mostly formed in communities established by Germans, were even less prepared than the more Francophone Cistercians for the dramatic revisioning of monastic spirituality wrought by the French and Italian scholars of the 1930s–50s.

In the first few conferences contained in this book, Merton presents a remarkable overview of the tradition and its modern expositors (who, often enough, were also its excavators). The later sections are less satisfying, consisting largely of summaries of Cassian's *Institutes* and some of the *Conferences*. By that point in the course, however, Merton's audiences should have begun their own dialogue with the texts. The fruit of Merton's initiative is evident in the series in which these lectures now appear. Would Cistercian Publications have happened without Merton? Probably not.

My first article was about John Cassian's teaching on unceasing prayer. At the time I had been reading a lot of Merton, and he had shaped much of my imaginative landscape of monasticism. I knew that Merton had taught his novices about Cassian, but his text had not been published. Even so, he was with me as I wrote about Cassian, and I concluded the article with a quotation from "Notes for a Philosophy of Solitude." I am delighted now for the opportunity we all have to learn even more from this great master of the monastic life.

Columba Stewart, OSB
Saint John's Abbey and University

INTRODUCTION

In October 1955 Thomas Merton (or Fr. Louis, as his monastic brothers knew him) was appointed master of novices at the Abbey of Gethsemani, replacing Fr. Walter Helmstetter, who had been elected abbot of Gethsemani's daughter house, Our Lady of the Genesee in upstate New York. In one way Merton was a logical choice for the office, having already served since 1951 as master of scholastics, in charge of the training of newly professed monks. But there was an element of unexpectedness and perhaps even of risk in his volunteering to take on the position, as well as in his abbot's acceptance of the offer, for Merton had been going through a recurring "vocation crisis" since the late 1940s, periodically seeking to transfer to an order, such as the Carthusians or Camaldolese, that would satisfy his longing for greater solitude.[1]

Immediately before this new development, a tentative compromise solution had been worked out between Merton and Abbot James Fox, and approved by the Cistercian Abbot General, Dom Gabriel Sortais, whereby Merton would continue as a Cistercian, but live a more solitary life as a fire watcher atop a tower a few miles from the abbey. Instead, Merton decided, as he put it to Dom Gabriel, "to reimmerse myself completely in the true spirit of my vocation"[2] by taking responsibility for the

1. See Michael Mott, *The Seven Mountains of Thomas Merton* (Boston: Houghton Mifflin, 1984), 270 ff. for a detailed treatment of the events surrounding Merton's appointment as novice master.

2. Thomas Merton, *The School of Charity: Letters on Religious Renewal and Spiritual Direction*, ed. Patrick Hart, ocso (New York: Farrar, Straus, Giroux, 1990), 93.

formation of the young men just beginning their monastic life.[3] While his restlessness did not disappear, Merton continued in this demanding position for almost a full decade before leaving in August 1965 for the hermitage where he would spend the final three years of his life.

One of the significant dimensions of this "reimmersion" in the spirit of his vocation was the preparation and presentation of conferences for the novices on monastic life and history. In becoming novice master, Merton pledged to represent fairly and fully the authentic Cistercian tradition, not an idiosyncratic personal vision. As he wrote to Dom Gabriel, "I have made a vow . . . not to say anything to the novices that would diminish their respect for the Cistercian cenobitic life and orientate them towards something else."[4] Yet it would be reductive and unfair to Merton to suppose that for ten years he simply mouthed a "party line" about the meaning and purpose of monasticism that he himself did not believe in. The novitiate conferences published in this volume and in subsequent volumes of this series provide insight into Merton's own deep love for and commitment to monastic tradition, at the very time when he was working to bring that tradition into a fruitful encounter and engagement with contemporary society and culture.[5] In introduc-

3. According to Mott, Dom James considered this "a major failure of nerve on Merton's part" (287), though as Mott himself points out, there was both the practical problem of Merton, a notorious non-driver, getting back and forth between fire tower and monastery, as well as the spiritual problem that Merton was not yet prepared for this kind of independent living arrangement. Merton himself evaluates his decision and its results some four months after becoming novice master in a letter to Dom Jean Leclercq: "My new life as master of novices progresses from day to day. It is an unfamiliar existence to which I often have difficulty in adapting myself. I sometimes feel overcome with sheer horror at having to talk so much and appear before others as an example. I believe that God is testing the quality of my desire for solitude, in which perhaps there was an element of escape from responsibility. But nevertheless the desire remains the same, the conflict is there, but there is nothing I can do but ignore it and press forward to accomplish what is evidently the will of God" (*School of Charity*, 95).

4. *School of Charity*, 93.

5. For an insightful discussion of Merton's integration of monastic tradition and contemporary culture, see Thomas Del Prete, "Culture and the Formation of Personal Identity: Dilemma and Dialectic in Thomas Merton's Teaching," *The Merton Annual*, 8 (1995), 105–21.

ing his subject Merton himself emphasizes this interaction of past and present: "Besides *renewal* of our own tradition we must of course obviously *adapt* ourselves to the needs of our time, and a return to tradition does not mean trying to revive, in all its details, the life lived by the early monks, or trying to do all the things that they did. But it means living in our time and solving the problems of our time in the way and with the spirit in which they lived in a different time and solved different problems" (6). These conference notes allow us to see what Thomas Merton considered the essential foundation of a balanced and healthy monastic life—for the young men entrusted to his care, and for himself as well.

In a letter to a Brazilian monk, written some ten months after he had left the novitiate for the hermitage, Merton outlined the course of studies as it had developed during his tenure as master: "During the novitiate, courses were given on the vows, on Cassian, on Monastic History, on Cistercian Fathers and history, on ascetic theology, Scripture and the Monastic Fathers, Liturgy, chant. All this was spread over two years."[6] Except for the training in chant, Merton taught all these courses himself for much of his tenure,[7] eventually turning over the scripture courses to a monk trained in the field.[8] While the pattern changed somewhat over the years, the conferences were generally given four times a week during a half-hour period before the mid-day office. (This does not include a further series of Sunday conferences on books of scripture or the lectionary readings of the day.[9])

6. To Dom Inácio Accioly, OSB, June 13, 1966 (*School of Charity*, 305).

7. Merton also added conferences on modern literature to the program in the final two years of his tenure: "For my own part I also at the end of my period as novice master gave some talks on literature, especially the poetry of Eliot, Rilke, and other modern poets, to novices and to all those in the monastic formation program" (*School of Charity*, 305).

8. See *School of Charity*, 185.

9. In "'The Great Honesty': Remembering Thomas Merton—An Interview with Abbot Timothy Kelly, O.C.S.O.," conducted by George A. Kilcourse, Jr., *The Merton Annual*, 9 (1996), Father Timothy mentions that scripture scholar Barnabas Ahern also came to Gethsemani to give scripture conferences once a month, and relates how this led to a temporary halt to Merton's own lectures on the Bible: "The next Sunday, Merton was giving the novices and juniors a conference based on the Scripture reading for the night office; we were reading the book of Jonah at the time. He waxed very eloquently in a poetic way about

Two or three series of conferences on different topics would typically be running concurrently over a period of months, generally (though with some flexibility) attached to particular days of the week. For example, in mid-1962, while Merton was giving conferences on Cassian on Saturdays, he was also lecturing twice a week on the meaning of the monastic vows and one other day on early Fathers of the Church.[10]

The Cistercian novitiate lasted for approximately two years, so the conferences were generally repeated, as Merton notes, according to a two-year cycle, but since there was no common time for beginning the novitiate, individual novices simply joined, and left, the ongoing sequence of the conferences at whatever points coincided with their own entry into the novitiate and profession of first vows.[11] The potential awkwardness of this arrangement was reduced by the orientation of the conferences, which was predominantly practical rather than academic. Brother Paul Quenon notes:

> Father Louis was in pursuit of wisdom. His teaching was not a matter of imparting knowledge, but was aimed at the formation of the whole person, a mature monk. Thus, it did not have an academic style, but was basically monastic and sapiential. Wisdom, *sapientia* in Latin, has the same root as 'to taste,' *sapere*. The purpose of education is to get a taste for truth and to taste it continuously, which in fact is meditation. . . . Understanding in this case is

---

Jonah, who was a very special person in his own life. It is in *The Sign of Jonas* (1953) in 'The Firewatch' he talks about Jonah and the mercy upon mercy that is our gift. One novice kept raising his hand, and finally he acknowledged him. He said, 'Fr. Barnabas said Jonah's nothing but midrash.' And with that, Merton closed his books, and he walked out and for a year or so never gave another Scripture conference" (198). He tells the same story to Gloria Kitto Lewis in "Learning to Live: Merton's Students Remember His Teaching," *The Merton Annual*, 8 (1995), adding "this guy raised his hand all the time and said that this professor had characterized Jonah completely differently, which, of course, was a poor understanding of what the professor had said and what Merton had said" (96).

10. This information is based on an examination of audiotapes of Merton's conferences, which began to be recorded in April 1962.

11. This information is based on interviews with Abbot Timothy Kelly, ocso, Brother Paul Quenon, ocso and Brother Harold Thibodeau, ocso.

mainly through experience. Father Louis kept this goal in mind: to start with the Word of God and go on to understanding it through experience. Ultimately, the goal is something only God can impart, and formal education is only the beginning.[12]

While packed with factual and interpretive material, the conferences' focus was on formation rather than information. Their purpose was not to have the novices master a body of knowledge but to immerse them in a tradition, to allow them to become acclimated to a way of life that reached back in a continuous line to the early centuries of the Church.[13] Abbot Timothy Kelly notes that Merton was instrumental in developing a formation program that was specifically monastic and Cistercian rather than generic or oriented more toward active orders such as the Jesuits.[14] Abbot John Eudes Bamberger, who studied under Merton as a scholastic, notes, "Those of us who sat in his conferences and classes, discussed spiritual matters with him and shared in the same community life were helped to

12. Quoted in Lewis, "Learning to Live," 91.

13. While the novices do not recall having to take examinations or write papers (personal interviews; see also Lewis, "Learning to Live," 92), apparently Merton did experiment with both at some point. Undated notes in the typescript of Merton's Cassian conferences include mention of "Exam—end June— on Cassian *Instituta* / constitutions / Term paper—consuetudines" ("Lectures on Cassian," 31v) and "Exam—Conf. 1,2,9,10" ("Lectures on Cassian," 67v).

14. Personal interview; see also Timothy Kelly, "Epilogue: A Memoir," in Brother Patrick Hart, ed., *The Legacy of Thomas Merton*, CS 92 (Kalamazoo, MI: Cistercian Publications, 1986), 223: "His instructions to the novices were based on the monastic tradition, much of which he was making available in English for the first time. His approach to the ascetic discipline of Trappist tradition created a new climate within the community with some ramifications throughout the Order." A similar point is made by John Eudes Bamberger, OCSO, in "Monasticism and Thomas Merton, Monk-Priest and Author: His Contributions to a Wider Understanding of Spirituality," *The Merton Annual*, 12 (1999): "Today monastic formation in our monasteries regularly includes conferences on major monastic writers such as Cassian, St Basil, Evagrius and the desert fathers. . . . While a variety of influences have been responsible for such interests, the fact remains that Merton regularly lectured on these authors at a time when only a few monks of our Order studied them for their spiritual contributions and their theological thought. His genuine involvement with their ideas and experiences was evident and contagious and acted as a stimulus for cultivating a personal interest in them" (26–27).

get a view of what is best in monastic culture and encouraged to assimilate it without denying what was valid in our experience of the world we were formed in."[15] Merton's primary concern for the contemporary pertinence of the material and its application to the lives of his novices is already evident in his carefully prepared notes, which were usually multigraphed for distribution to the novices, and even more so in the tapes of the actual conferences that were recorded in the later years of Merton's tenure (1962–1965).

* * * * * * *

Merton first gave the series of conferences on John Cassian immediately after becoming novice master. In a December 3, 1955 letter to his friend the Benedictine scholar Jean Leclercq, announcing his appointment as master of novices, he comments, "Meanwhile for my part I am happily lecturing on Cassian. What could be better material in my situation? Although I cannot live like Abbot Isaac, Nesteros, or Piamon, I feel that they are my fathers and my friends."[16] The choice of topic was a particularly appropriate one, especially for those just beginning monastic life, as Cassian is a seminal figure in the development and spread of monasticism. His writings served as a crucial bridge between the primitive monasticism of Egypt and the Christian East, where he was trained, and the first phase of monastic life in Europe, where he settled in the early years of the fifth century. He was a fundamental influence on St. Benedict and his *Rule*, and on the subsequent development of the Benedictine tradition up to and including the Cistercian reform of the twelfth century. He was deeply interested in proper monastic formation, as witnessed by his first work, the *Instituta* (*Institutes*), but he was also one of

15. Bamberger, "Monasticism and Thomas Merton," 25.

16. *School of Charity*, 94; see also letters of February 11, 1956 to Mark Van Doren (Thomas Merton, *The Road to Joy: Letters to New and Old Friends*, ed. Robert E. Daggy [New York: Farrar, Straus, Giroux, 1989], 28); April 10, 1956 to Jacques Maritain (Thomas Merton, *The Courage for Truth: Letters to Writers*, ed. Christine M. Bochen [New York: Farrar, Straus, Giroux, 1993], 27); and August 19, 1956 to Father Charles Dumont (*School of Charity*, 96), in all of which Merton mentions lecturing on Cassian.

the great early masters of prayer and contemplation, the focus of his most important work, the *Collationes* (*Conferences*).

Merton himself was an enthusiastic reader of Cassian from his earliest days in the monastery, as he notes in a 1965 letter to Nora Chadwick: "Certainly I agree with you about Cassian. Ever since I had him as a Lenten book in the novitiate, I have kept close to him, and of course use him constantly in the novitiate."[17] In his journal for March 3, 1953, he wrote: "Through Cassian I am getting back to everything, or rather, getting for the first time to monastic and Christian values I had dared to write about without knowing them."[18] At one point he was planning to write a book on Cassian[19] (presumably to be based at least in part on his novitiate notes), one of many projects that never reached fruition, but his interest in Cassian continued beyond his time as novice master: his brief work *The Climate of Monastic Prayer* (also published as *Contemplative Prayer*), which appeared shortly after his death, includes significant references to Cassian,[20] who

17. *School of Charity*, 283.

18. Thomas Merton, *A Search for Solitude: Pursuing the Monk's True Life—Journals, vol. 3: 1952–1960*, ed. Lawrence S. Cunningham (San Francisco: HarperCollins, 1996), 38 (see also 29).

19. See Thomas Merton, *Turning toward the World: The Pivotal Years—Journals, vol. 4: 1960–1963*, ed. Victor A. Kramer (San Francisco: HarperCollins, 1996), entry for March 2, 1962: "Question—more or less abstract—whether to write book on Cassian for the Benedictine Studies. Probably not, or not now. Too many people coming around, and what time I have is better spent alone in meditation" (207); entry for September 15, 1962: "The writing to be done . . . . Certainly the Cassian book—I will write it soon to please the Benedictines" (247).

20. See for example Thomas Merton, *The Climate of Monastic Prayer* (Washington, DC: Cistercian Publications, 1969), 67; *Contemplative Prayer* (New York: Herder & Herder, 1969), 57: "According to John Cassian, liturgical prayer bursts forth in a wordless and ineffable elevation of the mind and heart which he calls 'fiery prayer'—*oratio ignita*. Here the 'mind is illumined by the infusion of heavenly light, not making use of any human forms of speech but with all the powers gathered together in unity it pours itself forth copiously and cries out to God in a manner beyond expression, saying so much in a brief moment that the mind cannot relate it afterwards with ease or even go over it again after returning to itself.' Yet it is interesting that this is the conclusion of Cassian's commentary on the *Pater Noster*. 'Fiery prayer' is just the normal fruition that burst forth, by the grace of God, when vocal prayer is well made. 'The Lord's Prayer (says Cassian in the same chapter) leads all who practice it well to that higher state and brings them at last to the prayer of fire (*ignita oratio*) which is known and experienced by few and which is an inexpressibly high degree of prayer.'"

was also the subject of one of the weekly talks he gave to the community on Sunday afternoons during the hermitage years.[21] Cassian even makes a brief but important appearance in "Marxism and Monastic Perspectives," the talk he gave in Bangkok on the final day of his life.[22]

It may initially seem surprising that Merton gives a more thorough treatment in his notes to the less lofty, more pedestrian *Institutes* than to Cassian's masterpiece of the contemplative life, the *Conferences*. But this is explicable in terms of his audience. The material in the *Institutes* is both more readily accessible and more immediately suited to the training of novice monks than the teachings attributed to the great Egyptian hermits in the *Conferences*. But Merton, like Cassian himself, makes clear that even the most basic elements of training in ascetical practice and community formation are always oriented toward the goal of union with God. The Cassian material is actually composed of three sections roughly equal in length: a biographical survey of Cassian's life and writings, which incorporates brief overviews of a number of the *Conferences* that will not be treated in detail later; an extensive discussion of each of the twelve books of the *Institutes*, the first four on monastic formation and customs and the final eight on the eight principal vices; and an in-depth look at selected books of the *Conferences* (originally Books 1–2 and 9–10, with Books 4 and 16 added later).

While the lectures as first given focused exclusively on Cassian, they were later expanded (probably in 1959–60) to include a lengthy "Prologue to Cassian," at which point the series was given the title *Cassian and the Fathers*. The "Fathers" of this title

21. See Thomas Merton, *The Other Side of the Mountain: The End of the Journey —Journals, vol. 7: 1967–1968*, ed. Patrick Hart, ocso (San Francisco: Harper-Collins, 1998), 76 (April 6, 1968): "I came back to the hermitage, prepared a conference for the novices on Cassian and went down to give it."

22. Thomas Merton, *The Asian Journal*, ed. Naomi Burton Stone, Patrick Hart, ocso and James Laughlin (New York: New Directions, 1973), 340: "What is essential in the monastic life is not embedded in buildings, is not embedded in clothing, is not necessarily embedded even in a rule. It is somewhere along the line of something deeper than a rule. It is concerned with this business of total inner transformation. All other things serve that end. I am just saying, in other words, what Cassian said in the first lecture on *puritas cordis*, purity of heart, that every monastic observance tends toward that."

could be taken to refer both to the Church Fathers in general, since this prefatory material includes discussions of the Apostolic Fathers, the Alexandrians Clement and Origen, and the Cappadocians, and to the Desert Fathers of monasticism in particular, since they receive particular attention as forerunners of Cassian. The purpose for adding this material was to provide a context for situating Cassian as part of a developing ascetical and contemplative tradition. In the opening words of this "Prologue," Merton states, "It would be useless to study Cassian without some background. We have to know where he fits in to the history and development of Christian spirituality" (5). The principle of selection is based mainly (though not rigorously) on relevance to monastic life, both in the choice of figures to be discussed and in areas of focus on these figures. Thus Merton gives strong emphasis to the theme of virginity in the early Fathers, to Jerome's ascetical teaching, to Basil as monastic legislator and Gregory of Nyssa as spiritual guide, and to important monastic figures like the Pseudo-Macarius and Evagrius Ponticus, as well as the Desert Father tradition in general. Taken together, the two parts of the series provide a fairly thorough survey of the development of monasticism before the advent of Benedict (though it was replaced by a different set of lectures on *Pre-Benedictine Monasticism* in his final years as novice master).

* * * * * * *

Much of the value and interest of *Cassian and the Fathers*, as of the novitiate conferences in general, lies in the light it casts on Merton himself as teacher, novice master and monk. These notes provide a privileged standpoint for observing Merton functioning as an integral and important member of his monastic community. It is quite evident from the text that Merton took his duties as instructor of the young men in his charge very seriously. Merton's former novices recall him as an excellent teacher. According to Abbot Timothy Kelly, "As a teacher, he was always well prepared, a capable person, well organized. He knew exactly where he was going and how he was going to get there. . . . As novices we had to learn a certain amount of nuts and bolts and some specifics relative to the obligations for vows. He was very exacting in those areas, very precise. Yet, he could make the dry text come alive. He taught with a lot of respect—always."[23] Despite his various publishing projects and numerous other interests, he obviously invested considerable time and energy in preparing these classes; nor is there any evidence that he resented the demands made by this work—quite the contrary. Although the conferences themselves, as the tapes make clear, often have a tone of breezy informality, there is nothing superficial about Merton's preparation. While the lectures are certainly not intended as original scholarship, they do attest to the depth of Merton's own exploration of the material he is presenting. More than seventy-five major and minor sources can be traced for this one set of lectures. While he sometimes follows a single source quite closely, he typically synthesizes a wide variety of primary and secondary materials, and continues to incorporate new information in the successive recensions of his text.

For the Cassian section, he relies extensively for biographical details on Owen Chadwick's *John Cassian: A Study of Primitive Monasticism* (even though his endorsement of this volume in the text itself is somewhat restrained[24]). But his discussions of the *Institutes* and the *Conferences* themselves consist mainly of his own summaries and analyses. Moreover, though he occasionally quotes from existing translations, his primary dependence is directly on the original Latin texts, which he sometimes translates in the conferences themselves, but often leaves in the original (presumably to be translated as the occasion arises during the actual delivery of the lectures). This use of the Latin text is confirmed by the extensive marginal markings and underlinings in the Cassian volume of the *Patrologia Latina* that he used.[25]

---

23. Quoted in Lewis, "Learning to Live," 91–92.

24. He calls it "a fairly good book," noting also that Chadwick is not Catholic (7).

25. J. P. Migne, ed., *Patrologiae Cursus Completus, Series Latina*, 221 vols. (Paris: Garnier, 1844–1865), vol. 49. Merton's copy, now at the Thomas Merton Center at Bellarmine University, Louisville, KY, includes markings of *Instituta*: *Prefatio*; I:3,4,5,6,7,8,10; II:2,3,4,5,6,7,8,9,10,11,12,13,14,15,16,17; III:3; IV:6,7,8,12, 14,39; VII:7,14; VIII:11,17; IX:1,2,4,5,7,9,10,11,12; XI:2,3,6,7,8,9,10,11,13,14,15, 16,17,18; XII:15,31,32,33; *Collationes: Prefatio*; I:1,2,4,5,6,7,8,10,13,14,15,17,18,

Merton's sources for the "Prologue to Cassian" section are more varied, as one would expect given the range of material treated, but he does rely extensively on two sources that he mentions at the outset: the first volume of Pierre Pourrat's standard history of spirituality[26] provides a good deal of summary information and is also the source for a number of quotations from primary sources; even more important for Merton are the notes written by Fr. Francis Mahieu, the former novice master of the Cistercian Abbey of Scourmont (Chimay) in Belgium,[27] which serve both as a model for organization and as a source for material throughout the first part of the volume. But as with the

19,20,23; II:1,2,4,5,6,7,8,9,10,11,13,15,16; III:3,4,5,6,7,10; IV:1,2,3,4,5,6,7,8,9,10, 11,12,13,18,19,20,21; V:2,3,4; IX:2,3,4,5,6,14,15,18,19,21,22,23,25,26,27,29,30,31,32, 34,35,36; X:6,10,11,13, 14; XI:5,6,7,8,9,10,12; XIV:1,3,4,7,9,10; XVI:2,3,5,6,7,8,9,10, 11,12,14,15,16,17,18,19,22,24,26,27; XVIII:1,4,6,7; XX:8; XXI:12,22; XXIII:1,2,3,4,5, 7,8,10,12,13,18,21; XXIV:2,3,4,6,8,26. It should be noted that Merton does not use the more recent critical edition of Cassian in the *Corpus Scriptorum Ecclesiasticorum Latinorum* series, edited by Michael Petschenig: *Iohannis Cassiani Conlationes XXIIII, CSEL* 13 (Vienna: Geroldi, 1886); *Iohannis Cassiani De Institutis Cenobiorum et De Octo Principalium Vitiorum Remediis Libri XII, CSEL* 17 (Vienna: Tempsky, 1888).

26. Pierre Pourrat, *Christian Spirituality, vol. I: From the Time of our Lord till the Dawn of the Middle Ages*, trans. W. H. Mitchell and S. P. Jacques (1927; Westminster, MD: Newman, 1953).

27. Fr. François Mahieu, ocso, "A History of Spirituality," translated at Gethsemani, February 1956, 124 pp. [typed, single spaced, mimeographed]. Merton would cross paths with Fr. Mahieu again at the very end of his life. In July 1955 Fr. Mahieu arrived in India, where he was closely associated with Fr. Jules Monchanin, Fr. Henri Le Saux and Fr. Bede Griffiths in creating a form of Christian monastic life suited to India, and became known as Fr. Francis Acharya. He was principally responsible for the foundation of the Kurisumala Ashram, which was begun in early 1958 in the Syro-Malankara Diocese of Tiruvalla and was incorporated into the Cistercian Order in July 1998. (For details see Francis Mahieu, ocso, "Forty Years at Kurisumala Ashram," *Tjurunga*, 55 [1998], 91–97, and David Tomlins, ocso, "Homily for the Incorporation of Kurisumala Ashram," *Tjurunga*, 55 [1998], 98–101; also Dom Francis Acharya, ocso, *Kurisumala Ashram: A Cistercian Abbey in India* [Kattayam Dist.: Kurisumala Ashram, 1999].) Fr. Mahieu was present at the 1968 Bangkok conference, and was one of the six Cistercian signatories of the letter sent on December 11, 1968 to Abbot Flavian Burns of Gethsemani explaining the circumstances of Merton's death (*Asian Journal*, Appendix VIII, 344–47). A photograph of Fr. Mahieu standing next to Thomas Merton at one of the conference sessions is included in *The Seven Mountains of Thomas Merton*. Particular thanks are due to Brother Harold Thibodeau, ocso of Gethsemani for providing details of his own visit to Fr. Mahieu's ashram, and for locating the articles cited above.

Cassian material, when Merton moves from summarizing to a more detailed examination of a particular text, as he does with Athanasius' *Life of Anthony*, or Jerome's Latin version of the *Rule* of Pachomius, or the *De Oratione* of Evagrius, he goes directly to the primary source (whether in English translation, as with Athanasius,[28] or in Latin and French versions,[29] as with the other two). Merton also relies on his own work as a resource in this section, quoting and referring extensively to his selection of translations from the Desert Fathers, first published in a limited edition as *What Ought I to Do?*[30] and later to appear in an augmented version as *The Wisdom of the Desert*.[31]

It is quite apparent that the conferences are teaching notes, and must be read and evaluated as such, not as a finished literary product. The text is not without errors, as when he confuses one St. Nilus with another (90), or mistakenly writes Wilhelm Bousset's name as Bossuet (and then calls attention to the mistake by distinguishing him from the seventeenth-century bishop of that name) (89); these are generally not of major significance, but would presumably have been caught and corrected had the text been prepared for publication. At times the text is less than perfectly proportioned, as in the earliest pages, in which long quotations are not balanced by extensive commentary (7–16), or in the section on the Cappadocian Fathers, when a rather perfunctory treatment of Gregory Nazianzen is followed by a much more detailed consideration of Gregory of Nyssa, in whom Merton is obviously more interested, and whom he finds more relevant to monastic life (51–60); similarly, the rather bald summaries of the principal Syrian monastic figures, culled from Pourrat (69–71), are followed by a richly detailed consideration of the Egyptian hermits (71–80). There are also some awkward

28. *Life of St. Anthony*, trans. Sr. Mary Emily Keenan, scn, in *Early Christian Biographies*, ed. Roy J. Deferrari, The Fathers of the Church, vol. 15 (New York: Fathers of the Church, 1952), 125–216.

29. *PL* 23, cols. 65-92; Irenée Hausherr, "Le *Traité de l'oraison* d'Evagre le Pontique (Pseudo Nil)," *Revue d'Ascétique et de Mystique*, 15 (1934), 36–93, 113–70.

30. *What Ought I to Do?: Sayings of the Desert Fathers*, translated by Thomas Merton (Lexington, KY: Stamperia del Santuccio, 1959).

31. *The Wisdom of the Desert: Sayings from the Desert Fathers of the Fourth Century*, translated by Thomas Merton (New York: New Directions, 1960).

sections, as when Merton discovers, at some point after the pertinent material had already been written, that none of the works traditionally attributed to Macarius the Great was actually composed by this Egyptian hermit, and has to revise his discussion, which in consequence no longer fits its context as aptly as originally planned (81–88). There is also some repetition, as background material on early monasticism that formed part of the original Cassian lectures (108–109) is also found, in greater detail, in the "Prologue to Cassian" section (60 ff.).

This duplication highlights the fact that the conferences are a work in progress: not only do the "Lectures on Cassian" acquire a prologue half their own length, but the text is filled with literally hundreds of additions, many of them extensive, as well as occasional deletions and alterations. Merton was never content simply to repeat the lectures as they had been given during the previous cycle, even though he has a completely different audience. As already mentioned, at one point he incorporates lengthy discussions of two of Cassian's *Conferences* not previously considered (nn. 4 and 16; there are also fragmentary notes begun on *Conference* 14, which were never completed and presumably never used). While the addition of new blocs of text is relatively infrequent, practically every page of the original typescript includes additional handwritten material, as Merton continued to reflect on his subject and to do further reading about it. The successive versions of the text certainly provide evidence of his sense of responsibility as a teacher, both in keeping the material fresh for his students and in keeping himself abreast of recent developments in the field.

Merton's role as teacher is of course one dimension of his role as novice master, so that the conferences, as previously stated, have a focus that is more practical and experiential than detached and academic. Merton repeatedly looks for ways to engage his listeners with the material. Sometimes (especially when connections may otherwise seem rather remote) the approach is as basic as highlighting a picturesque detail, as when he tells the story of Anthony being beaten so severely by demons that he is thought to be dead and brought back to the church for burial, only to regain consciousness at midnight and head back to his retreat (33); or when he notes that in Pachomian monasticism even tweezers for extracting thorns from bare feet are held in common, and kept hanging conveniently by a library window (41); or when he includes among the miracles of St. Hilarion the cure of "a mad camel tied and dragged *magnis clamoribus* by thirty men!" (62).

He repeatedly applies the lessons of the past to present conditions, emphasizing the ways in which figures from the tradition can serve as models for aspiring monks. Early in the series, for example, he comments on the need in monastic life for a commitment like that of the martyrs: "Typical of the spirit of the martyrs, this strength and love of sacrifice is passed on and handed down by the martyr to the monk his successor. How necessary to have some of this spirit in our monastic life. Otherwise how feeble and inert we will be, how lacking in generosity, how tepid in fulfilling our sacred obligations" (12). He emphasizes the relationship of trust and love between an *abba* and his disciple as the ideal for authentic spiritual direction:

> The Desert Fathers were not necessarily *magic directors,*
> wizard gurus, who had a series of infallible answers on all
> points. They were humble and sagacious men, of few
> words, whom the Holy Ghost used for His purposes. We
> must know how to take advantage of direction in this
> sense. If we seek our director as a kind of oracle, he will al-
> ways fail us. If we are prepared to listen to him in simplic-
> ity and accept, with faith, some ordinary observation of his
> as coming from God, then he will be able to help us. This
> faith requires not absolute blindness of the reason and
> common sense: it requires a certain trust and response on
> our part, an awareness that this is fitting for our case,
> which faith intensifies and enables us to see in an entirely
> supernatural light (75–76).

Even rather unlikely figures can be seen to have something to teach contemporary monastics: after summarizing St. Hilarion's quite daunting regimen of fasting, he comments on the *"essential* importance of fasting in the ascetic and contemplative life. Not that everyone is obliged to keep the measure of St. Hilarion, but all must fast according to their measure. Fasting is not something one takes on for a time, hoping to give it up. It is a lifelong part of the monastic vocation, with of course room left for modifications in case of need" (61). He even draws inspiration from the pillar saints, the stylites, viewing their "uselessness" as a "witness to the divine transcendency, and to the superiority of the spirit" and as "a protest against the worldly preoccupation with politics, and politico-theological struggles, with earthly and ecclesiastical ambition" (70).

This does not mean that Merton adopts an uncritical or ahistorical perspective on the past: he is quick to point out those aspects of earlier figures and traditions that are culturally conditioned and that may even involve some distortion of authentic Christian doctrine or practice, as when he notes that "the monachism of Palestine and Syria represents an extreme against which St. Benedict himself is clearly in reaction. . . . Great deviations occurred, and monachism would quickly have been ruined if there had not been intervention on the part of men like St. Basil to bring in sobriety and organization" (70–71). But he also warns against the tendency "to make judgements that are too crude both of the nature of error and of the nature of true Christian spirituality," as well as the "danger of drawing very clear lines of demarcation, with all black on one side and all white on the other" (16). His call "for greater discernment" is heeded in his own discussions of Origen and Evagrius, for example, where he notes aberrations but stresses their positive contributions, as it is in another way in his treatment of St. Jerome, whom he is able to present as in many ways a valuable guide despite his "very *active* and aggressive" (64) temperament.

Merton continually draws attention to the influence of the lives and teachings of the early monks on the Benedictine, and more specifically the Cistercian, tradition, in order to make clear to his novices their own links with these monastic founders and forbears. Thus, for example, he points out that "We can see the sources of St. Benedict's chapter on the reception of novices" in the Pachomian *Rule* (44), and that Basil's emphasis on the surrender of self-will is a "principle . . . adopted by St. Benedict" (50). The teaching of the *Great Letter* of the Pseudo-Macarius is described as "genuine Benedictine spirituality" (82). Cassian, especially, is repeatedly cited as a primary influence on Benedict, who "considered Cassian an ideal author for monks—one who would help them lead their monastic lives more perfectly, one who would bring them into contact with God, for Whom they had left the world" (100). The "admirable simplicity of Benedictine prayer," in which meditation was "incorporated in the office itself . . . not a special exercise" is traced back to Cassian's instructions on the recitation of the divine office in Book 2 of the *Institutes* (143). *Conferences* 9 and 10 are considered "the solid foundation of Benedictine prayer" and "the textbook of prayer for St. Benedict" (231), while Cassian's emphasis on "healthy alternation between bodily and spiritual works, so that our faculties and powers apply themselves *in turn* in different ways to prayer" is cited as "the secret of Benedictine balance and sobriety, which we should always try to preserve at all costs because without it perpetual prayer is really impossible" (232). Following Cassian, "[t]he practice of using the *Deus in adjutorium* at all times, especially at the beginning of each new action or observance, was universal in Western monasticism" (254).

Merton sees both similarity and contrast between Origen's use of the imagery of bride and bridegroom from the Song of Songs and "St. Bernard's use of the very same idea, which is the starting point of his homilies on the Canticle preached at Clairvaux" (28). Likewise, "The influence of St. Gregory of Nyssa is considerable in the West, and especially on the Cistercian William of St. Thierry, through whom the theology of Gregory of Nyssa became part of the Cistercian heritage—hence his special importance for us" (54). The teaching of St. Anthony on the goodness of the soul in its natural state, in Athanasius' *Life*, "appears again in St. Bernard, speaking of the natural *rectitudo* of the soul and the state of the *anima curva* [in sin]" (35–36). The teaching of Abbot Chaeremon on perfection in the eleventh of Cassian's *Conferences* as love of the good for its own sake is described as "the heart of St. Bernard's mystical theology, the climax of his sermons on the Canticle of Canticles. Pure love which 'casteth out fear' is the way to wisdom, in which we act and are moved only '*sapore boni*'" (111). Cassian's discussion of Martha and Mary as symbols of active and contemplative lives is noted as "a doctrine which influenced St. Bernard and the Cistercians" (212), while Abbot Daniel's discussion of the three types of soul in *Conference* 4 is glossed by a reference to William of St. Thierry, who bases his famous *Golden Epistle* on a similar division (229–30). These are but a few of the connections Merton draws between primitive monasticism and the Western Benedictine and Cistercian tradition to which he and his novices belong.

Merton's primary emphasis is on the search for a usable past, on appropriating the authentic witness of early Christianity and transposing it into modern life, specifically modern monastic life. He often finds in the teachings of the early Fathers themes that are also characteristic of his own writings. He especially values and highlights elements in the tradition that point toward genuine self-discovery, as in his description of "the foundation stone" on which St. Anthony the Great's "asceticism is built. God created the soul beautiful and upright in His own image. This beauty is its natural state. To be perfect, we have only to be as God created us, that is to say we have only to 'live according to our (true) nature'" (35); this recovery of the true self is understood as a return to "the state in which man was created in Paradise, for which he was intended by God" (34). The centrality of the paschal dimension of Christian spirituality is noted, as in his discussion of Origen: "This idea of union with the Logos through union in love and suffering with Christ, the Word Incarnate, is the most fundamental idea in all Christian mystical theology" (28). Another characteristic emphasis is found in the section on Jerome, where he states that the monk "must base his whole monastic life on *eschatological hope*—the second coming and the new creation" (68); this echatological dimension is balanced by the equally important awareness of sacramentality, as in Origen's "contemplative wisdom, a broad, rich, penetrating view of the universe as 'sacrament' and 'mystery' in Christ" (25), or Evagrius' *theoria physike* (natural contemplation), "an intuitive penetration of reality—of 'nature' in so far as it reflects God . . . an intuition of the Creator in His Creation" (94). Throughout the lectures Merton focuses particularly on the Fathers' recognition of the goal of human life as union with

God, the deep contemplative awareness exemplified, for example, by Gregory of Nyssa's teaching on humans as created in the divine image: "Man is made in the *image of God*. Just as God is beyond all clear knowledge, so the image in us is beyond the clear grasp of our intelligence. Man's job in life is to reproduce in the depths of the soul his *divine likeness*. This consists in the right use of his *freedom*, which is his *royal dignity* and this is entirely summed up in the *return to God by pure love*" (56). Thus Merton's genuine enthusiasm for and resonance with the teachings of the pre-monastic and early monastic tradition he is discussing are evident throughout these lectures.

    This is of course preeminently true of his principal subject, Cassian,[32] whom he calls "*the* great monastic writer—the Master of the spiritual life par excellence for monks—the source for all in the West" (99).[33] For Merton, Cassian is an invaluable guide to authentic monastic life first of all because of his direct contact with the tradition of the earliest monks: "It is for us to catch from him something of the undying inspiration of the Desert Fathers" (109). (It should be noted that Merton gives little attention to the critical issue of how much of the teaching Cassian attributes to various Egyptian abbots actually comes from them and how much of Cassian's own ideas has been put into their mouths. His interest is elsewhere—he simply states that Cassian "is *not a mere compiler*" but shows "real literary talent and ability to organize ideas in an *original synthesis* valid for all" [99], and that he "was admirably fitted to make the great synthesis of monastic doctrine and adapt the Eastern tradition to the West" [139].[34]

32. For an interesting comparison of Merton and Cassian, which does not however draw on any of Merton's published or unpublished discussions of Cassian, see Frank A. Peake, "Self, Sexuality and Solitude in John Cassian and Thomas Merton: Notes from a Retreat," *The Merton Annual*, 2 (1989), 241–56.

33. Merton makes a similar statement in his essay "The Humanity of Christ in Monastic Prayer": "Cassian is perhaps the most important and influential writer in Western monasticism. It was he who, in the early fifth century, transmitted to the West the Origenist and Evagrian doctrines on monastic life and prayer which were, and remained, dominant in Hellenistic monachism" (Thomas Merton, *The Monastic Journey*, ed. Patrick Hart, ocso [Kansas City: Sheed, Andrews and McMeel, 1977], 90).

34. In "The Humanity of Christ in Monastic Prayer," Merton writes, "The ninth and tenth *Conferences* of Cassian represent not only what was probably

Merton is confident that Cassian conveys the genuine spirit of the Egyptian *abbas*, whatever creative adaptations and reformulations he has made.)

Merton's admiration for Cassian and his teachers is by no means uncritical. He is perhaps too ready, in fact, to accept the traditional judgement that Cassian deviated from authentic doctrine on the question of grace and free will, though he does note, "It is misleading to use the term 'semi-pelagianism' of Cassian, as if to imply that he sympathized with Pelagius and *adopted a modification of his heretical doctrine*" (102); and in the context of his discussion of Jerome in the "Prologue" section, after commenting that while Jerome had actually written a statement sounding considerably more "semi-pelagian" than anything by Cassian, the great scripture scholar's reputation had not been damaged because he had not run afoul of the Augustinian party in Gaul as Cassian had, he concludes: "We must be careful to remember that the stigma of heresy or doubtful orthodoxy clings tenaciously sometimes to men who have not taught otherwise than the saints of their time, but have somehow acquired a bad reputation due to 'politics'" (67).[35]

Merton also alerts his listeners to the occasional questionable piece of advice or illustration of a principle by one of Cassian's

---

the accepted doctrine on prayer in the monastic centres of lower Egypt, but also his own synthesis of the monastic ideology of Southern Gaul in the early fifth century" (*Monastic Journey*, 90). In a June 17, 1960 letter to John Harris, Merton presents a more popularized explanation, but one that he no doubt realized was overly simplistic: "You have never heard of Cassian? He is easily available in *Sources Chrétiennes* (Editions du Cerf) and makes very good reading, though perhaps he might appall you. He is the Boswell of the Desert Fathers, and wrote down everything they could be cajoled into saying. None of them were very talkative" (Thomas Merton, *The Hidden Ground of Love: Letters on Religious Experience and Social Concerns*, ed. William H. Shannon [New York: Farrar, Straus, Giroux, 1985], 397).

35. In his letter to Harris Merton again gives an explanation suited to his audience: "In the Oriental Church he is venerated as St. Cassian the Roman. In our Church he is suspect of heresy, but no one has ever stopped reading him on that account. And the heresy is just one little sentence he quoted from an old Desert Father one hundred years old who could no longer walk upright but crawled around on all fours. No wonder the poor old man could not be perfectly accurate on the fine shades of the doctrine of grace!" (*Hidden Ground of Love*, 397).

teachers, as when he remarks that Abbot Theodore's instruction to Cassian and Germanus "that the way to arrive at the understanding of Scripture is to ignore the commentaries and overcome the vices of the flesh" is an "example of a statement that must be accepted with qualifications!!" (162), or when he cautions that the same Father's story of "two boys who died in the desert rather than eat figs which they were carrying to a sick hermit" is "[a]gain, an exaggeration which is not true virtue" (162). While he praises Cassian for his "lifelike portraits of the Desert Fathers," who "remain 'models for imitation,'" he goes on to ask, "in what sense are they to be imitated?" and responds:

> *Not* in all their exterior actions—impossible to us—not at all suited to our situation; not in all their attitudes—they were extremists—they were often quite wrong. They are to be followed in their *faith*, their love of Christ, their zeal for the monastic state and their spirit of prayer and sacrifice. In reading the Desert Fathers one must: (1) DISCRIMINATE; (2) ADAPT, as did St. Benedict himself, who consciously and deliberately, wrote a *Rule* which some of the Desert Fathers would have condemned as soft (100–101).

In fact this process of discrimination and adaptation had already been well begun by Cassian himself, whom Merton has already described as "remarkable for his grasp of the *essentials* of monasticism, avoiding bizarre details" and as "a good observer and psychologist, a prudent Master of the spiritual life" (99).

It is this prudence and psychological acuity that Merton repeatedly calls attention to in his commentary on Cassian's writings. Thus in discussing Book 5 of the *Institutes*, on gluttony, the first of the eight principal vices, Merton notes Cassian's emphasis on the need for honesty in order to overcome self-deception: "The knowledge of self and of the remedies for sin was one of the keystones of the asceticism of the Desert. Ascetic practice was of no value unless it was based on a genuine knowledge of the state of affairs—not just on vague feelings and premonitions of guilt. . . . Hence the first thing is, with the help of God's light, to *dispel the ignorance* which leaves us at their mercy (c. 2; col. 204). Note the tremendous importance of insight, self-knowledge.

Good will, without knowledge, leads to disaster" (156–57). Again in the section on anger (Book 8 of the *Institutes*), Merton focuses on what he calls Cassian's "psychological finesse," as revealed in chapter 14: "He discovers the mechanism of 'projection' by which we place on others the blame for our own faults, impatience, etc. in order to rationalize these faults and overlook them. We blame our defects on the vices of others, and thus prevent ourselves from making any progress in virtue—a most important observation" (176–77).

What Merton values above all in Cassian is his fundamental good sense, his balance and moderation.[36] Referring to Cassian's critique of efforts to induce tears in prayer, Merton comments, "Cassian here lays down an important principle: violence and strain are not only useless in the spiritual life, but they are harmful and prevent the true spiritual life from developing properly. *They kill spontaneity* which is absolutely necessary in our relations with God, and which is what we must try as far as possible to preserve, {and} may distract us from the humility which makes prayer fruitful. Note Cassian's respect for the natural makeup of man, and for his psychic mechanism" (251). This passage, like many others throughout the text, reveals both Merton's ability to recognize broadly applicable principles in specific directives of Cassian, and to formulate them in language that can be immediately grasped by a contemporary audience. Merton does not settle for describing or summarizing Cassian's teaching: he is continually interpreting it so as to make it meaningful to the novices.

For Merton the heart of Cassian's teaching, and of his continuing value for monks, is to be found in his doctrine of purity

36. Merton notes this aspect of Cassian as early as 1949, in *The Waters of Siloe* (New York: Harcourt, Brace, 1949): "the great abbots of Egypt and Syria laid down the foundations of an asceticism that was full of wisdom and prudence, good sense and charity. All the sanity and moderation of St. Thomas Aquinas could find no better authority on which to rest, no safer model to follow, than the *Conferences* and *Institutes* of Cassian" (4). He makes a similar point about Cassian and the Desert Father tradition more than a decade later in "The Recovery of Paradise," part of "Wisdom in Emptiness," Merton's dialogue with D. T. Suzuki that was originally planned as an Introduction to *The Wisdom of the Desert*: "their instrument in opening the subtle locks of spiritual deception was the virtue of *discretio*. It was discretion that St. Anthony called the most important of all the

of heart,[37] which leads to pure prayer: "without a knowledge of his doctrine on purity of heart and discretion, we would fail to understand the true monastic attitude and miss the whole purpose of the monastic life. They show us that contemplation does not consist exclusively in solitude and silence and renunciation but that these are only means to purity of heart" (204).[38] This purity of heart, which Merton defines, following Cassian, as "the

---

virtues in the desert. Discretion had taught him the value of simple manual labor. Discretion taught the fathers that purity of heart did not consist simply in fasting and self-maceration. Discretion—otherwise called the discernment of spirits—is indeed germane to the realm of knowledge, since it does distinguish between good and evil. But it exercises its functions in the light of innocence and in reference to emptiness. It judges not in terms of abstract standards so much as in terms of inner purity of heart. Discretion makes judgments and indicates choices, but the judgment and choice always point in the direction of emptiness, or purity of heart. Discretion is a function of humility, and therefore it is a branch of knowledge that lies beyond the reach of diabolical comment and perversion. (See Cassian, Conference II, *De Discretione*, Migne, P.L., vol. 49, c. 523 ff.)" (Thomas Merton, *Zen and the Birds of Appetite* [New York: New Directions, 1968], 130).

37. Abbot John Eudes Bamberger writes of Merton's teaching on the true self, "This hidden self is deeper than psychological reality; it is not subject to direct control but must be approached through a process of discovery that involves a turning aside from the many layers of the person we appear to be not only to others, but even to our self. . . . Cassian's first Conference dealt with this theme, and so when Merton lectured and wrote on this teaching he was at one with the ancient author in showing how purity of heart was the immediate end of all the monk's efforts, and the final end was attaining to the kingdom of heaven. This concept serves as a norm by which the monk judges the usefulness of such matters as vigils, lectio, fasting and manual labor. What contributes to purity of heart is to be put into effect, but only in so far as it leads to this desired result" ("Monasticism and Thomas Merton," 30–31).

38. In "The Humanity of Christ in Monastic Prayer," Merton writes, "The whole monastic doctrine of Cassian is summed up in the equation: *perfecta caritas = puritas cordis = pura oratio*. The monk has left the world to seek the Kingdom of heaven, which is union with God in contemplation. . . . The monk fully enters the Kingdom of God when, through purity of heart, he receives the illumination of the Holy Spirit, the Spirit of Christ. His proximate end, as a monk, is to purify his heart by asceticism, thus attaining to a state of tranquillity, or *puritas cordis*, in which his spirit recovers a natural 'lightness' or freedom from material ties, and, like a dry feather in a light breeze, can be carried towards heaven by love. He is no longer weighed down by the cares and desires of a sinful or passionate existence. He is no longer distracted and dominated by earthly concerns, and hence he is able to pray without ceasing, thus fulfilling the Apostle's command in the most perfect manner (1 Thess. 5.17). It is for this end that men become monks" (*Monastic Journey*, 90–91).

ability to love God purely and to do His will for love's sake alone—disinterested love" (205)[39] is the bridge between ascetic renunciation and the heights of contemplation.[40] Merton finds in Cassian a unified presentation of the spiritual life in which all works together for good, in which the *scopos* (purity of heart) leads to the *telos* (the Kingdom of Heaven, union with God):[41]

39. In "The Recovery of Paradise," he writes: "Cassian . . . gives a characteristically Christian affective balance to the concept of purity of heart, and insists that it is to be defined simply as 'perfect charity' or a love of God unmixed with any return upon self" (*Zen and the Birds of Appetite*, 91).

40. In *The Wisdom of the Desert*, Merton writes, "the proximate end of all this striving was 'purity of heart'—a clear unobstructed vision of the true state of affairs, an intuitive grasp of one's own inner reality as anchored, or rather lost, in God through Christ. The fruit of this was *quies*: 'rest.' . . . The 'rest' which these men sought was simply the sanity and poise of a being that no longer has to look at itself because it is carried away by the perfection of freedom that is in it. And carried where? Wherever Love itself, or the Divine Spirit sees fit to go. Rest, then, was a kind of simple no-whereness and no-mindedness that had lost all preoccupation with a false or limited 'self.' At peace in the possession of a sublime 'Nothing' the spirit laid hold, in secret, upon the 'All'—without trying to know what it possessed" (4). In his essay "The Spiritual Father in the Desert Tradition," Merton writes of purity of heart, "John Cassian, in his first conference, defining the whole purpose of the monastic life, brings together three things which he identifies with monastic perfection. These three are simply aspects of the same spiritual reality. Perfection does not consist merely in solitude, asceticism, prayer, or other practices. All these may be sought for basically selfish motives, and they may in the end be simply more subtle and more stubborn ways of affirming one's own ego. True perfection is found only when one renounces the 'self' that seems to be the subject of perfection, and that 'has' or 'possesses' perfection. For Cassian this perfection is 'charity . . . which consists in purity of heart alone' and which he identifies with *quies*, since it consists in 'always offering to God a perfect and most pure heart, and in keeping that heart untouched by all perturbations'" (Thomas Merton, *Contemplation in a World of Action* [Garden City, NY: Doubleday, 1971], 273). It is instructive to compare these descriptions of purity of heart, which are filled with turns of phrase characteristic of much of Merton's mature spiritual teaching, with the more traditional explanation in *The Waters of Siloe*: "Purity of heart, *puritas cordis*, is a technical term in medieval ascetical writing. It harks back to the beatitudes, 'Blessed are the clean of heart, for they shall see God' (Matt. v:8). It means detachment not only from all illicit desires but even from licit pleasures and temporal interests and cares. More than that, it signifies the ability to rise above and beyond the images of created things and all dialectical reasoning in order to seize the truth by a pure and direct intuition" (xxviii, n. 7).

41. In "The Recovery of Paradise," Merton writes: "One thing, and this is most important, remains to be said. Purity of heart is not the *ultimate end* of the

"there is a vital and essential relationship between prayer and
all the virtues in the spiritual life (virtues—'strengths'). Since
the life of prayer is built on the foundation of virtues, it is useless to talk about it unless we keep in mind the virtues on which
it depends. This is just another way of linking prayer and purity of heart, because the function of all the virtues is to purify
the heart and remove those obstacles which make it difficult or
impossible to keep recollected and engage ourselves with God
alone" (233). But even in pointing toward the heights of contemplation, Cassian refuses to get lost in ethereal speculations: he
balances his description of the "prayer of fire,"[42] which "tends by
its very nature to soar beyond words and clear concepts" (240)
with his teaching on a simple method of prayer "a brief form of
prayer which can be constantly repeated and meditated in the
depths of the heart so that we return constantly to the presence
of God and keep ourselves in a perpetual state of prayer," which
in God's own proper time *"leads to contemplation* of the divine

---

monk's striving in the desert. It is only a step towards it. We have said above that
Paradise is not yet heaven. Paradise is not the final goal of the spiritual life. It is,
in fact, only a return to the true beginning. It is a 'fresh start.' The monk who
has realized in himself purity of heart, and has been restored, in some measure,
to the innocence lost by Adam, has still not ended his journey. He is only ready
to begin. He is ready for a new work 'which eye hath not seen, ear hath not
heard, nor hath it entered into the heart of man to conceive.' Purity of heart,
says Cassian, is the intermediate end of the spiritual life. But the ultimate end is
the Kingdom of God. . . . Purity of heart establishes man in a state of unity and
emptiness in which he is one with God. But this is the necessary preparation not
for further struggle between good and evil, but for the real work of God which is
revealed in the Bible: the work of the *new creation*, the resurrection from the dead,
the restoration of all things in Christ" (*Zen and the Birds of Appetite*, 131–32).

42. See "The Humanity of Christ in Monastic Prayer": "Here there are no
more words to utter, as the spirit is carried away beyond words and indeed beyond understanding into that *oratio ignita*, 'burning prayer' or 'prayer of fire', in
which flame-like movements of love burst out from within the depths of the
monk's being under the direct action of the Holy Spirit. This powerful surge of
inner spiritual life and love is the pure gift of God, expressed in prayer of 'most
pure energy uttered within us by the Holy Spirit interceding without our
knowledge'. . . . The highest form of prayer is, then, a prayer 'without forms',
a pure prayer in which there are no longer any images or ideas, and in which
the spirit does not take any initiative of its own, for all activity of the human
mind and senses is here completely surpassed" (*Monastic Journey*, 91–92).

mysteries" (253).[43] Thus for Merton the master of novices, the appropriateness of introducing Cassian to those beginning their monastic life is that in Cassian each pilgrim, wherever he may be on the spiritual path, is able to recognize himself and his current situation, while at the same time being reminded that he is already embarked on a journey that leads beyond himself to God, and being encouraged to persevere toward the goal of perfect unity with God and all God's creation.

* * * * * * *

This sense of recognition can even be extended, if somewhat obliquely, to include Merton himself. While there are virtually no direct personal references in the written text of the lectures, there are numerous comments throughout the conferences that cast a fascinating and intriguing, if indirect, light on Merton's own complex life as monk and writer. They range from the offhand remark, after quoting St. Anthony's advice to "write down your deeds as if you were telling them to another," that "there is some justification for keeping a Journal if even St. Anthony recommended the practice!" (38), to the startling assertion (given Merton's own repeated efforts to do precisely this) that "Desires to transfer to other monasteries . . . imagining all the perfections and advantages of other communities, seeing the drawbacks and deficiencies of our own vocation" are one of the signs of acedia, spiritual torpor (189).

While Merton is certainly faithful to his vow not to "orientate" the novices "towards something else" than the authentic Cistercian tradition, his own attraction to the hermit life can occasionally be glimpsed, as when he discusses the transition from eremitic to cenobitic monasticism in fourth-century Egypt:

43. See *Climate of Monastic Prayer*, 30–31; *Contemplative Prayer*, 20–21: "In John Cassian's *Conferences on Prayer* we see great stress laid by the early monks on simple prayer made up of short phrases drawn from the Psalms or other parts of Scripture. One of the most frequently used was *Deus in adjutorium meum intende*, 'O God, come to my aid!' . . . They were careful not to go looking for extraordinary experiences, and contented themselves with the struggle for 'purity of heart' and for control of their thoughts, to keep their minds and hearts empty of care and concern, so that they might altogether forget themselves and apply themselves entirely to the love and service of God."

With Pachomius, we find *organized community life*. And
here begins an old debate: between cenobites and hermits.
It was to last a long time, and the thread of argument runs
all through the Desert Fathers' literature. Some are for the
free, unorganized life of the hermit living alone with God.
Others are for the safer, more consistent, organized life of
communities. The argument sometimes gets quite heated,
and in the end the cenobites, for all practical purposes,
won out. The eremitical ideal remains still the highest *ideal*
of monasticism, especially in the Orient. But in practice
cenobitism is what is advocated. Rarely, from time to time,
in monastic tradition, the hermit life reappears. It is something that is always there and must always be there but it
will remain a special vocation. The life of the cenobite is
the "ordinary" and "normal" monastic way (39).[44]

This passage is noteworthy for its balanced presentation, which
refuses to take sides in the "old debate," and which affirms that
cenobitic life is the "ordinary" and "normal" monastic way; still,
the connotations of "free" and "living alone with God" have a
warmer tone than "safer, more consistent, organized life."

44. In *The Waters of Siloe*, Merton had written of the beginnings of cenobitic
life: "St. Pachomius discovered another kind of solitude. In the first great monastery of Egyptian cenobites, at Tabenna, the monk learned how to disappear—
not into the desert but into a community of other monks. It is in some ways a far
more effective way to disappear, and it involves, on the whole, an asceticism
that is peculiarly deep and lasting in its effects" (4). However on the next page
he presents St. Basil's critique of Pachomian monasticism without registering
any disagreement. (It should be recalled, of course, that Basil was just as critical
of the anchorites.) "St. Basil, who traveled up the Nile in the middle of the
fourth century, was quick to sum up the weakness of the monastic life that he
saw. The cenobitic system of Pachomius, he said, was too complex, too noisy,
too active. Tabenna was a huge affair—a town, or rather an armed camp, of five
thousand ascetics. They were divided up into platoons and regiments, under a
hierarchy of military officials dependent upon the abbot, who was the general-
in-chief. The vast machine worked efficiently enough, but with a kind of inhuman ponderousness. Labor was so arduous that it resembled modern sweatshop
production. So great was the number of monks that all life was depersonalized.
There was no intimate contact with superiors. Instead of real spiritual direction,
the monks were subjected to a system of formal humiliations and public insults.
It was only the extraordinary spiritual vitality of the monks themselves that kept
this process from being altogether brutalizing" (5).

While Merton gives Basilian monasticism, the standard form of cenobitism in the East, its due, noting its emphasis on love within and beyond the monastery walls, its recognition that the "good things of God are easily shared in community, and the sharing increases them," and that the "variety of duties offers scope for various talents and graces" (50–51), he does not hesitate to state that Basil shows "real bias" against the eremitic life and that he "does not give the hermits a fair hearing" (40). He himself recognizes that both forms of monastic life have built-in risks, but that both are ways of living out the Gospel:

> The danger for hermits is individualism and anarchy. The danger for cenobites is excessive organisation, totalitarianism, and mechanical routine. In either case, the only remedy is fidelity to grace, close union with the Holy Spirit Who breathes the divine life into souls and informs rules and regulations with the *spiraculum vitae* without which they are only empty forms. This is the hermit's own responsibility. In the cenobium, the responsibility rests first of all with Superiors, but the subject too must be careful not to let himself become merely a passive cog in a machine. A monastery must be an organism, not just an organization (44–45).

Coming to a passage such as this after reading some of Merton's negative comments on his own monastery in his private journals, one might interpret it as an indirect criticism of Gethsemani, but such a conclusion would be an oversimplification: the context is a defense of Pachomian monasticism, which despite its "fearsome" and potentially "misleading" appearance is clearly, in Merton's view, a healthy monasticism formed by the power of the Holy Spirit: "The spirit of St. Pachomius was not simply one of military efficiency, but of deep Christian charity. Charity was first and foremost in the cenobitic life" (44). But Merton here, as in many of the essays collected in *Contemplation in a World of Action*, is emphasizing the necessity of fidelity to the genuine spirit of monasticism, not just a conformity to external structures.

Perhaps the closest Merton comes to criticizing his own monastery is in his discussion of the seventh book of Cassian's

Institutes, on the Spirit of Avarice: after noting Cassian's treatment of love of possessions as a kind of cowardice, a failure to
trust in God, he asks, "Is our materialistic society one of weak
and degenerate souls that have no inner spiritual resources?"
and responds, "Perhaps more so than we think." He then adds
that monastic life is not automatically immune to the same
temptations: "In contemplative monasteries—when we start
going out of ourselves to place our hope in things that can be
bought and sold, we are confessing the inanity of our interior
life" (166). Such a comment might be seen as a covert stricture
directed at Gethsemani Inc. and Trappist cheese, but in fact
there is no effort to point up any specific application of what is
certainly a valid gloss on Cassian's own acute critique of the
survival of avarice in a monastic setting; and when Merton returns to the issue at the conclusion of his commentary on this
book it is clear that he recognizes that the temptation is not just
an institutional one but something that each person must con-
front personally:

> Throughout one's whole religious life one must firmly
> cling to a spirit of simple faith and avoid hesitation,
> double-mindedness and fear—we cannot serve God and
> Mammon (Matt. 6), and the "double-minded man is incon-
> stant in all his ways" (James 1). {N.B.} importance of this
> principle, from the psychological point of view. So much
> trouble, in religious orders, comes from this unconscious
> duplicity, which makes our life a pretense and a sham, al-
> though we manage to salve our conscience and create for
> ourselves a multitude of pretexts for evading our gift of
> self. Note, the way in which we create alibis for our-
> selves—is not merely by glossing over weakness with ex-
> cuses, but also by living in such a way that there is much
> *apparent zeal* and generosity, directed however to some-
> thing that does not matter while the really important
> things are forgotten. Our zeal for the non-essential is
> thought to justify our lives, and to excuse the evasion of
> the essential (171).

The ultimate question raised by the temptation to avarice concerns "the gift of self" weighed against a "zeal for the non-

essential" that becomes a form of self-justification, a theme that Merton frequently explores both in the journals and in the essays and reflections written for publication.

Far more frequent in the lectures than comments that might seem to reflect negatively on institutional monasticism are those that touch on issues related to Merton's personal struggles and tensions with his own vocation. What is particularly striking about the tenor of such comments is how they differ from many of his journal entries of the same period. For example, in summarizing *Conference* 18, he discusses Abbot Piamon's warnings about the sarabaites, wandering monks who live without a superior: "This gives us a deep insight into the nature of the monastic vocation. We proclaim our faith in God by preferring Him to all else—*not* our subjective feeling about Him, but His *Will* and his *Word*. Therefore the test—is to let *God run our lives*, and to let Him do so through His representatives, our superiors. From this we see how essential it is for the monastic life to be a life of complete dependence on God's Providence and a total submission of ourselves to His Will and His plans. Outside of this there is nothing but illusion" (119). Considering Merton's own struggles with his own superior, Dom James, one might be inclined to treat such statements as suitable instruction for the novices but not reflective of Merton's own attitudes, or perhaps as a remnant of his early conventional piety that will give way to a greater rebelliousness in coming years. But such a reading would be reductivist and overly simplistic. While Merton continued to chafe against what he sometimes saw as arbitrary exercise of authority, and cautioned against a kind of blind obedience that abdicated any role in the process of discerning God's will, he was clearly aware of the dangers of self-will, what he characteristically called the false self of egocentric desires, and of the role of obedience in the development of necessary self-discipline. When he goes on to say that "[t]he monk, insisting on running his own life and taking care of himself, is left to do so by God, and as a result leads a life that is a sterile and laborious succession of projects and anxieties," and that such a "lack of trust in God, lack of belief in God's promises . . . is a rejection of the Gospel, in order to seek worldly peace, worldly security, comfort, respect, a position in society without doing anything to deserve them" (120), he is best interpreted not as being disingenuous or hypocritical but as preaching to himself as well as to his novices.

Likewise, when in connection with Cassian's eighth book of the *Institutes*, on anger, he discusses *"True and false love of solitude,"* including "the delusion of those who want to change their Order or go into solitude, as a result of their projection of their own weaknesses upon the community or the brethren" he is surely aware of its pertinence to his own desires: "Far from being ready for solitude," he continues, "such souls are weak in virtue. Only the perfect can rest assured that their desire of solitude is based on a true love of contemplation rather than on pusillanimity. For those who go into solitude without being perfect not only do not get away from their vices, but become more deeply enmeshed in them" (177). As with the comment quoted earlier connecting the desire to transfer to another monastery with acedia, so here the linking of the same desire with anger surely functions on one level at least as a form of self-examination, even of self-criticism. It provides another, needed perspective on Merton's own wrestling with his desire for greater solitude, one that must not be disregarded in evaluating his own theory and practice of monastic life.

Similarly when he discusses the relationship of vanity to solitude, the personal implications are visible just beneath the surface: "far from being diminished in solitude it is even worse there, even though there is no one to admire us. For the solitary is capable of getting along with his own admiration of himself and is that much worse off for not needing the admiration of others. When we overcome it in single victories, it rises again all the more strong to combat us. Unlike other vices which diminish with age, this grows stronger as we grow older" (191–92). But if the problem is relevant to Merton's own life, the solution he proposes is quite characteristic as well; it is in fact one of the few places in the lectures where he does not base his discussion on his source:

> Cassian does not say so, but one of the only effective ways
> to fight vanity is to *admit* it and face it squarely, instead of

trying to keep it hidden by vain efforts to eradicate it, when these efforts are themselves prompted by vanity. The enemy to look out for is that false desire of perfection which cannot abide a fault in ourselves, which out of real vanity seeks to be spotless, and which is agitated when the slightest spot appears. To fight vanity we must be content to have faults, so long as we do not willingly indulge them. If a man is really vain [and we all are more or less] his whole desire for perfection is in reality inspired by vanity, that is to say by the need to be esteemed and to take complacency in self. Hence it is clear that it is much better to be imperfect in many things, as long as these imperfections spring only from weakness and do not imply a lack of zeal for the spiritual life, than to be perfect and at the same time vain of our perfection. If our imperfections lead us to trust fully and wholeheartedly in the mercy of God, then they are of great benefit to our souls. To be without vanity is to see oneself as an imperfect and sinful creature without feeling undue anxiety or shame, without fighting reality, without losing our peace, but trusting in God. It means accepting oneself as he really is (192).

Here, certainly, is the authentic Mertonian voice, undermining all attempts, including, at least implicitly, his own, to inflate the ego in such a way as to make self rather than God the source of one's own value. As he expresses the same idea shortly afterward: "We should accept ourselves, laugh at our own weakness, and turn our minds to something better by using a good book, or thinking about something more profitable, and more practical. The soul who really and culpably indulges vanity like this is generally one who is too proud to be ordinary and normal, too puffed up to descend to simple and ordinary means for avoiding these fantasies. Such ones are really badly infected. But the man who is humble enough to be ordinary and to work at his perfection with humble and ordinary means, will not be harmed by the inevitable fantasies of his imagination" (193). If Merton on occasion took himself too seriously, if he was not invariably "humble enough" to accept his ordinariness and so avoid harmful consequences of "the inevitable fantasies of his imagination," he certainly was one who regularly recognized his own faults and refused to become complacent—someone who on balance had the saving grace to be able to recognize, and laugh at, his own weaknesses and imperfections. He is one who, like Chaucer's clerk, would gladly learn and gladly teach,[45] one who even continues to learn in the process of teaching.

Thus part of the value and importance of these conferences lies in the insights they make possible about a major aspect of Thomas Merton's life as a monk that are not otherwise readily available. The "public" Merton has long been visible in his works written for publication, and has more recently been complemented by the "interpersonal" Merton disclosed in his correspondence and the "intimate" Merton revealed in his complete journals. While it would be overstating the case to claim that the novitiate conferences are comparable in significance to these other sources, they do provide access to yet another stratum of Merton's wide-ranging and immensely productive engagement with his world from the distinctive standpoint he had chosen within a tradition dating back more than sixteen centuries. While these lectures need to be used critically and cautiously in evaluating Merton's own perspectives and commitments, nevertheless they do need to be used. They are a salutary check against "over-privileging" the journals, which could and certainly did at times serve to express Merton's immediate feelings and reactions rather than his considered impressions and judgements, and so are not to be set up as an absolute standard for determining the "authentic" Merton. The dialectical relationship between Merton's private and more public statements, including those made to his novice classes, allows for and makes possible a more complex and thus a richer picture of his monastic identity and so of his personal identity. In learning about Cassian and the Fathers from Merton, one learns as well about Merton as monk, as heir to the great monastic teachers, and as teacher of a new generation of monks, an easily overlooked and undervalued, yet integral, even central component of his vocation for more than half his monastic life. Thus the publication of the novitiate conferences will fill a significant lacuna in Merton studies

45. Geoffrey Chaucer, *The Canterbury Tales*, "General Prologue," l. 308 ("And gladly wolde he lerne and gladly teche").

and contribute to a balanced, holistic comprehension and appreciation of Thomas Merton's life and work.

* * * * * * *

On April 27, 1962, Merton's novitiate conferences began to be recorded on audiotape, so that the brothers (who at the time had a separate novitiate) could listen to them as they worked in the abbey kitchen.[46] This practice continued throughout the rest of Merton's term as Novice Master (and was followed by the taping of his customary Sunday lectures to the community during the final three years of his life). More than six hundred different lectures were taped between 1962 and 1968, many of which have been made available commercially.[47]

Merton had already begun the third and final section of his Cassian lectures, on the *Conferences*, when the taping was initiated. Fourteen classes, from April 28, 1962 (the day after the first tape was made) through August 4, 1962, were recorded,[48] and

46. For details concerning the beginning of the recording of Merton's conferences, see Victor Kramer's interviews with Matthew Kelty, OCSO, "Looking Back to Merton: Memories and Impressions," *The Merton Annual*, 1 (1988), 69–70, and with Flavian Burns, OCSO, "Merton's Contributions as Teacher, Writer and Community Member," *The Merton Annual*, 3 (1990), 83.

47. Three sets of twelve tapes were produced by Electronic Paperbacks of Chappaqua, NY in the 1970s; more recently, over one hundred tapes have been produced by Credence Communications of Kansas City, MO.

48. No tape exists for the conference of May 5, immediately following the first of the Cassian lectures to be taped, presumably due to "technical difficulties" of some sort. Dating of the tapes is somewhat conjectural; many of the original tapes are not dated, and of those that are, many are clearly wrong: for example, the second Cassian tape is dated May 10 (a Thursday), but the tape immediately following refers to this conference having been given on a Saturday. The tape given the date of May 26 clearly follows that given the date June 2—apparently the dates were reversed. In the discussion that follows, the dates have been regularized to conform to the dating of the Saturdays between April 28 and August 4, as that clearly appears to be the day of the week on which the Cassian conferences were regularly given (six of the dated conferences fall on Saturdays; three are undated; five are dated inconsistently [four different days] on other days of the week—one of these is clearly wrong, and of the others, all but one correspond to weeks when no Saturday conference is listed; the only exception occurs on May 14, a Monday following the class [to be discussed below] in which the entire conference period was taken up with a discussion of the nuclear issue; that class probably did take place on the date given, to make

so make possible a comparison of the last part of Merton's text with the conferences as actually presented. The opportunity to observe his teaching technique and style as it moves from the study into the classroom enhances appreciation of both the written text and of the tapes, and makes clear that Merton handles his prepared material quite freely: the text as written serves as an outline for the classes, but is never slavishly followed.

The tapes provide a vivid sense of the actual atmosphere of the classes. Often the first few minutes of the conference period were taken up with practical matters.[49] For example, on May 12 Merton reminds the novices to turn out the lights if they are the last one to leave a room, and mentions that while brothers are allowed to grow beards, choir monks are not (if they were, he comments, their Father Master would have one). On May 26 he announces that May 31 is the profession day for the novice sisters at the nearby convent of Loretto (where his friend Sister Mary Luke Tobin was superior) and asks his novices to pray for them. On June 8, Merton gives a rather involved directive about towels (don't take a new one every time after showering; have two, and turn one of them in each week). On June 23 he gives the news that Fr. Matthew (Kelty), who entered Gethsemani as a priest, is making his solemn profession. On July 28 he announces changes in job assignments for the novices. On August 4 he compares a monk who had recently died to Dom Edmond Obrecht, the former abbot of Gethsemani.

He also uses this preliminary period on occasion to inform the novices of various current events that he thinks they should be aware of. On May 12 he tells them about the *Everyman*, a small boat that is sailing into the nuclear test area in the South Pacific to protest atmospheric testing; the ensuing discussion of the nuclear issue (kept going in the time-honored manner by the students' questions) continues through the entire conference period, so that Merton never gets to Cassian at all! On June 2, Merton

---

up for the "missed" class). On one Saturday, probably June 30, possibly June 23 (the relevant tape is dated June 24, a Sunday—almost certainly wrong), there was apparently no conference given.

49. These correspond to the notes Merton wrote on the verso pages of the typescript he used for the conference lectures.

lets the novices know (much more briefly) that the boat's crew had been arrested for their civil disobedience; on the same day, he mentions the most recent manned spaceshot, noting that the astronaut, Scott Carpenter, was from Aurora, Kentucky; that the stock exchange had dropped forty points; and that a group of Tibetan Buddhist monks, including the Dalai Lama's older brother, had settled in New Jersey, where among other things, they played badminton! It is evident, then, that Merton used the conference periods to keep the novices abreast of at least some of what was going on in the outside world, a reflection of his own conviction that the contemplative life could not and should not be cut off from issues and concerns of the society beyond the abbey walls.

As for the substance of the conferences themselves, Merton created a quite informal, casual, relaxed atmosphere, but without diffusing the focus on the material itself. The methodology used was not exclusively lecture but included a great deal of interaction. Merton would typically ask questions that depended on general knowledge rather than any close acquaintance with Cassian in particular—for example, why we are pulled between desires of the flesh and desires of the spirit (April 28), or which of the types of prayer best characterized an example he had just read (June 7). He regularly directed his questions to particular novices, not the group in general; if he didn't get the answer he was looking for he would sometimes ask another novice, sometimes give it himself, though he would often try to integrate the initial response in some way into this overall discussion.[50] When he was looking for certain answers, as when he wanted a Latin phrase or sentence translated, he apparently sought out someone he was confident could provide a correct answer. While there were occasional questions from the novices, these were much

50. Brother Harold Thibodeau recalls: "It was not a dry lecture. He was aware of his audience: If you were falling asleep or not paying attention, he would say, 'Well, what do you think of that, Brother so-and-so?' If you gave the wrong answer and everyone would laugh, he would say, 'Do you really think that?' And then he would like to interrogate for a while. Often if you might say something that was not really on target, he would weave it into his next theme and make it sound all right. If it was not far off, [but] not complete enough, he would even fill it out for you" (quoted in Lewis, "Learning to Live," 94–95).

less frequent than Merton's questions to them; they were usually handled rather expeditiously,[51] though if Merton considered the question a good one, he would take the time to consider it in detail, as when on April 28 one novice asked how to distinguish desolation caused by negligence or diabolical attack from that willed by God. (Merton's answer is that the last could be seen as taking even the first two into account, though discernment is also clearly necessary to recognize, and overcome, one's own shortcomings.)

Merton frequently incorporated stories not in his written text to make his points more vivid. Sometimes the stories were drawn from the traditional monastic literature. Discussing the early monks' reluctance to become priests, he tells the tale of one *abba* who fled when his fellow monks wanted him to be ordained, only to relent in the end when his hiding place was discovered by a donkey who had accompanied the other monks on their search for him (April 28). During his consideration of simplicity in prayer, he relates the story of two hermits living on an island who didn't know even the Lord's Prayer; after a visiting monk laboriously taught them the prayer, he left by boat, only to see the two hermits running toward him across the water to say that they'd forgotten the prayer and needed him to repeat it for them (June 7). On other occasions the examples are taken from the life of the monastery itself, as when Merton is discussing the tendency to substitute busyness for a kind of prayerful tranquillity, to "work overtime" on "self-willed projects," and mentions finding the newly professed monks (during his time as master of scholastics) undertaking a completely unauthorized (and less than aesthetically pleasing) decoration of the chapel after hours on the night before Christmas (May 26).

Merton occasionally makes reference to himself, usually in a self-deprecating manner, in the course of the conferences. For instance, speaking about busyness on May 19, he uses himself

51. According to Abbot Timothy Kelly, "He could be very curt. He would answer your question very specifically and was clear in his body language that he wanted no more; that is, time's up. Of course, our style was not open to much dialogue and questioning, so he really did not open classes up to questions. It was also foreign to his style. He sometimes asked questions to get the answers he wanted" (quoted in Lewis, "Learning to Live," 95).

as an example, listing letters to be written, class notes to be assembled, arrangements to be made with the cellarer, a conference with a postulant, and the "book business"—at that point two books in process and another one about to be begun. Speaking on June 7 about praying for others, he points out that it is not necessary to pray explicitly and in particular for every intention mentioned in chapter, but then adds that he can use all the prayers he can get, so they can pray for him whenever they want. Discussing conversions on May 14, he notes that a monk should have at least two conversions, one to get him into the monastery and another to make him a good monk; the second, he says, should take place about twenty years after entering the monastery, and adds, "I'm about due."

As a number of these examples suggest, there is a good deal of laughter, including Merton's own, throughout the conferences.[52] Merton often uses humor to make serious points, as when he is discussing the fact that constant prayer cannot mean explicitly "saying prayers" at all times, since "we are not made that way"; he says we don't want to pray all day any more than we want to eat all day, and after a well-timed pause adds, "sometimes we want to sleep!" Sleeping actually shows up a number of times with comic effect, as when on May 26 he is interpreting Cassian's phrase *"procumbentibus nobis ad pacem"*—the posture of prostration for prayer—and comments that it could well become "too popular" (people wouldn't get up); or when on June 7 he is discussing wordless prayer, and cautions that this doesn't mean applying a kind of syllogistic logic to the effect that as wordless prayer is the highest form of prayer, and I want to pray according to the highest form, I therefore should avoid all words: without the guidance of the Holy Spirit, he says, this will lead only to the prayer of sleep. While he wants the novices to take prayer and the monastic life seriously, he doesn't want them to take themselves too seriously. Humor is a kind of non-threatening

---

52. Asked by Merton how he found the conferences, Brother Columban Weber recalls that he "commented that his sense of humor surprised me and he said, 'If you have a sense of humor, you should use it.' He would often poke fun at various things we did around the monastery in a way that we could see the wisdom of it. Someone should do a study of Merton's sense of humor" (quoted in Lewis, "Learning to Live," 93).

way of juxtaposing ideals and reality, of gently undercutting
any tendencies to pious self-dramatizing, as when he notes that
meditation is simply focused, undistracted thought, whatever
its object, so that one could be deep in meditation about how to
rob a bank (June 2).

Merton's effort to apply the material to his novices' lives,
already quite evident in the written text, is heightened in oral
presentation both by addition and by subtraction. Usually the
comments Merton adds to his text have some sort of concrete
application in one way or another. Thus in discussing *Conference* 4, "On the Desires of the Flesh and of the Spirit" (April 28),
he places additional emphasis on the need for balance between
physical and spiritual dimensions, and warns his students to be
careful of apparently intense longings for spiritual things, especially for sensible fervor, which can be sought for its own sake
and so become as much of a trap as sensual desires. On May 14
he points out that trying to have an idea of God constantly in
one's mind can produce unnatural strain and tension, and tells
the novices that the real point is not to be always explicitly thinking about God but to have a heart constantly oriented toward
God, since it is love not knowledge that brings one into unbroken union with God. At the end of the same conference he emphasizes the need for simplicity in the monastic life, and points
out how difficult it is to be simple amid the complexities of life
in the world, where it is hard not to be at least two different
people, with one identity at home and another at work—though
he also points out that being content with a complicated life is
itself a way of being simple, and that one may certainly have
many interests, but all should contribute to one goal (ultimately,
the life of prayer). His extensive discussion of work and prayer
on May 19 and 26 emphasizes both the healthy alternation of
work, especially manual labor, and prayer in the monastic life,
as well as the temptation to find one's satisfaction in activity at
the expense of prayer. He alerts the novices to the inevitability
of dryness in prayer (May 26), the waning of the fervor that may
have brought them to the monastery, but reassures them that
this is a normal and necessary step, one that generally lasts for
many years, on the way to authentic contemplation. He returns

repeatedly to the frustrations of meaningless activity, comparing life "on the outside" to a treadmill where one has to use a tremendous amount of energy simply to remain in the same place (June 7). In explaining the petition of the Lord's Prayer, "Thy will be done" (July 7), he emphasizes that this is not only a passive but an active request, one that calls not merely for submission but for collaboration through a love that is creative and productive, not sentimental. These and similar statements take Cassian's words as a starting point, but then go on to apply them to situations that his listeners can readily relate to, showing the relevance of these ancient teachings to contemporary monastic life, and of contemporary monastic life to their own experiences.

Merton is not averse to streamlining his presentation to highlight certain points in his text by omitting others. He knows that the novices will eventually have a copy of the written lectures (in 1962 they were distributed on July 21, the third last class), so he feels no pressure to include everything that appears in the text in his oral presentations. He shows a good deal of flexibility, and a willingness on occasion to follow out a particular line of thought even when it gets away from the outline of the lecture, as with the discussion of balance on April 28, or of constant prayer on May 14. Relatively little of the written text is ever read word for word, aside from actual quotations from primary sources, and even these are sometimes summarized or paraphrased. While the written word provides the sturdy skeleton for the conferences, the flesh and blood, the living vitality of the presentations, comes from Merton's improvisations, his lively, often spontaneous interaction with his audience.

One final observation worth noting is Merton's punctilious fidelity to the monastic *horarium*. He stops immediately at the appointed time, with no running over or "rounding off" a topic (though he frequently seems to time his discussions fairly well so that he has brought a particular subsection to some sort of natural stopping point when the bell rings). This precision in itself could be taken as emblematic of the ways in which Merton "fit in" to the monastic pattern, at least in his public role, more compatibly than one might assume on the basis of some of his private comments alone. In fact the clear impression of Merton provided by the tapes is of someone completely engaged with his topic and completely present to his students, someone who is deeply interested in what he is doing and who enjoys doing it. While on certain levels he may have been longing for deeper solitude and for greater engagement in social issues, it seems quite evident that these desires do not distract him from his responsibilities to his novices nor detract from the effectiveness of his presentation. Listening to the conferences, as well as reading the text, strongly supports the supposition that his role as teacher was not a peripheral concern for Merton, and that if it did not completely content and fulfill him, it must have provided a considerable degree of satisfaction in work well done.

* * * * * * *

There are three major and one minor (but significant) witness to the text of _Cassian and the Fathers_. In the archives of the Merton Center at Bellarmine University is the actual typescript of the conferences used by Merton in his lectures. It consists of a title page, entitled "CASSIAN AND THE / FATHERS. Notes for / Conferences / Given in the Choir Novitiate, Abbey of Gethsemani" and two separately paginated sections. The first, forty typed pages,[53] is entitled on a separate page "PART ONE / MONASTIC SPIRITUALITY AND THE EARLY FATHERS / FROM APOSTOLIC FATHERS TO EVAGRIUS PONTICUS." with the title "PROLOGUE TO CASSIAN" on the first page of text and used as a running head thereafter.[54] A final page of this section, corresponding to material on pages 94–96 of this edition (from "Purity of thought" through the end of Part I), is missing in this

53. The pages are numbered consecutively 1–34, followed by 34a–b, followed by 35–37 (with pagination and running head "Prologue to Cassian" written by hand on pages of "APPENDIX TO CASSIAN. / EVAGRIUS PONTICUS ON PRAYER"); an unnumbered typed page marked "insert—Evagrius—" is found between pages 35 and 36, marked for insertion in the second paragraph of page 35. There is also an unnumbered handwritten page inserted between pages 34a and 34b which contains detailed instructions on Lenten practices, but no lecture materials.

54. The running head is generally abbreviated as "Prol. to Cass." or the like; on pages 18–21 and 24–25 the running head is "Intro. to Cass." while on page 26 it reads "Pref. to Cassian".

version of the text, though handwritten material on page 37v is marked for insertion on this missing page, which therefore was clearly part of the text when Merton was using it for his lectures. The second, eighty-five pages, of which seventy-six are typed,[55] is without a separate title page; it is headed "LECTURES ON CASSIAN" on the first page of text, with the running head "Cassian" (sometimes abbreviated). The text of both parts is typed on one side only, on three-ring binder paper.[56] It is evident that except for one short section, to be discussed below, this text was typed by Merton himself: it includes various on-line alterations that provide evidence that he was composing, or

55. The pagination of this second part is quite complicated: for the first sec-
ᵗ, up through the completion of the discussion of the *Institutes*, the pagina-
ᵗfter an unnumbered first page, is 2–5, 5 a–b (pencilled in on two typed
ᵗarked "Insert:" dealing with *Conference* 11), 6–18, 18a (a handwritten
ᵗook 3 of the *Institutes*), 19–46, 47 (misnumbered 46 and corrected in
ᵗ9; however pages 40–49 are renumbered 44, 45, 46, 47 cont'd, 48
ᵗt'd, 49–50, 51, 52, 53 to correspond with pagination of the first
ᵗpy [renumbering in pencil except for page 53, where "(mimeo-
ᵗ beneath "Cassian 49"]). Although the pagination of this section of
ᵗures on Cassian" runs through p. 49, the pagination of the section on
ᵗonferences that follows begins with page 46! The explanation is apparently
ᵗat the first pages numbered 46–49, on the twelfth book of the *Institutes* (Pride)
for some reason were not part of the earliest production of the typescript: discussion of Book 11 ends after eleven lines on page 45 and the rest of the page is blank, a practice not followed elsewhere in the typescript. The section on *Conferences* begins with an unnumbered handwritten page, followed by pages 46–58, two unnumbered handwritten pages on *Conference* 4, pages 59–70, one unnumbered handwritten page on the Later Conferences, three unnumbered handwritten pages on *Conference* 16, and one unnumbered handwritten page (four lines only) on *Conference* 14. Preceding the first page of the "Lectures on Cassian" there is also a handwritten page headed "Cassian—material for conferences" which was evidently Merton's earliest outline for his lectures; it is marked "(Skip this page)" and is not included in either of the other copies of the text (see Appendix A [261–62] for the text of this material).

56. The paper for the first part, the "Prologue to Cassian," has reinforced strips on the verso sides of the pages, except for the two title pages, the inserted page between pages 3 and 4, the non-text page between pages 34a and 34b, and pages 35–37 (the Evagrius pages); none of the pages in the second, "Lectures on Cassian," section has these reinforced strips except the first inserted page on *Conference* 4, the three handwritten pages on *Conference* 16 and the handwritten page on *Conference* 14. This difference reinforces other evidence that the two parts of the text were composed and typed at different times.

at least revising, in the process of typing.[57] The text also includes extensive handwritten additions by Merton himself, added at various times in different inks and occasionally in pencil. Some of the additions, generally shorter, are added on line, or interlined, or written in the margins, sometimes to replace cancelled words, phrases or sentences, more often as additions. Longer additions are written on the blank verso sides of the previous typed pages, and are customarily marked with arrows for insertion at the proper place; usually these are supplementary material, though in some instances they replace cancelled passages. Occasionally whole pages of material, either typed or handwritten, have been added: they are usually self-contained sections (e.g. material on a *Conference* not previously discussed). This is the most authoritative form of the text, and will be used as and referred to as the copy text. (The only material for which this typescript does not serve as the primary copy text is the "Appendix to Cassian" section, which will be discussed below.) Readings will depart from this version only when other versions have a more complete text (i.e. when the copy text directs the typist to "copy" a quotation not included in the typescript itself, or in rare cases when one of the other witnesses has a more developed version of the text that can plausibly be ascribed to Merton himself; all these instances are listed in Appendix A).

There are also two other extant typed versions of the text that were prepared and reproduced for distribution to the novices themselves. Both of these are included in Volume 18 of Merton's "Collected Essays," a series of bound copies of typescript reproductions of both subsequently published and unpublished ma-

---

57. For example, on page 6 of "Prologue to Cassian," Merton originally types "it is not mater" but x's it out and follows it on line with "the material is inferior . . ."; on page 10 of "Prologue to Cassian," Merton originally types "ascetic wa" but x's it out and follows it on line with "systematic way of asceticism . . ."; on page 6 of the "Lectures on Cassian," Merton originally types "Nesteros says" but x's it out and follows it on line with "The following night, Nesteros gives them . . ."; on page 9 of the "Lectures on Cassian," Merton originally types "think of them at all," but x's it out and follows it on line with "suffer any temptation or experience any phantasms proceeding from that kind of sin." Examples of this kind, which could easily be multiplied, make clear that Merton himself must have been doing the typing.

terials by Merton that was assembled at the Abbey of Gethsemani. Copies of the set are available both at the Abbey and at the Merton Center in Louisville.

The first, earlier typescript (henceforth referred to as "I") is entitled "Lectures on Cassian 1955–1956" and consists of 81 pages of ditto "spirit master" (i.e., purple) typed reproduction.[58] It is a witness to an early state of Merton's text. It includes only material on Cassian, without the "Preface to Cassian," and consists of a reproduction of the typescript and a relatively small percentage of the handwritten additions from Merton's own text of the "Lectures on Cassian." It is not completely certain when this version of the text was produced. The notation "1955–1956" on the title page suggests that it is the completed transcript of the conferences as delivered for the first time. The numerous handwritten additions from the copy text incorporated into this version could be considered evidence that this is actually a transcript of the second version of the text, plausibly dating from 1957–1958, and that the dates "1955–1956" could simply have been copied from Merton's own typescript.[59] However these handwritten additions are generally not extensive and could well represent notations Merton added in the process of delivering the lectures, before the typist had produced the copy for distribution. While the evidence is not completely conclusive, it seems best to assume that this version of the text dates from 1955–1956, the first time the course was given.

In the same volume of "Collected Essays" is a second version of the Conferences (henceforth referred to as "II"), reproduced in mimeographed form. It is entitled "Cassian and the Fathers" and includes both parts of the copy text, numbered separately: fifty-four pages of the "Prologue to Cassian" followed by ninety-four pages of the "Lectures on Cassian." It is clear that this version is based directly on the copy text, not on "I," for the material

58. The pages are numbered 1–18A, 18B–80; Evidently the typist failed to include a number on the nineteenth page, so a handwritten "A" was added on page 18 and "CASS. 18B" was handwritten on the top of what should have been page 19.

59. This was evidently the case for at least one other set of lecture notes: the bound copy of Merton's notes for the course on "The Rule of St. Benedict" is listed in the Table of Contents as "1960 reprint of '57 ed."

they have in common, since there are occasional correspondences between the copy text and II over against I, whether in a correct reading of a handwritten addition or in the inclusion of typed material inadvertently skipped in I; it would of course make little sense to use I as a basis for this new typescript, which includes the numerous handwritten additions made by Merton on his own typescript subsequent to the typing of I. (The typists of both I and II are generally quite accurate, and they are both skillful decipherers of Merton's sometimes obscure script, but each shows occasional instances of eyeskip or mistranscription.) This version includes most, but not all, of the additional handwritten additions present in the copy text.

The dating of this version of the text is again not definitive. A series of marginal notations in the copy text, consisting of dates from 6-22[-59] through 12-9-60 (corresponding to material on pages 19 through 145 of the present edition), were evidently made by a typist, and one strong piece of evidence points to his being the typist for this version of the text: after the date "7-1-60" near the bottom of the fourth page of the "Lectures on Cassian" section of the copy text (page 109 of this edition), there is a note reading "type last line only": the last line on this page reads "13th which contains the error on nature and grace."; the sixth page of the "Lectures on Cassian" section of II begins "which contains the error on nature and grace." While the correspondence is not exact ("13th" is the last word on the previous page of II), it seems more likely that the typist of 1959–1960 is the typist of II than that another typist (in 1961–1962) would have begun a new page at almost precisely the same point as his predecessor, since presumably the only reason for retyping would have been because there were numerous new handwritten additions to be incorporated into the text, which would have affected the pagination. There are relatively few handwritten additions in the typescript that are not included in II, but there are some, which also suggests that II is not a transcription of the final, 1961–1962 version of the lectures (though these additions are found almost exclusively toward the end of the text, so that an argument could be made that they were added after the typist had copied this section—according to the tape of the conference, the notes were distributed to the novices on July 21, 1962, the third last class session, when Merton was still in the midst of discussing the Lord's Prayer [page 247 of this edition]; the vast majority of the additions not included in II are either after or shortly before this point in the text). The strongest piece of evidence that would date II later than 1959–60 is a reference made to "Werner Jaeger's studies on Gregory [of Nyssa]—lectures at Harvard" in a handwritten note on page 21 of the "Prologue to Cassian" section of the copy text and included on page 28 of the corresponding section of II (page 53 of this edition); the reference is apparently to Jaeger's 1960 lectures at Harvard, published in 1961 as *Early Christianity and Greek Paideia*, which include an extensive section on Gregory of Nyssa. According to the marginal date in the copy text this page was apparently typed sometime in September 1959,[60] so that it could not have included a reference to lectures that had not yet been given, much less published. But this evidence for a later date for II is less persuasive than it first appears, since this page has been typed on a different typewriter than the first 26 pages of the text of II, so it could have been substituted at a later date, after the handwritten note on Jaeger had been added to the copy text. There were in fact four different typewriters used to type II, three of them in the "Prologue to Cassian" section, so that it is possible that II represents a hybrid text dating from more than one period.[61] Further complicating the matter is the possibility, to be discussed below, that the "Prologue to Cassian" material was not used at all in 1961–1962. While no final conclusion can be drawn, the evidence on balance seems to be more supportive of 1959–1960 as the date for the bulk of

60. The notation actually reads "9- -0" which might be taken as a reference to September 1960 (the previous notation reads "9-10-0") but subsequent references beginning with the following one to "10-7-59" seem to follow in sequence and clearly refer to October 1959 (and then jump to March 1960, followed by July through December 1960) so that the September date would appear to refer to 1959 despite the ambiguous use of "0" in the place generally used for the year.

61. The main typewriter for the "Prologue to Cassian" section of II is an elite model, which was used for pages 1–26, 30–31, 33–35; a second typewriter, with pica type, is used for pages 27–29, 32, 38–54, while yet a third machine, also pica, is used for pages 36–37. All the "Lectures on Cassian" section was typed on a single elite typewriter, but it is clearly not the same one used for the first part of the "Prologue."

the text of II, with some of the material from the "Prologue to Cassian" section having been revised and retyped later.

On March 27, 1958, Merton sent to his friend Sr. Thérèse Lentfoehr a three-page typescript with handwritten additions entitled "AN APPENDIX TO CASSIAN. / EVAGRIUS PONTICUS ON PRAYER." In the accompanying letter he writes, "Also if you get time I could use a copy of the Notes on Evagrius Ponticus although they are not really finished."[62] (Sr. Thérèse, who had typed much of Merton's lecture material while he was master of scholastics, was currently working on a typescript of his novitiate liturgy conferences.[63]) A comparison of the text sent to Sr. Thérèse, now in the Columbia University Library, with the pages on Evagrius that conclude the "Prologue to Cassian" section of the copy text, strongly indicate that these pages were typed by her, not by Merton—the only section of this typescript that does not come directly from Merton. Though the final page of this section is missing from the copy text (the only missing page, evidently misplaced after Merton had used it for his lecture, since there are handwritten additions on the opposite page marked for insertion in the now missing page), the surviving typewritten pages correspond almost exactly in text to the version Merton sent to Sr. Thérèse, but include the handwritten addition in typed form. There are however a few minor discrepancies between the two versions in which Merton's original copy preserves the proper reading.[64] Therefore the Columbia copy is, technically, the copy text for material present in both this text and in Merton's typescript, as well as for material from the missing final page of the "Prologue to Cassian" typescript, through "cf. Ruysbroeck: 'Superessential vision of the Trinity'" (for the rest of the missing material, which is not included in the Columbia copy, II serves as copy text). Merton's typescript continues to serve as

62. Unpublished letter of March 27, 1958 (Merton Center archives).

63. Unpublished letters of August 21, 1957, October 12, 1957, November 14, 1957, January 2, 1958, March 27, 1958, April 18, 1958, July 14, 1958, November 10, 1958 (Merton Center archives).

64. On page 90, the Columbia reading "definitively" is clearly superior to "definitely"; on page 93, "us to passion" was apparently misread by Lentfoehr as "me to passion" and on page 94, "untainted" was typed as "untained" (changed in II to "unstained").

copy text for all handwritten additions not found in the Columbia copy, as well as for the typed insert marked for inclusion on page 35 (pages 88–89 of this edition), which is also not included in the Columbia text.

The Cassian conferences were probably given four times. In 1955–1956, only the "Lectures on Cassian" were given, according to the evidence of I. There is no explicit evidence for the conferences being repeated in 1957–1958, but presumably they were, as this would correspond to the pattern of the cycle both in the previous and following years; probably only the Cassian lectures were given, perhaps with the addition of the Evagrius material, which is entitled "Appendix to Cassian" rather than "Prologue," "Introduction" or the like, suggesting it would have been given after the Cassian material rather than as part of a more extensive series of prefatory lectures corresponding to the "Prologue to Cassian." In 1959–1960, the evidence of the typist's marginal dates indicates that the entire course of lectures, both the "Prologue to Cassian" and the "Lectures on Cassian," was presented in this period, perhaps running over into the beginning of 1961.[65] The Cassian conferences were once again given in 1961–1962, as the tapes attest; but the evidence is unclear as to whether the "Prologue to Cassian" material was included in this cycle: there is a taped version of material on Clement and Origen based on the "Prologue to Cassian," but it dates from the summer of 1962,[66] after the "Lectures on Cassian" have been completed, and is part of a group of lectures on early Church Fathers otherwise different from the "Prologue to Cassian"; and

65. The typist's marginal dating stops after a final date of "12/9/60" but this only brings the lectures to the end of Book 3 of the *Institutes* (page 145 of this edition). It is of course impossible to tell what relation the schedule of typing had to the schedule of the actual delivery of the lectures. (In a February 4, 1960 letter to Dorothy Day, thanking her for offering to send a copy of a translation of Cassian that she had received, he remarks, "I am going to be lecturing on him shortly. Your offer is providential" [*Hidden Ground of Love*, 137], and in a letter to John Harris on May 13, 1960, he writes, "I have a conference on Cassian to give in a few minutes" [*Hidden Ground of Love*, 395], but the earliest notation on typing the "Lectures on Cassian" section is dated "7-1-60".)

66. According to Merton's preliminary remarks recorded on the tape (Credence Cassette # AA2082), the Origen conference takes place on the Feast of St. Louis, August 25.

while Merton makes reference to the Cassian lectures on the tape, there is no indication that this material on the Alexandrians had been part of a sequence of lectures immediately preceding the Cassian material, which at least some of the novices would presumably have been present to hear. This seems to suggest that perhaps only the Cassian lectures were given during this fourth and final cycle, or at least that the "Prologue to Cassian" material was not given in full.

The evidence of the tapes makes clear that neither part of the series was given after 1962. Instead, in 1963–1964 Merton developed and presented a new series of conferences entitled *Pre-Benedictine Monasticism*, not dependent on *Cassian and the Fathers* but covering much of the same ground. Originally the new course was intended to focus on European predecessors of St. Benedict, particularly in southern France, but as it developed it included extensive coverage of Pachomius and Basil as well as Cassian. But Merton does not draw on the same notes for these figures: in the Cassian section, he discusses some different *Conferences*, and when he discusses the same *Conferences* as in *Cassian and the Fathers* the treatment is noticeably different. In 1964–1965, the last year of his time as Novice Master, he presents a second series of conferences on *Pre-Benedictine Monasticism*, focusing particularly on Syrian and Palestinian monasticism; this series was completed on August 15, just before Merton moved into the hermitage permanently. While Merton refers to *Cassian and the Fathers* a number of times in the new course,[67] the two series of *Pre-Benedictine Monasticism* conferences effectively, if not intentionally, served as an alternative presentation of much of the same material. Thus *Cassian and the Fathers*, which in its earliest form dated back to the very beginning of Merton's term as Master of Novices, was not repeated during the final three years of that term.

* * * * * * *

67. For example, when he comes to Cassian in the first series of *Pre-Benedictine Monasticism* conferences, he writes, "As we have a whole course on Cassian, it is sufficient at this point to show in outline the doctrine of Evagrius as transmitted by Cassian to the West" (16), but he then goes on to spend eighteen pages discussing various *Conferences* (including *Conference* 14, begun but abandoned at the end of the present text).

This edition uses Merton's own typescript with its hand-written additions as copy text (except for the Evagrius Ponticus section of the "Prologue to Cassian," where Merton's typescript sent to Sr. Thérèse Lentfoehr takes precedence over her retyping of this text; for the brief portion of this section missing from both Merton's and Sr. Thérèse's typescripts, the II text serves as copy text). All substantive additions made to the text, in order to turn elliptical or fragmentary statements into complete sentences,[68] are included in braces, as are the few emendations incorporated directly into the text, so that the reader can always determine exactly what Merton himself wrote. No effort is made to reproduce Merton's rather inconsistent punctuation, paragraphing, abbreviations and typographical features; a standardized format for these features is established that in the judgement of the editor best represents a synthesis of Merton's own practice and contemporary usage (e.g., all Latin passages are italicized unless specific parts of a longer passage are underlined by Merton, in which case the underlined section of the passage is in roman type; all other passages underlined by Merton are italicized; words in upper case in the text are printed in small caps; periods and commas are uniformly included within quotation marks; patterns of abbreviation and capitalization, very inconsistent in the copy text, are regularized). Latin passages in the original text are left in Latin but translated by the editor in the notes. All references to primary and secondary sources are cited in the notes (cf. in particular unreferenced passages from Cassian and other patristic writers, which are cited by column and section number of the appropriate volume of the *Patrologia Latina*). All identified errors in Merton's text are noted and if possible corrected. All instances where subsequent research and expanded knowledge affect Merton's accuracy are discussed in the notes (e.g., the Macarian writings).

The textual apparatus does not attempt to record every variation between the different versions of the text. Errors in either

68. In an unpublished letter of May 21, 1955, Merton writes to Sr. Thérèse Lentfoehr concerning her typing of his "Monastic Orientation" lectures (given as master of scholastics), "When typing it, if you find any place that I have not made a proper sentence out of a note, will you please supply the necessary verb or preposition or whatever is needed?"

of the two later typescript copies of the text, whether of omission or of mistranscription, are not recorded since they have no independent authority vis-à-vis the copy text. No attempt is made to record on-line corrections Merton made in the process of typing (i.e., crossing out one word or phrase and immediately substituting another); changes in handwritten additions are recorded, however.

Notes on the text record:

a) all cases in which a reading from I or II is added to or substituted for the copy text—generally limited to the typist following Merton's own instructions for expanding the text; in those cases where Merton's direction to expand the text is not followed, the text is left as it is in II, the direction is recorded in the textual apparatus, and the addition is included in the explanatory notes;

b) all handwritten additions or alterations to the original typed text that are incorporated in I;

c) all handwritten additions or alterations to the original typed text that are not incorporated in I but are incorporated in II;

d) all handwritten additions or alterations to the original typed text that are not incorporated in either I or II.

Thus the textual notes allow the interested reader to trace the development of Merton's text through various stages and so make possible a study of how his thoughts on and presentation of his material in successive cycles evolved (with the caveat that the dating of the various stages is not absolutely determined, and that there may have been successive layers of additions within the extant versions of the text).

Also included as a second appendix is a table correlating the written text and the taped lectures, which facilitates comparison of Merton's version of the material as published in this edition with the conferences as actually delivered to the novices.

Finally, a list of suggestions for further reading is included as a third appendix, consisting first of other sources in Merton's published works where figures and topics from this volume are discussed, followed by a list of important recent studies on the major figures and topics of this volume, that will provide helpful updating on material discussed by Merton.

* * * * * * *

In conclusion I would like to express my gratitude to all those who have made this volume possible:

- to the Trustees of the Merton Legacy Trust, Robert Giroux, Anne McCormick and Tommie O'Callaghan, for permission to publish the *Cassian and the Fathers* conferences;
- to the late Robert E. Daggy, former director of the Thomas Merton Center, Bellarmine College (now University), Louisville, KY, for first alerting me to the project of editing the novitiate conferences, and for his encouragement in this and other efforts in Merton studies;
- to E. Rozanne Elder, director of Cistercian Publications, for graciously accepting my offer to participate in this project, providing encouragement and support along the way, and seeing it through to completion;
- to Jonathan Montaldo, former director of the Merton Center, for his gracious hospitality during my visits to the Center, for facilitating my research in ways both professional and inspirational, and especially for bringing to my attention the original typescript of the *Cassian and the Fathers* conferences;
- to Abbot Timothy Kelly, OCSO, Brother Paul Quenon, OCSO, and Brother Harold Thibodeau, OCSO for generously sharing their own recollections of Merton's novitiate conferences, and especially to Brother Paul for arranging and facilitating my research at Gethsemani;
- to Joshua Brands, former Gethsemani archivist, and Father Joachim Johnson, OCSO, for their very helpful assistance in orienting me to the Gethsemani library and in locating hard-to-find materials in the library and the abbey scriptorium;
- to Erasmo Leiva-Merikakis, who fortuitously—or providentially—suggested the location of the unpublished materials Merton used as sources for his lectures;

- to Brother Patrick Hart, OCSO, for his continued encouragement along the way and for choosing this volume to initiate the new Monastic Wisdom series of which he serves as editor;
- to the Gannon University Research Committee, which provided a grant that allowed me to pursue research on this project at the Merton Center and at the Abbey of Gethsemani;
- to John Euliano, formerly of the interlibrary loan department of the Nash Library, Gannon University, for his tireless efforts in locating and acquiring various obscure volumes; to library staff of the Friedsam Memorial Library of St. Bonaventure University, of the Columbia University Library, of the Hesburgh Library of the University of Notre Dame, and of the Divinity School Library, the Sterling Memorial Library and the Mudd Library of Yale University, for assistance in locating important materials in their collections; to my sons David and Michael, for faithfully and repeatedly supplying me with material from the Ohio State University and University of Notre Dame libraries, respectively;
- first, last and always to my wife Suzanne for her constant love, support and encouragement, and her willingness throughout the past thirty-three years to make ever more room for Thomas Merton on our bookshelves and in our life together.

CASSIAN AND THE FATHERS

Notes for Conferences
Given in the Choir Novitiate, Abbey of Gethsemani[1]

—Index of Contents—[2]

1. A handwritten notation (not by Merton) on the title page of II reads: "(late fifties) 1956–".

2. This index, found only in II, does not in all cases correspond precisely to the subheadings in the text itself; page numbers to the present edition are given only for the entries with page numbers in the typescript of II.

MONASTIC SPIRITUALITY AND THE EARLY FATHERS FROM APOSTOLIC FATHERS TO EVAGRIUS PONTICUS

PROLOGUE TO CASSIAN

It would be useless to study Cassian without some background. We have to know where he fits in to the history and development of Christian spirituality. We shall see later why he is considered so important for monks. Meanwhile—a few general remarks to start with.

Return to Sources

If for some reason it were necessary for you to drink a pint of water taken out of the Mississippi River and you could choose where it was to be drawn out of the river—would you take a pint from the source of the river in Minnesota or from the estuary at New Orleans? This example is perhaps not perfect. Christian tradition and spirituality certainly do not become polluted with development. That is not the idea at all. Nevertheless, tradition and spirituality are all the more pure and genuine in proportion as they are in contact with the original sources and retain the same content.

Pius XII insisted[3] that religious strive for *renewal* of their own authentic tradition, by a return to sources. Monastic spirituality

3. Pius XII's major statements on religious life are collected in Gaston Courtois, ed., *The States of Perfection According to the Teaching of the Church: Papal Documents from Leo XIII to Pius XII*, trans. John O'Flynn (Westminster, MD: Newman, 1961). While references to a founder's vision are present (cf. for example 52 [on Ignatius], 115 [on Benedict], 132 [on Joseph Calasanctius], 182–83 [on tradition and adaptation], 310, 319 [on superiors' fidelity to founders' aims]), the theme of renewal according to the spirit of the founder is considerably less prominent than it becomes in the Vatican II "Decree on the Appropriate Renewal of the Religious Life" (*"Perfectae Caritatis"*), which called for "a continuous return to the sources of all Christian life and to the original inspiration behind a given community" (article 2, in Walter Abbott, ed., *The Documents of Vatican II*

is especially traditional and depends much on return to sources—to Scripture, Liturgy, Fathers of the Church. More than other religious the monk is a man who is nourished at the early sources. Monastic life {is the} earliest form of religious life—the monk by his vocation belongs to the earliest kind of Christian spirituality. He must be able to go back *direct* to *his own* sources. The original monastic sources have contributed to the stream of spirituality that has branched out in all the other orders; but the monk should get the life-giving waters from his proper source and not channeled through other spiritualities of later date, which have in them elements that are alien to the monastic life.

Besides *renewal* of our own tradition we must of course obviously *adapt* ourselves to the needs of our time, and a return to tradition does not mean trying to revive, in all its details, the life lived by the early monks, or trying to do all the things that they did. But it means living in our time and solving the problems of our time in the way and with the spirit in which they lived in a different time and solved different problems.

Materials

In order to prepare the ground for a study of Cassian, some background reading might be suggested. Pourrat's *Christian Spirituality*, vol. I,[4] is a standard text and is especially concerned with early monasticism. Unfortunately it has its limitations— and these are inevitable in a broad survey. It is however a good standard book. We are fortunate to have a set of notes translated from the French of a former novice master of Chimay (Belgium),[5]

[New York: Herder and Herder, 1966], 468). However, in his commentary on the decree, Friedrich Wulf notes that in its balance between "a return to origins" and "an accommodation to the needs of the world," the one constant throughout the multiple drafts of the document, "we might almost speak of a topic that originated in the addresses of Pius XII" (in Herbert Vorgrimler, ed., *Commentary on the Documents of Vatican II* [New York: Herder and Herder, 1968], 2:305).

    4. Pierre Pourrat, *Christian Spirituality, vol. I: From the Time of Our Lord till the Dawn of the Middle Ages*, trans. W. H. Mitchell and S. P. Jacques (1927; Westminster, MD: Newman, 1953).

    5. Fr. François Mahieu, ocso, "A History of Spirituality," translated at Gethsemani, February 1956, 124 pp. [typed, single-spaced, mimeographed].

giving a very good introduction to Christian and especially monastic spirituality up to Cassian (but not including him). This is one of the best studies on the period and is particularly good on some of the Desert Fathers, v.g., St. Macarius the Egyptian. Other books—we have some of the early Christian writers, St. Ignatius, *The Didache*[6]—early biographies like that of St. Anthony by St. Athanasius[7]—a fairly good book on Cassian by Owen Chadwick[8] (non-Catholic) and a few others (an antiquated translation of the *Vitae Patrum*[9]). Patrologies are useful, particularly Quasten.[10] In your browsing in {the} library, etc., get to know Patristic and Monastic source books.

Early Christian Spirituality

The Early Church (first and second centuries)

These were the days of the great persecutions. Hence the Christian was above all confronted at any moment with MARTYRDOM.

6. *The Apostolic Fathers*, trans. Francis X. Glimm, Joseph M.-F. Marique, SJ, Gerald G. Walsh, SJ, The Fathers of the Church, vol. 1 (New York: Christian Heritage, 1947).

7. *Early Christian Biographies*, ed. Roy J. Deferrari, trans. Roy J. Deferrari *et al.*, The Fathers of the Church, vol. 15 (New York: Fathers of the Church, 1952).

8. Owen Chadwick, *John Cassian: A Study in Primitive Monasticism* (Cambridge: Cambridge University Press, 1950); a second edition, entitled simply *John Cassian*, appeared in 1968. Unless otherwise noted, references will be to the first edition.

9. Merton is apparently referring here to Thomas Challoner's compilation and translation, *The Lives of the Fathers of the Eastern Deserts*, 2 vols. (Boston: D. & J. Sadlier, 1852), a collection beginning with a life of John the Baptist and including abridged versions of about thirty lives of various Desert Fathers. The *Vitae Patrum* (*Lives of the Fathers*) is not a distinct work in itself but an early seventeenth-century compilation, by Heribert Rosweyde, in ten books, of the main sources of early Eastern Christian monasticism in Latin translation, including the *Lives of Antony*, *Pachomius* and many others, the *Historia Monachorum*, the *Historia Lausiaca*, the *Verba Seniorum*, etc.; it is reprinted in J. P. Migne, ed., *Patrologiae Cursus Completus, Series Latina*, 221 vols. (Paris: Garnier, 1844–1865), vols. 73–74 (subsequently referred to as *PL* in text and notes). Challoner's work includes a relatively small proportion of this material, as well as other writings not found in this collection.

10. Johannes Quasten, *Patrology*, 3 vols. (Westminster, MD: Newman, 1951–1960): vol 1: *The Beginnings of Patristic Literature*; vol. 2: *The Ante-Nicene Literature after Irenaeus*; vol. 3: *The Golden Age of Greek Patristic Literature*. (Though not written by Quasten, a fourth volume in the series, *The Golden Age of Latin Patristic Literature*, edited by Angelo di Berardino, appeared in 1986.)

This is the keynote to the spirituality of the first centuries. Together with martyrdom as an ever-present possibility and con-
ceived as the summit of the spiritual life, was also the ideal of
virginity. Martyrdom and virginity were considered as supreme
forms of union with Christ by the sacrifice of all that the world
holds dear. *Asceticism* went with this, hand in hand. The idea
was, in all literal fact, to take up one's cross and follow Christ
into the Kingdom where He reigns in glory. The Christian had
no perspectives in this present life.

The *life of the Christian* was centered in the unity of the
Church—a unity of perfect love, in which everything was still
very much in common, and in which the Sacred Liturgy, the reen-
actment of the Redemptive Sacrifice of Christ, was the great communal act, the source of all strength, life, courage to face
martyrdom, etc. The life of the Christian was an intense life of
love and self-forgetfulness in the community of the faithful,
closely united together in Christ by the Liturgy, and daily expecting to bear witness to their faith in Christ by death.

In this situation there was not much literature, not much
"pious reading." What was written was written to be read to the
community—or for the formation of catechumens. Examples
{include}—St. Ignatius and his *Epistles*; *The Didache* or "Teaching" (of the Twelve Apostles); the *Shepherd* of Hermas (allegorical and apocalyptic visions).[11] Note that the spirituality of the
early Church was strongly eschatological. We may discuss these
in detail at some other time. Meanwhile—a few samples.

The Didache: "There are two ways, one of life and one of
death; and great is the difference between the two ways"[12] (opening words). The way of life is simply the way of the Gospel and
in summarizing it the author repeats and summarizes the main
moral teachings of Jesus, quoted from the Gospel. READ for instance nn. 2 and 3 (*Apostolic Fathers*, p. 171).[13] READ especially

---

11. All of these works are included in *The Apostolic Fathers* (*op. cit.*).

12. *Apostolic Fathers*, 171.

13. "This is the way of life: 'First you shall love God who made you, secondly, your neighbor as yourself; and whatever you would not like done to
you, do not do to another.' The teaching of these words is as follows: 'Bless
those who curse you, and pray for your enemies, and fast for those who perse-
cute you. For what is the merit of loving those who love you? Do not even the

chapters 9 and 10 on the Eucharist—beautiful, simple, deep—
{the} first beginnings of the liturgy in spontaneous prayer. We
should keep this spirit and spontaneity in our own worship.
Chapter 10 {is} a model for the Mass, {and} can also be model
for our own prayer after communion (pp. 178–179).[14]

    St. Ignatius of Antioch[15] {was the} second successor to St. Peter
as Bishop of Antioch, {an} important city. {His writings are
marked by} ardent love for Christ, love for unity of the Church,
thirst for martyrdom. Study his conception of the Church and
of the Christian life. READ Magnesians 4–8 (pp. 97–98)—unity of
the Church;[16] Romans 1–5 (pp. 108–109)—his desire for martyrdom:[17] {the} whole epistle should be read and meditated. It is
tremendous.

---

pagans do this?['] But, 'love those who hate you,' and you will not have an
enemy."

    14. Chapter 9 presents short communion prayers, first in relation to the
cup, then to "the breaking of bread," and specifies that communion is to be re-
stricted to the baptized. Chapter 10 records a longer post-communion prayer,
followed by a note that prophets should be permitted to pray in their own
words.

    15. Merton will discuss Ignatius in greater detail in his conferences on "As-
cetical and Mystical Theology: From the Apostolic Fathers to the Council of
Trent" (1961), pages 14–17 of typescript.

    16. Chapter 4 emphasizes that to be a Christian not just in name but in fact
requires unity with the bishop and regular assembly for worship; chapter 5 contrasts the way of life and the way of death, of God and of the world, and stresses
the necessity of sharing in the Passion of Christ in order to have life; chapter 6 focuses on the three-fold office of bishops, priests and deacons, and again emphasizes unity with the bishop; chapter 7 proposes the unity of Jesus with the Father
as a model for Church unity; chapter 8 warns against being led astray "by new
doctrines or old fables," and focuses on the central Christian teaching "that there
is one God, who has manifested Himself in Jesus Christ His Son, who is His Word
proceeding from silence . . ." Church unity is the topic of Merton's 1961 essay
"Church and Bishop in St. Ignatius of Antioch" (in *Seasons of Celebration* [New
York: Farrar, Straus, Giroux, 1965], 28–44), which opens with a quotation from the
first chapter of the Letter to the Magnesians (28), in which Merton says Ignatius'
"whole ecclesiology, in fact his whole theology is contained in brief" (29).

    17. After an introduction praising the Roman Church, chapter 1 asks the
Romans not to try to rescue him from martyrdom; chapter 2 repeats this request
and presents his death as a sacrificial offering; chapter 3 asks for their prayers
that he "may be a Christian not merely in name but in fact"; chapter 4 expresses
his wish to become "God's wheat . . . ground by the teeth of the wild beasts
that I may end as the pure bread of Christ" (Merton quotes this passage, in another

Hence the spirituality of the age of the martyrs can be summed up as follows:

a) Everything is centered in the *unity of the Mystical Christ*—humility and meekness and the virtues that promote unity are paramount, and above all *charity*. READ quotes from Epistle of Clement (in Pourrat, vol. I, pp. 50–51):

> The heavens, set in motion by His command, obey Him in peace. Day and night fulfil the course He has laid down for them without interfering with one another. The sun, the moon, and the groups of stars follow according to His ordinance in harmony and without deviation the orbits He has prescribed for them. The fruitful earth in obedience to His will brings forth in due season an abundance of food for man and brute, and for all the creatures that live thereon. . . . The vast sea, confined within the bed which His creative hand has hollowed out, breaks not the bounds that He has set, but as He hath ordained, no farther doth it go. He hath said unto it: *Thus far shalt thou go, and here shall thy waves be broken in thy bosom.* . . . The seasons of spring, summer, autumn, and winter peacefully succeed one another. The winds in their abodes fulfil their functions at the appointed times undisturbed; the never-failing springs, made for man's refreshment and health, offer him an inexhaustible life-giving flow of life. . . . The sovereign Creator and Master of the universe hath ordained that all these things should abide in peace and concord (I Clem. xxi, 8).
>
> Make us submissive to Thy most mighty and excellent name, to our princes and governors in this world. For Thou, O Master, hast given them the power of reigning by Thy glorious and unspeakable might, in order that, knowing the glory and honour Thou hast assigned to them, we should obey them and not contradict Thy will. O Lord, grant unto them health, peace, concord, and stability, that they may wield without hindrance the sovereignty which Thou hast given them. For Thou, Master, and heavenly King of all the ages, givest unto the sons of men glory, honour and power over the things of the earth. Guide Thou, O Lord,

---

translation, in "Church and Bishop," 32); chapter 5 describes the hardships of the journey and the approaching suffering as of no import "so long as I get to Jesus Christ" (110).

their counsels according to that which is good, according
to that which is pleasing in Thy sight, so that they may use
with reverence in peace and mildness the power which
Thou hast given them, and enjoy Thy favor (Prayer for the
Roman emperors by Clement and the Roman Christians in
their liturgical gatherings: I Clem. lx, 4 to lxi, 2).

b) Special emphasis {is put} on the mystique of martyrdom—
the consummation of the Christian's consecration of himself to
Christ in baptism. Tertullian {writes}: "A prison provides a Christian with the same advantages that a desert gives to a prophet."[18]
This is interesting. Not only are the Desert Fathers heirs to the
vocation of the martyrs, but the martyrs are the heirs of those
pre-desert fathers, the prophets. In either case, {there is} the idea
of {the} *prophetic* vocation of the Christian saint as witness to the
presence of Christ in the world (classic example—St. John {the}
Baptist—model of martyrs, of monks, and of prophets). Tertullian
encourages martyrs in strength and love of suffering for Christ.

> Blessed martyrs, look upon every hardship you have to en-
> dure as fitted to develop in you virtues of soul and body.
> You are about to take up the good fight in which the living
> God will award the prize. . . . Christ Jesus, who has
> anointed you with the Holy Spirit, has willed before the
> day of battle to take away your freedom and to deal with
> you stoutly to toughen your strength. Athletes, as we know,
> in order to harden themselves, withdraw from their fel-
> lows to undergo a regime of greater severity. They abstain
> from all indulgence, all dainty fare, and all too pleasant
> drink. They do themselves violence, undergo pain, tire
> themselves out, being surer of winning the more thoroughly
> they are trained. And yet all this is, as the Apostle says (I
> Cor. ix. 25) "that they may receive a corruptible crown: but
> we an incorruptible one." Let us then regard the prison as
> the place where we are trained to suffer, that we may be
> broken in to it when we are led forth to the tribunal. For a
> hard life increases virtue, softness on the contrary destroys
> it (Tertullian, *Ad Martyr.*, 3).[19]

18. Tertullian, *Ad Martyros*, 2, quoted from Pourrat, I:52 (which reads ". . .
as a desert . . .").
19. Quoted from Pourrat, I:52-53.

St. Cyprian writes, in his *Exhortation to Martyrs*:

> The world becomes a prison, in time of persecution: but
> the heavens are opened. Antichrist threatens but Christ
> comes to the rescue; death is inflicted, but immortality fol-
> lows; the martyr who is put to death loses the world, but
> restored to life he gains paradise. Temporal life is snuffed
> out but eternal life is given in exchange. What dignity and
> what joy to go hence from this life in joy, to sally forth in
> glory from the midst of torture and afflictions: in one mo-
> ment to close those eyes which saw men and the world and
> open the same immediately in order to see God and Christ.
> *Tam feliciter migrandi quanta velocitas.* [Note possible allu-
> sion to the *Pascha Christi, transitus.*] Thou art instantly taken
> out of this world in order to be placed in the kingdom of
> heaven. This ought to be embraced by our thought and
> meditation, this ought to be turned over in our minds day
> and night. If persecution comes upon such a soldier of God,
> his strength girded for battle cannot be overcome.[20]

Typical of the spirit of the martyrs, this strength and love of sacrifice is passed on and handed down by the martyr to the monk
his successor. How necessary to have some of this spirit in our
monastic life. Otherwise how feeble and inert we will be, how
lacking in generosity, how tepid in fulfilling our sacred obligations. St. Cyprian wrote another characteristic treatise on *The
Good of Patience* which refers to the sufferings of the martyrs and
by extension applies to all Christian suffering, as the way of overcoming every vice.[21] The age of the martyrs looked at union with
Christ Crucified, by martyrdom, as the ideal way of fulfilling
one's vocation to union with Christ and swallowing up all sin
and burying sin and punishment alike in the Blood of Christ.
But not all were martyrs—nor was it sufficient to hope for mar-

20. St. Cyprian, *Ad Fortunatum, de exhortatione ad martyr[em]*, 13: Merton's
translation of the Latin in Pourrat I:53, n. 2; "What dignity and what joy" is
properly translated "What dignity and what security" [*securitas*]; the words left
untranslated mean: "How happily [and with] what speed of movement."
"*Pascha Christi, transitus*" means "Christ's Pasch, passing over."
21. See the Latin quotation from chapter 20 of this work in Pourrat I:55, n.
1, which praises patience as "tempering anger, reining in the tongue, governing
the mind, guarding peace, enthroning discipline, breaking the force of lust," etc.

tyrdom as the exclusive and unique way of being a perfect Christian. What if one did not die a martyr? How should one live? One should live as if preparing for martyrdom. But the Christian virtues should be practiced in a very special way by certain groups within the Church. Here we find *virgins and ascetes* (ascetes applying to men leading lives of chastity, prayer and penance) and the *widows*: three forms of continent and mortified life. Origen says: in the parable of the sower, the three degrees of fruitfulness of the seed sown in good ground refer to the following: those who bear a hundredfold—the martyrs; sixtyfold—the virgins (and ascetes); thirtyfold—the widows.[22]

The Ideal of the Virgins and Ascetes:

a) The life of virginity is also a life of union with Christ. The virgin is the Bride of Christ (Tertullian). *Nupsisti enim Christo, illi carnem tuam tradidisti. Age pro mariti tui disciplina* (Tertullian);[23] cf. {also} Clement—quotes from the *Paidagogos* below.[24]

22. Merton is in error here. He has adapted this from Mahieu, 46: "After *Origen* and *St. Cyprian*, the yield of the seed in the parable of the Sower, is understood in the following way: A hundredfold is the martyr[;] sixtyfold is the virgin[;] thirtyfold is the widow." Mahieu does not actually say that Origen used this interpretation, and in his definitive discussion of the history of interpretation of this passage, Antonio Quacquarelli specifically says that he did not: see *Il triplice frutto della vita cristiana: 100, 60 e 30 (Matteo XIII-8, nelle diverse interpretazioni)*, 2nd ed. (1953; Bari: Edipuglia, 1989), 27. Cyprian equates the hundredfold with martyrdom and sixtyfold with virginity, but does not discuss the thirtyfold (*De habitu virginum*, 21; Quacquarelli, 23; see also *Ep*. 76:6, not mentioned by Quacquarelli). There are in fact a number of variations of this arrangement, including a hundredfold to the martyrs, sixtyfold to the virgins and thirtyfold to the faithful in general, and a hundredfold to the virgins, sixtyfold to the widows and thirtyfold to the lawfully married (Quacquarelli, 31). The martyr, virgin, widow triad is actually best known, perhaps, from Jerome's letter to Pammachius (*Ep*. 48; *PL* 22, col. 500), which disagrees with inclusion of martyrdom in the series because it excludes married people (Quacquarelli, 46); Jerome's own preferred interpretation is virgins, widows, spouses (43–44). While Quacquarelli in one place lists martyrs, virgins, widows along with virgins, widows, spouses as the two major interpretations of the parable in the West (63), in his conclusion his two classifications are martyrs, virgins, spouses and virgins, widows, spouses (118).
23. "For you have become betrothed to Christ; you have handed over your flesh to him. Practice discipline for your husband's sake": Tertullian, *De oratione*, 22, quoted in Pourrat I:41, n. 3.
24. There is no bridal imagery in the passages from the *Paidagogos* to which

b) Those who embrace the life of virginity do not merely renounce marriage and legitimate pleasures of the flesh, but in general they embrace lives of greater mortification. While all the faithful fast on Wednesday and Friday, these have an even stricter rule of life. "We often meet with Christians who might marry and thus spare themselves the aggravation of the struggle between the flesh and the spirit. They prefer to refrain from exercising their right, but to lay upon themselves hard penances, to keep under their bodies by fasting, to bring them under obedience by abstinence from certain foods, and thus in every way to mortify by the spirit the works of the flesh" (Origen, *In Jeremiam Hom.* xix, 7 [*PG* 13:517]). "Virginity requires a strong and generous nature, which soars with a vigorous beat of wing above the tide of pleasure and makes for loftiest heights of heaven, a steadfast nature which never goes back upon its resolution to keep its virginity, until it has passed beyond the borders of this world and reached heaven to contemplate in all its brightness Purity in itself as it proceeds from the stainless soul of the Almighty" (Methodius, *Feast* i, 1 [*PG* 18:37]).[25]

c) Since perfect chastity is a special gift of God, then it must be asked for and preserved *by a life of constant prayer*. But prayer is not only associated with the virginal life because of its difficulties. Also, the life of virginity fits one to offer special praise to God. It becomes a life of praise, a life devoted (later on) to the *opus Dei*.[26] The virgins follow the Lamb singing hymns wherever He goes. Apocalypse 14:1-6:

> And I saw, and behold, the Lamb was standing upon Mount
> Sion, and with him a hundred and forty-four thousand hav-

Merton refers (see below, pages 21–22); Merton may be thinking of his references to Origen's writings on the Song of Songs (see below, pages 27–29).

25. The information about fasting as well as the two quotations is taken from Pourrat I:45; the reference is to J. P. Migne, ed., *Patrologiae Cursus Completus, Series Graeca*, 161 vols. (Paris: Garnier, 1857–1866) (subsequently referred to as *PG* in text and notes).

26. Literally "the work of God," used in reference to the divine office; see *The Rule of St. Benedict in Latin and English*, ed. and trans. Justin McCann, OSB (London: Burns, Oates, 1952), c. 7 (46); c. 22 (70); c. 43 (102); c. 44 (104, 106); c. 47 (108); c. 50 (116); c. 52 (118); c. 58 (130); c. 67 (152).

ing his name and the name of his Father written on their
foreheads. And I heard a voice from heaven like a voice of
many waters, and like a voice of loud thunder; and the
voice that I heard was as of harpers playing on their harps.
And they were singing as it were a new song before the
throne, and before the four living creatures and the elders;
and no one could learn the song except those hundred and
forty-four thousand, who have been purchased from the
earth. These are they who were not defiled with women;
for they are virgins. These follow the Lamb wherever he
goes. These were purchased from among men, first-fruits
unto God and unto the Lamb, and in their mouth there was
found no lie; they are without blemish.

It is especially fitting that pure souls should devote themselves
to the praise of God—they are able to love and understand Him
better; they are on more intimate terms with Him; praise in the
mouth of a pure person is more pleasing to God, etc. This life of
prayer early took the form of an embryonic divine office: *Vigils*—
all Christians assisted at vigils of reading and psalmody in
church from Saturday to Sunday (from this arose {the} office of
matins). Virgins and ascetes habitually prayed at set times of
the day, especially morning, noon and evening. The prayer life
of all was centered, of course, in the Holy Eucharistic sacrifice.[27]

d) The life of prayer and penance was also accompanied by
good works. Virgins and ascetes were assigned officially to certain works of mercy in the Church, as part of their vocation.
Hence the virginal life is an angelic life (*bios angelikos*), a special
spiritual gift coming down from heaven. But it must be accompanied with humility and works of charity. (St. John Chrysostom
will later point out that the foolish virgins with no oil in their
lamps lacked works of mercy and were attached to their possessions. See our Breviary.[28]) The pure love of the virgins, far

27. The information on common prayer is taken from Pourrat I:46.
28. See Mahieu, 46: "Nevertheless, the Fathers did not leave untouched the
relative value of virginity. They give warnings against the vanity that can be
drawn from it. They want it to be accompanied by all the virtues and works of
charity. (The oil which the foolish virgins forgot: Cf. St. John Chrysostom, Brev.
Comm. Of Virgins, Others Lessons, III Noct.)." The reference is to the *Breviarium
Cisterciense*, 4 vols. (Westmalle, 1951), 145–46 (in all 4 volumes), a reading from

from being sterile, is spiritually fecund (*gloriosa fecunditas*) in the Church, not only spiritually but even temporally. St. Ambrose was to say later: "Where virgins are few in number there the population diminishes, but where virginity is held in honor there too the number of inhabitants increases,"[29] and he refers to Alexandria as an example.

Aberrations in the First Centuries

In order to understand the Christian tradition of the early centuries we must also know about the aberrations from the true tradition, which had a significant effect. On the other hand we have to be careful in studying such things: not because we are likely to be led astray by the errors themselves, but because we are apt to make judgements that are too crude both of the nature of error and of the nature of true Christian spirituality. {There is a} danger of drawing very clear lines of demarcation, with all black on one side and all white on the other, {and so a} need for greater discernment. For instance, much that was good in Neoplatonism has in fact passed over to the Fathers, v.g. St. Augustine.

Chrysostom's *Homily 79* (error for *78*) *in Matt.* See Philip Schaff, ed., *Nicene and Post-Nicene Fathers*, 1st series, trans. George Prevost (1888; reprint: Grand Rapids, MI: Eerdmans, 1969), 10:470-71: "He putteth forth this parable sufficient to persuade them, that virginity, though it should have everything else, if destitute of the good things arising out of almsgiving, is cast out with the harlots, and He sets the inhuman and merciless with them. And most reasonably, for the one was overcome by the love of carnal pleasure, but these of money. . . . Therefore also He calls them foolish, for that having undergone the greater labor, they have betrayed all for want of the less. But by lamps here, He meaneth the gift itself of virginity, the purity of holiness; and by oil, humanity, almsgiving, succor to them that are in need. . . . For nothing is more sullied than virginity not having mercy; so that even the multitude are wont to call the unmerciful dark." Chrysostom makes this point repeatedly in his homilies, generally punning on the words for oil (*elaion*) and mercy (*eleon*): cf. also *Homily 20 on Acts, Homily 18 on Romans, Homily 6 on Timothy, Commentary on Galatians 6:9-10*.

29. *De habitu virginum*, 35; substantially the same translation (as part of a longer passage) is found in Mahieu, 47; Pourrat I:146 includes this passage, but in a different translation, and with no mention of Alexandria, which is found in Mahieu.

Encratism (from *egkrateia*—abstaining): exaggerated asceticism—hatred of the flesh is not Christian. This error condemned all marriage and all use of meat and wine as evil. On the contrary St. Methodius gives the true doctrine: "in marriage God associates man with His own creative work."[30] True asceticism supposes a balance: perfection consists not in denying oneself but in charity. Asceticism is a means to an end and not an end in itself. Eusebius[31] gives an example of true Christian spirit in the martyr Alcibiades of Lyons (Pourrat I, 62). In prison, he was severely abstaining from certain foods. But when it was pointed out that this was troubling others who thought they might be obliged to do the same, "he made use of everything indifferently, thanking God, for the martyrs were not bereft of the grace of God, but the Holy Spirit was their counsellor."

Montanism {was the} great heresy of the second century. {It} claimed Tertullian as one of its adherents. {In it} false asceticism and false mysticism {were} combined.[32] {It} contains elements common in movements of similar type down the ages:

1. Crude idea of eschatology: {the} end of the world {is} about to happen any day now.

2. The reign of the Holy Spirit had begun. Hence {there is an} obligation for all to practice extreme asceticism.

3. Perfection consists in extraordinary mystical (?) gifts and experience. Montanus {was a} priest with his two prophetesses, Priscilla and Maximilla. Frequency of visions and ecstatic madness, spectacular manifestations of "possession by the Holy Spirit," convulsions[33] etc. {marked the movement, which was} condemned by the Church.

Neoplatonism: The above were heretical movements. Neoplatonism is not a Christian deviation—it is a Hellenistic philosophical and mystical school of thought. It falls short of Christianity

---

30. *The Feast of Virgins*, II, 2, quoted in Pourrat I:61.
31. *Historia Ecclesiastica*, V, 3 (PG 20:436D–437B).
32. Pourrat (I:62) likewise notes the combination of "an exaggerated asceticism" with "a false mysticism."
33. Pourrat (I:63) also mentions "the convulsions of the Montanists"; on the previous page he provided the names of the two women.

and was opposed to it, but it cannot be dismissed lightly. {It} flourished at Alexandria—*Plotinus, Proclus*, etc. {were} its main lights. {It represented a} development of Plato's philosophy with religious elements from the Near East included; {thus it was} syncretistic. Much of the Christian tradition on "contemplation" is in fact full of the influence of Neoplatonism. The word "contemplation" does not occur in the Gospel. The idea of abstracting oneself from all things, purifying one's mind of all images, and ascending by self-denial to an ecstatic intellectual contact with God the Supreme Truth—ending up by being "alone with the alone"[34]—all this is characteristic of the Neoplatonic approach. It has been taken over by a whole tradition of Christian writers and has become Christianized. But still we must remember in dealing with such writers that we are handling a characteristically Greek type of thought and must take care not to lose sight of Christ Himself and His teachings in order to follow a more or less pagan line of thought from which Christ is all but excluded.

One specifically Neoplatonic element {is the} idea that contemplation (*gnosis*) is for a *select elite* and others cannot attain it. It is true St. Paul speaks of perfect Christians and carnal minded Christians[35]—but that is not quite the same thing.

Another element {is} *dualism*, {in which} body and soul {are considered as} separated: soul belongs to the realm of spirit, body to the realm of matter, and the material is inferior if not even evil. Origen was led astray by this idea. Hence {arises the} conclusion that to live a "purely spiritual" life is better; hence {also the} emphasis on *apatheia* (complete freedom from passion) as

34. Plotinus, *Enneads*, VI.9.11.51; these are the famous closing words of the entire work.

35. See Mahieu, 33: "St. Paul distinguishes between 'sarkikoi'—carnal men (I Cor. 3, 2–3, Rom. 7, 14) and 'teleioi' – perfect men (I Cor. 14:20; Eph. 4:13; Col. 1:28; 4:12)"; the same distinction is found on page 53 in Mahieu's discussion of Origen. In fact, in I Corinthians 2:6, 3:1, Paul seems to be using the term "perfect" (*teleioi*) polemically, to undercut the pretensions of those who "claimed to be a spiritual elite" but were in fact "of the flesh" (*sarkikoi*): see Birger Pearson, *The Pneumatikos-Psychikos Terminology in I Corinthians* (Missoula, MT: Scholars Press, 1973), 28. In Philippians 3:12 Paul explicitly denies being perfect, though Ephesians 4:13 speaks of the goal of attaining perfect manhood in Christ.

the climax of ascetic life. Nowhere in the New Testament do we find such an ideal of complete deliverance of the soul from the body. On the contrary, the New Testament envisages the spiritualization of the whole man, body and soul together, pointing to the Resurrection of the Flesh. But ideas like *apatheia* became part and parcel of Christian ascetic theory and practice, especially in the Orient. They must always be qualified with Christian correctives.

Gnosticism: a deviation from Christianity (an attempt to "improve" on it), cruder, more oriental, more elaborate than Neoplatonism. {It was also} more esoteric (that is, salvation and sanctification are more exclusively for an elite of initiates). There is a very curious mythological and magical content in gnosticism, {which posited} a "Pleroma" of mythical personages, some friendly to God and some inimical to him. Note the creation of personages like "Sabaoth" due to misunderstanding of {the} Septuagint. (They thought the Lord Sabaoth [Lord of Armies] was a special personage called "Sabaoth"—a kind of demiurge.) However gnosticism is centered on Jesus. A fantastic ascent through the thirteen aeons brings the perfect soul at last to Jesus Himself, the supreme Mystery of Light, above all the celestial archons; Gnosticism was an attempt to unite Christianity with astrology and magic, rejecting the Old Testament and substituting for it the pseudo-sciences of the day. Dualism {was present} even in divine things: God of the Old Testament {was} evil (enemy of Jesus), God of the New Testament good; body {was} evil, "tomb" of the soul, etc. {The} universe came from an evil principle called Ialdaboth. {These ideas were} taken up by Manichaeans later.

We can recognize similar trends all down through the history of the Church. Such trends arise when there are times of unrest, when the masses are spiritually hungry and going through a period of transition. Such trends are associated with ignorance (excluding Neoplatonism of course) and misinterpretation of Christian revelation—and with relatively crude natural appetites for spiritual experience. They flare up and lead to many excesses, but when they die down the spirit of whole classes or groups is left "burnt out" and helpless.

The Christian Teachers of Alexandria

Clement of Alexandria—Origen

It is very important to know something of this great school. Pourrat[36] is rather shallow and superficial and gives a false idea of it, especially of Clement. The work of this school was the establishment of Christianity as a spiritual and intellectual movement acceptable to the upper classes and to the intellectuals. Clement and Origen adopted as much of Greek thought as could be harmonized with Christianity. Note—the large and influential Jewish colony at Alexandria included many intellectuals who for generations had been working to reconcile Platonism and Jewish thought. Clement interpreted Exodus 11:1-3, about borrowing precious vessels from the Egyptians, in the sense that the Church should appropriate all that was good in pagan philosophy.[37] In this he followed an interpretation already favored by the Alexandrian Jews. At the same time Clement believed that Plato, Socrates, etc. had been saved by their knowledge of God arrived at through philosophy. Knowledge was their "covenant" as the Law was the covenant of the Jews.[38] Tertullian on the contrary thought Greek philosophy came from the devil.[39]

Clement considers the Christian life as a progress from *faith to gnosis.*[40] In this he is perhaps too intellectual and remains too

36. Pourrat discusses Clement on pages 68–71 and Origen on pages 71–73 of his first volume.

37. While this interpretation of Exodus 3:22, 11:2, 12:35-36 is found in Irenaeus, *Adversus Haereses* 4:30, in Origen's *Letter to Gregory* (PG 11:87-91), and most familiarly in Augustine's *De Doctrina Christiana* 2:40 and *Confessions* 7:9:15 (major source of its repeated use in the Middle Ages), it was apparently not used by Clement (nor by Philo).

38. See Quasten, 2:12-13, which summarizes Clement's position "that philosophy is given by God and was granted to the Greeks by divine providence in the same way as the Law to the Jews," and quotes *Stromata*, 1.5.28: "Philosophy, therefore, was a preparation, paving the way for him who is perfect in Christ."

39. This is rather an overstatement: while Tertullian, like patristic writers generally, equated the Greek gods with demons (see Quasten, 2:258), his disparagement of pagan philosophy, while intense, does not go so far as to declare it demonic: see Quasten, 2:320-21, which includes discussion of the famous question, "What indeed has Athens to do with Jerusalem?"

40. See Pourrat I:69; Merton discusses the idea of Christian gnosis in Clement in greater detail in "Ascetical and Mystical Theology," 20–22, 23.

close to pagan philosophical terms. But his work is of great interest and importance. {He} wrote three books, guides to the Christian life: Christ presented in three aspects:

1. The *Protreptikos* (Converter)—How the Lord converts souls and awakens them to the new life of faith: an apologia of Christianity for the Greeks.

2. The *Paidagogos* (Teacher of Small Children)—Christ teaches and guides us in the beginnings and ordinary paths of Christianity. Written for "Christians in the world," it throws many lights on the social life of Alexandria in the second century. See quotes from the *Paidagogos* in Fremantle, *Treasury of Early Christianity*, about food etc. (v.g. p. 49);[41] and later, Christian table manners, etc.[42] READ from *The Educator*, nn. 4, 6, 9 (pp.

---

41. Anne Fremantle, ed. *A Treasury of Early Christianity* (New York: Viking Press, 1953): "Some men, in truth, live that they may eat, as the irrational creatures, 'whose life is their belly, and nothing else.' But the Instructor enjoins us to eat that we may live" (48–49); Clement goes on to emphasize the need for discrimination with regard to food, recommending that which is "simple, truly plain," conducive to "health and strength." When invited to dinner, the Christian should eat what is set before him, as Paul recommends: "We are not, then, to abstain wholly from various kinds of food, but only are not to be taken up about them. We are to partake of what is set before us, as becomes a Christian, out of respect to him who has invited us, by a harmless and moderate participation in the social meeting" (49); but one is to be temperate, avoid delicacies, and retain a sense of what is truly significant: "it is the mark of a silly mind to be amazed and stupefied at what is presented at vulgar banquets, after the rich fare which is in the Word" (50). (This same material [in a different translation] can also be found in Clement of Alexandria, *Christ the Educator*, trans. Simon P. Wood, CP, Fathers of the Church, vol. 23 [New York: Fathers of the Church, 1954] 94, 101–103 [Book II, chapter 1]; this is the version Merton refers to as *The Educator* immediately below.)

42. Clement counsels the Christian to keep "the hand and couch and chin free of stains," to "guard against speaking anything while eating," and not "to eat and to drink simultaneously" (51). He adds, "Frequent spitting, and violent clearing of the throat, and wiping one's nose at an entertainment, are to be shunned. . . . If anyone is attacked with sneezing, just as in the case of hiccup, he must not startle those near him with the explosion, and so give proof of his bad breeding; but the hiccup is to be quietly transmitted with the expiration of the breath, the mouth being composed becomingly, and not gaping and yawning like the tragic masks. . . . To wish to add to the noises, instead of diminishing them, is the sign of arrogance and disorderliness. . . . In a word, the Christian is characterized by composure, tranquillity, calmness, and peace"

5, 7, 10),[43] {which} show his beautiful spirit of faith and intimacy with Christ in all departments of life; also 99, 100, 101 (pp. 274–275), {which give the} basic principles of Christian education by Christ.[44]

3. The *Stromata*—Clement's greatest work: *Stromata* {which} means "Carpets," {consists in} various unsystematic thoughts—especially on {the} relation of Christian wisdom to pagan learning. Pagan philosophy paves the way for Christ. {In it Clement} also argues against gnostics and opposes to them the true Christian gnosis. In his ascetic teaching Clement insisted too much on the division between the ordinary Christian and the "gnostic" (contemplative)—and also demanded that the perfect Christian be completely above all passion (*apatheia*). (Read Pourrat, vol. I, p. 70, par. 2.[45])

---

(55); for the same material in the Wood translation see Book II, chapter 1 (104–105) and Book II, chapter 7 (145–46).

43. In #4 (Book I, chapter 2) Clement presents Christ, "God immaculate in form of Man," as the model for the Christian, who is to strive "to resemble Him in spirit as far as we are able . . . to be as sinless as we can" (5–6); in #6 (Book I, chapter 2) Clement speaks of "the Word" as "our Educator" and "the only true divine Healer of human sickness . . . . Wisdom Himself, the Word of the Father, who created man, concerns Himself with the whole creature, and as the Physician of the whole man heals both body and soul" (7–8); in #9 (Book I, chapter 3) Clement points to "the Word, keen of sight, penetrating into the secret places of the heart," as an unerring guide on the spiritual journey: "let us see in His commandments and counsels direct and sure paths to eternity" (11).

44. These sections (Book III, chapter 12) are the very conclusion of the work (except for a final "Hymn to the Educator"): Clement encourages his readers to become "hearers indeed of the Word, . . . this Educator, the Creator of the world and of man, become the Educator of the world, also, in His own person." After a prayer to the Word, asking Him to "bestow all things on us who dwell in Thy peace, who have been placed in Thy city, who sail the sea of sin unruffled, that we may be made tranquil and supported by the Holy Spirit, the unutterable Wisdom, by night and day, unto the perfect day, to sing eternal thanksgiving to the one only Father and Son, Son and Father, Educator and Teacher with the Holy Spirit . . ." he concludes with a final exhortation "to offer to the Lord, in return for His wise education, the eternal offering of holy thanksgiving."

45. "The true Gnostic, indeed, is not only freed from the lusts of the flesh, and is not only the master of his passions, but, further, he suffers nothing of the senses in himself. 'The only impressions he consents to experience are those that are necessary for the preservation of life, such as hunger and thirst.' Pain and even death will find him indifferent. He will suppress all emotions that are

Origen—There is a kind of fashion among superficial minds to dismiss Origen as a heretic and have nothing to do with him. This is very unfortunate because Origen is certainly one of the greatest and even holiest of the Church Fathers and was certainly the most influential of the early Fathers. His contribution to Catholic theology and spirituality was inestimable, and if he unfortunately did fall into theological errors (which was not to be wondered at in these early times when theological teaching had not been at all systematized), it is not difficult to separate his errors from the great mass of his orthodox teaching. Of all the Eastern Fathers Origen is perhaps the one who remained the most influential in Western monasticism, not excluding St. Basil. St. Bernard's commentary on the Canticle of Canticles, which is typical of the whole theology and spirituality of the Cistercians and of medieval monasticism as a whole, goes back directly to Origen, and is often merely an elaboration of the basic ideas found in Origen (many of which in turn go back to Philo Judaeus).

{Origen was} born {in} 185 of Christian parents—his father Leonidas died as a martyr under Severus (202). Origen was prevented by a trick from offering himself up to the persecutors (his mother hid all his clothes). He lost all his patrimony in the persecution, {and} at 18 he began teaching in the school of Alexandria, abandoned by Clement.[46] {The} Catechetical School of Alexandria grew up on the confines of the great pagan university—{it} had been started by a converted Stoic, Pantaenus (a kind of Newman Club)—converts were instructed, curious pagans came for lectures, Christians were prepared for Orders. {The} master received

---

at all perturbing or agitating, such as joy, grief, impatience, anger. He will live in an imperturbable inward calm. He will rise above creatures, and become quite indifferent to what men think or say. In short, he will keep his soul in perfect serenity." The quotation is from *Stromata*, VI, 9, and the summary that follows is based on *Stromata*, VII, 11.

46. See Jean Daniélou, *Origen*, trans. Walter Mitchell (New York: Sheed and Ward, 1955), 9–10, who points out, following G. Bardy, that it is an oversimplification to see "Origen's appointment to this high teaching post in succession to Clement, and Clement in turn . . . as the successor to Pantaenus"; in fact Origen's catechetical school was not a direct successor to Clement's "school," his instruction of a group of disciples: "the impression of a permanent institution providing advanced teaching in theology and having Clement and Origen as its principal lecturers" is a misleading later interpretation.

pupils in his own house. For some—simple study of the Creed was enough. Others received a full intellectual training in science, philosophy, letters—with an apologetic slant. {The course} culminated in *ethics*, where dialectical training began—questions, v.g. good and evil, leading up to theology. According to Eusebius he lived a life of strict asceticism and evangelical poverty, fasted, slept on the floor.[47] However, in misguided ascetic zeal he castrated himself—a grave error.

At first he taught secular subjects—dialectics, physics, mathematics, astronomy, Greek philosophy—{and} attracted pagans by these courses. ({He} himself studied under Ammonius Saccas, founder of Neoplatonism.) Later {he} devoted himself entirely to Christian theology. {In} 216, he moved to Palestine. Not yet ordained, he was invited to *preach* (as distinguished from *teach*); this created a scandal in Alexandria: his bishop opposed it. The bishops in Palestine ordained Origen. Demetrius of Alexandria protested that the ordination was illicit since Origen had castrated himself, {and} excommunicated Origin. {The} bishop of Caesarea adopted him and ignored the excommunication—Origen continued to teach at Caesarea. Origen was imprisoned and tortured under Decius, and died at Tyre in 253 as a result of his sufferings. In effect, he gave his life for the faith. But he had many enemies during life and many after death.

There was a storm about Origenism about 400 and finally the Council of Constantinople in 543 anathematized certain propositions of Origen. His errors are due to his excessive Platonism. His *main errors* condemned by the Church concern:

1. The pre-existence of the human soul.
2. The Resurrection—the manner of the resurrection of the body.
3. The *apocatastasis*—that Christ will somehow renew His Passion for the demons and the damned and that the punishments of hell will be brought to an end.

As a result of the controversies, much of his original writing disappeared, and what remains was largely preserved in

47. Eusebius, *Historia Ecclesiastica*, VI, 3 (*PG* 20:525D–529D), cited in Pourrat I:72; the reference to castration is also cited by Pourrat, from Eusebius, VI, 8 (*PG* 20:536B–537B).

Latin. There were supposed to have been between two and six thousand treatises by him in existence.

His works on Scripture {include}:

The Hexapla—six-column translation (original Hebrew, Hebrew in Greek characters, and four Greek translations annotated by Origen).

Commentaries—Origen, the first great Christian exegete, commented on practically every book of the Old and New Testaments. The commentaries are often in the form of homilies addressed to the people, but are generally deep and mystical. Origen is a master of the spiritual, mystical or typological sense of Scripture, and also is rich in tropological (moral) interpretations of the sacred books. His writings on Scripture are, with his treatise *On Prayer*, the most important for monks. His scriptural commentaries are rich and full of inexhaustible ideas—as long as we do not expect from him *scientific* interpretations. But his mystical interpretations are not mere fancy and subjectivism. He treats the Scriptures as a whole new world of types and symbols, and the end result is a contemplative wisdom, a broad, rich, penetrating view of the universe as "sacrament" and "mystery" in Christ, for which there is plenty of warrant in the New Testament. The greater part of his commentaries have disappeared except for fragments found in Anthologies (*Catenae*).[48] Those which remain fill several volumes of Migne,[49] and the texts we have are often the Latin translation rather than the Greek original.

Other important works {are}:

De Principiis—the fundamentals of knowledge, especially as {a} basis for theology.

On Prayer—a very fine treatise: the oldest Christian treatise on prayer, in two parts—{it} deals with (1) Prayer in general—{the} validity of petition; (2) the Our Father (a commentary); conditions for true prayer: 1) One must be earnestly striving to

---

48. See, e.g., J. A. Cramer, ed., *Catenae Graecorum Patrum in Novum Testamentum*, 8 vols. (Oxford, 1838–1844).

49. Origen's surviving works are contained in *PG* 11–17; the commentaries are found in vols. 12–14.

detach himself from sin; 2) One must be struggling to become free from domination by the passions, especially those which cause conflict with our neighbor; 3) One must strive to avoid distractions. But after all one must remember that *prayer is a gift of the Holy Ghost.* Origen recommends that we pray standing, facing east—(Christ = rising sun).

Contra Celsum—defence of the Christian faith against paganism.

Exhortation to Martyrdom.

Spiritual Doctrine of Origen—He sees degrees of spiritual life in {the} Sapiential Books: 1) Proverbs—for beginners; 2) Ecclesiastes—for proficients; 3) Canticle of Canticles—for perfect. See excellent outline in the notes of Fr. Francis Mahieu.[50] Here we simply jot down a few main points. Origen's doctrine of the active and contemplative lives comes from Philo, who got it from Plato and Aristotle.

Ascetic—or active life—*Praxis*:

1. Self-knowledge[51]—a theme taken up later by St. Bernard,[52] {and} based on Canticle of Canticles—this is the *first step* to perfection.

2. Struggle to renounce the world. As we begin to know our *passions* (object of self-knowledge) and realize our implication in the perishing world, by reason of passion, we begin the struggle to extricate ourselves. This means renunciation, sacrifice, self-denial. Origen places great emphasis on continency and chastity {and is} a strong defender of virginity.[53] Life-long asceticism is necessary.

3. Imitation of Christ—the ascetic seeks to be re-formed in the likeness of Christ. This gives the soul stability, security in good, and restores lost union with God by charity. This involves crucifixion with Christ, and sharing in His virtues.

50. Mahieu, 47–53.
51. See Mahieu, 49, which refers to Origen's *In Cantica* II (*PG* 13, col. 125B).
52. See Étienne Gilson, *The Mystical Theology of St. Bernard*, trans. A. H. C. Downes (New York: Sheed & Ward, 1940), 69–70 and 232, n. 89.
53. See Pourrat I:72: "To encourage the practice of perfect chastity and virginity, Origen praises virgins in terms as enthusiastic as those of St. Cyprian and St. Methodius."

4. Origen bases his asceticism on the fact that man, created in the *image* and *likeness* of God, has lost his likeness to Him, but remains the image of God. *This likeness has to be recovered by grace and love.* St. Bernard took over this doctrine and made it the basis of his teaching.[54]

Contemplative life—Theoria (Gnosis):

1. When one has become purified by self-denial, crucifixion with Christ, and interior trials, one begins to receive a higher light of knowledge of Christ—*principally by a penetration of the spiritual meaning of Scripture.* But preparation by interior suffering in union with Christ is essential. This is the characteristic feature of Origen's mysticism—here we find a blending of Neoplatonism and Christianity, intellectualism and sacramentalism.

2. The perfect man is the spiritual man, *pneumatikos*, moved by the Spirit: "He who carries the image of things celestial according to the inner man is led by celestial desires and celestial love." (The *pneumatikos* is guided by the Spirit of love.) "The soul is moved by this love when having seen the beauty of the Word of God she loves His splendor and receives from Him the arrow and the wound of love" (*In Cantica*, Prol.).[55]

3. The soul aspires *to mystical union with the Word of God.* She cannot be satisfied with a mediate knowledge of God through human ideas or even through Scriptural symbols.

> When the mind is filled with divine knowledge and understanding through no agency of man or angel, then may the mind believe that it receives the very kisses of the Word of God. (Therefore the soul prays: Let Him kiss me with the kiss of His mouth.) As long as the soul was not able to receive the full and substantial teaching of the very Word of God she had the kisses of His friends, knowledge that is from the lips of teachers. But when she begins of her own accord to see things hidden, . . . to expound parables and riddles . . . then may the soul believe that she has now received the very kisses of her Lover, the Word of God (*In Cantica*).[56]

54. See Gilson, 53 and *passim*.
55. Substantially the same translation is found in Mahieu, 50.
56. This passage from Book I of Origen's commentary, not in Mahieu, is found in substantially the same translation in Quasten, 2:89.

This is considerably more intellectual than St. Bernard's use of the very same idea, which is the starting point of his homilies on the Canticle preached at Clairvaux.[57] Origen also introduces the idea of "the wound of love" (see above) which is developed in Christian mystical tradition. In the Oriental Church, a mystic is referred to as "a man kissed by God."[58] In the last analysis, for Origen, the martyr is the one perfectly united to the Word in mystical marriage. This idea of union with the Logos through union in love and suffering with Christ, the Word Incarnate, is the most fundamental idea in all Christian mystical theology.

4. But normally, the life of the soul seeking Christ is a *constant search* with alternations of light and darkness, presence and absence. "Frequently I have seen the Spouse pay me a visit and remain often with me. Then He withdrew suddenly and I could not find Him for whom I was looking. That is why I again long for His visit, and often He comes back, and when He appears as if snatched out of sight by hands, He disappears again, and while He is taken away He is desired afresh" (*In Cantica*, 1).[59] This idea is also very prominent in St. Bernard, who discusses at length the *vicissitudo* of the soul seeking Christ.[60]

57. Gilson points out that "[t]he multiplicity of 'oscula', which for St. Bernard stands for that of affective experiences, signifies in Origen that of the meanings of Scripture thus revealed. The effect of this union therefore lies in the spiritual and mystical understanding of Scripture . . . . It is given to the soul by divine love . . . and received in joy; nevertheless Origen seems to consider it as essentially cognitive" (216, n. 7).

58. See the final words of Merton's farewell talk to the novices on August 20, 1965: "The ambition of the Greek monks on Mount Athos is that you get to the point where you're kissed by God. There's a picture of an Athonite hermit in some old book, all beat-up, ragged old guy with a crow sitting on his shoulder and the caption is, he was kissed by God" (Thomas Merton, "Life and Solitude," Tape 8-B, *The Merton Tapes* [Chappaqua, NY: Electronic Paperbacks, 1972]; the text was transcribed and published as Thomas Merton, "A Life Free from Care," *Cistercian Studies*, 5.3 [1970], 217–26). See also Merton's essay on "Mount Athos" in *Disputed Questions* (New York: Farrar, Straus & Cudahy, 1960): "Not everyone can become a hermit: this depends on the permission of monastic superiors who jealously guard the privilege and grant it only to those who have proved their spiritual strength and purity of heart and are ready to be 'kissed by God'" (73–74).

59. Substantially the same translation is found in Mahieu, 50; n.b. this is the first homily, not the first book of the commentary.

60. See Gilson, 143 and 241, n. 215, which cites Bernard *In Cantica* 32:2 and 74:4; Mahieu, 50, refers to *In Cantica* 72.

5. It is necessary to have *discernment* (*discretio*) to recognize the comings and goings of the Spouse, and to distinguish temptations and false lights among the true lights that come from God. As we grow in experience, we develop the use of the *spiritual senses* which give us a kind of experience of ineffable and divine realities, "sight for contemplating supracorporal objects, hearing, capable of distinguishing voices which do not sound in the air; . . . smell which perceives that which led Paul to speak of the good odor of Christ; touch which St. John possessed when he laid his hands upon the Word of Life" ({*Contra Celsum*, I:48}[61]). The spiritual senses do not develop unless we mortify the carnal senses.

6. With the development of the spiritual life, one ascends to the "embrace" of the Word, to "divine inebriation," and to ecstasy (which does not imply a state of alienation from sense, but a transport of spiritual joy and wonder).[62] But it does imply subjection to the power of the Holy Spirit.

7. The summit: union, "mingling of the soul with the Word."[63]

In summary, whatever may be said for or against Origen, he is the most powerful influence on all subsequent mysticism, East and West, *particularly West*. We find Origen in Cassian, in St. Bernard, St. John of the Cross, the Rhenish mystics, etc., etc. He is practically the source (after the New Testament itself) of Christian mystical thought.

The First Desert Fathers

Egyptian and Palestinian monasticism arose in the desert, when the *ascetes* (and even some of the virgins) of whom we have

---

61. Substantially the same translation is found in Mahieu, 51, though Merton omits "taste, for savoring the living bread come down from heaven to give life to the world" after "hearing . . . air" (but inserts ellipses before rather than after this phrase – they have been moved). Merton erroneously cites *In Cantica*, 1 as the source of this passage, probably because this was the source of a second quotation found in the same paragraph in Mahieu, who himself erroneously attributed the passage to the *De Principiis*.

62. Mahieu, 51.

63. Mahieu, 51.

spoken above, decided that it was necessary for them to withdraw still further from the world. *What prompted this movement
to the deserts?* It grew in force when the Church became worldly,
but *began before* that: 313—the *Edict of Milan*—{is} an important
date in early Church history. Constantine, "converted" (but not
baptized) in 312, recognized Christianity and gave it freedom
and a place in society. From then on, the Emperors themselves
were to be at least exteriorly Christians. As St. Jerome said, summing up the idea common to Christians of his time and to later
tradition: "When the Church came to the princes of the world,
she grew in power and wealth but diminished in virtue."[64] *Conversions* became more numerous but less fervent. The level of
Christian life sank and there was more of a tendency for the
Christian to become hardly different from his pagan neighbor.
Those seeking the perfect Christian life of renunciation were
thus placed in difficulties. First, *stricter rules* and a more *systematic way* of asceticism were enjoined upon the ascetes. For instance, virgins were formally bound to stay at home, unless real
necessity called them outside (beginnings of enclosure).[65] The
hours of the office, Tierce, Sext and None, became customary
everywhere, with of course the night office (*anastasis*).[66] Year-
round fasting was prescribed. Ascetics *began to live in communities*—in towns or near them, just outside. However, this was not
enough. Visitors disturbed them; the town was near. There were
many distractions and temptations. Yet we must not think that

64. St. Jerome, *Vita S. Malchi monachi*, 1, quoted in Latin in Pourrat I:75, n. 1;
translated by Merton.
65. See Pourrat I:75: "At the beginning of the fourth century, to guard ascetics and virgins from the dangers that threatened them, many churches bound
them to a stricter rule than that of earlier days, and to a style of life which in
some respects resembled that of the monks of later times. . . . Virgins might go
on living in their own homes, but they had to avoid running out unnecessarily,
to pray at stated times, to fast and to give alms."
66. See Pourrat I:75-76: "The set prayers consisted in the recitation of the
Psalms at the traditional hours of Tierce, Sext, and None, in honour of our
Lord's condemnation, crucifixion, and death. In the night, at the hour of
Christ's resurrection, they had to get up to chant Psalms. . . . In Jerusalem, the
continent of both sexes (*aputacticae*) met in the church of the *Anastasis* at the
same hours of the day and night to recite the Psalms along with the clergy."
("*Anastasis*" is the Greek word for "resurrection.")

they went into the desert expecting to avoid temptation. The desert was a place of deeper and more spiritual temptation, not just a refuge from the world. What led them to the desert? The examples of St. John Baptist, Elias, and above all of Christ Himself.[67] READ—III Kings 17:1-9 (Elias at the Brook Kerith—cf. Ideal of Carmelites[68]). {The} ideal {was one} of silence, solitude, dependence on God. Direct dependence on God is the vocation of the solitary. Perfect abandonment {is} proper to the monastic state, because it is a literal and exact fulfillment of the Gospel.

St. Anthony[69]

Let us study the conversion and monastic life of St. Anthony of the Desert. It was the classic example of a monastic conversion, and the life of Anthony, written by St. Athanasius for some Western monks between 356 and 357, is the most important monument of tradition on the monastic origins. {It} should be read by all monks. In the *Life of St. Anthony* we find all the essential elements of the early monastic ideal. Note—the idea that vocations to the desert came with the edict of Constantine is not quite accurate. There were already many hermits in the desert before that. St. Anthony embraced the hermit life about 270, and went into the desert at Pispir about 285. He had gathered many disciples around him before 313.

The Vita Antonii. Anthony {was} born at Coma,[70] Middle Egypt, about 251 A. D.

67. References to being disturbed by visitors and to Elias and John the Baptist (though not Christ) as forerunners are found in Pourrat I:77.

68. Merton is probably referring here to his essay "The Primitive Carmelite Ideal" (*Disputed Questions*, 218–63), which discusses Elias as a model of the solitary on pages 221–29, and the early Carmelite interpretation of this Scriptural text on pages 225–26.

69. Merton summarizes this material, with some additional comments, in his conferences on "Pre-Benedictine Monasticism," first series (1963–1964), pages 6–9 of typescript.

70. This information is found not in the *Life* but in the *Historia Ecclesiastica* of Sozomen (I:13); in his translation of the *Life*, however, Robert T. Meyer notes, "This may be a confusion arising from the fact that Athanasius repeatedly speaks of the home 'town' or 'village' (*kome*) of Antony" (St. Athanasius, *The Life of Saint Antony*, trans. Robert T. Meyer, Ancient Christian Writers, vol. 10 [Westminster, MD: Newman, 1950], 106, n. 5).

First stage (270–285)

1. At the very first, Anthony had ascetic inclinations. He wanted like Jacob "to dwell a plain man in his house"[71]—avoided the company of other children. {He was} simple and obedient, loved Church services and listened carefully to the Word of God when it was read—{this is} important, because here he got his vocation.

2. (270 A. D.) He had been meditating on the vocation of the Apostles who left all to follow Christ, and on the renunciation of the first Christians (READ Acts 4:35[72]). Entering church, he hears read the classical passage from Matthew 19, that of the vocation offered the rich young man (READ[73]). Anthony took this as addressed to himself, and immediately went out, sold all he had, gave to the poor and to his sister.

3. Later, hearing another precept of Christ in the Gospel, "Do not be anxious about tomorrow" (Matt. 6:34), he takes a further step, places his sister (of whom he had care) in a convent; he becomes an ascete outside his home village.

4. In the first stages of his ascetic life—he works with his hands—he seeks out models of virtue in the other ascetes; prays constantly; pays close attention to the reading of Sacred Scripture. (Note: he did not know how to read himself, but remembered long passages of Scripture by heart, "his memory serving him instead of books."[74]) READ—*Life of St. Anthony*, chapter 4 (*Early Christian Biographies*, 137).[75]

5. First temptations: the Enemy is soon on the scene, and strives to break Anthony's resolution with temptations—their order is significant. *First—anxiety about property*, his sister, food;

71. Gen. 25:27, cited in chapter 1 of *Life of St. Anthony*, trans. Sr. Mary Emily Keenan, SCN, in *Early Christian Biographies* (134).

72. *Life*, chapter 2, describes Anthony's reflecting on this verse in Acts, when the early disciples, "selling their possessions, brought the price of what they had sold and laid it at the Apostles' feet for distribution among the needy" (135).

73. "If thou wilt be perfect, go, sell what thou hast, and give to the poor, and thou shalt have treasure in heaven; and come follow me": Matthew 19:21, as quoted in *Life*, chapter 2 (135).

74. *Life*, chapter 3 (137), which reads ". . . memory later serving . . ."

75. This chapter focuses on how Anthony observed and imitated the particular virtues of the various ascetics he visited, and won the approval of all the villagers.

worry about weakness of body and his ability to persevere. *Second*—violent temptations of the flesh. Anthony replies by meditation—on what? "He extinguished the illusion by meditating on Christ and reflecting on the nobility that is ours through Christ, and on the spiritual nature of the soul."[76] Note the positive and optimistic basis of monastic asceticism—{the} Incarnation has raised us to {the} level of sons of God, highest nobility. Our aim should be to live up to this. *Third* temptation—pride. The devil flatters him, tries to make him take pride in the fact that he is a "great ascetic" and "not like other men."[77] Anthony contemns him. The Saviour triumphs in Anthony.

6. Anthony consolidated his gains by *discretion*, studying the manifold wiles of the enemy, and by *self-discipline*. {Showing} great fervor and zeal, he is able to practice extraordinary mortifications, passing nights without sleep and eating only bread and water. "The state of the soul is vigorous when the pleasures of the body are weakened."[78]

Second Stage (285–305)

1. He goes out to the tombs, near the town {and} lives as a recluse in a tomb. Here {is a} new phase of struggle. The devils beat him and leave him for dead. He is taken back for burial to his village church, but gets up at midnight and returns to the tombs. The temptations are renewed; {the} devil tries to terrify him. (READ p. 144.[79])

2. The Lord appears, and declares that He had waited to see Anthony's struggle—compare St. Stephen's martyrdom and chapter 10 of the *Vita Antonii*.[80]

3. Anthony, after this "novitiate," starts out for the Desert. {He} lives as a recluse in an ancient fort—struggling with the

76. *Life*, chapter 5 (139), which reads: "he extinguished the burning oil of that illusion . . ."

77. See *Life*, chapter 6, where the devil says to Anthony, "I have deceived many, and I have overthrown many; yet now, when I attacked you and your works, as I have attacked others, I was powerless" (140).

78. *Life*, chapter 7 (142), which reads, ". . . . soul, he said, is vigorous . . ."

79. In *Life*, chapter 9, the demons attack Anthony in the form of various wild beasts, but Anthony scorns this approach as proof of their weakness.

80. Cf. 145: "Looking up, Anthony saw the roof opening, as it were, and a ray of light coming down toward him; . . ." and compare Acts 7:56.

demons. {He} spent *twenty years* in this fort and becomes a perfect ascetic and monk (*megaloschemos*). (READ c. 14, p. 148.[81]) He
has reached *apatheia*—"The temper of his soul was faultless . . .
etc. . . . who has *remained in his natural state.*"[82] Important—
Anthony has recovered the state in which man was created in
Paradise, for which he was intended by God.

    4. As a proof of his *apatheia*—he is unharmed by ferocious
animals (cf. crosses a canal infested with crocodiles, unharmed,
with the aid of prayer[83]). Also, at this point numerous disciples
join themselves to him. We mention these points not as biographical data alone, but because of their importance in theological
tradition. See also the life of St. Benedict by St. Gregory.[84] When
Benedict reaches ascetic perfection and becomes a contemplative, souls are also brought to him to be formed.

The Doctrine of Anthony

    Chapter 16 begins a sequence of chapters containing An-
thony's doctrine. It is presented as a discourse somewhat like
the Lord's Sermon on the Mount at the beginning of His public
ministry. Here is the essence of his teaching:

81. This chapter relates how after twenty years Anthony emerged from the
fort with his body unchanged and his spirit tranquil; he healed many of those
present of bodily and spiritual illnesses, spoke graciously to all, and drew many
to the solitary life. The chapter concludes with the famous words, "So from that
time there have been monasteries even in the mountains, and the desert was
made a city by monks who had left their own city and enrolled themselves for
citizenship in heaven" (149).

82. The complete passage reads: "The temper of his soul, too, was faultless,
for it was neither straitened as if from grief, nor dissipated by pleasure, nor was it
strained by laughter or melancholy. He was not disturbed when he saw the crowd,
nor elated at being welcomed by such numbers; he was perfectly calm, as befits a
man who is guided by reason and who has remained in his natural state" (148; the
emphasis is Merton's). Merton's comment following this quotation makes the same
point as the translator's note on the passage, which glosses "natural state" as "The
state in which Adam and Eve were created, but which was damaged by the Fall."

83. *Life*, chapter 15 (149).

84. Gregory the Great, *Dialogues*, trans. Odo Zimmerman, OSB, Fathers of
the Church, vol. 39 (New York: Fathers of the Church, 1959), Book 2, c. 3 (66):
"As Benedict's influence spread over the surrounding countryside because of
his signs and wonders, a great number of men gathered around him to devote
themselves to God's service. Christ blessed his work and before long he had established twelve monasteries there."

a) Scripture and tradition. The scriptures are in themselves sufficient but also there is their relationship with their elder (Anthony) in which they tell him their difficulties and he relates to them what he knows on the point from his own experience and from the accumulated experience of the ages.[85]

b) Zeal and energy—determination to grow in ascetic perfection in this life in order to reign with God in eternity—the triviality of trial in time, compared with the eternal reward. (READ c. 17, p. 151.[86]) Corollary to this {are} poverty: renounce possessions in this life; seek rather to gain virtues (treasure in heaven); constancy: sustained efforts, not giving up—avoid neglect; need of watchfulness; "synergy": the Lord works with those who give themselves generously to ascetic effort (the Pelagian controversy in the West would lead to clarifications in this matter); charity—and daily thought of death, so that we forgive others at all times; the thought of hell—its power in dispelling carnal temptation. "Perfection is within our reach." (READ c. 20, p. 153.[87])

c) The goodness of the soul in its natural state. Here we come to an important argument, the foundation stone on which his asceticism is built. God created the soul beautiful and upright in His own image. This beauty is its natural state. To be perfect, we have only to be as God created us, that is to say we have only to "live according to our (true) nature." This sounds exactly the opposite to what we read in ascetic treatises today: that sin consists in following nature, and virtue in going against nature. Explain: two different views of nature. Modern writers consider nature in its fallen condition; Anthony and the Fathers (up to Augustine, who is pessimistic) consider nature in its original integrity. "Rectitude of soul . . . consists in preserving the intellect in its natural state, as it was created" (p. 154). (This appears again in St. Bernard,[88] speaking of the natural *rectitudo* of the

---

85. *Life*, chapter 16 (150).

86. This chapter emphasizes that to renounce even the whole world for the sake of the kingdom of heaven is to give up little, and that as all will soon be left in dying, all should be left now for the sake of virtue.

87. This chapter, which includes the statement "Perfection is within our reach," focuses on the presence of the kingdom of God within, and perfection as recovery of the natural state willed by God in creation.

88. See Gilson, 53–54 for a discussion of this imagery.

soul and the state of the *anima curva* [in sin]). "If . . . perfection were a thing to be acquired from without, it would indeed be difficult; but, since it is within us, let us guard against our evil thoughts and let us constantly keep our soul {for} the Lord, as a trust reserved {from} Him . . . so that He may recognize His work as being the same as when He made it" (p. 154).[89]

d) Demonology—Special vices: Two great groups, "anger" (irascible passions) and concupiscence (desires for gratification) (cf. Freud's *thanatos* and *eros*, and others[90]—libido and desire for power). These passions are incited within us by demons, and they are various "spirits" against which we must guard with constant watchfulness. (This reappears as the essence of Cassian, as we shall see.) These demons are not absolutely evil in themselves; they were created by God and all creatures of God are good. But they envy men and try to prevent them from rising to heaven whence the demons fell. The demons were the "gods" of the pagans. We need the gift of *discernment of spirits* to detect their wiles. The tactics of the demons (*Read* c. 23, p. 156[91]): 1) evil thoughts; 2) phantasms; 3) false visions and prophecies; 4) terrifying visions (p. 157). Their whole purpose is to make us renounce our resolution to be monks. They use extraordinary and spectacular means, but they also use subtle and less obvious means—for instance: urging to indiscreet fasts and prayers (breaking our sleep); trying to cause despair at our past sins;

89. In this quotation Merton adds "our" to the text and writes "from" for "for" and "for" for "from" (these have been corrected); he also indicates an ellipsis where there is none in the text.

90. Literally "death" and "love" or "desire" (Gk.); Freud first proposed a conflict between a death instinct and a life instinct in *Beyond the Pleasure Principle* (1920). (It is noteworthy that the most widely available edition of this text [New York: Bantam, 1959] had an introduction by Dr. Gregory Zilboorg, with whom Merton had a difficult encounter at Collegeville, MN in 1956: see Michael Mott, *The Seven Mountains of Thomas Merton* [Boston: Houghton Mifflin, 1984], 290–98.) See also Herbert Marcuse, *Eros and Civilization* (Boston: Beacon Press, 1955), especially the final chapter, "Eros and Thanatos" (622–37).

91. The first three of the tactics are described in chapter 23, the fourth in chapter 24.

causing *acedia* and disgust; quoting the scriptures vainly. After chapter 28, Anthony goes on to explain in greater detail the ways of the devils and how they can act on us as immaterial beings {as well as} their combined powerlessness (due to the victory of the Cross) and hatred of us. "Therefore we must fear God alone, and despise these evil spirits, having no fear of them at all."[92] (READ c. 41, p. 172.[93]) He warns especially against the prophecies and specious visions they bring to ascetics. This should all be regarded as a temptation; we should serve God not for extraordinary powers, but for love of Him. This doctrine is that of St. John of the Cross (*Ascent of Mount Carmel*, esp. Bk. II).[94] The main weapons against the devil are the Holy Name of Christ Jesus and the Sign of the Cross. The Holy Name becomes the foundation stone of Oriental monastic prayer. The long discourse ends with chapter 43. (READ c. 44—The Desert Paradise, p. 175; cfr. Isaias.[95])

---

92. *Life*, chapter 30 (163).

93. In this chapter Satan appears to Anthony and complains that he is being blamed without cause, since he has been deprived of all power and now is no longer in control even in the desert.

94. See for example *Ascent* II.16.6: "I say, then, that with regard to all these imaginary visions and apprehensions and to all other forms and species whatsoever, which present themselves beneath some particular kind of knowledge or image or form, whether they be false and come from the devil or are recognized as true and coming from God, the understanding must not be embarrassed by them or feed upon them, neither must the soul desire to receive them or to have them, lest it should no longer be detached, free, pure and simple, without any mode or manner, as is required for union" (St. John of the Cross, *Complete Works*, trans. E. Allison Peers, revised ed. [Westminster, MD: Newman, 1953], I:124-25). The entire second half of Book II of the *Ascent* is largely taken up with the question of visions and other paranormal phenomena.

95. The chapter quotes Numbers 24:5-6 to describe the monastic settlement of the desert: "How beautiful are thy tabernacles, O Jacob, thy tents, O Israel! As woody valleys: as watered gardens near the rivers: as tabernacles which the Lord hath pitched: as cedars by the waterside." The reference to Isaias is evidently to the various passages in Deutero-Isaiah that describe the blooming of the desert (cf. 41:18-19; 43:19-20; 51:3). For this theme in Merton's own writing about the desert of solitude, see his essay "The Recovery of Paradise" in *Zen and the Birds of Appetite* (New York: New Directions, 1968), 116–33 (part of his dialogue with D. T. Suzuki), and his review essay "Wilderness and Paradise" in *The Monastic Journey*, ed. Patrick Hart, OCSO (Kansas City: Sheed, Andrews & McMeel, 1977), 144–50.

The Later Life of Anthony (305–312)[96]

He seeks martyrdom in Alexandria, but in vain (c. 46).[97] His reputation for miracles brings crowds to him. So he retires to Pispir.[98] (READ chapter 50, p. 180.[99]) {There follows} a further exposition of his doctrine, at Pispir. The later teaching of St. Anthony is more mild—{with an} emphasis on controlling anger, and on what resembles examination of conscience: "write down your deeds as if you were telling them to another" (185).[100] Hence there is some justification for keeping a Journal if even St. Anthony recommended the practice! But it must be objective. His virtues and his miracles are emphasized (c. 56 ff.),

96. The date of Anthony's death is usually given as 356; whether Merton originally intended these dates to represent a third but not a final stage in Anthony's life, or simply is in error here, is not clear; he may have copied these dates from Mahieu, 56, where 312 is the last date given (for Anthony's retirement further into the desert).

97. This is the persecution of Maximin Daja, c. 311–13; Anthony ministered to the needs of the confessors in prison and strengthened those appearing in court, continuing to be present even when all monks had been banished from the city (*Life*, 177).

98. Merton is mistaken about this location. While Pispir is never mentioned by name in *The Life of Anthony*, according to its location as described by Palladius in *The Lausiac History*, it is to be identified with the "outer mountain" (*Life*, chapter 73, [198]) where Anthony spent his twenty years in solitude but which has now become crowded with monks (see Palladius, *The Lausiac History*, trans. Robert T. Meyer, Ancient Christian Writers, vol. 34 [Westminster, MD: Newman, 1965] 21:1 (71), and 185, n. 194; see also *Life of Saint Antony*, trans. Meyer, 110, n. 52: "the 'Outer Mountain' where St. Antony spent twenty years in retirement . . . is at Pispir on the east bank of the Nile, about fifty miles south of Memphis"). The "inner mountain" (*Life*, chapter 51 [181]) to which Anthony withdraws at this time is identified as "Mt. Colzim, lying in the open desert on the South Qalala Plateau, approximately 100 miles south-east of Cairo, 75 miles east of the Nile, and 20 miles west of the Red Sea. The mountain, with the ancient Monastery of St. Antony, is still called Dêr Mar Antonios" (*Life of Saint Antony*, trans. Meyer, 120, n. 177). It should be noted that in his introductory paragraph on Anthony, Merton has correctly stated that the saint "went into the desert at Pispir about 285" (31).

99. This chapter describes Anthony's settlement of his new home, his cultivation of his own food, and his freedom from crop damage due to beasts after he catches one and tells it not to molest him further.

100. The passage, from chapter 55, reads: "Let us note and write down our deeds and the movements of our soul as if we were to tell them to each other . . . . [I]f we write our thoughts as if to tell them to one another, we shall guard ourselves the better from foul thoughts through shame of having them known."

his orthodoxy especially ({cc. 68–70}[101]). He makes a wise apologia against paganism (c. 74 ff.[102]—these chapters probably reflect the doctrine of St. Athanasius as much as that of Anthony). His prediction of Arianism[103] and his death[104] {bring the work to a close}. This *Life* is a great document of monastic tradition, perhaps the very greatest, second to no other, even to the *Rule* of St. Benedict. It is one of the great sources of Eastern and Western monasticism, and shows the monk as a soldier of Christ, a man of God and a man of the Church.

St. Pachomius and the Cenobites[105]

With St. Anthony we have seen the beginning of monasticism in its purest and most primitive form: that of the anchorites. These had a species of community life, in the sense that there were groups of hermits living in certain regions and coming together at times for Mass. Of these some lived altogether by themselves, some lived two or three in a cell. But their life was *not organized*, and was not meant to be organized. With Pachomius, we find *organized community life*. And here begins an old debate: between cenobites and hermits. It was to last a long time, and the thread of argument runs all through the Desert Fathers' literature. Some are for the free, unorganized life of the hermit living alone with God. Others are for the safer, more consistent, organized life of communities. The argument sometimes gets quite heated, and in the end the cenobites, for all practical purposes, won out. The eremitical ideal remains still the highest *ideal* of monasticism, especially in the Orient. But in practice cenobitism is what is advocated. Rarely, from time to time, in monastic tradition, the hermit life reappears. It is something that is always there and must always be there but it will remain a special vocation. The life of the cenobite is the "ordinary" and "normal" monastic way.

101. Typescript reads "ch. 69 ff".
102. This address evidently does take place at "the outer mountain," i.e., at Pispir: cf. chapter 73 (198).
103. See chapter 82 (206–207).
104. Chapters 92–94 (214–16).
105. Merton will return to Pachomius in greater detail in "Pre–Benedictine Monasticism," first series, 34–61.

St. Basil visited Egypt and returned with a strong bias in favor of the cenobites and against the hermits. Reasons: the cenobite is sanctified more easily and more surely by obedience and charity, Gospel virtues. The hermit life is more subject to dangerous illusions. St. Basil manifests real bias on these points. {He} does not give the hermits a fair hearing. Perhaps he had witnessed too many abuses in Egypt. The *Verba Seniorum* on the other hand bear witness to the beauty and simplicity of the eremitical way. *St. Benedict* followed St. Basil in preferring the cenobitic life for monks as a whole. He does not exclude hermits, but they are the exception, and need long preparation in the cenobium (*Rule*, c.1). *St. Theodore Studite* in the East, strongly emphasized cenobitism at the monastery of Studion, Constantinople. *Cîteaux and Cluny* were both strongly cenobitical, yet note that both allowed exceptional vocations to live in solitude. This however was rare. Note: *St. Romuald, St. Bruno* (Camaldolese and Carthusians) bring a renewal of emphasis on hermit life in the West (11th century). There were always and everywhere men living as hermits in the middle ages—also recluses.

Life of St. Pachomius: 292—Pachomius was born of pagan parents in Upper Egypt; 313–314—in the army of Constantine; edified by charity of Christians to prisoners, after discharge he becomes a Christian; {a} vision shows him the way to the cenobitic life, a life of "sweetness" filling the whole earth; 317—however Pachomius first begins to lead a traditional hermit life, under the guidance of Abbot Palemon; {he} spends four years as a hermit, {and receives} a second vision like the first: the cenobitic life represented as honey covering the earth; 324—after his third and fourth visions, {he} establishes the cenobium at Tabenna; 346—death of St. Pachomius.[106]

The Rule of St. Pachomius

A Latin digest of the *Rule* of St. Pachomius has come down to us from the hand of St. Jerome (Migne, *PL*, vol. 23[107]). It is especially interesting because in it we recognize not only the broad general outline of the cenobitic life as we know it, but also many

106. Merton follows Mahieu (59) closely in this summary.
107. Cols. 65–92.

familiar details of monastic regularity. Here we come face to face with the familiar structure of monasticism as an *institution*.

1. The monastery is a large community subdivided into smaller groups. Pachomian monasticism was built on a military plan. The various groups are under the command of subordinate officers, responsible to superior officers. Each group is responsible for a certain share in the monastic work, or liturgy. They take turns in furnishing certain goods or services. The monastery is surrounded by an *enclosure* from which women are excluded. Monks cannot go out without permission. The head of the whole monastery is the *higumenos*. Under him are the *houses* presided over by *chiefs*, forty in a house. The houses are divided into squads of twenty under a lieutenant. {There are} about thirty or forty houses in a monastery (i.e. about 1500 monks). The houses are charged with certain jobs, or trades. Hence the members of each house generally do the same work and carry on the same trade. They also take turns weekly in fulfilling community services—providing cooks, etc. *Seniority* in fulfilling communal offices is determined by the time of entrance into the monastery, as in St. Benedict.[108] The cowls bore special insignia for the monastery and for the "house" (cf. Cambridge—colleges).

2. The material side of the life: *work and poverty*. Strict common life was prescribed for the Egyptian cenobites. Articles of clothing were issued from the common store; each was allowed a mat to sleep on, clothes, and nothing more. No one was allowed to keep food in his cell, or to bring food there with him when he returned from infirmary. No one could cook on his own, or build a fire on his own. All such things were in common. No wine was allowed except to the sick. Food was cooked and distributed from a common kitchen and, except on great occasions, was picked up there and eaten in the *domus*. No one could pick fruits or vegetables from garden on his own. Cooks were not to prepare anything for themselves that was beyond the common rations. No closed cells were allowed, but apparently each had his own cell. It was even decreed that tweezers for taking thorns out of bare feet could not be had except in common, and were to hang in the window where the books were kept.

108. *Rule*, c. 63 (McCann, 143, 145); cf. Jerome's *Prefatio*, 3, col. 66.

The business of the monastery was strictly and efficiently regulated. Each week the *domus* had to furnish an account of production to the *higumenos*. Materials and tools were distributed at a central point and work was done in the *domus*. Tools were kept for a week, and redistributed at the end of the week. Work was distributed every evening for the following day. There was an annual shakeup in the distribution of jobs and everything: in the month of August, *"instar jubilaei remissionis dies exercentur."*[109] Not only were the jobs redistributed, {and} the officers changed, but also sins and public penances were remitted, and monks were supposed also to make up all quarrels and start afresh from scratch. (This may throw light also on our Palm Sunday excommunication.[110])

Regularity: Whereas for the hermit the great thing is individual generosity in prayer, solitude, compunction and penance, for the cenobite external regularity becomes very important. The life is built on it. Prayer life is integrated in the regular exercises. *Trumpets* announce the hours of prayer. As soon as the trumpet sounds, the monk drops everything and praying mentally (this is insisted on), starts for the place of prayer. Great emphasis is placed on punctuality, on doing everything together and in order. The Pachomian monastery had an air of strict military discipline.

Penances: A regular system of penances protected the framework of regularity, penances for tardiness, for losing things, etc. (One had to go three days without the lost article before it was replaced.) Those who were late had to stand in a place apart. If one left garments out on the line to dry for three days, he was

109. "Days of remission are held comparable to the Jubilee" (*Prefatio*, 8, col. 68, which reads "*Jubilaei*").

110. See *Regulations of the Order of Cistercians of the Strict Observance* (published by the General Chapter of 1920) (Dublin: M. H. Gill & Sons, n.d.), 114 (#239): "In Chapter, after the Sermon, the ceremony of excommunication takes place. The religious rise at the same time as the Superior and turn in choir. The Reverend Father Abbot puts on a purple stole over his cowl, takes the crozier, and holding in his right hand a lighted candle, pronounces the formula of excommunication, as it is found in the Ritual. While saying the last words, **fiat, fiat,** he throws the candle on the ground, then lays aside the crozier and gives back the stole to the sacristan. In the absence of the Abbot, this ceremony is performed by the Father Prior."

penanced. Penance {was} prescribed for one who did not immediately make known the flight of one of the brethren—or for a *Praepositus*[111] who does not immediately correct a fault in a subject. Laziness and idleness were severely reproved. The monk had to keep occupied with work or prayer or both. {There were} severe penances for taking objects assigned to others, or from {the} common store.

Prompt and universal obedience were emphasized at all times. Independent activities were reproved, even in the smallest things. {There were} severe reprimands for those who argued with superiors. The monk should not presume to go out in a boat without permission, to cut his hair or that of another unless appointed for the job, to work on his own, etc. Yet at the same time there was much *room for individuality* in the spiritual life. The spiritual life was not strictly regimented. Individuals could arrange their meals according to inspirations of grace, fast more or less as their conscience dictated (with approval of a director)—some ate at none, some ate in the evening only, etc. This was easy since there was not much cooked food, and most ate only bread and raw vegetables, olives, fruits. Nothing was to be preferred to the work of God.

Community life: silence was insisted upon—also a certain recollection and solitude. The monks were discouraged from being intimate with one another, and were told to keep to themselves (had to stay always one cubit apart at least, and not go for walks together). There were disputations (conferences) twice a week by *Praepositus*—penances for sleeping at them. The monks discussed among themselves what was said at them. Great emphasis is placed on charity and meekness in community and there is much legislation to curb disobedient, rebellious, or discontented monks. Even those who sit around with sour expressions (*perfrictae frontis*)[112] are admonished.

Guests: There was a certain latitude in visiting one's relatives or being visited by them. One could go home for special occasions, with a companion. One received visitors also with a companion (as in orders of nuns today). One could eat food brought

111. I.e., the superior or chief of each house.
112. Col. 86 (c. 165).

by guests, but when they left the extra food had to be turned in for the sick. Clerical visitors came to choir with the monks.

Novices: The formation of the new monks was given special care. We can see the sources of St. Benedict's chapter on the reception of novices:[113]

a) They were to be kept waiting at the gate a few days: a postulancy in which they are taught the Our Father and a few psalms. His motives are tested—to see whether he is entering out of fear of punishment for crime or for some other trouble—whether he can really renounce his family and possessions, and if he is potentially a man of prayer (*aptus ad orationem*).[114] As part of his formation the postulant is taught to read and write, and it is prescribed that he have classes at Prime, Tierce and Sext if necessary. "*Etiam nolens legere compelletur et omnino nullus erit in monasterio qui non discat litteras, et de Scripturis aliquid teneat.*"[115] It is said that they had to know by heart the Psalms and the New Testament before fully becoming monks.

b) When it is decided that he is good material, he is taught the other rules and observances at the gate, still. And this preparation (novitiate) goes on for some time.

c) Finally the gatekeeper brings him in to the community, he is stripped of secular clothes and vested in monastic habit and joins the monks.

Summary—St. Pachomius

The detailed picture of Pachomian cenobitism may seem a little fearsome. It is misleading, seen only from the outside. The spirit of St. Pachomius was not simply one of military efficiency, but of deep Christian charity. Charity was first and foremost in the cenobitic life. However, when one legislated for such a big monastic organization, and created such a complex system for the monks, there was always grave danger of it becoming a machine, a big business, or an army outfit. The danger for hermits is individualism and anarchy. The danger for cenobites is exces-

---

113. *Rule*, c. 58 (McCann, 128/129–132/133); cf. Pachomius, col. 73 (c. 49).

114. Col. 73 (c. 49), which reads "*aptum ad orationem.*"

115. Col. 82 (c. 140): "Also, one unwilling to read will be compelled to do so, and there will be no one at all within the monastery who has not learned his letters and memorized some of the scriptures."

sive organisation, totalitarianism, and mechanical routine. In either case, the only remedy is fidelity to grace, close union with the Holy Spirit Who breathes the divine life into souls and informs rules and regulations with the *spiraculum vitae*[116] without which they are only empty forms. This is the hermit's own responsibility. In the cenobium, the responsibility rests first of all with Superiors, but the subject too must be careful not to let himself become merely a passive cog in a machine. A monastery must be an organism, not just an organization.

St. Basil came to Egypt as a critic of the anchorites and a reformer of the cenobitic life.

St. Basil[117]

{Basil was} born about 329 {in} Caesarea, Cappadocia. His family was Christian and ascetic. His elder sister Macrina had a vow of virginity—she took part in his education. Later his mother and Macrina retired to country property of theirs called Annesi on the banks of the Iris and began to live the monastic life together with other virgins, and with his younger brother Peter, who acted as kind of cellarer. {In} 351, at the same time as his sister retired to solitude, Basil went to Athens to study. There he met Gregory Nazianzen, and spoke to him of monastic life. His other brother retired to solitude in 352. Basil travelled to Alexandria, Egypt, Palestine {and} saw monastic life at first hand. {In} 358, returning from studies and travels, Basil sells all his goods and retires to {the} banks of the Iris at Annesi to live as a monk. He is joined by Gregory Nazianzen. {In} 364 {he} writes *Rules*, or begins the redaction of them. {He} kept returning to this work and revising throughout his life. {In} 365 {he was} called to Caesarea by Bishop Eusebius, to aid him in the chancery {and was} ordained priest. {In} 370, Basil becomes Bishop of Caesarea. {He} continued ascetic life—longed for monastery—{and} founded a hospital at Caesarea which he *confided to monks* (monks in active life now): a "city of charity." As Bishop, Basil struggled for peace of the Church against Arianism. Athanasius was a Church

---

116. "breath of life".
117. Merton discusses Basil in greater detail in "Pre-Benedictine Monasticism," first series, 61–76.

politician, Basil primarily a theologian. He was in the Nicene-Origenist tradition. {He} hates controversy, strives to bring Church back to simplicity of faith, defends Divinity of Holy Spirit. His theology is oriented to *contemplation* as much as it is to dogmatic controversy. He is not just a disputer and rebuker (n.b. {the} same can be said of St. Athanasius, but to a lesser degree). (Gregory of Nyssa is the most contemplative of the Cappadocian Fathers. He is Basil's brother.) READ Von Campenhausen, *Fathers of the Greek Church*, pp. 91–93—good summary of St. Basil: his idea of pure and primitive Christianity, as against the political and controversial Christianity of his time.[118] {In} 379 {occurs the} death of St. Basil.

　　The Writings of St. Basil: Dogmatic—*Adversus Eunomium*; *Homilies on Creation* etc.; *De Spiritu Sancto*; *De Baptismo*. (See below—under St. Gregory of Nyssa—we must *not* separate Theology and Spirituality in the Greek Fathers.) Ascetic and Monastic —generally grouped together as the *Asceticon*, or *Opera Ascetica*— books on the following subjects: The Renunciation of the world; Ascetic Discipline; Judgement, and Faith; Letters; and above all the *Rules*: The *Long Rules*—*Regulae Fusius Tractatae*—a kind of spiritual directory for the monastic life; The *Short Rules*—*Regulae Brevius Tractatae*—a catechetical series of solutions to cases and problems in the monastic life. (The collection called *Ascetical Works* of St. Basil in English, in the Fathers of the Church se-

---

118. Hans Von Campenhausen, *The Fathers of the Greek Church*, trans. Stanley Godman (New York: Pantheon, 1959): "Basil's true greatness becomes apparent only when he is studied in the context of the conflicts of his age and his role is properly understood. As an ecclesiastical politician Basil did not display the rocklike strength of Athanasius; as a theologian he did not possess the harmony and universality of his younger brother, Gregory of Nyssa; as a monk he did not possess the subtle refinement of some of the later mystics. But these things must not be interpreted as moral weaknesses. On the contrary, it was his very devotion to the needs of the hour which compelled him constantly to vary his tactics and made it impossible for him to develop his rich talents in peace. He found his work as an ecclesiastical politician so difficult because he was not only wiser and more far-seeing but also more profound and more honest than most of his colleagues. It is thanks to him in the first place that the State Church of the Nicenes, which had been built so quickly, not only celebrated easy victories but retained a real theological life and intellectual freedom" (91–92).

ries,[119] contains most of the above [not the *Short Rules*] and also some *homilies on the ascetic life* which are very good.)

Doctrine on Perfection

All Christians are called to perfection and sanctity, by consecration to God and by faithfully carrying out His holy will. But monks above all have given themselves completely to the pursuit of perfection, to seeking God. The characteristic of St. Basil's doctrine of monastic perfection is that he seeks to be more prudent and discreet than the Fathers of Egypt, to avoid their exaggerations, and to lead all, or at least greater numbers, more safely to God in a wisely regulated monastic life. Also he adapted the monastic life to the rigorous climate of Cappadocia (very rugged and cold in winter).

{Monks act} in the interests of *charity* above all, since perfection consists in charity. The second question in the *Long Rules*, which is fundamental, establishes before all that the monastery is a place where the natural seed of charity planted by God is nurtured and grows. (Read *Ascetical Works*, p. 233.[120]) St. Basil emphasizes the cenobitic life and indeed rejects the hermit life as *selfish* and "unnatural." (See *Long Rules*, Q. 3, p. 239—Read.[121]) This is an extreme judgement in which not all the Fathers concur. Then, like St. Bernard in *De Diligendo Deo*,[122] St. Basil gives some of the reasons for loving God. Monastic life {is} built on gratitude for God's love. The monastic *family life* in which the

119. St. Basil, *Ascetical Works*, trans. Sister M. Monica Wagner, csc, Fathers of the Church, vol. 9 (Washington: Catholic University of America Press, 1950).

120. "[S]imultaneously with the formation of the creature—man, I mean—a kind of rational force was implanted in us like a seed, which, by an inherent tendency, impels us toward love. This germ is then received into account in the school of God's commandments, where it is wont to be carefully cultivated and skillfully nurtured and thus, by the grace of God, brought to its full perfection" (*Ascetical Works*, 233).

121. "Who does not know that man is a civilized and gregarious animal, neither savage nor a lover of solitude! Nothing, indeed, is so compatible with our nature as living in society and in dependence upon one another and as loving our own kind." Basil does not directly address in this chapter the issue of eremitism vs. cenobitism, which is the topic of Q. 7 (247–52), which includes the famous question, "Whom, therefore, will you wash? To whom will you minister? In comparison with whom will you be the lowest, if you live alone?" (252).

122. See Gilson's discussion (87 ff.).

elders are full of fatherly or brotherly concern for the juniors, is
the supreme means to perfection in charity. Emphasis is placed
on *obedience, docility and humility* as the characteristic monastic
virtues. (Read *Long Rules*, Q. 41, p. 314.[123]) But *poverty* and *austerity*
remain absolutely essential. The monastic life is essentially peni-
tential and austere. In this connection St. Basil insists on *manual
labor as a penance* and inveighs against laziness. The labor is governed by strict obedience to superiors and not by the caprice of
the monk himself. However St. Basil also recommends *intellectual
work*—especially the study of theology and of Sacred Scripture.

   Prayer however is above everything else the first duty of the monk.
Of very great importance is self-custody and guarding against
distraction. (Read Q. 5, p. 241 and 243.[124]) The purpose of the
life of prayer is not only to glorify God but also to lead the soul
to perfect union with Him. However St. Basil speaks little of
contemplation. He is primarily an active soul, and his brother
Gregory of Nyssa is the contemplative of the family. Note that in
the cenobitic tradition the keynote has been given by active, ascetic, organizing, administrating saints like Basil rather than by
interior and contemplative saints like Gregory of Nyssa. These
appeal more to solitaries.

   123. "He who denies himself and completely sets aside his own wishes
does not do what he wills but what he is directed to do. Nor, indeed, does reason permit that he himself make choice of what is good and useful, since he has
irrevocably turned over the disposal of himself to others who will appoint the
task for which they in the Lord's Name may find him suited. . . . Now, just as
it has been shown to be unfitting that one should rely upon oneself, so it is forbidden also to refuse to submit to the decision of others" (*Ascetical Works*,
314–15); see also the reference to preventing "the limits of docility and obedience from being transgressed" (316).
   124. The question is entitled "On Avoiding Distraction," and uses the anal-
ogy of learning a trade or skill by intense concentration on that one activity: "As
each kind of mastery demands its own specific and appropriate training, so the
discipline for pleasing God in accordance with the Gospel of Christ is practiced
by detaching oneself from the cares of the world and by complete withdrawal
from its distractions" (*Ascetical Works*, 242); Basil goes on to apply this general
principle to particular circumstances: "we should watch over our heart with all
vigilance not only to avoid ever losing the thought of God or sullying the memory of His wonders by vain imaginations, but also in order to carry about the
holy thought of God stamped upon our souls as an ineffaceable seal by continuous and pure recollection" (243).

Spiritual Progress: St. Basil does not admit of a spiritual life in which everything is static. One does not fly to the monastery and then remain in the same state for the rest of his life. We must *grow* in perfection.

a) The evil of sin. The monk lives face to face with the truth that *sin* is the great obstacle between himself and God. Hence his life is first of all a combat against sin, a struggle for liberation from all sin. The only evil is that which depends on our own power. "Evil" which comes from outside ourselves can be turned to good. But sin, which comes from within us, always harms us, is always a true evil. In his teaching on liberation from sin St. Basil resembles and follows the *Stoics*.

b) The starting point in the spiritual ascent is *self-knowledge* and self-custody (see above). (*Read Homily* 21, especially pp. 487, 488.[125])

c) Then {comes} resolute entrance into the *spiritual combat*,[126] the struggle against passion and self-love. St. Basil analyzes the various vices and describes the action of the virtues that oppose them. The early monks were psychologists and observers of human nature. The most important of the virtues is *humility* (at least from the point of view of the spiritual combat). Why this special importance devoted to humility? Because by it we return to our *original (natural) state* (cf. St. Anthony).[127] Our natural state is that of sons of God, men made in the image and likeness of God. Humility restores us to our complete dependence on God from whom we have received, and must yet receive, all that we are and all that we have. St. Basil especially emphasizes the renunciation of one's own will to do the will of God. *Quidquid quis fecerit a propria voluntate . . . alienum est a*

---

125. Basil depicts the Devil as a brigand lying in wait along the way, and instructs his listeners, "If, then, we would safely traverse the road of life lying before us, and offer to Christ our body and soul alike free from the shame of wounds, and receive the crown for this victory, we must always and everywhere keep the eyes of our soul wide open, holding in suspicion everything that gives pleasure. We must unhesitatingly pass by such things, without allowing our thoughts to rest in them" (*Ascetical Works*, 488).

126. See for example Basil's "Introduction to the Ascetical Life" (*Ascetical Works*, 12).

127. See above, 35–36.

pietate.[128] This principle was adopted by St. Benedict (see *Rule*, c. 49).[129]

d) The notion of the three divisions of the spiritual life—purgative, illuminative and unitive, is present in St. Basil, but not emphasized.

e) *Union with God*: is the summit of the spiritual life because he who is fully united to God, and resembles Him most perfectly, gives Him the greatest glory. This means—the *intellect* is filled with God's truth. And one is able to share that truth with others. The *will* is filled with His love which unites us closely to God so that no suffering can separate us from Him.

Basilian Cenobitism

Pachomian monasticism was *organized* but the spirit remained more individualistic. The Pachomian monastery was not a family, or a real community, but a collection of small groups, cemented together by organization and discipline. St. Basil emphasizes the *social and communal* heart of the cenobitic life. The value of the cenobitic life is not to be sought in organization but in love—something deeper and more interior. The monastic community is a family, a body, and the members *share in* the life and activities of the body. The good of one is the good of all. *No one seeks his own good* in the monastic community. Each is for all and all are for each. Each helps the other, and in helping others helps himself. Each makes up for what the other lacks. No one has to be complete and self-sufficient; what he has not, another will supply. Nothing is wasted in the monastic life—even spiritually. One who is weak and poor, can still contribute whatever small talent he has, and go on, supported by the others. Thus, the perfect life is accessible to all. The good things of God are

128. "Whoever does anything according to his own will is far removed from piety" (*Regulae Brevius Tractatae*, PG 138, col. 1174, quoted in Mahieu, 110).

129. Speaking of Lent in this chapter, Benedict counsels, "Let each one, over and above the measure prescribed for him, offer God something of his own free will in the joy of the Holy Spirit," yet warns this must be done only with the "consent and blessing" of the abbot, "because what is done without the permission of the spiritual father shall be ascribed to presumption and vainglory and not reckoned as meritorious" (McCann, 115). Renunciation of self-will is also Benedict's second degree of humility (c. 7 [41]).

easily shared in community, and the sharing increases them. The cenobitic life offers greater protection against the devil. The variety of duties offers scope for various talents and graces—some can take care of guests, of the sick etc., others are free to devote themselves more exclusively to prayer. In the monastery, there is always the power of living example. The good of the community is the divine will. Hence in community life the divine will is easy to know and follow. The great enemy is *self-will*. Everything else in the monastery can be consecrated to God, but not this.

Other Cappadocian Fathers: The Two Gregories

In passing we ought to pause at least long enough to make the acquaintance of two great monastic theologians, friends and confreres of St. Basil. One of them, Gregory of Nyssa, is the saint's blood brother. The other is his close friend.

St. Gregory Nazianzen

{Gregory was} born about 330. {He} studied with St. Basil in Athens {and} had also studied at Caesarea (where Origen had taught) and Alexandria—hence an Origenist. {In} 359 {he} became a monk with Basil, on the banks of the Iris. {He} devoted himself to asceticism and study {and} composed the *Philocalia*, an anthology of the best passages from Origen[130] (not to be confused with another *Philokalia*—Orthodox texts on prayer[131]). {In} 362, {he is} reluctantly ordained priest but afterwards returns to solitude, but was recalled to active life and supported orthodoxy in the Arian conflict. {In} 371 {he is} reluctantly consecrated bishop of Sasimes by St. Basil, but afterwards regrets it and flees once again to solitude; {he} enjoyed contemplative life for a while in the monastery of St. Thecla at Selucia. {In} 379, he consents to take over the Diocese of Constantinople, overrun with Arians.

130. See the critical edition by J. A. Robinson, *The Philocalia of Origen* (Cambridge: Cambridge University Press, 1893) and the English translation by G. Lewis (Edinburgh: T. & T. Clark, 1911).

131. *The Philokalia: The Complete Text*, compiled by St. Nikodemos of the Holy Mountain and St. Makarios of Corinth, trans. and ed. by G. F. H. Palmer, Philip Sherrard and Kallistos Ware, 4 vols. to date (London: Faber & Faber, 1979–95).

His center {is} a small semi-private chapel, where he gives discourses, etc. and gradually wins over intellectuals and influential people to orthodoxy. The Arians had established a bishop of their own in the see, but Theodosius supported Gregory and had him enthroned and acclaimed in Sancta Sophia. Gregory was acknowledged by {the} Eastern Council of Constantinople, 381, but then, opposed by Egyptian and Macedonian bishops who came late, he resigned. {In} 381–383 {he} administered {the} vacant diocese of Nazianz {and in} 381–389 retired to solitude, and died there.

It is clear from this outline that Gregory did not adapt well to the active and episcopal life. Not that he was not a gifted bishop, but he had *no flair for politics*. He was a truly spiritual man, and a true contemplative. His simplicity made him unfit for politics. He was sensitive and sincere, hence was greatly hurt by betrayals and insincerities of others. Generous and unselfish, he would not fight for his own interests. Although he preferred the contemplative life, he sacrificed that life several times, sincerely desiring to do what seemed to be the will of God. But he was unable to become a "politician" and returned to solitude. His life is a series of repeated failures in the active world, and repeated returns to contemplation. His chief greatness is as a *theologian and preacher*, inheriting the mystical tradition of Origen.

His works: *Sermons*—especially those preached at Constantinople in 380, against the Arians; *Poems*—mostly written during the last contemplative period of his life: on moral and dogmatic topics, and one long autobiographical poem *De Vita Sua*; *Letters*—mostly of historical interest. St. Gregory Nazianzen has left us little that is of specific importance for monastic theology and spirituality.

St. Gregory of Nyssa[132]

St. Gregory of Nazianz was a dogmatic theologian and an orator. His writings were more popular in the eighteenth and nineteenth centuries, because they had an apologetic trend. But he is not as useful to monks as St. Gregory of Nyssa, who has

132. See also "The Mysticism of the Cappadocian Fathers," which focuses almost entirely on Gregory of Nyssa, in "Ascetical and Mystical Theology," 30–42.

come into our own as a *great contemplative theologian* especially strong in the monastic tradition. Fr. Daniélou's book *Platonisme et Théologie Mystique*[133] and the French translation of *De Vita Moysis*,[134] both of which appeared during World War II, started a revival of studies and admiration for St. Gregory of Nyssa, as did also the work of Fr. Hans Urs Von Balthasar.[135] It can be said that Gregory of Nyssa is one of the most important figures in the contemplative revival of Patristic studies that has been going on in the '40s and '50s of this century and which is a significant spiritual movement of our time. Note also—Werner Jaeger's studies on Gregory—lectures at Harvard.[136]

Life: {Gregory was} born about 330. {He was} ordained lector while young, but was seduced by {the} revival of pagan culture under Julian. He became a professor of rhetoric and then married. But exhorted by St. Basil and St. Gregory Nazianzen, he left the world to join them and live as a monk on the banks of the Iris (about 361). After ten years of solitude, he becomes bishop of Nyssa, 371. Gregory was not happy at Nyssa. {He} was opposed by the emperor, framed and deposed on charge of wasting funds (374) {but was} restored as bishop in 377. On {the} death of St. Basil, January 1, 379, Gregory took over his theological and ecclesiastical work, and carried on where Basil had left off. {He} was involved in all the political struggles of this time (380 ff.). He too was not very adept at politics, but as a theologian he played an important part in the Council of Constantinople (381) and was one of the outstanding figures there—gained a reputation as a great preacher in Constantinople. The Council of

133. Jean Daniélou, *Platonisme et Théologie Mystique: Doctrine Spirituelle de Saint Grégoire de Nysse* (Paris: 1944); 2nd ed. (Paris: Aubier, 1954).

134. Grégoire de Nysse, *La Vie de Moïse*, ed. Jean Daniélou, Sources Chrétiennes, vol. 1 (Paris: Éditions du Cerf, 1942; 2nd ed. 1955).

135. Hans Urs von Balthasar, *Présence et Pensée: Essai sur la philosophie réligieuse de Grégoire de Nysse* (Paris: Beauchesne, 1942); *Presence and Thought: Essay on the Religious Philosophy of Gregory of Nyssa*, trans. Mark Sebanc (San Francisco: Ignatius, 1995).

136. In the 1960 Jackson Lectures at Harvard, published as *Early Christianity and Greek Paideia* (Cambridge: Harvard University Press, 1961), Jaeger focuses in the last two of the seven lectures on the role of the Cappadocians, and of Gregory of Nyssa in particular, in integrating the Greek cultural and educational tradition (*paideia*) with Christian life (cf. 68–102).

Constantinople was the triumph of St. Basil's ideas and of those of St. Gregory. After {the} Council of Constantinople he went to Arabia and Egypt on Church business. Returning, in Jerusalem he was accused of Apollinarism {but} goes to Constantinople, in high favor; 380–386 {marks} the peak of his career. {From} 387 onward, in retirement, he devotes himself to *writing*.

Of the three great Cappadocian Fathers Gregory of Nyssa is the greatest as *mystic and spiritual theologian*. He is the greatest contemplative of the three, the deepest, most mystical, and most spiritual. His theology is drawn from *experience* and it is evident that his experience was the deepest of all the Greek Fathers, including St. Maximus and Pseudo-Denys. But besides being a mystic he is also a philosopher, a speculative thinker. This combination makes his work very original and significant. As a theologian he is an Origenist. The importance of Gregory of Nyssa is as a *source of Christian mystical theology*. He transmits the tradition of Origen, purified and deepened by a more spiritual experience, to later theologians like Pseudo-Denys. St. Gregory of Nyssa stands side by side with another Origenist and mystic, Evagrius Ponticus (a Desert Father)—who is more an intellectualist. Gregory gives the primacy to love. The influence of St. Gregory of Nyssa is considerable in the West, and especially on the Cistercian William of St. Thierry, through whom the theology of Gregory of Nyssa became part of the Cistercian heritage[137]— hence his special importance for us.

Theological Writings: The dogmatic and controversial writings of St. Gregory of Nyssa are less important for us—the main one is *Contra Eunomium* {which} carried on controversy begun by St. Basil with the Arian bishop Eunomius. (Eunomius held that the essence of God was innascibility, and hence the Son could not be God; also that the essence of God could be clearly known by man: Gregory stands up strongly for the "darkness" which obscures the mind of man in presence of the transcendent mystery of God—this is one of the most important ideas in his mys-

---

137. See Jean Marie Déchanet, osb, *William of St. Thierry: The Man and His Work*, trans. Richard Strachan, CS 10 (Spencer, MA: Cistercian Publications, 1972), 39–40, and in greater detail, the same author's *Aux sources de la spiritualité de Guillaume de St.-Thierry* (Bruges: Beyart, 1940), 22–59.

tical theology: to know God "by unknowing.") *Contra Apollinarem* —against the Apollinarist heresy that in Christ the Word took the place of the human mind; *Oratio Catechetica*—exposition of dogmas of Trinity, Incarnation, Redemption.

Spiritual Writings: First it should be remarked that this distinction between "theological writings" and "spiritual writings" is very misleading in St. Gregory of Nyssa. His spirituality is his theology and his theology is entirely spiritual. Nowadays there is a gulf separating theology (technical dogma and moral) from spirituality (meditations, devotions, psychology of the spiritual life, mysticism and asceticism). For St. Gregory and the Greek Fathers the two are inseparable, and especially for St. Gregory. For example his treatise on the creation of man, *De Hominis Opificio*, is not merely theological and philosophical in the technical sense, but is also a study of man as a creature destined for contemplation. Hence {there is} spiritual, mystical theology in this work. What we might call more technically theological works of the Greek Fathers are works of *controversy* with emphasis on special technical points. But we have seen above that even Gregory's *Contra Eunomium* has important implications for the mystical life.

Conclusion: for the Greek Fathers theology is above all and essentially *mystical* theology, and all learning culminates in true theology, the vision of God. St. Bonaventure above all carries on this tradition in the scholastic era, but scholasticism in general tends to degenerate into technical knowledge *about* God, and tends less and less to lead to contemplation of Him.

The writings:

De Virginitate—His first book, written to aid St. Basil in establishing {his} monastery. Theme: Christian perfection. The virgin soul is the spouse of Christ. The monastic life is the best means of living a *bios angelikos* (angelic life) and cultivating perfect purity of heart.

Short treatises on perfection, mortification, the Christian life. A biography of his sister *St. Macrina*.

In Hexameron (379)—a parallel to St. Basil's treatise on the Hexameron. Purpose—To throw new light on the facts exposed by Basil; to show the deep underlying causes and purposes at work in creation.

De Hominis Opificio—about the same time—completes St. Basil's treatise on creation. St. Basil had not taken the sixth day, creation of man. Man {is} made for contemplation. This treatise had considerable influence on William of St. Thierry[138] and enters into Cistercian tradition (through the mediation of John Scotus Erigena). The conception of man in Gregory of Nyssa and William of St. Thierry: man {is} made up of *psyche* (animal nature—body); *nous, mens, ratio* (rational nature, mind); *pneuma—spiritus—* (spiritual life—grace—divinization). Concept {is} that perfection is the perfect balance and ordering of *all these three*: body, mind and spirit—not just the development of the mind in a purely mental spirituality at the expense of body and spirit. Man is made in the *image of God*. Just as God is beyond all clear knowledge, so the image in us is beyond the clear grasp of our intelligence. Man's job in life is to reproduce in the depths of the soul his *divine likeness*. This consists in the right use of his *freedom*, which is his *royal dignity* and this is entirely summed up in the *return to God by pure love*.

Spiritual Interpretation of Scripture:

Following Origen and Philo, but going much deeper than either one, Gregory interprets Old Testament books as describing the spiritual ascent of the soul to God.

De Vita Moysis—one of the greatest mystical works of the Greek Fathers—{is} divided into two parts:

1. *Historia*—the literal sense, but not scientific; emphasis is moral and hortatory, really a kind of saint's life, rather than a scriptural study. Remember that for the early Fathers, the "saints" were for the most part the saints of the Old Testament (except for the martyrs). Here he follows Philo closely, often word for word.[139]

138. "What strikes one about the book on the soul is the fact that three-quarters of it comes from St. Gregory of Nyssa's *De hominis opificio*" (Déchanet, *William of St. Thierry*, 39).

139. See Daniélou's introduction to his edition of *La Vie de Moïse*, xiv–xv, for specific parallels between Gregory and Philo's *Life of Moses* (translated by F. H. Colson in the Loeb Classical Library [Cambridge, MA: 1935]).

2. *Theoria*—the mystical interpretation. Especially notable {is} the idea that Moses' ascent of the mountain into the cloud symbolizes contact of the soul with the transcendent "darkness" of God. This is the mysticism of "night"—of darkness (apophatic mysticism) which forms one important tradition in Christian mystical theology contrasted with the mystics of "light" (cataphatic) in another tradition. The most important mystics of darkness: St. Gregory of Nyssa, Pseudo-Dionysius, St. John of the Cross, Eckhart. Mystics of light: Origen, St. Bernard, St. Theresa of Avila etc. The latter are the more common. St. Gregory says (concerning Exodus 19—READ):

> Religious knowledge starts out as light (the burning bush) when it first appears: for then it is opposed to impiety, which is darkness, and this darkness is scattered by joy in the light. But the more the spirit, in its forward progress attains, by a greater and more perfect application, to the understanding of the realities and comes closer to contemplation, {the more} it realizes that the divine nature is invisible. Having left behind all appearances, not only those perceived by the senses but also those which the intelligence believes itself to see, the spirit enters more and more into the interior until it penetrates, by its striving, even unto the Invisible and the Unknowable, and there it sees God. The true knowledge of Him that it seeks and the true vision of Him consists in seeing that He is invisible, because He transcends all knowledge, and is hidden on all sides by His incomprehensibility as by shadows (*De Vita Moysis*, ii:162).[140]

See also St. John of the Cross. (READ *Ascent of Mount Carmel*, II:3-4, vol. 1, p. 70 ff.[141]) We must also take note of the typical sense of

140. *La Vie de Moïse*, 81; apparently Merton's own translation; n.b. "(the burning bush)" is not in the original text.

141. St. John of the Cross, *Ascent*, chapter 3, entitled "How faith is dark night to the soul. This is proved with arguments and quotations and figures from Scripture," focuses on faith as a "certain and obscure" habit of the soul that transcends the understanding, so that "for the soul, this excessive light of faith which is given to it is thick darkness" (I:67); chapter 4, entitled "Treats in general of how the soul likewise must be in darkness, in so far as this rests with itself, to the end that it may be effectively guided by faith to the highest contemplation," emphasizes that the soul "must be like to a blind man, leaning

Exodus, brought out by St. Gregory, in which the events of Exodus signify sacred and sacramental events of the New Testament and of the Mystery of Christ. The origin of this is in St. Paul. READ I Corinthians 10:1-6 (all baptized in the sea). The crossing of the Red Sea signifies baptism. The tabernacle is Christ (cf. Hebrews).[142]

Other Scriptural exegesis:

On the Psalms: Here he finds other material on the ascent to perfection.

On Ecclesiastes: The illuminative way—subtle and rich discussion of the disillusionment of the soul with material and temporal things, as it ascends to God. He studies the concept which Pascal called *"divertissement"*[143]—very important for contemplatives. Man *seeks distraction.* He vainly hopes to forget his troubles not so much in enjoying pleasures or acquiring wealth, as in the *pursuit* of these things. It is the pursuit, the expectation, that gives joy. Hence man lives more and more outside himself and "beyond" himself, and his life becomes a race, a running away from the present into the future, perpetual motion. This is the *vanity* of Ecclesiastes. The first step to stability is then to be content with what we have and with what we are.

On the Canticle of Canticles: Follows the commentary on Ecclesiastes and completes it, going on to the unitive life. {It} also *adds to* mystical theology of Origen's commentary on Canticles, carries it further. {It} was a more influential work than Origen's, deeper—describes in some detail the gradual approach to Union—the steps by which the Word makes Himself known to the soul—as a faint "perfume," as a voice, and finally as food for the soul that is "tasted" and sweet. Finally {it} describes burn-

---

upon dark faith, taking it for guide and light, and leaning upon none of the things that he understands, experiences, feels and imagines. . . . For, as we say, the goal which it seeks lies beyond all this, yea, beyond even the highest thing that can be known or experienced; and thus a soul must pass beyond everything to unknowing" (I:71-72).

142. Heb. 8:2 ff., 9:11 ff.

143. "diversion": see Pascal's *Pensées,* nn. 139, 142–43, 166–68, 170 (Blaise Pascal, *Pensées; The Provincial Letters,* trans. W. F. Trotter and Thomas McCrie [New York: Modern Library, 1941], 48–52, 53–54, 59–60).

ing love of God which is proper to union and renders the soul impatient of all that separates it from God—themes that reappear in St. John of the Cross, *Living Flame of Love*.[144] Origen does not have this warmth and ardor born of deeper experience.

Two New Testament treatises: *On the Lord's Prayer*—stresses the idea of sonship and *parrhesia* (freedom and spontaneity of speech with God) implied by the prayer—man's vocation to help God establish His Kingdom on earth, in souls, by driving out sin. *On the Beatitudes*—one of many Patristic commentaries on the eight Beatitudes (Matthew 5) which treats them as an ascent to mystical perfection, with special emphasis on the sixth ("Blessed are the pure in heart") as referring to contemplation. Here we meet the familiar Patristic doctrine—the soul made in the image of God. The image has been obscured by sin. It must be restored to its perfection by love—then God will again be perfectly mirrored and experienced in the mirror of the soul. READ *Beatitudes* (Eng. trans., p. 149–150).[145] The great problem is the purification of the heart—this is treated at length in the sermon.

Three Biographies: St. Gregory also wrote three lives, less important for biographical data than for remarks on spirituality:

144. See in particular the commentary on Stanza 3, "The deep caverns of sense" (St. John of the Cross, *Complete Works*, III:62-86 [first recension], 154–80 [second recension]) for discussion of both the "unctions" and "ointments" of the Holy Spirit (66, 157) and the "hunger . . . for the perfection of love" (63, 155); the image of the "living flame" is explored repeatedly, particularly in the commentary on Stanza 1: "Oh, living flame of love" (17–20 [first recension], 106–109 [second recension]); commentary on Stanza 2: "Oh, sweet burn!" (36–38 [first recension], 127–28 [second recension]); commentary on Stanza 3: "Oh, lamps of fire" (53–58 [first recension], 145–50 [second recension]).

145. St. Gregory of Nyssa, *The Lord's Prayer; The Beatitudes*, trans. Hilda C. Graef, Ancient Christian Writers, vol. 18 (Westminster, MD: Newman, 1954), 149–50: "For the Godhead is purity, freedom from passion, and separation from all evil. If therefore these things be in you, God is indeed in you. Hence, if your thought is without any alloy of evil, free from passion, and alien from all stain, you are blessed because you are clear of sight. You are able to perceive what is invisible to those who are not purified, because you have been cleansed; the darkness caused by material entanglements has been removed from the eyes of your soul, and so you see the blessed vision radiant in the pure heaven of your heart. But what is this vision? It is purity, sanctity, simplicity, and other such luminous reflections of the Divine Nature, in which God is contemplated" (Sermon 6: "Blessed are the clean of heart, for they shall see God").

1) St. Basil—his brother; 2) St. Macrina—his sister; 3) St. Gregory the Wonderworker (because he was a disciple of Origen).

Conclusions: For all the various reasons expressed above St. Gregory of Nyssa is the most important and most interesting of the Cappadocian Fathers, at least for *contemplatives*. He requires to be studied more deeply, however. Perhaps the moment has not yet come when he is accessible to the average monk with ease—at least not in English. He may perhaps remain difficult and inaccessible to most.

PALESTINIAN MONASTICISM[146]

St. Hilarion—St. Jerome

About 390, St. Jerome wrote the life of St. Hilarion (i.e. about the time Cassian was in Egypt). Hilarion, as a founder of Palestinian monachism and disciple of St. Anthony, is an important if somewhat legendary figure. Jerome presents him as the model monk, the type of Palestinian monachism. Hilarion was also praised by St. Epiphanius, one of the founders of Palestinian monachism.

Life of St. Hilarion: {He was} born at Tabatha, near Gaza, in Palestine, {of} pagan parents. {He} was sent to study in Alexandria, and there became a Christian. Attracted by {the} fame of St. Anthony, {he} went to see him, became a monk, spent several months with him, then returned to Palestine to live the monastic life. He was then fifteen years old. {He} retired to {a} desert place on the coast, infested with robbers: *contempsit mortem, ut mortem evaderet*.[147] {He} embraced a life of strict fasting, labor, solitude and penance, suffered temptations like those of St. Anthony, cut his hair once a year—at Easter, never washed his hairshirt, alleging that cleanliness was useless in one who wore a hairshirt.

His fasts: from twenty one to twenty four, {he} ate {a} half-pint of lentils soaked in water once a day; 24 to 27—ate only dry

146. Merton will discuss Roman monasticism in Palestine, with a focus on Melania the Elder and Younger, Jerome (especially the controversy with Vigilantius), and the *Pilgrimage* of Aetheria [Egeria], in "Pre-Benedictine Monasticism," first series, 77–94.

147. *PL* 23, col. 31 (c. 3): "He scorned death that he might escape death."

bread with water and salt; 27–31—ate wild herbs and raw roots; 31–35—6 oz. of barley bread a day, with a few herbs; 35–64— "But perceiving his sight to grow dim, and his body to be subject to an itching, with an unnatural kind of scurf and roughness, he added a little oil to this diet" (Butler—following Jerome);[148] 64–80—cut down one ounce on the bread, ate only 5 oz.; 80— "When he was fourscore years of age there were made for him little weak broths or gruels of flour and herbs, the whole quantity of his meat and drink amounting to the weight of four oz. Thus he passed his whole life; and he never broke his fast until sunset, not even upon the highest feasts, nor in his greatest sickness."[149] Point of this—*essential* importance of fasting in the ascetic and contemplative life. Not that everyone is obliged to keep the measure of St. Hilarion, but all must fast according to their measure. Fasting is not something one takes on for a time, hoping to give it up. It is a lifelong part of the monastic vocation, with of course room left for modifications in case of need. But we should not seek them without necessity, or be looking for pretexts to give up fasting. (Note: St. Benedict stresses that obedience is more important than fasting.[150])

When he was 18, robbers came to him, and said: What would you do if robbers found you? His reply: nudus latrones non timet. *Occidi potes*, they continue. *Possum, inquit, possum*, et ideo latrones non timeo, quia mori paratus sum.[151] They were edified and converted. Note—the hermit life involves the facing of *every possible danger*. {At the} age of twenty two {he} worked his first miracle which was the cure of a barren woman. After that his life is a catalogue of miracles. {He} cures men from all over the

148. Alban Butler, *The Lives of the Fathers, Martyrs and Other Principal Saints*, 2 vols. (Dublin: Coyne, 1853), 2:719; n.b., these sentences are not found in the revised version of this classic work: Herbert Thurston, sj and Donald Attwater, eds., *Butler's Lives of the Saints*, 4 vols. (New York: P. J. Kenedy & Sons, 1956), 4:163-65.

149. Butler, 2:719 (c. 11, cols. 33–34); Merton's typescript omits "scarce" before "amounting" and reads "until" for "till" and "nor" for "or".

150. The reference is evidently to chapter 49 of the *Rule*, which specifies that during Lent the monks are to submit their regimen of fasting to the approval of the abbot (McCann, 115).

151. Col. 34 (c. 12): "The naked person is not afraid of robbers." "You can be killed." . . . "I could," he said, "I could, and so I am not afraid of robbers because I am ready to die."

world, and animals, including a mad camel tied and dragged
magnis clamoribus[152] by thirty men! {He} converted many Pagans
(note missionary aspect of his hermit life). The *Laura* {is} typical
of Palestinian monachism (village of cells around a church).
Note—excessive austerity of some, like *Adulius*—(see Pourrat,
vol. I, p. 85).[153] From his twenties to his seventies, working miracles everywhere, he became the center of a great attraction and
cult. Finally, seeing himself surrounded by many monks and
pilgrims at all times, he lived in great sorrow, weeping daily,
saying, "I have returned to the world—I am receiving my reward in this present life."[154] In the lives of solitary and monastic
saints, apostolate *is charismatic* and is fruitful *because of contra-
diction*. He had prophetic knowledge of the death of St. Anthony.

Although a crowd of 10,000 pilgrims tried to hold him back,
he went into the desert of Egypt with a few monks to see that
place where St. Anthony had lived and died. St. Anthony had
been buried in a secret place, at his own command, lest his bones
be taken away and made a center of pilgrimage. After this, he
fled into Sicily, where he was unknown. Avoiding the ports,
where he might be recognized by oriental traders, he fled in-
land and lived as a beggar, bringing firewood to town on his
back for a livelihood. He was discovered through an announcement made by the devil in a possessed person, who came and
threw himself down to be cured at the hut where Hilarion was
living in the hills. The miracles begin again. Hilarion then went
to Dalmatia, then Cyprus. Finally {he} found a very remote
place in some mountains of Cyprus where there were no Christians {and} lived there in peace five years (cf. Charles de Fou-
cauld). There he died at the age of 80.

152. Col. 41 (c. 23): "with loud cries."
153. Pourrat (I:85) quotes chapter 43 of the *Lausiac History* of Palladius,
who writes that Adulius "practised asceticism beyond the powers of humanity.
. . . For on account of his excessive abstinence and vigils he was suspected of
being a ghost. During Lent, indeed, he ate once in five days, and at all other
times once every other day. . . . From the evening (until the monks met to
pray), on the Mount of Olives, on the hill-top where the Ascension of Jesus took
place, he remained standing singing and praying all the time. And whether it
snowed or rained, there he stood and never moved."
154. Col. 44 (c. 29).

ST. CHARITON—From Iconium in Asia Minor. He lived in a cave in the Wadi Pharan north of Jerusalem, from 322 on. Here disciples gathered and a monastery was founded. {In} 355 he moved on to {the} other side of Jordan to {the} mountain where Jesus fasted—another monastery was founded {which is} still there today (Greek monks). Finally he found an inaccessible cave in the desert of Juda—but a third monastery was founded near it—Deir Suka.

ST. EUTHYMIUS (d. 473), from Armenia, began as a hermit at Wadi Pharan, near St. Chariton, started a cenobium, then founded famous Laura of St. Euthymius, near Bethany (428); it was transformed into a cenobium after his death.

ST. SABAS (439–532), {a} Cappadocian, formed in cenobium of St. Euthymius, lived as {a} hermit in {the} Kedron valley near Jerusalem. Then {he} organized the *great Laura* of *Mar Saba* (478), {which still} exists today, clinging to the side of a cliff. *St. John Damascene* was a monk here—and here wrote all his books. It has three churches, in which liturgy used to be celebrated in three languages according to three rites—Armenian, Syrian and Greek. Today about 30 monks—Greek Orthodox—live in cells which are partly caves. The monks of St. Sabas also maintained hospitals. He instituted the *Typikon*—basis of oriental monastic liturgy.

Cyril of Scythopolis—a disciple of St. Sabas, lived in great Laura and composed lives of saints.

John Moschus (6th–7th cent.) {was} a late compiler of monastic stories and legends—the *Pratum Spirituale*[155]—popular—full of "wonders."

ST. JEROME

The most famous monk in Palestine was to be *St. Jerome* whom we will here treat quite briefly. Although a Desert Father, St. Jerome really falls outside the whole scope of these lectures, as a Father and Doctor of the Church and a translator and commentator on Scripture. His vocation was much vaster and more

---

155. John Moschos, *The Spiritual Meadow*, trans. John Wortley, CS 139 (Kalamazoo, MI: Cistercian Publications, 1992).

spectacular than that of a simple Desert Father—the same could of course be said for Sts. Basil, Gregory of Nyssa etc.

Life of St. Jerome: {He was} born at Stridon, Dalmatia, about 347, {the} child of Christian parents, but was not baptized until later in life. Meanwhile, during his studies in Rome, {he} led a somewhat dissolute life. Baptized about 365 (age 18), {he} started living as a monk near Aquilaeia in Italy. Here his association with *Rufinus* began. {He} moved east (about 374), and lived as a monk in the desert of *Chalcis*, near Antioch, Syria. This was already a monastic center. {He was} ordained priest at Antioch about 378. {The years} 382–385 {mark} his visit to Rome under Pope Damasus. {He} now has a great reputation. {He} served Damasus as secretary. It was under Damasus that Jerome gave himself definitely to work on *Scripture*. He made himself unpopular in Italy by criticizing lax Christians and tepid clergy. From now on he was definitely to be a fighter, and in every battle of his time. Here he met Paula and Eustochium, whose direction he assumed, and they were led by him to monastic life in Palestine. He went with them to Palestine in 385 when, after {the} death of Pope Damasus, violent opposition to Jerome was let loose in Rome. Occasion was taken to calumniate St. Jerome and his relations with the noble matrons he had directed at Rome, teaching them to read Scripture in original Greek and Hebrew. *St. Paula* (feast: Jan. 26; d. 404) was mother of St. Eustochium and St. Blaesilla. {She} became a widow at 34, came under influence of St. Jerome, led {a} consecrated life, was Abbess of {a} convent founded by him at Bethlehem, where she also conducted a hospital—a remarkable instance of nuns living contemplative life—with notable elements of *scholarship* and *works of mercy*.

The monastic life as influenced by the presence and character of St. Jerome takes on a very *active* and aggressive character, although remaining contemplative. For this reason we have to be careful of taking Jerome as a typical "Desert Father"—on the whole he is not the best of models for contemplatives. He inspires rather those whose spiritual life is aggressive, ascetical, active and controversial: but these are often people who stir up monastic orders and cause dissension—though when they are really saints they may accomplish much good.

On arriving in Palestine with Paula, Eustochium and a bevy of other friends, St. Jerome went for a trip around all the holy places, accompanied by them. He continued on down into Egypt, but did not visit Nitria as he hoped. Heat in Alexandria in 386 (summer) drove them all back north. They settle in Bethlehem— two monasteries, one of women, one of men, both founded by St. Paula. St. Jerome finishes his life here, thirty-five years of very fruitful activity, surrounded by his monks. From 390 to 405 he is engaged in translation of {the} Bible (Vulgate)—learned Hebrew from Rabbis who slipped in to monastery under cover of darkness (and collected a good fee for their lessons). {He} wrote commentaries on various books of the Bible at this same time, carried on *controversies*, wrote innumerable *letters*. Sulpicius Severus described Jerome thus: "He is constantly immersed in study, wholly plunged in his books he gives himself no rest either day or night; he is incessantly occupied in reading or writing."[156]

We shall see later, in discussing Cassian, Jerome's place in the *Origenist* controversy. Jerome went against Origen, breaking with the Bishop (John) of Jerusalem, who nearly had him thrown out of Palestine, and breaking also with his best friend, *Rufinus*, who remained faithful to Origen. Jerome, in his *Apology against Rufinus*, accuses the latter of heresy, duplicity etc. *Rufinus* had followed Jerome to Palestine, a little after the grand tour. {He} arrived in Palestine with *St. Melania* the Elder (another ascetic woman of great prominence)—he founded monastery on the Mount of Olives. So did she. Like Jerome, Rufinus was a scholar-monk. {He} translated much of Origen {and is} important for his (translation) work—the *Historia Monachorum in Aegypto*.

The controversy with Jerome was very unpleasant and was exceptionally hot due to various misunderstandings, Jerome's quick temper and sharp tongue, etc. Rufinus was much more moderate, discreet, and probably the more sensible of the two in this controversy. He made less of an exhibition of violence. The breach was repaired in 397.[157] The controversy is important

156. Sulpicius Severus, *Dialogues*, I:9 (*PL* 20, col. 190A).
157. The reconciliation was temporary, however; after Rufinus returned to the West the conflict was renewed. For a summary of the stages of the controversy, see John N. Hritzu's introduction to his translation of Jerome's *Apology*

in monastic history. During the controversy, Rufinus had moved to Italy. Driven out by Visigothic invasion, he died in Sicily where he was with Melania the Younger, in 411.

Other controversies in the life of St. Jerome: among his very numerous controversies, we enumerate those which have some importance for monastic history.[158]

Against *Helvidius* who attacked the virginity of the Blessed Mother (said she had other children after Our Lord). This defence of Our Lady's virginity was also important for consecrated (monastic) virginity.

Against *Jovinian* who attacked the life of chastity and continency and preached faith without works. Jerome's defence is important for monastic ascetic doctrine.

Against *Vigilantius* a priest from Spain who had been hospitably received in Jerome's monastery and afterwards wrote a book condemning monastic life and veneration of the saints.

Jerome, in collaboration with St. Augustine, helped by Orosius (Augustine's messenger) delved into the *Pelagian* controversy—looked up material on Pelagius for St. Augustine. He joined in the controversy also, and as a result the Pelagians pillaged his monastery. (We shall return to the question of Pelagianism in talking of Cassian.) St. Jerome was especially opposed to the doctrines of *apatheia* (possible freedom from all passion by ascetic works, without grace) and *impeccability* (the ascetic could by his own efforts, when free from passion, become sinless). (There is a phrase in St. Jerome which has a semi-pelagian flavor: *nostrum incipere, illius perficere*.[159] Our part is to begin [the work of salvation], His is to perfect it. This is certainly stronger

---

against *Rufinus* in St. Jerome, *Dogmatic and Polemical Works*, Fathers of the Church, vol. 53 (Washington: Catholic University of America Press, 1965), 47–58.

158. The same controversies are discussed in the same order in Pourrat I:147-55. The detail that Vigilantius had visited Jerome, not mentioned in Pourrat, may have been taken from Nora K. Chadwick's *Poetry and Letters in Early Christian Gaul* (London: Bowes & Bowes, 1955), 81, a work to which Merton refers below; Chadwick notes that Vigilantius was sent to Jerome by Paulinus of Nola "with a letter of high commendation" but returned disillusioned with what he considered "extreme asceticism and superstitious practices," criticized in the now lost treatise to which Jerome responded.

159. *Dialogi contra Pelagianos Libri Tres*, 3:1 (*PL* 23, col. 596C).

than any of the semi-pelagian-seeming phrases in Cassian, yet
in Jerome it is always successfully excused, and regarding Cassian, suspicion remains. This is because Cassian was opposed
by the strong Augustinian party in the West; Jerome was not.[160]
We must be careful to remember that the stigma of heresy or
doubtful orthodoxy clings tenaciously sometimes to men who
have not taught otherwise than the saints of their time, but have
somehow acquired a bad reputation due to "politics.")

St. Jerome's Monastic Doctrine:

St. Jerome was a great preacher and apostle of monastic renunciation. His doctrine contains nothing new: what is original
in him is the *fire and power of exhortation*. (Quote from Letter xiv
to Heliodorus: Pourrat, vol. I, p. 139):

> Why are you a Christian with such a timorous heart? Look
> at the Apostle Peter quitting his nets; look at the Publican
> leaving his office for the receipt of custom to become a mis-
> sionary on the spot. The Son of Man had not where to lay
> His head, and will you be making use of great doorways
> and spacious dwellings? If you look for your inheritance in
> this world, you cannot be the co-heir of Christ. . . . You
> have promised to be a thorough Christian. . . . But a thor-
> ough Christian has nothing but Christ, or if he has anything
> else he is not perfect. . . . What are you, my brother, doing
> in the world, you who are greater than the world? . . . Do
> you dread the poverty of the desert? But Christ says that
> the poor are blessed. Are you afraid of work? But no ath-
> lete wins a prize without toiling hard. Are you thinking of
> the food you will get here? But if your faith is strong you
> will not fear being hungry. Are you afraid of bruising your
> limbs on the bare ground after they have been emaciated
> by fasting? But the Lord lies down with you on the
> ground. Do you dread wearing your hair unkempt on your
> unwashed head? But Christ is your head. Do you shrink
> from the infinite spaces of the desert? But in your thoughts

160. See, however, N. Chadwick, 47, who notes that Jerome's "resentful
contempt for opponents had created in Gaul as elsewhere dislike of his person
and criticism of his orthodoxy" (citing Sulpicius Severus, *Dialogues* I:9 [*PL* 20,
col. 189CD], who, however, defends Jerome against his detractors).

you will tread the heavens; and whenever you are borne
thither in mind you will be no more in the desert. . . . The
day will surely come when this corruptible and mortal flesh
will put on incorruption and immortality. "Blessed is that
servant whom, when his lord shall come, he shall find
watching" (Luke xii:43). On that day when the trumpet shall
sound, the nations of the earth shall be smitten with fear,
and then you will rejoice!

Importance of this document: the monk leaves all to live united
with Christ. He has an *obligation* to do this for, being a member
of Christ, he is greater than the world and should not remain
subject to what is beneath him. He must bravely face the hardships of desert life and deprivation, trusting in Christ, not in his
own power. Finally he must base his whole monastic life on *eschatological hope*—the second coming and the new creation.

Jerome urged men and women fearlessly to defy the world
and their families in order to renounce worldly life and follow
Christ with courage. This emphasis on courage and dauntless
faith is what makes St. Jerome's letters such necessary reading
for monks and contemplatives (cf. his influence on St. Teresa[161]).
READ the classic diatribe in which he urges Heliodorus to trample on his father's prostrate body if the latter lies down across
the threshold to prevent him going forth to follow his vocation.

> Remember the day of your profession of the Christian faith,
> when you were buried with Christ in baptism and prom-
> ised on receiving the sacrament that you would spare nei-
> ther your mother nor your father if the name of Christ
> required it. See how the enemy is trying to kill the Christ
> in your heart. See how the other side is grieved at your re-
> ception of the gift of Christ which you were to use in the
> fight! Even if your grandnephew were clinging to your neck
> and your mother with her scanty hair and her garments
> rent asunder were to bare the breasts that you had sucked
> to make you give way, even if your father were to fling him-

161. In the third chapter of her *Life*, Teresa writes that it was reading the letters of St. Jerome that gave her the courage to tell her father that she wished to
become a nun. (See *The Collected Works of St. Teresa of Avila*, trans. Kieran Ka-
vanaugh, OCD and Otilio Rodriguez, OCD [Washington, DC: Institute of
Carmelite Studies, 1976], 1:40.)

self down upon the threshold to bar your way, trample him beneath your feet, and onward without a tear towards the standard of the cross (Pourrat, vol. I, p. 140).

We should all be familiar with these exhortations and meditate on them often. Courage and determination are *essential* to a real monastic vocation. Without them, we fail to correspond to grace. *Pray for determination* and fidelity to God's call.

Monasticism in Mesopotamia and Syria[162]

Here the ascetic element is even more emphasized. The monks of Palestine and Mesopotamia in general were more rigid and extreme than the monks of Egypt.[163]

Theodoret of Cyr—{is} the main source for information about these monks.

St. James of Nisibis, bishop, d. 361, hermit and then bishop—{is} typical of Syrian monachism—lived on wild herbs, without fixed abode, slept in a cave in winter, outdoors in summer.

St. Aphraates—{was a} Persian abbot and then bishop.

St. Ephrem, deacon, lived temporarily as anchorite outside Edessa—famous Syrian liturgical poet.

St. John Chrysostom lived for a time (6 years) as monk and hermit alternately, outside Antioch {and} wrote in defense of monastic life and on compunction. {He is} noted more as bishop and Doctor, defender of orthodoxy. We shall see later that he welcomes Cassian and Egyptian Origenist monks to Constantinople.

The Stylites—first made their appearance in Syria—column sitters. St. Symeon Stylites, born in Antioch, died 459, {is} one of the great saints of the fifth century. {He} first chained himself to a rock, then got a pillar ten feet high, changed to one 30 feet high and finally on one 63 feet high—renowned throughout the world for his miracles. After {the} death of Symeon there was a bitter struggle for his relics between the Patriarch of Antioch and the

162. Merton will focus on this topic in "Pre-Benedictine Monasticism," second series (1964–1965) (87 pp.), especially Theodoret of Cyrrhus, Aphraat, St. Ephrem and Philoxenos.

163. Information on the following figures apparently comes from Pourrat: Theodoret is mentioned on page 85, James of Nisibis and Chrysostom on page 86, Aphraates and Ephrem on page 103.

monks who had settled around his pillar. Patriarch got them—with the help of soldiers. But afterwards the relics were taken to Constantinople. A huge basilica was built around the abandoned pillar and was a great center of pilgrimages, comparable to Lourdes or Fatima today. Celebrations were held there in 1959—fifteenth centenary of his death.

How did stylites live? St. Symeon spent 37 years on top of pillars—thirty of them on the 63-foot pillar. He *stood* without shelter, protected by a railing. He prayed with *metaniae* (repeated genuflections). (A pilgrim once counted up to 1244 successive prostrations.) He was tied to a post in Lent when he *fasted the whole 40 days.* Other stylites had *shelters.* Food was hauled up in a basket—provided by faithful and disciples. They preached to the crowds, gave spiritual direction. Those who wanted a "private" interview went up a ladder. Pilgrims came from all over the world—Gaul, Britain, Turkestan. . . .

Other stylites: St. Daniel, St. Symeon the younger, St. Jonas. Attempts at stylitism in {the} West were stopped by bishops.

What attitude should we take toward this kind of sanctity? The fashion has been to disparage it, to treat it as something absurd and grotesque. This is not the full truth. {It was a} witness to the divine transcendency, and to the superiority of the spirit. Precisely its *uselessness* was what made this witness powerful. If we are to fully understand our contemplative vocation, we must be able to understand the uselessness, the "folly" of the stylites. The folly of God is greater than the wisdom of men. It was a protest against the worldly preoccupation with politics, and politico-theological struggles, with earthly and ecclesiastical ambition, etc. Symeon converted thousands of pagans.

Defects of Palestinian and Syrian Monachism

However it must be admitted that the monachism of Palestine and Syria represents an extreme against which St. Benedict himself is clearly in reaction. We have a story of St. Benedict reproving a hermit who chained himself to a rock.[164] St. Benedict inveighed against the *independence* and *irresponsibility* of monks who

164. *Dialogues*, Book III, c. 16 (144).

wandered about without superiors.[165] The Sarabaites and Gyrovagues flourished mostly in Syria etc., monks without ecclesiastical control. Great deviations occurred, and monachism would quickly have been ruined if there had not been intervention on the part of men like St. Basil to bring in sobriety and organization. On the other hand, we must not imagine that Basilian monachism was something tightly and rigidly organized either. But there was the control of *obedience* and the sobering influence of *discretion*.

THE HERMITS OF NITRIA AND SCETE

We now come to the heart of our subject: the great monastic centers of northern Egypt, where Cassian and Germanus wandered about consulting the "old men"—the land of the *Apothegmata* (*Verba Seniorum*), and of the other famous Desert Father texts. First, let us list summarily the more famous *collections* of stories, proverbs and other Desert Father material. This is in addition to the *Vita Antonii*, etc. mentioned above.

1. *Historia Monachorum*—translated by Rufinus—original lost (*PL* 21).[166]

2. *Historia Lausiaca*—by Palladius, disciple of St. John Chrysostom (in *PL* 73)[167]—gets {its} name from {the} fact that it

165. *Rule*, c. 1: "The third kind of monks is that detestable one of the Sarabaites. . . . They live in twos or threes, or even singly, without a shepherd, in their own sheepfolds and not in the Lord's. Their law is their own good pleasure: whatever they think of or choose to do, that they call holy; what they like not, that they regard as unlawful. The fourth kind of monks are those called Gyrovagues. These spend their whole lives wandering from province to province, staying three days in one monastery and four days in another, ever roaming and never stable, given up to their own wills and the allurements of gluttony, and worse in all respects than the Sarabaites. Of the wretched observance of all these folk it is better to be silent than to speak" (McCann, 15, 17).

166. *PL* 21:387-462; Merton is mistaken about the Greek original—it was first edited by E. Preuschen, *Palladius und Rufinus* (Giessen: Rickersche, 1897) 1–131, and more recently by André Festugière (Brussels: Société des Bollandistes, 1961); for an English translation see Norman Russell, *The Lives of the Desert Fathers*, CS 34 (Kalamazoo, MI: Cistercian, 1980); the additions of Rufinus are included in an appendix to this translation. Merton has an extended discussion of this work in "Pre-Benedictine Monasticism," first series, 9–16.

167. This is the Latin translation, included in Rosweyde's *Vitae Patrum* as the eighth book (col. 1065–1234); the Greek version, superseded by Butler's edition, is found in *PG* 34, col. 991–1278.

was dedicated to Lausus, chamberlain of Theodosius II. Dom C. Butler made a famous English translation and edition (1904).[168] {It was} written before Cassian's *Conferences*, in 419–20. One should know at least in outline some of the scholarly arguments about the *Historia Lausiaca*:

    a) It was attacked by the German critic Reitzenstein[169] as unhistorical.

    b) Butler defended the historical value of the *H. L.* He also contended that the Greek text which still exists was the original and authentic text.[170]

    c) Draguet has established that the original (Coptic) text has not yet been found and that the Greek text is corrupt.[171] Further he contends that the *H. L.* is not the pure spirit of the Desert

168. Cuthbert Butler, OSB, *The Lausiac History of Palladius*, 2 vols.: vol. 1 Prolegomena; vol. 2: The Greek Text with Introduction and Notes (Cambridge: Cambridge University Press, 1898, 1904). Merton is mistaken about the inclusion of an English translation in this edition; an English version was produced by W. K. L. Clarke, *The Lausiac History of Palladius* (Translations of Christian Literature, Series I: Greek Texts [London: SPCK, 1918]), and later by Robert T. Meyer (1965).

169. Richard Reitzenstein, *Historia Monachorum und Historia Lausiaca: Eine Studie sur Geschichte des Mönchtums und der frühchristlichen Begriffe Gnostiker und Pneumatiker* (Göttingen: Vandenhoeck und Ruprecht, 1916).

170. Butler asserted that the shorter of the two ancient Greek recensions was the authentic one (see Meyer, *Lausiac History*, 9, 12); see also his later articles, "Palladiana I: The Lausiac History: Questions of Text," *Journal of Theological Studies*, 22 (1921), 21–35; "Palladiana II: The *Dialogus de Vita Chrysostomi* and the *Historia Lausiaca*: Authorship," *Journal of Theological Studies*, 22 (1921), 138–55; "Palladiana III: Lausiac History: Questions of History," *Journal of Theological Studies*, 22 (1921), 222–38.

171. Merton is mistaken in the idea that Draguet thinks the entire original text was Coptic; he does propose Coptic sources for two chapters: see R. Draguet, "Le chapitre de l'*Histoire Lausiaque* sur les Tabennésiotes dérive-t-il d'une source copte?" *La Muséon: Revue d'études orientales*, 57 (1944) 53–145; 58 (1945) 15–95; "Une nouvelle source copte de Pallade: le ch. VIII (Amoun)," *La Muséon*, 60 (1947) 227–55. On the Greek text, see R. Draguet, "Un nouveau témoin de texte G de l'*Histoire Lausiaque* (MS Athenes 281)," *Mélanges Paul Peeters* (*Analecta Bollandiana* 67) (Louvain, 1949), 300–308; R. Draguet, "Butler et sa *Lausiac History* face à un ms. de l'édition, le Wake 67," *La Muséon*, 63 (1950), 203–30; D. J. Chitty, "Dom Cuthbert Butler and the Lausiac History," *Journal of Theological Studies*, n.s. 6 (1955), 102–10; and R. Draguet, "Butleriana: Une mauvaise cause et son malchanceux avocat," *La Muséon*, 68 (1955), 239–58; for a recent survey of the textual scholarship, see G. Bunge, "Palladiana," *Studia Monastica*, 32 (1990), 79–129.

Fathers but just the distillation of the doctrine of one of them, *Evagrius Ponticus,* a late arrival and an intellectual (see below). It is a kind of popular catechism of Evagrian spirituality.[172] Draguet has been preparing a more critical text to replace Butler—based on an older ms. from Mount Athos which Butler had not seen, and with reference to oriental sources which Butler had not consulted.[173]

3. *The Apothegmata* or *Verba Seniorum* (see *PL* 73).[174] This is without doubt *the best source* for the spirituality of the Desert Fathers, better even than Cassian. Its advantages:

a) This collection represents predominantly the spirit of the *hermits of Scete,* and Scete was the center of the purest and most perfect eremitism in Egypt.

b) It is completely simple and colloquial, without frills or decorations, and seems to go back faithfully to the actual manner of expression of the Fathers themselves. In doing so, it gives us a picture not of exalted and extraordinary men, living in an atmosphere of marvelous spiritual events, but of simple and humble hermits, fleeing everything savoring of pride and display, preferring all that is obscure and unobtrusive.

c) It is concerned with the spiritual life and not with strange and marvelous tales.

172. R. Draguet, "L'Histoire Lausiaque', une oeuvre écrite dans l'esprit d'Evagre," *Revue d'Histoire Ecclésiastique,* 41 (1946), 321–64; 42 (1947), 5–49. For an extensive overview of Palladius in the context of the Origenist controversy as a whole, see E. D. Hunt, "Palladius of Helenopolis: A Party and its Supporters in the Church of the Late Fourth Century," *Journal of Theological Studies,* n.s. 24:2 (1973), 456–80.

173. For the Athos ms, see R. Draguet, "Un Texte G de l'*Histoire Lausiaque* dans le Lavra 333 Γ 93," *Recherches de Science Réligieuse,* 40 (1951–1952), 107–15. Draguet's critical edition of the Greek text has never appeared; Draguet did publish an edition and translation of material from the *Lausiac History* in Syriac: *Les Formes Syriaques de la matière de l'Histoire Lausiaque,* Corpus Scriptorum Christianorum Orientalium, vols. 389–90 (Louvain: Secretariat du Corpus SCO, 1978). In the Preface to this work, he states that he had never intended a new Greek edition (though this had been the expectation—see Meyer, *Lausiac History,* 13), but rather a translation accompanying the Butler text in the Sources Chrétiennes series, and he announces that this project has been abandoned (7*, n. 9).

174. The *Verba Seniorum* occupy the third and fifth through seventh books of Rosweyde's *Vitae Patrum* (cols. 739–814, 851–1066); the fourth book is composed of excerpts from Sulpicius Severus and Cassian.

d) The Fathers are content to confine themselves exclusively to *practical* and simple matters of everyday life. They generally refuse even to venture a comment on Scripture or any form of theological doctrine. They just discuss the ways of confronting problems of ascetic life.

e) The stories are taken from life, many of them consisting simply of "words of salvation" or fragments of spiritual advice given by a master to a disciple.

f) The doctrine of the *Apothegmata* is marked above all by its simplicity and discretion. It is a doctrine that can be followed and is basically healthy, as opposed to the exaggerations that are found in some of the other sources.

g) The *Apothegmata* are more purely *Coptic*. The other sources represent mixtures from Syrian and other Oriental sources (a few of these creep into the *Apothegmata* later). We can distinguish clearly between the humble and practical spirituality of the original Coptic monks, and the intellectualism of Evagrius for instance—Macarius also.[175]

Various elements in the *Apothegmata*—They are composed of several collections:

1. The "Alphabetic" collection—from Alpha—(Anthony)—to Omega—(Or)—attributed to the more famous Abbots—only in Greek (*PG* 65).[176]

2. The collection arranged according to "virtues"—Greek original lost[177]—preserved in Latin (*PL* 73, col. 855 ff.) Consists of 18 books or chapters: Lib. I—*de Profectu Patrum*; Lib. II—*de Quiete*; Lib. III—*de Compunctione*—etc. etc.

3. A third Latin collection, following the above in *PL* 73[178]—again divided according to virtues and vices. This is less good than the former.

175. But see the discussion of Macarius below, in which Merton recognizes that the works attributed to Macarius are not his.

176. Cols. 71–440.

177. Jean-Claude Guy discusses his recent rediscovery of manuscripts containing the Greek version of this topical collection in *Recherches sur la tradition grecque des Apophthegmata Patrum*, Subsidia Hagiographica 36 (Brussels: Société des Bollandistes, 1962), 118.

178. In the forty-four chapters of the seventh book of the *Vitae Patrum* (cols. 1025–66) vices are more prominent in the chapter headings than in the initial se-

For our purposes, (2) above is the best. There is a slight variety of materials:

a) Apothegmata, properly so called, "words of salvation"—brief proverbial statements, and

b) longer stories with a practical moral, illustrating a truth about the hermit life.

The Spirituality of the Desert as reflected in the Sayings of the Fathers:

The primary concern of the desert life {is} to seek God, to seek salvation. The salutation common among Desert Fathers was *"sotheis"*—mayest thou be saved.[179] Many of the sentences are simply answers to the question, "What ought I to do?" Hence the answers are simple, succinct summaries of some of the main obligations of a monk in the primitive sense. But remember:

1. These were bits of advice given to *individuals*—hence they are responses to special individual needs, and are not in themselves the universal answer to *all* questions. They must be pieced together and seen in perspective—must be seen in light of special *circumstances*.

2. Remember that there was *no set rule* for the hermit—only certain rather free prevalent customs. He had to make his own rule of life, based on the individual teaching and advice received from the Fathers. He had to know what to accept and what to discard as useless to him. The memorable phrases which have been preserved are remarkable not so much for their special depth, as for the fact that someone was struck very deeply by them and held on to them as coming from God. They became a rule of life for *him*. There was no irresponsible license in the true Desert Fathers. The Desert Fathers were not necessarily *magic directors*, wizard gurus, who had a series of infallible answers on all points. They were humble and sagacious men, of few words, whom the Holy Ghost used for His purposes. We must

---

ries; Merton does not mention either the two hundred twenty paragraphs (not grouped into chapters) in Book III (cols. 739–814) or the four "libelli" that make up Book VI (cols. 991–1024), which is a kind of appendix to Book V, though he makes use of both these collections in *What Ought I to Do?* and in *The Wisdom of the Desert*.

179. See Mahieu, 70, citing Marc. 3 (*PG* 65, col. 296C) [properly "σωθειης" (*"sotheies"*)].

know how to take advantage of direction in this sense. If we seek our director as a kind of oracle, he will always fail us. If we are prepared to listen to him in simplicity and accept, with faith, some ordinary observation of his as coming from God, then he will be able to help us. This faith requires not absolute blindness of the reason and common sense: it requires a certain trust and response on our part, an awareness that this is fitting for our case, which faith intensifies and enables us to see in an entirely supernatural light. For this, we must be *open* and *trusting*. We must be able to let go a little. If we cannot trust any director—then we will have more trials and difficulties. Confidence in a director is a grace to be prayed for. In any case we all should be attentive to special "words of salvation" that come to us in reading, sermons, conferences or direction, as God's *special will for us*.

What should the monk do? A few examples taken at random from our small collection *What Ought I to Do?*[180] (numbers refer to the sayings as collected there):

A general summary of the virtues of monastic life (n. vii): "An elder said: Here is the monk's life-work / obedience / meditation / not judging others / not reviling / not complaining. For it is written: You who love the Lord / hate evil. So this is the monk's life—not to walk in agreement with an unjust man / nor to look with his eyes upon evil / not to go about {being} curious / and neither to examine nor to listen to the business of others. Not to take anything with his hands / but rather to give to others. Not to be proud in his heart / nor to malign others in his thoughts. Not to fill his stomach / but in all things {to} behave with discretion. Behold / in all this you have the monk" (p. 8).[181]

"Have no confidence in your own virtuousness, do not worry about a thing once it has been done, control your tongue

---

180. *What Ought I to Do?: Sayings of the Desert Fathers,* translated by Thomas Merton (Lexington, KY: Stamperia del Santuccio, 1959). This limited edition of 100 sayings from the *Verba Seniorum* was later published in an expanded edition of 150 sayings as *The Wisdom of the Desert: Sayings from the Desert Fathers of the Fourth Century* (New York: New Directions, 1960). All references to individual sayings will also be recorded in the notes according to the numbering of this more easily accessible edition, as well as to its location in Migne.

181. (8–9) *Wisdom of the Desert,* ix (28–29); *PL* 73, col. 857CD.

and your belly" (i).[182] This saying of St. Anthony {is} simple and wise, *basic*—humility, trust, and temperance. Note the wisdom of the Desert Fathers who insist on not worrying about things that can no longer be changed. What is done is done. Don't fret over it, but do not do it again—true penance.

To accept illness and temptation with thanksgiving—(ii, xxxviii);[183] Purity of intention and obedience (ii, xlvi, lxi);[184] Work—the monk must not be idle—but must spend his life in solitary work supporting himself and aiding the weaker brethren (vi).[185]

Silence—meaning not mutism but wise control of speech, especially refraining from all vainglory in talk, all showing off knowledge, all desire to prove one's point or justify oneself (see ix, xiii, xiv, xv, xvii [detraction], xxx, xl, xlix, lxv).[186] Silence is for the sake of contemplation—li,[187] cf. Arsenius, xiii—*Fuge, tace, quiesce*.[188] The *fuge tace quiesce* of Arsenius—reminds us that the monk is above all one who renounces the world and flies from it. Why?—because possessions lay one open to attacks of demons (xx).[189] Hence importance of poverty, and even strict poverty in the monastic life itself—no compromise with spirit of proprietorship, even in the best and most necessary of things. One should not have anything he is not willing to part with—even if it is taken violently and unjustly (lxxiii, lxxvii).[190] Though the monk makes his own living, he does not bargain and haggle or try to "make money" like the people in the world (lxxviii).[191] There should be *perfect trust* in divine Providence, no hoarding

182. (7); *Wisdom of the Desert*, i (25); *PL* 73, col. 855A.

183. (7, 17); *Wisdom of the Desert*, ii, xlvii (25, 42); *PL* 73, cols. 856A, 801BC.

184. (7, 19–20, 23); *Wisdom of the Desert*, ii, lv, lxxvii (25, 45, 51); *PL* 73, cols. 856A, 927CD, 950AB.

185. (8); *Wisdom of the Desert*, vi (26–27); *PL* 73, col. 857A.

186. (9, 10, 11, 14–15, 18, 20, 24); *Wisdom of the Desert*, x, xii, xiv, xv, xix, xxxix, xlix, lxi, lxxxi (29, 30, 32, 39, 43, 40, 53); *PL* 73, cols. 857D, 858AB, 864AB, 865B, 870D, 909AB, 922A, 931C, 960D.

187. (20–21); *Wisdom of the Desert*, lxv (47); *PL* 73, col. 939C.

188. (10); *Wisdom of the Desert*, xii (29); *PL* 73, col. 858AB: Merton translates "*Fuge, tace, quiesce*" as "fly, be silent, rest in prayer."

189. (11–12); *Wisdom of the Desert*, xxii (32–33); *PL* 73, col. 888BC.

190. (26, 27); *Wisdom of the Desert*, xciv, xcvii (59, 60); *PL* 73, cols. 971CD, 1029BC.

191. (27–28); *Wisdom of the Desert*, xcix (61); *PL* 73, col. 1030CD.

up of possessions for the morrow (lxxxvii)[192]—because ambition and vainglory are the ruin of souls in the world—and because of the dangers of the flesh, sensuality etc.—also because the mere conversation of men obscures and dulls the spirit. Hence *solitude*—one must "stay in the cell, the cell will teach you all things" (x, xxvi).[193] The desert life should lead to contemplation, but by the way of humility. A monk should not just be content with his little ascetic routine: he should seek to become "all fire" (lv).[194] He should be "all eye like the cherubim and seraphim" (lii).[195]

But the way to contemplation is barred by insuperable obstacles, in anyone who is *uncharitable and despises others* (xxxiv, lxxi),[196] who is *attached to exterior penance* for its own sake (xxxv, xxxvi),[197] or is in any way proud, attached to himself, noisy, turbulent, arrogant, etc. The hallmark of the true saint in the desert as everywhere else is *charity*. And this simple charity is both active and passive: active in the sense that it is all ready to perform works of mercy, when the occasion arises, and passive in the sense that it supports every injury and trial with heroic patience. The charity of the Desert Fathers is outstanding and it is what most impresses the readers of the *Verba Seniorum*. In other collections, their asceticism and miracles tend to be more prominent.

Some other characteristics of desert spirituality:

Xeniteia—*peregrinatio*—the quality of being a stranger or an exile, a man without any fixed abode or home, in the likeness of Christ who had nowhere to rest His head. But this includes stability in a cell, except certain cases like Bessarion who "wandered about the desert without any more cares than a bird of the heavens [but always stayed in the same general area—other-

192. (31–32); *Wisdom of the Desert*, cxi (66–67); *PL* 73, col. 772CD.
193. (9, 13); *Wisdom of the Desert*, xiii, xxviii (30, 34); *PL* 73, cols. 859C, 902AB.
194. (21); *Wisdom of the Desert*, lxxii (50); *PL* 73, col. 942A.
195. (21); *Wisdom of the Desert*, lxiii (47); *PL* 73, col. 934A.
196. (15–16, 25–26); *Wisdom of the Desert*, xlii, lxxxvii (40, 54); *PL* 73, cols. 911AB, 966AB.
197. (16, 16–17); *Wisdom of the Desert*, xliv, xlv (41–42); *PL* 73, cols. 915AB, 916D–917A.

wise no stability] . . . no house, no desire to travel, no books, . . . entirely freed from all bodily desires, resting only on the firmness of his faith"[198] etc.

Anachoresis—solitude. The Desert Fathers repeat the Neoplatonic maxim—"alone with the Alone"[199]—*solus ad Solum*. (This does not exclude charity as we have seen.) *Solitude*, with *work* and *prayer*, forms one of the three great obligations of the desert monk. These three together are his very life itself. For this see Sayings xxxv[200]—advice of Abbot Ammonas to an ascetic. But solitude is combined with the strict obligation of *hospitality and instruction*. The guest sent by God is to be received as Christ Himself, and entertained. The obligation of fasting yields to the primary obligation of charity—one breaks fast to eat with guest. A disciple or a tempted brother must be counseled and helped. In this matter see the stories about "not watering the vegetables."[201]

Humility is the essence of charitable social relations, on both sides. See Sayings lxv ff. to lxxi, lxxxv, lxxxviii, xcviii, xcix[202] (how the Desert Fathers reacted against vanity in the pursuit of perfection).

Penthos—compunction also is of the very essence of desert spirituality, allied with fear of the Lord and humility: cf. Sayings xiv[203]—against useless and empty laughter. The life of the Desert Father is serious, and *penthos* is an instrument for interiority. It drives one into the depths, makes one thoughtful, hesitant to trust in his own words and opinions, ready to listen, aware of his failings. But it is combined with courage and hope in God. It is not mere morbid pessimism. Abbot Isaias was told by Abbot Macarius: "Flee from men" (this was a word of salvation) but

---

198. See Mahieu, 71 (Bessarion 12 [*PG* 65, cols. 141D,144AC]), where the translation is very close but not identical.

199. See Mahieu, 71 (Alonius 1 [*PG* 65, col. 134A]).

200. (16); *Wisdom of the Desert*, xliv (41); *PL* 73, col. 915AB.

201. *Wisdom of the Desert*, viii (27); *PL* 73, col. 741B–742A; not included in *What Ought I to Do?*

202. (24–26, 30–31, 32, 36); *Wisdom of the Desert*, lxxxi–lxxxvii, cx, cxii, cxxviii, cxxix (53–54, 65–66, 67, 73); *PL* 73, col. 960D, 961A, 964B, 964C, 965CD, 966AB, 752C–753A, 777D–778A, 906C, 909C.

203. (10); *Wisdom of the Desert*, xiv (30); *PL* 73, col. 864AB.

he asked for explanation. Fleeing from men, according to Macarius, implies: "to remain seated in your cell and to bewail your sins."[204] Hence the connection between *penthos* and *anachoresis*, *euche* (prayer) and humility—also stability. This shows the important and vital interconnection between all the virtues in an organic whole, in the desert life. Note also—devotion to Our Lord and to the Blessed Mother {is} connected with *penthos*. Abbot Poemen comes out of ecstasy and says: "My spirit was there where holy Mary the Mother of God, wept at the foot of the Savior's Cross. And I would very much like always to weep like that."[205] This sort of thing, thought to be characteristic of *devotio moderna*, is often found in the simplicity of the Desert Fathers.

Diakrisis—Discretion. As we have seen from St. Anthony, discretion is the most important virtue in the monastic life because without it all the others go astray. This is also the teaching of St. Thomas on Prudence.[206]

Amerimnia—The absence of all cares, especially material ones. This was sometimes an impossible ideal (cf. John the Dwarf).[207]

Parrhesia[208]

Hesychia—As we have seen above, "*quies*" or sweet repose in contemplation is the crown of the desert life, the reward of all the hermit's strivings and the foretaste of heaven. But the Fathers were very simple and retiring about this also—they did not seek to be known or admired for their prayer but to keep it hidden and consequently they have little to say about it. However, there were great speculative theologians in the desert, notably *Macarius* and especially *Evagrius*. It is time to consider these theologians of contemplation.

204. See Mahieu, 80 (Macarius 27 [*PG* 65, col. 274B]): same translation.
205. See Mahieu, 81 (Poemen 144 [*PG* 65, col. 358B]): same translation.
206. *Summa Theologiae*, ed. Thomas Gilby, OP, 61 vols. (New York: McGraw-Hill, 1964–80), 36:21-27 (II–II, Q. 47, art. 6 and 7); see below, pages 220–21 for specific information on the teaching of Aquinas on this point.
207. *What Ought I to Do?*, xxxvi, xci (16–17, 33); *Wisdom of the Desert*, xlv, xci (41–42, 56–57); *PL* 73, cols. 916D–917A, 894A.
208. "free speech": see Merton's discussion of prayer as parrhesia in *The New Man* (New York: Farrar, Straus, Giroux, 1961), 71–98.

St. Macarius

There were two saints by this name in the desert, contemporaries and friends. The first was a monk of Nitria, Macarius of Alexandria, called *"politikos"*—the "city man."[209] He left no writings. (A third—Macarius of Magnesia—is sometimes confused with these two.) *Macarius the Great*, the one who concerns us, was practically the founder of Scete and was the master of Evagrius of Pontus. Hence he is really the fountainhead of the desert school of mystical theology.

{He was} born about 300–310. He lived to be ninety years old. {He} came to Scete when he was 30 {and} became famous for miracles and prophecies—was ordained priest on this account at the age of 41. In Migne (*PG* 34) there are many works ascribed to Macarius, but most of them are almost certainly by someone else. For example, there are some 50 homilies, which seem to have been written for cenobites, and are said to have Messalian tendencies—belong to a later date,[210] some monk of Asia Minor or Syria. There are also treatises (which are just selections from the homilies) and letters. The *Epistola ad Monachos*[211] was long thought to be genuine, but even this is almost certainly not by Macarius. In Greek Mss. the author is called Macarius, but now the same letter in Arabic is ascribed to one *Symeon*.[212] Who was he? A shorter version of the same letter was

209. So Palladius in the *Lausiac History* 20:2: see Meyer 71 and 184, n. 191; Palladius provides information on Macarius the Alexandrian, whom he had met, in chapter 18 of the *Lausiac History* (Meyer, 58–67), and on Macarius the Egyptian (the Great), who had died the year before Palladius came to Scete, in chapter 17 (Meyer, 54–58), which includes the information found at the beginning of the following paragraph.

210. The most thorough recent study of this material dates it "in the second half of the fourth century, probably in the 380s": see Columba Stewart, OSB, *'Working the Earth of the Heart': The Messalian Controversy in History, Texts, and Language to AD 431* (Oxford: Clarendon Press, 1991), 70.

211. *PG* 34, cols. 409–441.

212. This was first noted by Werner Strothmann in his 1931 Göttingen dissertation, "Die arabische Makariustradition." See Werner Jaeger, *Two Rediscovered Works of Ancient Christian Literature: Gregory of Nyssa and Macarius* (Leiden, Brill, 1954), 152. This Symeon is first identified with a Messalian leader of the same name by Hermann Dörries in his *Symeon von Mesopotamien: Die Überlieferung der messalianischen "Makarios"-Schriften*, Texte und Untersuchungen, 55:1

also ascribed to St. Ephrem. The *Epistola ad Monachos*—ascribed to Macarius—deals with the ideal of the monastic life, the "conversion" to that true good which man desires by his very nature and which God makes accessible to him by grace. He considers *the way of perfection* in the spiritual life, especially *apatheia* and the need for humility. Prayer he says is the leader of all the choir of virtues. Dom Wilmart[213] and Fr. Francis of Chimay[214] have studied this doctrine and compared it with the spirituality of St. Benedict, coming to the conclusion that this is genuine Benedictine spirituality. Indeed it is the proper spirituality of monks and contemplatives, although rather limited in its views. It is an early *psychology* of the contemplative life. But we must realize that there are other very important perspectives which are omitted from this. So much for the spirituality of the "Great Letter of Macarius" *as it appears in Migne.* Recently this letter has been in the "news" among Greek scholars, and Werner Jaeger[215] has *proved that the letter in Migne PG is not really the text of "Macarius'" letter at all* but is a faulty compilation of a *lost treatise* on the ascetic life by Gregory of Nyssa, recently discovered.[216] At the same time, the *full text of the Great Letter* has also been discovered and is being edited. The Greek text has been printed by W. Jaeger.[217] What is this text? It is an *expanded copy*—with explanations and comments—of Gregory's lost ascetic treatise—a way of adopt-

---

(Leipzig: J. C. Hinrichs, 1941); see also the same author's *Die Theologie des Makarios-Symeon* (Göttingen: Vandenhoeck & Ruprecht, 1978).

213. Merton has apparently misunderstood his source here: Mahieu's translation of the "Great Letter" is based on the text published in André Wilmart, OSB, "La Lettre Spirituelle de l'Abbé Macaire," *Revue d'Ascétique et de Mystique,* 1 (1920), 58–83, but there is no discussion of the relation of Macarius to Benedictine spirituality there.

214. Mahieu, 95–101.

215. Jaeger, *Two Rediscovered Works,* 37–47.

216. The text of the treatise generally called *De instituto Christiano* had been published in what Jaeger calls an "abridged and mutilated form" (3, n. 1) in *PG* 46, cols. 287–306; the authentic text appears in Jaeger's edition of *Gregorii Nysseni Opera vol. VIII, I: Gregorii Nysseni Opera Ascetica* (Leiden: Brill, 1952), 1–89.

217. Jaeger, *Two Rediscovered Works,* 231–301. A more recent edition of both the *Great Letter* and the *De Instituto Christiano* is that of Reinhart Staats: *Makarios-Symeon: Epistola Magna. Eine messalianische Mönchsregel und ihre Umschrift in Gregors von Nyssa 'De instituto christiano'* (Göttingen: Vandenhoeck & Ruprecht, 1984).

ing and passing on useful monastic material.[218] The newly discovered letter shows that the author *added his own* material copiously when talking about the common life. This is the work of a fifth-century cenobite, probably in Syria—and is *not* by Macarius. In the new letter, there is considerable discussion of problems raised in community life by the fact that "more perfect" monks were allowed extra time for prayer while others had to work.

The Macarian Writings

We have seen that in addition to the letters ascribed to Macarius the Great, which are few in number, there remain a large number of homilies ascribed to him.[219] For a long time it was thought that the letters were really by Macarius and the Homilies by some unknown Messalian. Werner Jaeger has shown that both are by the same person, an admirer and copier of Gregory of Nyssa, probably some Syrian cenobite of the fifth century.[220] Now these Macarian homilies are important for the history of oriental spirituality because of the great influence they had on the development of the *Hesychast movement*. Hence it is necessary here to consider the teachings on prayer of the homilies of Pseudo-Macarius. But since these homilies are full

218. This conclusion of Jaeger (174–207) that the *De instituto Christiano* was the source of the *Great Letter*, rather than vice versa, has subsequently been widely challenged by other scholars, who consider that Gregory or his disciples produced a revised text of the *Great Letter*: see Reinhart Staats, *Gregor von Nyssa und die Messalianer*, Patristische Texte und Studien, 8 (Berlin: De Gruyter, 1968), as well as his 1984 edition of the two texts (see previous note); M. Canévet, "Le 'De Instituto Christiano' est-il de Grégoire de Nysse?" *Revue des Études Grecques*, 82 (1969), 404–23; Vincent Despres, Introduction to *Pseudo-Macaire: Oeuvres Spirituelles: Homélies propres à la Collection III*, Sources Chrétiennes, vol. 275 (Paris: Éditions du Cerf, 1980); arguments summarized by George A. Maloney, sj in the Introduction to his translation of *Pseudo-Macarius: The Fifty Spiritual Homilies and the Great Letter* (New York: Paulist, 1992), 10–11 and 28, n. 5.

219. For a summary description of the four overlapping Greek manuscript traditions, see Maloney, Introduction to *Pseudo-Macarius*, 5–6, and Stewart, 'Working the Earth of the Heart,' 71–74.

220. See Jaeger, *Two Rediscovered Works*, 154: "Whatever his true name, there can be no doubt that he is identical with the author of the so-called Macarius homilies." Jaeger provides further evidence of the influence of Gregory of Nyssa on the homilies on pages 208–30. More recent scholarship considers Gregory and the author of the homilies to be contemporaries, and demonstrates that the influence of the two is mutual rather than in one direction only.

of Messalian tendencies, we have to stop first of all to consider the meaning of the *Messalian heresy.*

Messalianism—a heresy which gave exaggerated emphasis to prayer and to the sensible experiences that occur during prayer. For the Messalians, contemplation and the quasi-physical experience of "divine things" was all-important, and the sign of true spiritual perfection. Without such "experiences" no real perfection was possible. Such subjective experiences outweighed in importance the liturgical and sacramental life of the Church. By experiences of prayer one was sanctified and made perfect. {It was} condemned in a general way at the Council of Ephesus (431);[221] the heretical doctrines of the Messalians were summarized and condemned by St. John Damascene,[222] Theodoret[223] and others.[224] Briefly, the main errors of the Messalians were these:

1. Original sin gave the devil possession of man's inmost heart, so that everyone is born *possessed* by the devil. Baptism itself is powerless to deliver man from this state of possession. But *perpetual prayer* is able to get the devil out of man's heart and leads eventually to complete possession by the Holy Spirit. Hence it is a perpetual spiritual prayer which is the main sanctifying force in man's life.

2. In order to practice perpetual prayer, they neglect work and remain in a state of silence and inertia for long periods (i.e. overemphasis on a quietistic type of contemplation); in this contemplation they *claim to see God with the eyes of the body* at certain times—at other times they are moved to sudden impulsive actions, dancing, "shaking" etc. and "shooting imaginary arrows" at the devils.

221. For a thorough discussion of the three phases of opposition to Messalianism, culminating at Ephesus, and the various synodal and conciliar condemnations, see Stewart, 'Working the Earth of the Heart,' 12–52.

222. In *Liber de haeresibus*, 80 (*PG* 94:728A–737C).

223. Theodoret of Cyrrhus, *Historia ecclesiastica*, 4:10 (*PG* 82:1141D–1145B), and *Haereticarum fabularum compendium*, 4:11 (*PG* 83:429B–431C).

224. Lists are also found in Timothy of Constantinople, *De iis qui ad ecclesiam ab haereticis accedunt*, and in Severus of Antioch, *Contra additiones Juliani*. For a thorough discussion and comparison of these lists, see Stewart, 'Working the Earth of the Heart,' 52–67; the complete lists themselves are presented by Stewart in synoptic form in Appendix 2 of 'Working the Earth of the Heart,' 244–79.

3. By the practice of perpetual prayer (from which they were also called *Euchites*)[225] one arrived at *apatheia*, complete immunity to all passion. One also arrived at mystical marriage with the Divine Spouse, which was in some way physically experienced. Not only that but the soul and body are completely transformed into God so as to become really divine, having a divine nature. They claimed full sensible awareness of the indwelling Spirit—also of sin and of grace.

4. There were also several dogmatic errors, concerning the Trinity, Incarnation, etc. They allowed women to be "priests" among them,[226] if they were "spiritual" or enlightened. They neglected the Eucharist, and also taught, as some quietists, that the "perfect" could sin bodily without being affected spiritually.

Traces and tendencies of this kind of teaching are found in the Pseudo-Macarian homilies, and also recur in later Oriental mystical writings. For instance Symeon the New Theologian places great emphasis on the sensible experience of divine light. However, the errors thus presented in a crude form must not mislead us when we read the Orthodox mystics: words must be carefully weighed, and the Hesychasts (those who experienced sweetness and rest) are not all to be treated automatically as Messalians. But the fact remains that the hesychast aspiration to *experience* in full the divine light can be misleading, especially when this experience is described as quasi-physical.

Pseudo-Macarius

It is still hotly disputed whether the writer of the Homilies by "Macarius" was really a Messalian or not. In the '20s—it was taken as established, by Dom Villecourt[227] *et al.*, that the Pseudo-

225. Both Messalleyane and Euchites mean "those who pray," in Syriac and Greek, respectively: see Maloney, Introduction to *Pseudo-Macarius*, 8.

226. This is not a completely accurate description of the accusation, which occurs only in the list of Timothy of Constantinople: "These people promote women as teachers of the doctrines of their heresy; they permit these [women] to rule over not only men but also priests, making women their own head, and dishonouring the one who is the head, Christ our God" (quoted in Stewart, 'Working the Earth of the Heart,' Appendix 2 [278]).

227. Louis Villecourt, OSB, "La grande lettre grecque de Macaire, ses formes textuelles et son milieu littéraire," *Revue de l'Orient Chrétien*, 22 (1920), 29–56,

Macarius was purely and simply a Messalian and that the homilies were full of the Messalian heresy. However Werner Jaeger has disputed this, and it has been shown that the Homilies of Pseudo-Macarius, while *sounding* Messalian, are really not so.[228]

---

and "La date et l'origine des 'Homélies spirituelles' attribuées à Macaire," *Comptes Rendus des Séances de l'Académie des Inscriptions et Belles-Lettres* (Paris: Picard, 1920), 250–58. A similar position was taken by Irenée Hausherr, sj in "L'erreur fondamentale et la logique du Messalianisme," *Orientalia Christiana Periodica*, 1 (1935), 328–60.

228. Jaeger argues that since Messalian doctrines had first been condemned as early as 380, but the works of Macarius were not written until after the work of Gregory of Nyssa on which they depend, which he dates to the early 390s, they could not have been the source of the ideas rejected as Messalian (226); he also maintains that "it seems much more likely that Macarius interpreted those of his beliefs that scholars have compared with what little we know of the Messalian sect in a more spiritual sense, and did not take them from this heretic group but from some common monastic tradition" and that "on closer inspection the difference between Macarius and the Messalian ideas appears very great" (225). The first point has not been generally accepted, both because scholars question the priority of Gregory's *De instituto Christiano* and because the later anti-Messalian lists, particularly that of John Damascene, clearly show verbal similarities to the Pseudo-Macarian writings. However, a number of scholars, notably Hermann Dörries in *Die Theologie des Makarios/Symeon*, who recognize the "Messalianism" of Macarius, maintain that the doctrines condemned as Messalian represent a misunderstanding or distortion of Macarius' work; this view, summarized by Stewart in *'Working the Earth of the Heart,'* "avoids the trap of declaring the texts to be 'Messalian', by holding that the list of condemned propositions preserved by John of Damascus quotes out of context, and thereby saves the embarrassment of concluding that centuries of Eastern Christian monastic life have been fed on a Messalian diet" (14, n. 4). From this perspective, "The Ps.-Macarian texts themselves may have been intended by their author as a corrective to extreme positions within ascetical circles" (14; cf also 235: "Furthermore, evidence in the collections of internal disagreements . . . and the suggestion of modern scholars that the Ps.-Macarian texts represent a reforming tendency in whatever ascetical milieu produced them remind the eager investigator that under the label 'Messalian' may have come several groups, sharing the emphasis on religious experience, but differing among themselves about the role of sacraments, ecclesiastical structures, hierarchical authority. It is impossible to know if Ps.-Macarius was actually a member of a targeted 'Messalian' group"). In Stewart's own view, "Much of this defensiveness may well have been misplaced" (69), because not only Pseudo-Macarius but Messalianism itself may have been misunderstood by its critics. His study maintains on the basis of a very careful and detailed examination of distinctively Pseudo-Macarian vocabulary that "The imagery and terminology associated with Messalianism is no more and no less than a dramatic manifes-

(Problem of establishing what is really Messalian—no original Messalian documents exist, and one has to judge by what those who condemned it alleged that it was.) Recently, the spirituality and the heritage of Pseudo-Macarius have been defended by Meyendorff[229] (authority on Gregory Palamas) who contrasts two trends in oriental Christian mysticism: (1) Platonist, intellectualist and pagan, stemming from Evagrius Ponticus; (2) Biblical, stemming from Pseudo-Macarius. This distinction is based on two different views of man. In the former it is the mind, *nous*, that is the seat of spirituality and of prayer. In the latter it is the "heart"—which stands for the whole man, body and soul spiritualized by grace. This follows the Biblical terminology in which the "heart" is regarded as the psycho-physiological center of man, and the seat of his deepest, most spiritual powers. The first kind of spirituality regards man as a mind imprisoned in matter. The second takes man as a whole, and is entirely sanctified by grace. Two ways of prayer follow from this. The Evagrian line leads to highly intellectual contemplation, in which the body has no part. The Macarian line leads to the "Prayer of the Heart,"

---

tation of Syrian Christianity in Greek guise, and can be considered utterly heterodox only from the viewpoint of the orthodoxy of a Greek-speaking imperial Church" (10). The dynamic, experiential and figurative language used by Pseudo-Macarius and others in a more "Semitic" milieu may well have been misjudged to be heterodox from the perspective of a more static, essentialist Hellenic environment. In other words, "Categorical denunciation of Messalian errors may be seen to rest largely on misunderstanding of unfamiliar terminology, and culture joins with (and perhaps supplants) doctrine as the basis of controversy" (69).

229. Jean Meyendorff, *St. Grégoire Palamas et la mystique orthodoxe* (Paris: Éditions du Seuil, 1959), 18–28. ET: John Meyendorff, *St. Gregory Palamas and Orthodox Spirituality*, trans. Adele Fiske (Crestwood, NY: St. Vladimir's Seminary Press, 1974), 20–29. Meyendorff later returns to this material in "Messalianism or Anti-Messalianism? A Fresh Look at the Macarian Problem," in Patrick Granfield and Josef Jungmann, eds., *Kyriakon: Festschrift in Honor of Johannes Quasten* (Münster: Aschendorff, 1970), 2:585-90. For a view that finds Evagrius and Macarius "on the same wavelength" and considers "[t]he contradistinction of 'intellect' and 'feeling,' mind and heart . . . at bottom false," see Alexander Golitzin, "Temple and Throne of the Divine Glory: 'Pseudo-Macarius' and Purity of Heart, Together with Some Remarks on the Limitations and Usefulness of Scholarship," in Harriet A. Luckman and Linda Kulzer, OSB, eds., *Purity of Heart in Early Ascetic and Monastic Literature* (Collegeville, MN: Liturgical Press, 1999), 129.

familiar at Mount Athos, the "Prayer of Jesus" in which the body has a place in prayer. This is sometimes compared to yoga, and condemned, as "Christian Yoga."[230] But it must be studied carefully before it can be condemned. We have not yet reached the point where we can give final judgement in this matter. It is a matter of great contemporary interest in spiritual theology.

EVAGRIUS PONTICUS ON PRAYER[231]

One of the great masters at Scete[232] in the time of Cassian was Evagrius of Pontus. He was generally considered as the greatest theologian of the desert—and was a follower of Origen. {He} is indeed one of the fathers of Christian mystical theology. He came from Asia Minor (Pontus) and was a friend of St. Basil and a disciple of St. Gregory Nazianzen. {He} lived in the "Desert of Cells." He died on the feast of the Epiphany, 399. After his death the great Origenist conflict broke out, leading to the departure of the Origenists from Scete. The memory of Evagrius was blackened and he then fell into oblivion.

In the earlier works on Desert Monasticism, Evagrius has a good name and is regarded as a holy and learned father. In the later works, after the fifth century, he has a very bad reputation. Moschus, *Pratum Spirituale*, records {a} story that his cell was said to be haunted or inhabited by a devil. {He} also said that he was in hell among the heretics.[233] St. John Climacus condemns him.[234] In general this is due to the fact that he was a noted Origenist and he fell with the Origenist party, thereafter stigma-

---

230. See Meyendorff, 64–65 (ET: 62), who stresses that despite a similarity in technique, the Christian "prayer of the breath" places strong emphasis on the necessity of grace and on a sacramental context; see also 118 (ET: 114).

231. See also Merton's discussion, "Evagrius Ponticus, the 'Prince of Gnostics'" in "Ascetical and Mystical Theology," 42–56.

232. More accurately, at Kellia, the "Desert of the Cells" located some twelve miles from Nitria, whereas Scete was about forty miles away through the desert; see the Introduction by John Eudes Bamberger, OCSO, to Evagrius, *The Praktikos; Chapters on Prayer*, trans. John Eudes Bamberger, CS 4 (Spencer, MA: Cistercian Publications, 1970), xlii–xliii.

233. *Spiritual Meadow*, 146–47, 18.

234. St. John Climacus, *The Ladder of Divine Ascent*, trans. Archimandrite Lazarus Moore, 14:12 (New York: Harper & Brothers, 1959), 141.

tised as a "deviationist." Yet his work not only survived, but strongly influenced even those who despised his memory. The *De Oratione*—is proved to be his definitively by Hausherr (*RAM*, Jan. 1959[235]). The Syrian and Arabic mss. continue to ascribe it to him after the Greek etc. ascribe it to Nilus. Reason—the Syrians and Arabs have no reason for condemning Evagrius. St. Maximus the Confessor, one of the great mystics among the Fathers, while twice condemning Evagrius by name, nevertheless is not only full of Evagrian doctrines, but can even be said to base his whole doctrine on Evagrius (see articles of M. Viller in *RAM*, April 1930 ff.[236]). "The relations that exist between them are such that clearly from a spiritual point of view, Maximus appears to us to be a disciple of Evagrius."[237]

There are some works of Evagrius in the *PG* 40[238]—the *Practicos*, the *Mirror of Monks*, the *Letter to Anatolios*. But more works of his are preserved in Syrian and Armenian and are more recently studied (by Bossuet[239]—not the Bishop of Meaux—and Frankenberg[240]). Another mystic influenced by him is Isaac of Niniveh, a Nestorian bishop and theologian who is also beginning to interest students in the West. Isaac calls Evagrius "the Blessed Mar Evagrios" "the wise one among the saints" "prince of gnostics."[241] Note—Isaac of Niniveh, full of Evagrius, was translated into Greek and much influenced Byzantine tradition; the translators, where Isaac praised Evagrius, simply inserted some other name, like Gregory of Nazianz.

235. I. Hausherr, SJ, "Le Traité de l'oraison d'Evagre le Pontique," *Revue d'Ascétique et de Mystique*, 40 (1959), 3–26, 121–46, 241–65, 361–85; 41 (1960), 3–35, 137–87.

236. M. Viller, "Aux Sources de la Spiritualité de S. Maxime: Les Oeuvres d'Evagre le Pontique," *Revue d'Ascétique et de Mystique*, 11 (1930), 156–84, 239–68.

237. Viller, 159–60.

238. Cols. 1213–86.

239. Wilhelm Bousset [n.b., not Bossuet!], *Apophthegmata: Studien zur Geschichte des ältesten Mönchtums* (Tübingen: Mohr, 1923). (Bousset is also regularly referred to as Bossuet in the English translation of Mahieu.)

240. W. Frankenberg, *Evagrius Pontikus* (Berlin: Weidmannsche Buchhandlung, 1912).

241. See Isaac of Niniveh, *Mystic Treatises* (Wiesbaden: Sändig, 1969): "the sage among the saints, Mar Euagrius" (72); "the blessed Euagrius" (297, 306, 333, 345); "the holy Euagrius" (334); "one of the holy Fathers, Euagrius, one of the initiated" (383).

Importance of Evagrius—his systematic presentation of the great theology of the first Fathers, especially Origen and Gregory of Nyssa—in a form that became definitive in the East. He is really the cornerstone of oriental mystical theology—a cornerstone that was rejected. We have seen that St. Maximus is based on Evagrius. So is the Pseudo-Denys (6th cent.). Even John Climacus is largely based on Evagrius.

The chief work of Evagrius, the *DE ORATIONE*, survived and was very popular—but it was ascribed to St. Nilus (an oriental monk who settled in southern Italy[242]). It exercised very considerable influence. The teaching of Cassian on prayer is very similar to that of Evagrius; indeed it is a kind of digest of the more profound and complete treatise of the Master. It will greatly aid us to understand the monastic tradition on prayer if we acquaint ourselves a little with Evagrius. The treatise is perfectly free from suspect "Origenism" and is one of the great Christian texts on interior prayer. The Treatise *DE ORATIONE* (published in French translation, with commentary by Père I. Hausherr, in *Revue d'Ascétique et de Mystique*, January–April 1934[243] and again in a new version, January 1959 ff.[244]) consists of a Prologue and 153 short *capitula*. Earlier than the works of Pseudo-Denys, this treatise of Evagrius definitively set the course for the mysticism of the Oriental Church. "It is through Evagrius that the great ideas of Origen and Gregory of Nyssa came down from their inaccessible heights to the level of the average intelligence," says Father Hausherr.[245]

What does Evagrius mean by Prayer? He is talking of what we would call mental prayer. He distinguishes prayer and psalmody.

---

242. Merton is confusing St. Nilus of Rossano (Nilus the Younger) (c. 905–1005), who was a founder of Greek monasticism in Italy (actually born in Calabria), with St. Nilus of Ancyra (often mistakenly called St. Nilus of Sinai on the basis of an unhistorical biography) (d. c. 430), to whom the *De Oratione* was mistakenly ascribed: see the articles by P. W. Harkins (Nilus of Ancyra) and B. J. Comaskey (Nilus of Rossano) in *New Catholic Encyclopedia* (New York: McGraw Hill, 1967), 10:490.

243. Irenée Hausherr, "Le *Traité de l'oraison* d'Evagre le Pontique (Pseudo Nil)," *Revue d'Ascétique et de Mystique*, 15 (1934), 36–93, 113–70.

244. This subsequently appeared as an independent volume entitled *Les Leçons d'un Contemplatif: Le traité de l'Oraison d'Evagre le Pontique* (Paris: Beauchesne, 1960).

245. Hausherr (1934), 169–70.

These are necessarily distinct and complementary, according to Evagrius. They are the two wings of the eagle, by which we ascend into the heights (*Oratione* 82—all the numbers given in brackets, unless otherwise stated, refer to *capitula* of the *De Oratione*). Psalmody belongs more to the active life; it "appeases the passions and lulls the intemperance of the body" (83). It is a more active and exterior form of devotion, and quantity is more important than in "*oratio*," which is interior, contemplative, and depends more on quality. In particular, the function of psalmody is to calm the passions, and especially anger. Prayer (*oratio*) is the exercise of the intelligence in a purely interior and spiritual contact with God (*Oratione* 3). Psalmody belongs more properly to the lower degrees of the spiritual life, prayer to the higher (85). Evagrius speaks of both prayer and psalmody less as practices than as *charisms*, which are to be prayed for as special gifts from God (87). We must not however think of "prayer" as purely spiritual and always without words or concepts or acts. On the contrary, in time of temptation especially, prayer is to be "short and intense"—acts (with or without words) having the character of ejaculations (98). Although prayer is higher than psalmody, Evagrius does not mean that one leaves psalmody behind altogether and ascends to a life of "pure prayer" that is continuous and without any exterior practices. However, when on occasion one has arrived at a deep interior contact with God, one should not abandon it merely because one has previously determined to recite psalms. One should not let go of what is better in order to revert to a mechanical practice. So he says: "If a profitable thought comes to thee, let it take the place of psalmody [he is not thinking here of a choral office necessarily]. Do not reject the gift of God merely in order to cling to the traditions of men . . ." etc. (quoted by Hausherr in note on *Oratione* 151[246]).

Prayer Defined—Mental and contemplative prayer is for Evagrius primarily an activity of the intellect, and is the highest activity of this faculty. In this intellectualist emphasis Evagrius is later corrected by St. Maximus who gives more place to charity in contemplation—but note that Evagrius's contemplation is

---

246. Hausherr (1934), 167 (from the *Paraeneticus*).

not exclusively intellectual. However the chief characteristic of Evagrius is that for him the monk is one who seeks above all a *continuous state of intellectual contemplation.* Everything else in Evagrius is ordered to this supreme end. Intellectual contemplation is the fruit and the expression of perfect charity and it is what love seeks exclusively and above all, according to him. It is pure prayer that makes man "equal to the angels" and one must leave all else, he says, in order to seek this blessed angelic state. Angels are *pure intelligence* and the contemplative also tends to be "all eyes" (in contemplation) or "all fire." Such also is the true "theologian." In contemplation man also returns to his first, pure, paradisiacal state. *Oratione* 3—"Prayer is a conversation of the intellect with God . . . without intermediary." The word "conversation" must not lead us into error here: he is not thinking of words, nor even of thoughts, for the highest prayer is an intellectual contact with God, in a direct intuition (not however clear vision), that is beyond words and thoughts. This definition however covers various degrees of prayer—including a lower degree of *supplication* which takes the form of ejaculatory acts in time of struggle, as we have already seen above. The lower kind of pure prayer is merely *disinterested petition.* The higher kind—is prayer without concept or image. Pure prayer—prayer without intermediary—means not a pure intuition in the sense of the beatific vision, but an intuition of God that does not require the mediation of a created object—angel—or even the sacred humanity of Jesus. The degrees of purity in prayer are degrees of immediacy. The highest prayer is intellectual intuition of the Holy Trinity. Other degrees, as we shall see, involve the intuition of spiritual beings, such as angels.

The first degrees of prayer demand purification from *passionate thought.* The highest degree demands perfect "nudity" of the intellect clothed in no thought at all. The lower degrees of "pure prayer" are compatible with suffering and sorrow. In the higher degrees there is only peace, tranquillity and joy. But *no* pure prayer is compatible with inordinate passion or with any vice. In another place he says the highest perfection of the intellect is prayer without distraction (34a): "Prayer without distraction is the highest operation of the intelligence." The object of the life of prayer is to ascend from the valley of shadows, attachment to passionate thoughts, to the summit of the mountain of contemplation of the Holy Trinity. In the lower degrees of prayer we are more engaged in "supplicating" to be purified. After first renouncing *things* themselves we begin by begging to be purified of *passions*. Then, in the intermediate stage, we ask to be purified of *ignorance*. Finally, in order to reach the summit, we need to be purified of all *darkness and dereliction*. In other words, the spiritual life is an ascent to greater and greater spiritual purity and intellectual clarity (37). However Evagrius and his followers agree that those who reach the heights of contemplation are *very rare* and even fervent monks spend their whole lives trying (vainly) to completely conquer "passionate thoughts" —few ever get to the degree where they struggle directly with ignorance or darkness. When he reaches the summit the contemplative has reached the highest dignity for which the intelligence was created—for God made the mind of man in order that we might contemplate the Most Holy Trinity. This highest act of the intelligence, contemplation of the Holy Trinity, leads to pure love (118).

Degrees of Prayer

1. *Preliminaries*: In order to enter upon the life of prayer one must be *detached from objects*. Evagrius distinguishes detachment from objects and from the thoughts of objects. Here we are pretty much on the same ground as in Cassian, *Conference* 3 (Paphnutius on the 3 *Renunciations*—cf. Lectures on Cassian[247]).

2. *Apatheia*—The true life of prayer begins when one has not only left behind the *things of earth*, but is beginning the struggle with *thoughts of those things*. The first step in the life of prayer is the struggle with "passionate thoughts," i.e. thoughts that move us to passion, whether anger, lust, etc. Here *meditation* is important, including the constant meditation of death and the last things, until the soul begins to be free. Here the big thing is *virtue*. Note—combat with evil spirits is crucial. According

247. See below, pages 126–27, for a brief discussion of the conference; Merton actually discusses it in much greater detail in "Pre-Benedictine Monasticism," first series, 21–24.

to Evagrius (*Or.* 49), the chief purpose of the battle waged by devils against the monk is to *prevent* or to *frustrate* interior prayer. The devils tempt us to those vices most contrary to prayer, especially *lust* and *anger*. *Apatheia* is the victory of the soul over *all* the devils (i.e. all the passions). Note that *apatheia* is not mere insensibility. It is compounded of humility, compunction, zeal and *intense love for God*. "*Apatheia*" is the state of a soul that is no longer moved by passionate thought. The thoughts of such souls are "simple," that is to say, untainted by passion: they have no "charge" of passion in them; we simply see objects as they are, in simplicity. At this point one reaches the stage of "meditation on simple thoughts." Note that prayer is inseparably connected with virtue. Without virtue, one cannot resist passion, and if one is dominated by passion, he has no control of thoughts and cannot pray.

However, Evagrius always insists that prayer is a *pure gift of God*; it is not attained by our own ascetic efforts but we must beg Him for the gift of prayer (*Or.* 58). However—a distinction: *Theoria Physica* is on our level and we can attain to it—but Contemplation of the Holy Trinity is a *pure* gift. When we have good will, even though imperfect, we can receive the gift of the Holy Spirit who comes to dispel *passionate thoughts* and to *produce peace* through *love* (*Or.* 62).

Purity of thought begins therefore with purity of life. If the intelligence is distracted it is not yet "monastic," but worldly. Here the Holy Spirit begins to act on the whole person through the intelligence. The presence and action of God in the intelligence calms the body and leads to greater tranquillity and purity. In the soul, the Holy Spirit stirs up the desire of a more spiritual and perfect prayer (62–63).

3. *Spiritual Contemplation—Gnosis* and *Theoria Physica*. The mind is now beyond simple thoughts but it receives in itself the form of the essences of things—an intuitive penetration of reality—of "nature" in so far as it reflects God. This, in other words, is an intuition of the Creator in His Creation. The *logoi* of creatures are reflections of the divine attributes. He says that in *theoria physica* we "receive letters" from God, but in the highest contemplation we speak to Him and He speaks to us. Cf. St. John

of the Cross, *Spiritual Canticle*, 2:3.[248] In the highest contemplation God is present directly to the mind *without form or concept*. In "Spiritual Contemplation" (*gnosis*), though the soul possesses *apatheia*, the devil can still tempt it—but now not with *passions*—rather he injects into the mind *spiritual forms, images and visions* which claim to "represent" God or divine things (*Or*. 67–68). In the highest contemplation (*Theologia*) the soul is beyond the reach of the devil because it no longer uses any concepts whatever and is pure of "all forms," and cannot be deceived by any false idea. This supposes that it is directly illuminated by God. How? It is not clearly explained.

4. *Theologia*—Union with God without intermediary of His creatures. In what sense *immediate*? Evagrius {is} not concerned with {the} technical problem. The mind is now above all essences. —cf. Ruysbroeck: "Superessential vision of the Trinity."[249] *Or*. 60:

248. See St. John of the Cross, *Complete Works*, II:37-45: the commentary on stanza ii focuses on the soul's "use of intercessors and intermediaries with her Beloved, begging them to tell Him of her pain and affliction; for it is a characteristic of the lover, when she cannot commune with her Beloved because of His absence, to do so by the best means that she may" (37); the commentary on stanza iii begins: "Not content with prayers and desires, and with making use of intercessors in order that she may speak with the Beloved, as she did in the preceding stanzas, the soul, over and above all this, sets to work herself to seek Him" (41).

249. The third and final book of Ruysbroeck's *Adornment of the Spiritual Marriage* (or *Spiritual Espousals*) is traditionally entitled "The Superessential Life," and focuses on the highest level of the mystical life, in which one transcends one's created existence to experience one's eternal life in God. See John of Ruysbroeck, *The Adornment of the Spiritual Marriage; The Sparkling Stone; The Book of Supreme Truth*, trans. C. A. Wynschenk (London: Dent, 1916), 167, 169–70, 172: "Yea, the lover who is inward and righteous, him will it please God in His freedom to choose and to lift up into a superessential contemplation, in the Divine Light and according to the Divine Way. . . . Now if the spirit would see God with God in this Divine light without means, . . . he must have lost himself in a Waylessness and in a Darkness, in which all contemplative men wander in fruition and wherein they never again can find themselves in a creaturely way. In the abyss of this darkness, in which the loving spirit has died to itself, there begin the manifestation of God and eternal life. For in this darkness there shines and is born an incomprehensible Light, which is the Son of God, in Whom we behold eternal life. And in this Light one becomes seeing; . . . All the riches which are in God by nature we possess by way of love in God, and God in us, through the unmeasured love which is the Holy Ghost; for in this love one tastes of all that one can desire. And therefore through this love we are dead to

"If you are a theologian you will truly pray and if you pray truly you are a theologian." For Evagrius: Theologian equals Mystic.

Summary and Conclusion: Is Evagrius Dangerous?

Evagrius is an extremist and several dangers are often pointed out in his teaching:

a) Angelism: There is a possibility that his doctrine on purity of prayer may tempt people to the idea that man is capable of living like a pure spirit without a body and without passions, and that the perfection to which we should tend is superhuman—total spiritualism. Does he ignore the reality of man? And despise God's Creation?

b) Is his doctrine pagan (Platonist) rather than Christian? Certainly there are many Platonic elements in it and Christ appears very little in it, almost not at all. However, the Holy Spirit plays a central role.

c) There is danger of pride and self-sufficiency. It is not altogether true that Evagrius exaggerates man's ascetic power and underestimates grace. But it is a spirituality centered on one's own purity and perfection. In the long run Evagrius is too idealistic and presents a program that is inaccessible to men.

There is truth in all these criticisms, but they are not absolute. They must be taken with a grain of salt too. Evagrius can usually be interpreted in a way that gives his doctrine value for all time, and for the whole Church. It is a high contemplative ideal, aspiring perhaps to an exaggerated spiritual perfection which is not preached in the Gospel. In any case the Evagrian ideal is what Cassian encountered in the desert, tempered by the simplicity of the more humble Desert Fathers as we have seen it in the *Apothegmata*.

End of Part One

---

ourselves, and have gone forth in loving immersion into Waylessness and Darkness. There the spirit is embraced by the Holy Trinity, and dwells for ever within the superessential Unity, in rest and fruition. And in that same Unity, according to Its fruitfulness, the Father dwells in the Son, and the Son in the Father, and all creatures dwell in Both" (*Adornment*, III:1,3). (In the "Appendix" version, #4 is a handwritten addition in ink by Merton to this point; the rest of the text is lacking.)

PART TWO

LECTURES ON CASSIAN

I. The Importance of Cassian

He is *the* great monastic writer—the Master of the spiritual life par excellence for monks—the source for all in the West. He is a *classic*, profoundly attached to tradition. He is a perfect source for the whole tradition of Oriental monasticism—basically the doctrine of Origen, adapted for monks by Evagrius—resuming all that we have so far discussed in Patristic thought. He is remarkable for his grasp of the *essentials* of monasticism, avoiding bizarre details, in contrast to Palladius for example. {He} is *not a mere compiler*—{he shows} real literary talent and ability to organize ideas in an *original synthesis* valid for all. {He} propagated in {the} West {the} doctrine of Active and Contemplative Lives. {He} is interesting, human, a good observer and psychologist, a prudent Master of the spiritual life—every monk should know him thoroughly. {He} *influenced all the early monastic founders* in the West—including St. Honoratus of Lérins, St. Caesarius;[250] in Spain, St. Isidore and St. Fructuosus.[251] He even influenced the early monks of Ireland.[252] In the East {he is} revered by all—*called a Saint*. {He} is included in {the} *Philokalia*[253] {and} praised by St. John Climacus as "The Great Cassian."[254] In modern times—after influencing St. Thomas, Cassian also had a profound effect on St. Ignatius and the Jesuits, on De Rancé and the Trappists, on Port Royal, on Fenelon, etc.

250. See O. Chadwick, 168: "The Rule of Caesarius owes something of its detail to the *Institutes*."
251. See O. Chadwick, 168, n. 3.
252. But see O. Chadwick, Appendix D, "Cassian and the Celts" (201–203), which concludes that "The literary evidence for knowledge of Cassian's writings in Ireland is not early" (203).
253. See *The Philokalia: The Complete Text*, 1:72-108: "On the Eight Vices" (73–93; abridged from *Inst*. 5–12); "On the Holy Fathers of Sketis and On Discrimination" (94–108; abridged from *Conf*. 1–2).
254. *Ladder*, 4:105 (91).

St. Benedict considers Cassian and the Desert Fathers ideal reading material for Compline (*Rule*, c.{42}).[255] It is due to Cassian that the Compline reading exists and from his work it gets its name *Collatio*. Compline reading has a special formative importance in St. Benedict's eyes. It draws the monks together after the varying business of the day and brings them face to face with the essentials of their vocation, before they retire for the night. The Compline reading is designed especially for *recollection* and *edification*. Hence St. Benedict considered Cassian an ideal author for monks—one who would help them lead their monastic lives more perfectly, one who would bring them into contact with God, for Whom they had left the world. In chapter 73—summing up his rule, admitting that the *Rule* is a map for the "active life" of beginners, and looking forward to the progress of his monks in contemplation, St. Benedict again recommends Cassian. He designates three kinds of reading that will help the monk reach the perfection of his vocation:

1. The Scriptures—"every page of which is a most accurate norm to live by"—*rectissima norma vitae humanae;*

2. The works of the Catholic Fathers—which enable us to go directly to God—*recto cursu;*

3. "The *Conferences* of the Fathers and the *Institutes* [i.e. the two main books of Cassian] and their lives, together with the Rule of our Holy Father St. Basil."

These are described as "examples of good-living and obedient monks, and instruments of virtue."[256] This is one of the things most striking about Cassian—lifelike portraits of the Desert Fathers. They remain "models for imitation." But—in what sense are they to be imitated? *Not* in all their exterior actions—impossible to us—not at all suited to our situation; not in all their attitudes—they were extremists—they were often

255. 24 in text; see McCann, 101: "let a brother read the Conferences of Cassian or the Lives of the Fathers, or something else that may edify the hearers" (n.b. "of Cassian" supplied by the translator: simply *"Collationes vel Vitas Patrum"* in the Latin).

256. This translation is not from McCann (160) and has not been otherwise identified; it may be Merton's own.

quite wrong. They are to be followed in their *faith*, their love of Christ, their zeal for the monastic state and their spirit of prayer and sacrifice. In reading the Desert Fathers one must: (1) DIS-CRIMINATE; (2) ADAPT, as did St. Benedict himself, who consciously and deliberately, wrote a *Rule* which some of the Desert Fathers would have condemned as soft.

Cassiodorus: "The priest Cassian, who wrote about the *formation of faithful monks*, should be diligently read and frequently heard; in the beginning of our vocation, he said, eight principal vices ought to be avoided. This writer *so skillfully describes the evil movements of man's soul*, that he helps one to see and avoid faults, whereas before he was in confusion and did not know what they were. However, Cassian was rightly blamed by St. Prosper for his errors about free will, and so we advise that he should be taken cautiously in this matter, in which he was mistaken."

Cassian fell into semi-pelagianism. But this error only appears in one or two places, and the fact that Cassian continued, in spite of it, to be the standard reading of all monks, is only an additional proof of his great authority in the ascetic field. The saints and Fathers of St. Benedict's day and of the Middle Ages would never have tolerated *any* of the works of a man suspected of heresy, if they had not been convinced that his writings were of the greatest value and importance, that in general their orthodoxy was beyond reproach. Compare what happened to Evagrius, who only survived under another name. The name of Cassian was always held in the highest respect.

St. Dominic and St. Thomas Aquinas: St. Dominic seized upon the writings of Cassian as a most apt means of learning how to become a saint of God. "He took up the book which is called the Conferences of the Fathers, and read it carefully. He set his mind to understand the things which he read therein, to feel them in his heart, and to carry them out in his actions. From this book he learned purity of heart, the way of contemplation, and the perfection of all virtues" (*Life of St. Dominic*). This gives us an idea how we ought also to read Cassian—or any other spiritual classic. St. Thomas loved to read Cassian in his spare moments. In other words Cassian was for St. Thomas a beloved spiritual book, favorite spiritual reading. The saint had {three}[257] reasons for this reading:

1. To keep his abstract speculations from cooling the ardor of his spiritual life—as an antidote to too much study;
2. To enable him to recollect his mind and ascend to the contemplation of divine things;
3. He was also consciously imitating St. Dominic.

Cardinal Turrecremata, commenting on chapter 42 of the *Rule*, says that the prescription that Cassian be read before Compline was most wise and holy—it would enable the monks, in the time of silence, to raise their hearts to the contemplation of God. "For this purpose the books of Cassian were rightly chosen . . . for in them the doctrine of all perfection, and edification, and sanctity, is contained" (these quotes from Migne, *PL* 49—cols. 46–50—Introduction to Cassian).[258]

Gilson—points out the all-important influence of Cassian on the Cistercian Fathers. Cassian helped form our tradition, especially St. Bernard.[259]

Cassian's Error

Before we go on to the study of Cassian's doctrine, we may briefly dispose of the error in his teaching:

1. It is misleading to use the term "semi-pelagianism" of Cassian, as if to imply that he sympathized with Pelagius and *adopted a modification of his heretical doctrine*. A writer has said that it would be fairer to call Cassian's error "semi-augustinianism"[260]

257. Text reads "two" but Merton subsequently added the number "3" in pen to the last line without changing this word.
258. *PL* 49, col. 45C–52D (*"Illustrium Virorum de J. Cassiano Testimonia"*): Benedict (c. 42): 45D; (c. 73): 46C; Cassiodorus: 47B; Dominic: 49A; Thomas: 49C; Turrecremata: 49D–50A.
259. Gilson calls "the substitution of love for fear by the Holy Spirit . . . the very centre of the ascesis of St. Bernard," and declares that "for its origin we must go back once more to Cassian," citing *Conf.* 11:8 and *Inst.* 4:39 (31); cf. also 72, which again cites Cassian as source in its discussion of the "displacement of fear by charity by way of the practice of humility" as "the whole of St. Bernard's ascesis, its beginning, its development and its term."
260. See J. F. Bethune-Baker, *An Introduction to the Early History of Christian*

—whatever may be the value of this suggestion, it remains true that *Cassian is closer to St. Augustine than he is to Pelagius.* Book 12 of the *Instituta*, on pride, is probably directed against the Pelagians. In his anti-nestorian writings, Cassian explicitly condemns Pelagius' denial of the Redemption. *Pelagius* held that man was entirely capable of achieving his own salvation, even after original sin, and that Jesus had come only as an "inspiration" and a "model of virtue." Cassian appears to teach that grace is necessary to achieve the perfection of sanctity, and to imply that without grace one can *begin the work* of our sanctification, but not bring it to completion (*Inst.* 12:14)[261]—in other words, that without grace we can do *something* to save our souls. Cassian can, however, be defended from this error by texts in which he says that Jesus declared that He could do nothing of Himself and that *a fortiori* we must say the same (*Inst.* 12:17).[262]

2. In the dispute about semi-pelagianism, the argument centers around the *initium fidei*, the first step towards believing. The heretics held that man could take this first step without grace. Cassian, however, explicitly says in the third *Conference* that even the *initium salutis* is a gift of God (*Conf.* 3:10).[263] Also he says *"Paulus declaravit . . . initium conversionis ac fidei nostrae, ac passionum tolerantiam donari nobis a Domino"* (*Conf.* 3:15—cf.

Doctrine, fourth ed. (London: Methuen, 1929), 321, n. 1: "Semi-Augustinianism would be at least as accurate a designation, and would beg no question"; see also N. Chadwick, *Poetry and Letters*, 179–80: "The controversy . . . has been commonly known since the early seventeenth century as 'semi-Pelagianism', though 'semi-Augustinianism' would be quite as true a description. Indeed, the opponents of St Augustine repudiate categorically any adherence to the doctrines of Pelagius." (Merton may not yet have read Chadwick, who refers to Bethune-Baker, at the time he makes this comment, which comes from the earliest stratum of his text.)

261. Cols. 444A–447A: "For as we say that human efforts cannot reach perfection without the help of God, so we declare that the grace and mercy of God are bestowed only on those who labor and exert themselves, and are granted, according to the words of the Apostle, to those who desire and who run."

262. Col. 452B–453A: "He says, in the person of his assumed humanity, that he is able to do nothing of himself; and do we, dust and ashes, think that in those things that pertain to our salvation we do not need the help of God!"

263. Col. 574B: *"et initium nostrae salutis Domini vocatione fieri"* ("even the beginning of our salvation happens through the call of the Lord").

Phil. 1:29).[264] The grace of God, he declares, is necessary every day and at every moment (*id.* 22).[265]

3. However, the most disputed text of Cassian on this point is in the thirteenth *Conference*, the one reproved by St. Prosper, a disciple of St. Augustine. In 432 Prosper wrote a direct attack on Cassian.[266] His motive is to defend St. Augustine against those who attacked his works on grace by appealing to Cassian. Even in attacking Cassian, Prosper calls him a "priest who excels among all others,"[267] and he does not attribute the doctrine on grace directly to Cassian, but to the Desert Father (Chaeremon) whom he is quoting.[268] He praises Cassian for starting out the thirteenth *Conference* with the statement that God is the principle not only of our good acts but also of our good thoughts—that man has need of grace in all things. However, the language of the thirteenth *Conference* later becomes erroneous. Cassian says (quoting Chaeremon), "When Divine Providence sees in us a beginning of good will . . . *then God begins to give us grace.*"[269]

264. Col. 577B: "Paul declared that the beginning of our conversion and faith, and the endurance of sufferings, is given to us by the Lord." ("*Paulus*" is not in the text, and "*declaravit*" follows the rest of the quotation.)

265. Col. 584B: "we have wished to demonstrate that the help and grace of God is necessary every moment of every day."

266. *Contra Collatorem*, PL 51, col. 213–76.

267. *Contra Collatorem*, c. 2 (*PL* 51, col. 218A); also quoted in the "*Testimonia*," *PL* 49, col. 45C.

268. Prosper actually writes: "The writer clearly shows that he approves and makes his own the abbot's teaching. So, we need not deal with the abbot, who would perchance say these opinions are not his or explain what seems wrong in them, but with the writer, who deliberately proposes a teaching that cannot but be a tool in the hands of the enemies of God's grace" ("On Grace and Free Will, Against Cassian the Lecturer," in Prosper of Aquitaine, *Defense of St. Augustine*, trans. P. de Letter, SJ, Ancient Christian Writers, vol. 32 [Westminster, MD: Newman, 1963], 72–73). O. Chadwick comments, "We must follow the example of Prosper, who, in attacking *Conference* XIII of Abbot Chaeremon, assailed Cassian and not Chaeremon, in recognizing this literary form to be convention" (32); see also Boniface Ramsey, OP, ed. and trans., John Cassian, *The Conferences*, Ancient Christian Writers, vol. 57 (New York: Paulist, 1997), 403: "Indeed, referring to Chaeremon's role in the thirteenth conference, Prosper of Aquitaine (*C. collatorem* 2.1) speaks of him as an invention of Cassian; this opinion, though, is probably to be explained by Prosper's pique at Cassian's divergent view of grace in that conference."

269. A paraphrase (rather than a direct quotation) of c. 8, cols. 912A–913A: "*Qui cum in nobis ortum quemdam bonae voluntatis inspexerit, illuminat eam confes-*

He immediately says that God has sown this seed, but seems also to leave a possibility that the seed might also have been sown by our own efforts. It is a "beginning of good will" that comes *either* from God *or* from ourselves. But there is no either / or. . . . It must all come from God. Cassian, in the thirteenth *Conference*, adopts without criticism Chaeremon's doctrine that the first beginnings of salvation *sometimes* come from God and sometimes from man. Cassian's error on this point was not merely a question of hazy terminology, but he actually deviated from the true doctrine (of St. Augustine), seeking a "middle path" between Augustine and Pelagius. As a dogmatic theologian, then, Cassian failed on this point.

The Second Council of Orange, in Southern France (529), settles the whole question (Denzinger—179:[270] see Canons 6,[271] 7, 8, 9; cf. 13,[272] 14, 18,[273] 19,[274] 20). We here give six canons from the Council of Orange. Does any one of these deal directly and specifically with Cassian's error?

---

tim atque confortat, et incitat ad salutem, incrementum tribuens ei quam vel ipse plan-tavit, vel nostro conatu viderit emersisse" ("When he has seen in us a certain arising of good will, he immediately enlightens and strengthens it and urges it toward salvation, giving increase to that which he himself has implanted or which he has seen to have arisen through our own effort").

270. *Enchiridion Symbolorum: Definitionum et Declarationum De Rebus Fidei et Morum,* ed. Henricus Denzinger & Adolfus Schönmetzer, SJ, 33d ed. (Freiburg: Herder, 1965) (179 is the marginal number of canon 6; all the quoted canons are found on pages 133–35); English translation in *The Sources of Catholic Dogma,* trans. Roy J. Deferrari (from the 30th ed.) (St. Louis: Herder, 1957), 75–81.

271. This canon declares that anyone who claims that mercy is given without grace to anyone who believes, wills, acts, etc., rather than acknowledging that the power to believe, will and act comes from the Holy Spirit, opposes Paul's words in I Cor. 4:7 and 15:10.

272. This canon declares that free will weakened by original sin cannot be repaired except through baptism, and quotes to that effect Prosper of Aquitaine, *Sententiae,* 152 [*PL* 45, col. 1871].

273. This canon, a quotation from *Sententiae,* 297 [*PL* 45, col. 1885], declares that while good works deserve a reward, grace, which is unmerited, precedes good works.

274. This canon, a quotation from *Sententiae,* 308 [*PL* 45, col. 1886], declares that no one can be saved without God's mercy, and that as even before the fall human nature could not save itself without divine assistance, so in its fallen state it is even more dependent upon grace to recover what has been lost.

Canon 7. Si quis per naturae vigorem bonum aliquid, *quod ad salutem pertinet vitae aeternae, cogitare, ut expedit, aut eligere, sive salutari, id est evangelicae praedicationi consentire posse confirmat absque illuminatione et inspiratione Spiritus Sancti,* qui dat omnibus suavitatem in consentiendo et credendo veritati, *haeretico fallitur spiritu, non intelligens vocem Dei in Evangelio dicentis: "Sine me nihil potestis facere," et illud Apostoli: "Non quod idonei simus cogitare aliquid a nobis, quasi ex nobis, sed sufficientia nostra ex Deo est."*[275]

Canon 8. Si quis alios misericordia, alios vere per liberum arbitrium, *quod in omnibus, qui de praevaricatione primi hominis nati sunt, constat esse vitiatum, ad gratiam baptismi posse venire contendit, a recta fide probatur alienus. Is enim non omnium liberum arbitrium per peccatum primi hominis asserit infirmatum, aut certe ita laesum putat,* ut tamen quidam valeant sine revelatione Dei mysterium salutis aeternae per semetipsos posse conquirere. *Quod quam sit contrarium, ipse Dominus probat, qui* non aliquos, sed neminem ad se posse venire testatur, nisi *"quem Pater attraxerit," sicut et Petro dicit: "Beatus es Simon Bar-Jona, quia caro et sanguis non revelavit tibi, sed Pater meus, qui in coelis est"; et Apostolus: "Nemo potest dicere Dominum Jesum (Christum) nisi in Spiritu Sancto."*[276]

---

275. "If anyone affirms that without the illumination and the inspiration of the Holy Spirit,—who gives to all sweetness in consenting to and believing in the truth,—through the strength of nature he can think anything good which pertains to the salvation of eternal life, as he should, or choose, or consent to salvation, that is to the evangelical proclamation, he is deceived by the heretical spirit, not understanding the voice of God speaking in the Gospel: *'Without me you can do nothing'* [John 15:5]; and that of the Apostle: *Not that we are fit to think everything by ourselves as of ourselves, but our sufficiency is from God* [II Cor. 3:5; . . .]" (Deferrari, 77).

276. "If anyone maintains that some by mercy, but others by free will, which it is evident has been vitiated in all who have been born of the transgression of the first man, are able to come to the grace of baptism, he is proved to be inconsistent with the true faith. For he asserts that the free will of all was not weakened by the sin of the first man, or assuredly was injured in such a way, that nevertheless certain ones have the power without revelation of God to be able by themselves to seek the mystery of eternal salvation. How contrary this is, the Lord Himself proves, who testifies that not some, but no one can come to Him, except *whom the Father draws* [John 6:44], and just as he says to PETER: *'Blessed art thou, Simon Bar-Jona, because flesh and blood hath not revealed it to you, but my Father, who is in heaven'* [Matt. 16:17]; and the Apostle: *No one can say Lord Jesus except in the Holy Spirit* [I Cor. 12:3 . . .]" (Deferrari, 77).

Canon 9. Divini est muneris, cum et recte cogitamus, *et pedes nostros a falsitate et iniustitia continemus;* quoties enim bona agimus, Deus in nobis atque nobiscum, ut operemur, operatur.[277]

Canon 14. Nullus miser de quantacumque miseria liberatur, nisi qui Dei misericordia praevenitur, *sicut dicit Psalmista: "Cito anticipet nos misericordia tua, Domine"* (Ps. 78:8), et illud: "Deus meus, misericordia eius praeveniet me" *(Ps. 58:11).*[278]

Canon 20. Multa Deus facit in homine bona, quae non facit homo; nulla vero facit homo bona, quae non Deus praestat, ut faciat homo.[279]

Canon 22. *Nemo habet de suo nisi mendacium et peccatum.* Si quid autem habet homo veritatis atque iustitiae, ab illo fonte est, quem debemus sitire in hac eremo, ut ex eo quasi guttis quibusdam irrorati non deficiamus in via.[280]

II. Cassian's Life and Background

His place of birth is unknown—speculations about it name him as native of southern France, Rumania, etc. etc.[281] Syria is

277. "'*The assistance of God.* It is a divine gift, both when we think rightly and when we restrain our feet from falsity and injustice; for as often as we do good, God operates in us and with us, that we may work'" (Deferrari, 77; this is a passage taken from *Sententiae,* 22 [*PL* 45, col. 1861]).

278. "'No wretched person is freed from misery, however small, unless he is first reached by the mercy of God' [St. Prosper], just as the Psalmist says: *Let thy mercy, Lord, speedily anticipate us* [Ps. 78:8]; and also: '*My God, His mercy will prevent me*' [Ps. 58:11]" (Deferrari, 78; the quotation is from *Sententiae,* 211 [*PL* 45, col. 1876]).

279. "'*That without God man can do no good.* God does many good things in man, which man does not do; indeed man can do no good that God does not expect that man do'" (Deferrari, 79; the passage is quoted from *Sententiae,* 312 [*PL* 45, col. 1886], based on Augustine's *Contra duas epistolas Pelagianorum* [*PL* 44, col. 586]).

280. ". . . No one has anything of his own except lying and sin. But if man has any truth and justice, it is from that fountain for which we ought to thirst in this desert, that bedewed by some drops of water from it, we may not falter on the way" (Deferrari, 79; the passage, which begins "*Those things which are peculiar to men,*" is quoted from *Sententiae,* 323 [*PL* 45, col. 1887] based on Augustine's *In Johannem,* 5:1 [*PL* 35, col. 1414]).

281. See O. Chadwick, 190–98, for an extensive discussion of Cassian's birthplace.

improbable as birthplace. He was born about 360 or 365. In his early youth he entered a monastery at Bethlehem, before St. Jerome came there. He had already received a complete classical formation. Why did he choose a monastery at Bethlehem? Out of veneration for the mystery of the Divine Infancy, and faith in the efficacy of that mystery as a source of grace for monks. In other words, he did not merely pick this place because it had been made famous by Our Lord, or because it recalled His memory: but above all because of the *efficacy of the mystery* of His childhood. Note: {the} importance of this mystery in the Cistercian Fathers, and in a modern Cistercian, Dom Vital Lehodey.[282] "*Ubi Dominus noster Jesus Christus natus ex Virgine, humanae infantiae suscipere incrementa dignatus, nostram quoque adhuc in religione teneram ac lactantem infantiam sua gratia confirmavit*" (*Inst.* 3:4).[283] *Notice* the emphasis on *grace* in the earliest beginnings of religious life—compare the canons we just discussed! Is *confirmavit* a strong enough word?

He perhaps entered the monastery at the same time as his friend Germanus, who accompanies him on his voyage to Egypt.

Palestinian Monasticism

Monasticism had been imported to Palestine from Egypt by St. Hilarion in the first part of the fourth century. (See above, "Prologue to Cassian."[284]) Cassian arrived a few years after the death of St. Hilarion—who was one of the first monastic confessors to receive a liturgical cult like that of the martyrs. The monasteries of Palestine were *lauras*—not quite cenobia, but more compact than the hermit colonies of St. Anthony. Cassian and Germanus probably lived together in the same hut. Palestinian

282. Dom Vital Lehodey, OCR, *Holy Abandonment*, trans. Ailbe Luddy, O.Cist. (Dublin: M. H. Gill, 1934), 117: "Could we but follow the life of Our Lord in its minutest details, we should find everywhere the love, the confidence, the docility, the abandonment of a little child."

283. Col. 127A: "Where Our Lord Jesus Christ was born of the Virgin, and deigned to undergo the development of a human child, He also strengthened by His grace our own infancy in religious life, when we were still delicate and nursing."

284. Pages 60–62.

monasticism emphasized exterior practices more than did that of the Egyptians. Cassian frequently remarks that the Palestinian monks made perfection consist in austerity, in long prayers, and special mortifications, while the Egyptians had a better idea of the essence of perfection—union with God, but at the same time were often more austere than the monks of Palestine. When Cassian visited Egypt for the first time, around 385, his discovery of the spirit of the monks of the desert came to him as a revelation, and thereafter he could not think of returning permanently to Palestine. It is for us to catch from him something of the undying inspiration of the Desert Fathers.

Cassian in Egypt

Around 385 Cassian and Germanus received permission to visit Egypt. Cassian is about 20 years old. {The} length of their stay was not determined, but they had to make a vow that they would return. {The} vow {was} made in {the} Cave of the Nativity. Their first stay in Egypt was to last about seven years. They returned for another seven. They land at Thennesys, in the Delta, and are met by a local bishop, and go to visit three solitaries who live in the marshes nearby (Panephysis): they are *Chaeremon, Nesteros,* and *Joseph.* These are the ones who supply material for the second part of the *Conferences*—11 to 17, including the thirteenth which contains the error on nature and grace.

At Panephysis

In the opening chapters of *Conference* 11, Cassian describes his arrival in the Delta, among "those old monks whose age is evident from their bowed frame and whose holiness shines forth in their expression, so that the mere sight of them is a lesson to the beholder" (*Conf.* 11:2).[285]

Abbot Chaeremon—They find the anchorites living on lonely islands in the salt marshes. Chaeremon, a hundred years old, is no longer able to walk upright. He excuses himself, and tries to

---

285. Col. 849B.

avoid giving them lessons in asceticism, because he is no longer able to observe the full austerity of his rule. Chaeremon then gives them conferences on the three ways of combating the vices and reaching the perfection of charity, which restores to the soul the image and likeness of God (*Conf.* 11—*De Perfectione*).

Conference 11 on Perfection

The first five chapters are introductory. This is the first conference Cassian and Germanus hear in Egypt. We are introduced to Chaeremon, living in the marshes, a man of very great age, humility and wisdom. They tell him they have come to learn *something in order to make progress* (*profectus nostri amore*[286]). This is the starting point of the conference.

Chapter 6—Chaeremon begins with the assumption that perfection means the overcoming of vices. This is axiomatic for Cassian and the Desert Fathers. But besides the mere fact of "not sinning," what constitutes the deeper perfection of the spiritual life is the motive, the way in which we avoid evil and do good. The various motives for not sinning and doing good are:

a) fear of hell or of violating the law;

b) hope of reward and of the good that we will enjoy as a result of virtue;

c) LOVE OF GOOD AND VIRTUE AS SUCH, for their own sakes.

It is this third that constitutes perfection: doing good without fear and without any interested motive, out of "perfect love" that is centered on the good alone, or even on love alone. {It is} love for love's sake (that is, for God's sake). Chaeremon associates faith with fear (servile attitude), hope with the "mercenary" attitude, and charity with perfection. Important: *Tertium specialiter Dei est, et eorum qui in sese imaginem Dei ac similitudinem receperunt. Ille solus ea quae bona sunt, nullo metu, nulla remunerationis gratia* SED SOLO BONITATIS AFFECTU OPERATUR.[287] (This is of

---

286. Col. 851C: literally, "out of love for our own progress."

287. Col. 852C, which reads *"Ille namque . . . gratia provocante . . ."*: "The third belongs particularly to God and to those who have received in themselves the image and likeness of God. For he alone does works that are good, moved neither by fear nor by the favor of a reward but solely by a love of goodness."

course the heart of St. Bernard's mystical theology, the climax of his sermons on the Canticle of Canticles. Pure love which "casteth out fear" is the way to wisdom, in which we act and are moved only *"sapore boni"*—see Cistercian Breviary, III Nocturn, Feast of St. Bernard.[288]) When this love is present, there is perfect resemblance to God Who gives all without stint to good and evil alike, who is not troubled by insults, always remaining in His own perfect goodness which does not visualize itself in contrast to evil.

Chapter 7—*Beginners (servi)* must start with fear. *Proficients (mercenarii)* are moved by hope of reward. The *Perfect (filii)*[289] believing that all which belongs to their Father belongs to them, are perfected in the image and likeness of God. (Note: like St. Bernard,[290] Cassian here refers to the *Prodigal Son*.) Here we love God as He has loved us. Just as He has saved us out of pure love for us, so we receive His grace out of pure love for Him. *Quemadmodum nullius alterius nisi nostrae salutis gratia prior nos ille dilexit, ita eum nos quoque nullius alterius rei nisi sui tantum amoris dilexerimus obtentu* (c. 8; col. 855).[291] He uses expressions which are basic in the mystical theology of the Fathers: *per indissolubilem caritatis gratiam*[292] (suggesting perfect and inviolable union with God by love); *Patris imaginem ac similitudinem recipere*[293] (distinction between image and likeness—perfect likeness, perfect union, perfect charity—pure love without admixture of any other motive). (Note: c. 9; col. 855—the expression *delectatione*

288. *"Nec duxerim reprehendendum, si quis sapientiam saporem boni definiat"* (*In Cantica* 85), *Breviary* (*Aestas*), 589: "I would not think someone should be criticized for defining wisdom as a taste for the good."

289. Col. 853A: *"servi"* = "slaves"; *"mercenarii"* = "hirelings"; *"filii"* = "sons".

290. This is evidently a reference not to Bernard's *De Diligendo Deo* 12–14, his most extensive discussion of the three-fold division of slaves, mercenaries and sons, which does not refer to the Prodigal Son, but to *Sermones de Diversis* 8 (*PL* 183, col. 561–65), *"De diversis affectionibus vel statibus, quibus anima est sub Deo"* ("On the different affections or states in which the soul is related to God"), which does use the Prodigal Son parable as a basis for discussing the progression of the soul toward divine union, which concludes not with the figure of the son but of the spouse.

291. "Just as He loved us first for no other reason than for our salvation, so we should love Him with nothing else as a motive except love for Him alone."

292. Col. 854A: "through the indissoluble grace of love."

293. Col. 854A: "to receive the image and likeness of the Father."

virtutum,[294] {the} actual words used at the end of chapter 7 of *Rule* of St. Benedict; read it: McCann, p. 48, 49 top.[295]) Why this love for love's sake is perfection:

1. It does not depend on the opinions of others, or their favor.

2. It purifies the heart of all interior evil inclinations and thoughts. Where there is perfect love of good for its own sake, all that is contrary to it is detested *summo horrore*[296]—and this not out of fear of punishment or hope of reward, but simply because of the opposition between evil and good.

3. In this case there is more perfect *freedom and spontaneity in good*. One is not motivated by an outside force, but by the good itself, which has become so to speak part of one's own being.

4. Hence there is perfect *stability in the good, and therefore peace*.

5. Man is then his own judge (implication that he is no longer in need of a judge). He can judge and guide himself because he is perfectly united with God Who is Love—*ama et quod vis fac*, says St. Augustine.[297] {This} must be properly understood. Cassian says: *ubique secum semperque circumferens arbitram non solum actuum sed etiam cogitationum suarum conscientiam, illi potissimum studere contendit, quem etiam circumveniri, nec falli, nec subterfugere se posse cognoscit.*[298] Love of good for God's sake alone, merely to please Him: this then is perfection according to Cassian. And this is in fact the traditional teaching of the Church and of the saints, down through the ages.

Further developments may be treated in brief:

294. "delight in virtue(s)."

295. "*universa . . . incipiet custodire: non jam timore gehennae sed amore Christi, et consuetudine ipsa bona et delectione virtutum*"("he will begin to observe . . . all these precepts . . . no longer for fear of hell, but for love of Christ and through good habit and delight in virtue").

296. Col. 855C–856A: "with the greatest horror."

297. Properly "*Dilige, et quod vis fac*" ("Love, and do what you will"): *Homilies on I John*, 7:8 (*PL* 35, col. 2033); see also the *Commentary on Galatians*, 57: "*Dilige, et dic quod voles*" ("Love, and say what you will") (*PL* 35, col. 2144).

298. Col. 856C–857A: "Carrying about his conscience with him everywhere and always, as a witness not only of his acts but also of his thoughts, he strives most intently to please it, which he knows he cannot cheat, nor deceive, nor evade."

1. The soul united to God in perfect love has no more anger, and hence does not judge sinners but has only compassion for them (c.10) (cf. *compassio* of St. Bernard).[299]

2. Such a man is perfectly humble, recognizing that it is purely by the grace of God that he is able to love in this fashion and keep free from sin himself (cf. the *fiducia* of St. Bernard).[300]

3. Such a one is able sincerely to love his enemies. This is an aspect of the true likeness to God (cf. Matt. 5).

4. Conversely, this love of enemies is test and proof of the purity of one's love for God (col. 859). Read end of chapter 10 (col. 861).[301] He who condemns others with severity for their sins proves that he himself is full of the same vices.

The remainder of the conference is devoted to clarifying details about servile and filial fear, diverse degrees of love and fear, and finally Germanus raises the question of perfect chastity which is put off until the next conference.

299. See for example *"Sermo II in Tempore Resurrectionis"* (*PL* 183, col. 285BC): *"Qui sic flebat super se, putas quia non compassus sit fratri? Hic itaque compassionis affectus multis quidem prodest, quia animus liberalis contristare, quem pro se viderit anxium, erubescit."* ("Do you think that one who weeps over himself will not be compassionate toward his brother? Thus this feeling of compassion benefits many, because an honorable soul is ashamed to sadden one whom he sees to be concerned about him.") For a broader discussion of *"compassio"* in Bernard, see Gilson, 73 ff.

300. See for example *"Sermo V in Vigilia Nativitatis Domini"* (*PL* 183, col. 108B): *"Nam sibi quidem ipsi fidere, non fidei, sed perfidiae est: nec confidentiae, sed diffidentiae magis, in semetipso habere fiduciam. Is vere fidelis est, qui nec sibi credit, nec in se sperat, factus sibi tamquam vas perditum, sed sic perdens animam suam, ut in vitam aeternam custodiat eam."* ("For one who trusts in himself does not exhibit faith but treachery; faithfulness is not a matter of self-confidence but of self-distrust. The truly faithful one does not place his faith or his hope in himself, but seems to himself like a vessel of destruction, but in thus losing his own life, he guards it for life eternal.") See also Gilson, 24, 113, and 240–41, n. 213.

301. The closing section of this chapter emphasizes that perfect love shares in the compassion of Christ who forgave his persecutors on the cross, and that a judgemental attitude toward the failings of others is a clear sign that one is not yet purified of the stains of vice, since he is unable to bear the burdens of another. Cassian concludes, "It is therefore quite certain that a monk will fall into the very same vices which he condemns with merciless and inhuman severity in another. For a stern king brings evil on himself, and 'One who stops his ears lest he hear the weak will cry out himself, and there will be no one to hear him' (Prov. 21)."

The twelfth *Conference* (Chaeremon's second) is on chastity—
{it} specifically deals with the problem whether it is possible for
one to be so perfect in chastity that he can avoid all motions of
fleshly concupiscence. Chaeremon says that it is possible, but
not by our own efforts. Yet he prescribes great mortifications in
order to attain it—fasts, solitude, silence, vigils, etc., etc. This is
what leads to the problem that is discussed in the thirteenth
Conference—on free will and grace. For Germanus cannot understand how it is possible that man should have to make so many
efforts, and yet the victory should be attributed to God's grace.

It is to be noticed that the error on free will and grace comes
in this context—the struggle for "perfect" chastity, which preoccupied the Desert Fathers. This should teach us to avoid their
extremism. It is for us, with St. Paul, to learn the lesson that God's
grace is sufficient, and that holiness demands the acceptance of
our human frailty and the willingness to face trial with patience.
This is a way of realism and of humility.

Abbot Nesteros—Abbot Nesteros, a man versed in the mysteries of Scripture, gives them a conference on "Spiritual science" (*Conf.* 14). This conference is on the twofold "science" by
which we reach perfection. The *scientia practica* (active life) which
purifies our conduct and our hearts, and the *scientia theoretica*
(contemplative life) which "consists in the contemplation of divine things and in the knowledge of the hidden meanings of
Scripture" (*Conf.* 14:1).[302] The first is absolutely necessary. It may
be had without the second, but the second cannot be had without the first. By "contemplation" Nesteros means only the penetration of the meaning of Scripture, first through the *historical*
sense, then in its *spiritual* sense (tropological, allegorical, ana-
gogical). The understanding of Scripture, says Nesteros, cannot
be attained without purity of heart and humility. We reach it—
non inanis jacantiae vitio, sed emundationis gratia.[303] In addition,
we need of course *diligence* in reading and study, but then above
all zeal in seeking the perfection of the "active life" (practice of
all the virtues). "It is impossible for the soul that is even slightly

---

302. Col. 955A.
303. Col. 965B: "not through the vice of empty boasting, but by the grace of
purification."

occupied with worldly preoccupations to merit the gift of knowledge, or to become the fruitful recipient of spiritual understanding, or even to persevere tenaciously in the labor of reading" (*Conf.* 14:9).[304] He explains that the worldly doctors who teach in the schools and who seem to have a great knowledge of Scripture actually do not know the word of God. They only know the outer surface; they have not penetrated the inner mystery, the secrets of God—they are like the pharisees, who knew all about the Scriptures but did not know Christ, the Heart of the Scriptures.

Note: Desert Fathers' insistence on experience, based on *practice*.

In short, two important considerations arise from this conference:

1. For the Desert Fathers—the Scriptures are the center of the monastic life. The purification of our hearts by asceticism is ordered to *theoria* by which we are enabled to know God in the mysteries of Christ, as revealed in Scripture.

2. The contemplative life is one in which the monk, purified by his life of humility and self-denial, is guided and enlightened by the Holy Spirit in his understanding of the Scriptures.

The following night, Nesteros gives them a second conference (*Conf.* 15) on miracles—(*De charismatibus divinis*).[305] It is on true and false miracles, and on the problem raised by the fact that false prophets and bad monks have sometimes seemed to work wonders. The conclusion is that we should not judge the value of a saint's life by the wonders he has worked, but by the charity and spiritual perfection which are seen in him. Not the working of miracles, but *humility* is the true foundation of the structure of sanctity, says Nesteros (*Conf.* 15:7). "It is a greater miracle to get rid of the *fomes*[306] of lust in our own flesh than to expel the impure spirits from the bodies of others, and it is a far more striking sign if by the virtue of patience we restrain the surging movements of anger, than if we command the powers

304. Col. 966B.
305. "On Divine Gifts."
306. "incitement".

of the air. It is a far greater thing to put out of our heart the gnaw-
ing power of sorrow than to drive out bodily fevers from others" (*Conf.* 15:8).[307] Note the importance of controlling *sorrow:*
—*tristitia* and *acedia.* This is {a} very important aspect of virtue
and perfection, to cultivate a humble joy, or rather to dispose
oneself to receive joy from God by patient and humble *content-
ment and acceptance* of all that He wills. *Sorrow comes from our
rebellions and refusals.*

Abbot Joseph—Nesteros gives this conference while they are
walking to the hermitage of Abbot Joseph. Joseph delivers *Conference* 16 on Friendship, which we will take up in detail. Then
he follows with another problematical *Conference* 17, *De
definiendo,*[308] in which we are on somewhat risky ground. They
take up the problem of their vow to return to Bethlehem, and
say they want to remain in Egypt. He tells them that their vow
does not bind them, because they are seeking a life of higher
perfection. This and other matters in the conference (including
Cassian's mild view of lying) raise too many problems, so we
will pass them over. *Conference* 17 is not to be read without care
and caution. After the conference of Abbot Joseph, they sent a
letter to their superior in Bethlehem, announcing that they intended to continue their journey. They set out for Scete. But on
the way they stop at Diolcos, in the Nile Delta.

Diolcos: Abbot John; Abbot Piamon

This is a monastic city near Rosetta, between a mouth of the
Nile and a lagoon. It is their first encounter with a big *cenobium.*
Here they meet Abbot John, who after twenty years as a hermit
has returned to the cenobitic life, finding it a safer way to perfection (*Conference* 19). Near the cenobium is a long sand-spit where
monks retire to live in solitude. Some think that Cassian and Germanus made their first attempt to live as hermits here—and that
Conference 24, of Abbot Abraham, refers to their first falterings as
hermits, and their desire to return to their own climate. (Read
Conf. 24, c. 1—see Abraham's answer—cc. 2 and 3.)[309]

307. Col. 1007B–1008A.
308. "On Making Promises."
309. Col. 1279D–1288A: The opening chapter of this final conference, after

The Abbot and priest of these solitaries is one who stands out "like a great lighthouse"[310]—Abbot Piamon. This hermit gives them a conference (n. 18) on "The three kinds of monks and the fourth kind that has lately come into existence." *Piamon* is anti-Syrian in his monasticism, and urges them strongly to conform to the wisdom of the Egyptians, "embracing without distinction and in all humility the wisdom of the ancients of Egypt."[311] They must, he says, not be like other Syrians who come to Egypt just to go around visiting and receiving entertainment, without learning anything new. Piamon distinguishes the three kinds of Egyptian monks—Cenobites, Anchorites, and Sarabaites. The latter are worthless. "There are three kinds of monks in Egypt, of which two are excellent and the third is tepid and altogether to be avoided" (*Conf.* 18:4).[312] Piamon then proceeds to give the history of monasticism, as he conceives it: the institution of the cenobites goes back to the Apostles, he says (cfr. our *Exordium Magnum*[313]). *Cenobitarum disciplina a tempore praedicationis apostolicae sumpsit exordium.*[314] He then quotes Acts 4 ("The multitude of the believers was of one heart and one soul . . ." etc. and "They divided unto each according as he had need" [*id.*]). At that time, the primitive Christians made the whole Church a cenobium. But now the true cenobites, who fully live the Gospel

---

relating the number of conferences to the mystical number of the elders in the Book of Revelation, focuses on the temptation of Cassian and Germanus to return to their homeland, where they would receive material and social support and be able to give good example that would lead others to conversion. Abraham responds by accusing the two monks of a superficial renunciation and a continued attachment to the world. He points to the example of the Egyptian monks, who have abandoned all things for the sake of the Gospel, even though material and moral support could easily be available to them, and who live in arid places so as not to be distracted from their true goal.

310. Col. 1091A (c. 1).

311. Col. 1092B (a paraphrase).

312. Col. 1093B–1094A.

313. Conrad of Eberbach, *Exordium Magnum Cisterciense*, ed. Bruno Griesser, Corpus Christianorum Continuatio Medievalis, vol. 138 (Turnholt: Brepols, 1994), I:2: "That the tradition of the common life began with the Primitive Church, and that from this the institution of monastic religious life has taken its beginning."

314. Col. 1094B–1095A (c. 5): "The way of life of cenobites dates its origin from the time of the apostolic preaching."

vocation, are a special minority, called monks because they abstain from marriage. This interpretation is not strictly historical—
Piamon thinks that monks originated long before Anthony and
Pachomius—but it is important because it reflects the idea of the
Desert Fathers about the "apostolic" character of their vocation—
an idea which was handed on through the ages to the first Cistercians and which we find in St. Bernard.[315]

A second error of Piamon is to imagine that cenobitism preceded the solitary life in order of time, as if eremitism was born
from the cenobia. *Hermits*—were evidently attacked as escapists.
Piamon says they are most justified in seeking the "hiddenness"
and secrecy of the desert for perfection and contemplation. Further, they go out to meet the demons in open conflict and pitched
battle (cf. St. Benedict[316]).

Sarabaites—appear in St. Jerome's twenty-second Letter
under the title of REMOBOTH.[317] The sarabaites—take their name
from the Coptic word meaning the "separated ones"—they break
off from ordinary communities and from discipline: "to take care
of their own needs!" He fancifully traces their origin to Ananias
and Sapphira—again the value of this statement is spiritual rather
than historical: it is a way of life in which self-love is the rule,
and love of self is placed before true charity. The sarabaites are
characterized by the fact that they refuse the discipline of the
cenobium, reject the authority of a superior, do not follow a rule

315. See Merton's essay, "St. Bernard, Monk and Apostle" (*Disputed Questions*, 274–90), which emphasizes the synthesis of the contemplative and the apostolic in Bernard and in monasticism: "St. Bernard promised all men a quick
and easy way in which to run to God: the way of apostolic renunciation which
is found in the monastery. . . . This is the *vita fortissima* in which we find Christ
by giving Him all we have and imitating the first Apostles. Indeed, there were
some at Clairvaux who had left 'more than boats and fishing nets' to rejoice that
they had found Jesus." Merton cites *Sermones de diversis* 37 (*PL* 183, col. 642D),
which speaks of monks being called to the prophetic, the apostolic and even the
angelic level; after mentioning those who have left more than boats and nets,
Bernard adds that while the original apostles followed Christ in the flesh, later
generations of "apostles" are blessed because they are those who have not seen
and yet have believed (Jn. 20:29).

316. See *Rule*, c. 1: "Hermits, . . . having learnt in association with many
brethren how to fight against the devil, go out well-armed from the ranks of the
community to the solitary combat of the desert" (McCann, 15).

317. *PL* 22, col. 419.

sanctioned by tradition and consequently *do not learn to over-come their own will*. They are monks in appearance only, and he explains why: they have sought only to evade the obligations and responsibilities of life in the world. They have sought a re-tired life in order to have peace and comfort, without struggle and without the cares of family life (*Conf.* 18:7). They also seek the admiration of men without striving to be true monks. They pose as monks. Because they do their own will, they do not in fact have any peace, for they are not truly following Christ and the Gospel. On the contrary, they work much harder and longer hours than other monks, and wander around seeking to satisfy their own whims: *"Their chief concern is to evade the yoke of au-thority and carry out their own will*, and to go about wherever they like. They desire only the freedom to do as they please and they spend their days and nights doing far more work than is done in the cenobium—yet this work is done without the same faith or the same intentions" (*Conf.* 18:7).[318] Cassian goes on to ex-plain that they are not only solicitous for the morrow but for years ahead. They spend their lives taking care of themselves and thus they make God a "liar" by their lack of faith which takes no account of His promises.

This gives us a deep insight into the nature of the monastic vocation. We proclaim our faith in God by preferring Him to all else—*not* our subjective feeling about Him, but His *Will* and his *Word*. Therefore the test—is to let *God run our lives*, and to let Him do so through His representatives, our superiors. From this we see how essential it is for the monastic life to be a life of com-plete dependence on God's Providence and a total submission of ourselves to His Will and His plans. Outside of this there is nothing but illusion. St. Benedict heartily agreed, and this con-ference of Cassian enables us to understand St. Benedict's words that the sarabaites "live in their own sheepfolds and not those of the Lord: they have for their law the impulsions of their own desire; whatever they choose or decide, they call holy etc.—and not being tried by a Rule like metal in the fire, they are as soft as lead, by their works they still show their allegiance to the world,

318. Col. 1105AB.

and their tonsure is a lie before God" (*Rule*, c. 1).[319] Interesting consequences of this doctrine applied to us:

1. The sarabaite spirit—is a spirit of separation from the Church and from Christ—a good example of what it means to live "in the flesh," when presuming to appear spiritual—even when mortifications are involved.

2. The essence of this spirit is the fact that we follow our own will rather than the will of God as manifested *through the Church*, that is through our superiors. The sarabaite opposes to the superior his own preferences, and he thinks holiness consists in following what pleases his own fancy and his own attractions, rather than the will of the superior and the traditions of the ancients.

3. It is a spirit of faithlessness which deprives the monastic life of its sanctifying strength, separating the monk from the life-stream of the Spirit coursing through the Church and from the will of God.

4. The monk, insisting on running his own life and taking care of himself, is left to do so by God, and as a result leads a life that is a sterile and laborious succession of projects and anxieties. He can have no peace.

5. The root of this is lack of trust in God, lack of belief in God's promises to those who leave all and follow Him. It is a rejection of the Gospel, in order to seek worldly peace, worldly security, comfort, respect, a position in society without doing anything to deserve them.

Piamon then goes on to declare that the sarabaites are found everywhere outside of Egypt. On a voyage to Armenia where Valens the Arian emperor had imprisoned chain gangs of Egyptian monks in the mines, and where Piamon went to bring them relief from their brethren, he found nothing but sarabaites everywhere.

The sarabaites are false cenobites. There is a fourth class of monks, even worse, the false hermits: this class has "recently arisen"[320]—he does not give them a special name; he just says

319. The quotation reverses the order of the clauses in the *Rule*; the translation is not McCann's.
320. Col. 1109A.

that after "a fervent beginning"[321] in the monastery, they retire to solitude to avoid the trials of common life, and to retain the appearance of virtue without giving up self—and without having to be tried by others (*Conf.* 18:8). Instead of growing in virtue they just hide their vices in solitude.

Piamon then goes on to speak of true humility which is the sign of a real monastic vocation, and tells the story of Abbot Serapion and the lazy monk who wanders about from cell to cell talking about virtue—who accuses himself of all crimes and is too "humble" even to sit on a mat, but must sit on the ground. When Serapion gently admonishes him that a young man of his health and strength ought to do a little work and earn a living for himself in order to fulfill the precepts of St. Paul, the youth immediately falls into sadness and discouragement, not to say indignation. He is in fact thoroughly insulted. Piamon ends with a discourse on perfect patience, essential to the true monk. To this we will probably return.[322]

At Diolcos they then return to the cenobium for a great gathering of monks for the anniversary of the death of the former abbot—here at the common meal they see the public humiliation of the young monk slapped by the Abbot Paul—an example of perfect humility and patience. Here they converse with Abbot John on cenobites and hermits (see *Conf.* 19). Then they leave Diolcos and retrace their steps to visit Abbot Pinufius.

Abbot Pinufius

Pinufius was an old friend of Cassian and Germanus. In the days when they had shared a cell (hut) together at Bethlehem, Pinufius had run away from Egypt because, having been ordained and appointed abbot of a great cenobium, "he thought that he was already receiving his reward in the human praise of his virtues that was spread far and wide."[323] Fearing thus to lose his eternal reward, he fled first to Tabenna—preferring to conceal himself in the great community rather than live as a solitary

321. Col. 1109A.
322. Merton does not in fact return to this discourse.
323. Col. 1149C (c. 1).

in the desert. He presented himself as a postulant in secular clothes and spent many days "in tears"[324] at the gate, throwing himself at the feet of all and asking their prayers. Having been admitted to be tried, he was placed under obedience to a young monk (*adolescenti fratri*[325])—spent three years here in great humility and obedience, but was recognized. Pinufius attributed this discovery to the devil, and escaped again, this time taking ship to Palestine—where he lived with Cassian and Germanus.

In the fourth book of the *Instituta* (cc. 32 ff.), Cassian reports an address given by Pinufius to a novice making profession in his monastery at Panephysis. It is a summary (*breviarium*) of the whole way of monastic perfection. Pinufius first of all stresses that *renunciation* is essential to the monastic state. The monk lives under the sign of the Cross. By his renunciation, Christ lives in him. The monastic life is a continual carrying of the Cross. And the Cross of the monk is spiritual—the *fear of the Lord* which restrains his desires and his own will. (*Read Instituta*, c. 35).[326] Then come the following points:

1. The beginning of salvation and wisdom is the fear of the Lord;

2. This brings forth compunction of heart;

3. Which leads us to strip ourselves of everything for love of God;

---

324. Col. 1149C.

325. Col. 1150B.

326. Col. 195B–196B: "Our cross is the fear of the Lord. Thus, as one who has been crucified no longer has the power of moving or turning his members in any way by the impulse of his own mind, so also we should attach our wishes and desires, not according to what is pleasant and delightful to us at present, but according to the law of the Lord, however it restricts us. And as one who is fastened to the yoke of the cross no longer dwells on present things, nor thinks about things he likes, nor is stretched out by care and concern for tomorrow, nor is upset by a desire for possessing, nor is enkindled by any pride, or strife, or jealousy, nor grieves over present injuries, nor recalls past ones, and even while he still breathes in the body considers himself dead to all the elements of this world, sending on the consideration of his heart to that place where he does not doubt to pass quickly; so it is right that we also, crucified by the fear of the Lord, should be dead to all these things, that is, not only fleshly vices, but also the very elements of the world, and should have the eyes of our mind fixed there where at every moment we should hope to travel. For in this way we can mortify all our desires and fleshly affections."

4. This in turn brings about humility;

5. When we are humble, then we *mortify our wills;*

6. This enables us to get free from vice and practice virtue;

7. This leads to purity of heart which is the perfection of charity.

Puritate cordis Apostolicae charitatis perfectio possidetur (*Inst.* 4:43).[327] The two visitors are very much humbled by all this, and imagining themselves to be at the bottom of the ladder, ask Pinufius to tell them what at least is true compunction so that they can climb the first step. Pinufius praises their humility, tells them they are well advanced, and gives a conference (*Conf.* 20) on how long one must do penance to satisfy for one's sins. The answer, in brief, is "until they are completely forgotten"[328]—that is to say until we no longer suffer any temptation or experience any phantasms proceeding from that kind of sin. Should we deliberately call to mind the shame of past sins? Yes, he says, except in the case of sins of the flesh, for "as long as one bends over a sewer and stirs up the filth, one will inevitably be suffocated by the evil smell."[329]

The Desert of Scete—and Nitria

Location {is a} twin mountain range west of Nile, near the coast, with two big desert valleys, one of which contains several salt lakes. Between the desert of Scete and Nitria, in the uplands, was the desert of the "cells," famous place of more solitary hermitages. Palladius said there were about 5000 monks living on the mountain at Nitria—some alone, some in twos. A big church, a common bakery supplies all the monks. Nitria was the first foundation of Abbot Macarius. From Palladius's description (of Nitria):

> On this mountain there are seven bakeries serving the monks of Nitria and the hermits of Scete (who number six

---

327. Col. 202B: "The perfection of Apostolic love is gained through purity of heart."

328. Col. 1157A–1158A (c. 7).

329. Col. 1167C (c. 9).

hundred) . . . . On this mountain there is a great church, near which stand three palm trees, on each of which a whip is suspended—one for solitaries who commit a fault, one for thieves, one for tramps. (?) . . . Next to the church is a guest house, in which the traveller is received until he desires to leave—even though he may stay two or three years. The first week, he is allowed to remain idle, but after that he is sent to work in the garden or the bakery or the kitchen. But if he is worthy of consideration, they give him a book and do not allow him to talk to anybody before the appointed time. To this mountain there come also doctors and pastry cooks. Wine is used and sold there. At the same time, the monks make linen with their hands, so that none of them lack anything. Each day, about the hour of none, one can go out and listen how the sound of psalmody comes forth from each cell, so that one would think himself in heaven. As for the church, no one comes there except on Saturday and Sunday. Eight priests serve this church, where, as long as the senior is alive, no one else celebrates or preaches or passes judgement in any case: but the others just sit around the senior without saying anything.[330]

Scete

Cassian was very eager to get to Scete, the "home of all perfect living."[331] He found there four churches, therefore four congregations of hermits, each one directed by a priest. Scete is the home of the most experienced and tried hermits—*probatissimi patres*.[332] It is the place where the most erudite and illuminated of the contemplatives are to be found—"*perfectione et scientia omnibus qui erant in Aegypti monasteriis praeeminabant*" (*Conf.* 10:2).[333] Cassian spent most of his first seven years here and re-

---

330. Presumably Merton's own translation (from *PL* 73, col. 1098AD [= *PG* 34, col. 1022AD]), as he assigns the third whip conjecturally to "tramps" (the Latin reads "*tertium vero ad corrigendos eos qui forte veniunt, et in aliqua delicta incidunt*" [1098B] ["the third to correcting those who come by chance, and fall into some offences"]). Working from Butler's critical Greek text, Meyer translates the third group as "any robbers that happen by," as contrasted with the second group, "any robbers that attack" (40).

331. Col. 482C (*Conf.* 1:1): "*omnium sanctorum morabatur perfectio.*"

332. Col. 481C–482C: "the most tested fathers."

333. Col. 822A–823A: "they surpassed in perfection and in knowledge all who were in the monasteries of Egypt."

turned after his visit to Bethlehem for seven years more. The most important of the conferences are those which he based on the teachings of the Fathers at *Scete*. *Scete* was a center of monastic wisdom—here were collected and written the *Verba Seniorum* (*Apothegmata*)—sayings of the great Desert Fathers from St. Anthony (early fourth century) to Arsenius (second half {of the} fifth century)[334] (see details above). These were the words of men taught by the Spirit of God. Even though an Arsenius was an educated and cultured man, he relinquished his knowledge in order to be wise in the wisdom of the Spirit. Poemen {is} a central figure in the *Apothegmata*, also Pastor,[335] Moses, etc. The *Verba* consist of:

a) Sentences, or "words of salvation" (proverbs);

b) Anecdotes—stories of the Fathers, illustrating a point;

c) Parables—stories of symbolic deeds, or allegorical sayings.

The great theme of all these *Verba* is *salvation*. When the Desert Fathers met one another, their greeting was "*sotheies*" ("Mayest thou be saved"). They travelled together a way of salvation that began with flight from the world. The monastic life is the *work of God*, having three divisions—solitude, work and prayer. Their aim {was} peace, liberty of spirit, purity of heart, freedom from all desires, living with God alone, like Bessarion who lived "without any more cares than a bird in the heavens . . . no house, no desire to go anywhere, . . . no books, entirely freed from all bodily desires . . . living only on the hope of eternal bliss, resting only in the firmness of his faith . . . going hither and thither persevering in nakedness and cold, or scorched by the fires of the sun, stopping in gorges like a strayed traveller or wandering over the far stretching desert as if over the ocean."[336] This picture of a desert wanderer is idyllic, but represents something of the ideal of the Fathers (except that most of them favored a strict stability in the cell!). Some had

---

334. Cf. Mahieu, 69, and 69–70 for the three types of *verba*.

335. Poemen and Pastor are in fact the same person: his Greek name is retained in the third book of the *Vitae Patrum* but elsewhere in the Latin collections of *Verba* is translated as Pastor.

336. Cf. Mahieu, 71, a close but not identical translation.

disciples, others lived in strict solitude, like Arsenius, 32 miles from the nearest cell. About the same time that Cassian visited Scete, or a little later, *Palladius* also came there. He afterwards wrote the *Historia Lausiaca* (so called because written at the request of Lausus—a courtier of Emperor {Theodosius II}[337]). A few years later, in 395, seven monks of Jerusalem visited the whole of Egypt from south to north and their experiences were described in the *Historia Monachorum.*[338]

The hermitage of Scete had been founded by St. Macarius about 330. He died about 390 and was still alive when Cassian visited the desert. Cassian refers to him as the "Great Man."[339] Cassian probably visited Evagrius Ponticus also in the Desert of Scete.[340] Cassian writes nothing of the teaching of these great men, but he has left us portraits of others, upon whose teaching he bases his conferences.

1—Paphnutius "The Buffalo"—He was the priest of Scete. Cassian speaks of Scete as "our monastery"[341] which means he was admitted there for a time as a monk. Paphnutius lived in a cell five miles from the church, and would not change to a closer one in spite of his great age. He had no spring nearby and had to carry a week's supply of water when he came back after Mass on Sunday. He would not let a younger brother do this for him. He did this for 90 years. After a brief formation in the cenobium he had hastened to the desert out of love of contemplation. He soon learned to hide himself so well that even the most experienced could not find him, and consequently he received the name of "buffalo" because he could, like that animal, hide himself in the wilderness.

Paphnutius gives the *third Conference* on the *Three Renunciations.* This deals with "three kinds of vocation":

1. In which one is called directly by God—as was St. Anthony;

---

337. Merton has erroneously written "Theodore" here; he correctly identified him earlier: cf. page 72 above.

338. Though they did not go to Scete, which "proved too dangerous for the seven to visit" (*Lives of the Desert Fathers*, 137 [xxiii, n. 2]).

339. *Inst.* 5:41 (col. 265A): "*tanti viri.*"

340. More precisely, in the Desert of Cells (Kellia).

341. Col. 557C (c. 1).

2. In which one is inspired by the example of holy souls, or by their teaching;

3. In which one is driven by necessity—by fear of death, or of damnation, by the loss of dear ones or of money, etc. Even though this third is the weakest kind of vocation, it has resulted in men becoming great saints.

After the three vocations, he goes on to the three renunciations:

1. Giving up all our possessions;

2. Giving up our former habits and way of life;

3. Turning our minds away from all that is passing, and living for eternal goods.

2—Abbot Daniel—gives the fourth *Conference* on the struggle between flesh and spirit. He was Paphnutius's deacon. Equal to the others in all virtue, he outshone them by his humility, and because of this had been chosen deacon. Paphnutius planned that Daniel should succeed him as the priest of Scete. Indeed, he was ordained priest, but never exercised any other function than that of deacon as long as Paphnutius was alive (note this background for St. Benedict's idea of the humility of the priest in the monastery[342]). In the end, Daniel died before Paphnutius and never got to exercise his priestly order. The conference on the conflict between flesh and spirit is really about *distractions* and trials that make the interior life difficult. This calls for a complete treatment, which we will give later.[343]

3—Abbot Serenus—They are invited to a "banquet" with this Desert Father ("a most sumptuous repast"—see *Conf.* 8, c. 1[344]). The "banquet" of Abbot Serenus consisted of bread—dipped in sauce—salt—3 olives each—5 chick peas. "To eat more would be a sin in the desert."[345] (Ordinary regime—2 lbs. of bread daily, of which some might be set aside for guests.) {Abbot Serenus is}

---

342. See *Rule*, c. 60, which stresses that a priest admitted to the monastery may, with the permission of the abbot, celebrate Mass and pronounce blessings, but "[o]therwise, let him not presume to do anything, knowing that he is subject to the discipline of the Rule; but rather let him give to all an example of humility" (McCann, 137).

343. See below, pages 226–30.

344. Col. 719C.

345. Col. 721A.

eminent for his chastity, never troubled at all by the flesh even in sleep. He had worked for this by prayers day and night and fasts and vigils. At the end of these, an angel in a dream had cut out of his loins a flaming tumor, after which he was never again molested. He gives *Conference* 7 on distractions and the temptations of the devil, and 8 on the different orders of angelic spirits. *Conference* 7—stresses the importance of *controlling one's thoughts,* which requires effort and "great sorrow of heart" (c. 6).[346] We have the grace of God to help us reject all evil thoughts. Devils cannot force the inmost sanctuary of the will, but can only tell how their suggestions are received by observing outward signs. (*Read* c. 16.[347])

4—*Abbot Theonas*—who had been married, according to the desire of his parents, while still young, had brought gifts as a layman to Abbot John. The latter had addressed {to} him a strong exhortation, saying "if you give away the tithes of your goods, you are fulfilling the perfection of the Old Law. But if you seek evangelical perfection, you must give away all that you have and follow Christ."[348] Theonas tries to persuade his wife to leave the world so that he also can become a monk, and when she refuses, he believes himself inspired by God to run away to the desert anyway. Cassian hastens to say this is not a general rule, but that it was justified in this particular case. Theonas gives them three conferences. The first (*Conf.* 21) is on the lack of fasting during Paschal Time. Cassian is curious to know why the monks of Egypt are so careful *not to fast* in Paschal Time, and why they pray standing up, and avoid kneeling during that

346. Col. 676B.

347. Col. 691AB: "For as some thieves are accustomed to check out hidden wealth of people in the homes they desire to break into secretly, and by carefully sprinkling by hand tiny particles of sand in the deep darkness of night they are made aware of concealed riches which they cannot catch sight of, through the sound of a slight ringing or scratching as the sand falls, and so attain quite reliable knowledge of the object and its metallic makeup, which is revealed by the sound produced, likewise these [demons] also, in order to explore the treasure of our heart, sprinkle in us certain poisonous suggestions like grains of sand; and when they see the fleshly response that has arisen according to the nature of their suggestions, they recognize what is hidden in the depths of the inner man, as if by a kind of ringing issuing forth from innermost chambers."

348. Col. 1171B–1179C: a summary (not a direct quotation) of chapters 2–7.

season while so many in Syria continued fasting etc. Theonas's reasons:

1. The tradition of the Fathers;
2. The principle of Ecclesiastes—"All things have their season" (Eccles. 3). Applying this principle—nothing of man's indifferent actions can be good if the circumstances do not help to make it good. Also, he says that fasting is not abstaining from food as from an evil. "If we fast in such a way that we think we would contract a sin by eating [i.e. by eating as such] we not only reap no fruits from our abstinence but we are guilty of the crime of sacrilege"[349] (and he supports this by quoting I Tim. 4:3-4). Note the importance of this—against the heresies of the time, especially gnosticism and manichaeism, which were inordinately "spiritual" and held material things to be "evil." Hence it follows that if food is not evil in itself fasting is not good in itself: both are relative. Fasting is one of those *media bona*[350]—indifferent in themselves but made good by intentions and circumstances. It is a means to an end—charity, mercy, patience, purity of heart. It is not an end in itself and does not constitute perfection.

3. Scripture, he says, teaches that we must *not* fast always (Matt. 9). We must not fast when Christ is with us. But Paschal Time is the time in which the Church relives the mystery of Christ's risen life on earth, with His disciples. *Ergo* . . . Christ is present with us in a very special way during the Paschal Season, Abbot Theonas believes. However, we must not think that the Desert Fathers advised much eating in Paschal Time. It was merely a matter of eating the same plain food, but earlier (at None instead of Vespers, generally).[351]

The second conference of Theonas is on Nocturnal Illusions (*Conf.* 22). {It was} given in response to the question why those who fast are often more tempted by the lust of the flesh than others who keep a less strict fast. He offers three explanations:

1. Perhaps gluttony of the past has an influence;
2. Perhaps the soul has not guarded purity of heart;

349. Col. 1188A (c. 12).
350. Col. 1187B: "neutral goods."
351. Col. 1199A (c. 23).

3. The envy of the devil tries to disturb souls who are striving to be fervent.

A modern observer might add another answer—somewhat akin to this third, that the trouble might be caused by nervous and mental strain. Those who give themselves to asceticism with *inordinate tension* must expect their system to take its revenge.

{A} problem raised by Germanus {is} whether one should go to communion the day after a nocturnal illusion. Theonas answers—provided there is no fault *in causa*—possumus et debemus *ad gratiam salutaris cibi confidenter accedere.*[352] We *should* receive the necessary food of our souls. The conference concludes with a discussion of the fact that no saint is so pure that he does not suffer from some human weakness or indeliberate faults. We are wrong if we expect "perfection" in this life to deliver us from all human frailty.

This leads into the next conference of Theonas (*Conf.* 23)— *De velle bonum et agere malum.*[353] The problem is raised by St. Paul—in Romans 7—"It is not what I wish that I do, but what I hate that I do . . ." etc. (vss. 15-25). This text has been much misused by heretics. Theonas begins by making it clear that this does not apply to deliberate sins. The words are spoken by St. Paul, who was a saint and full of every virtue. The "good" that he desires and which he cannot have at will must be something higher than virtue. It is *theoria*—the perfect purity of heart which belongs to pure charity and contemplation (1246). The goodness he aspires to is the goodness of God dwelling in us, by comparison with which goodness our virtues are as filthy rags (Isa. 64). The purity he aspires to is that of the Gospel, compared with which the virtues of the Law are as nothing. The burden Theonas complains of is the burden of a self laden with illusion and falsity due to original sin—often even our good intentions are full of hidden evil. The souls to be pitied are not the ones who feel this—it is a salutary suffering, but the souls that cannot feel it and think everything is perfect with them. At the same time we must not be pushed into discouragement and sadness. So in these

352. Col. 1223B: "we can and should approach the gracious gift of saving food with confidence" (*in causa* means personal responsibility for the occurrence).
353. "On Willing Good and Doing Evil."

words, according to Theonas, Paul is saying that in spite of all his efforts and virtues, he laments the fact that he cannot always contemplate God in purity of heart, but is troubled and disturbed by his nature, in temptations, trials and indeliberate or semi-deliberate sins.

The problem of this conference is, in fact, the problem of *distractions*, and of *indeliberate weakness and faults*. The saints, Theonas reminds us, have a very acute sense of sin and suffer much from these imperfections. But the view of their miseries produces in them *true* humility (1260). They realize that they cannot do the impossible, that they will undoubtedly be left with their faults and sins until the end of their days, but for the grace of God which alone can deliver them from "the body of this death." Hence, accepting their faults, their limitations, in true humility, they rely no more on their own powers but prostrate themselves before God in humble prayer. Hence they eat their "spiritual bread" (which is Christ) in the sweat of their brow (1263). And thus they share the common lot of men (1264). They must truly recognize themselves as sinners, like the rest of men. *But they are "saints" by their greater humility and greater confidence in God*, more than by their other virtues. They confidently go forward, not giving up in despair, and the fact that they know themselves to be sinners does not keep them away from communion, but rather—*sed ad eam magis ac magis est, et propter animae medicinam et purificationem spiritus* avide festinandum (1279).[354] In a beautiful eucharistic passage which closes the conference, Theonas reproves the presumption of those who only communicate once a year, with the implication that communion is only for those who are most pure and perfect saints. Hence they believe themselves worthy, once a year. But it is much better to receive the Lord each Sunday conscious of our needs and miseries, going to Communion as to the necessary medicine for our frailties. Hence, here too we see great emphasis on humility, on trust in God's mercy, and above all on love for the Blessed Eucharist, the source of sanctity. This is important because it is something often overlooked in the spirituality of the Desert Fathers.

354. "One should hasten to it more and more eagerly, as both the medicine of the soul and the purification of the spirit" (c. 21).

Other Fathers, about whom Cassian gives us fewer details, are *Abbot Moses* (Basic Conference on the meaning of the monastic life—*Conf.* 1),[355] *Abbot Isaac* (the two very important conferences on prayer—*Conf.* 9 and 10), *Abbot Abraham*—last conference, n. 24, on mortification; also *Abbot Theodore*, who lives in the desert of the Cells, plateau between Nitria and Scete, who discusses with them the problem of the death of the Palestinian hermits, killed in the desert of Juda by Saracens (*Conf.* 6). His reply is that there is no problem if living by faith, we have the true idea of good and evil. Death is no evil to the Christian, since Christ has overcome death. What is good, is to do the will of God. What is evil is to disobey God. In between come things that are neither absolutely good or evil in themselves, and whose value depends on how we use them. Life and death are among these. In this conference (*Conf.* 6) he also takes up other questions, such as stability (c. 15), temptations (c. 11), the value of trials, and making good use of suffering and temptation.

The Origenist Conflict

During the time of Cassian's journey to Egypt, the Origenist conflict arose. It is important in the history of monastic spirituality for it marks the end of the great age of Egyptian monasticism. Origenism—as condemned by the Church, consists chiefly of errors flowing from Origen's teaching on the *preexistence of souls*—and the *apocatastasis* (or a final settlement when *all*, even the damned, return to God); also his Trinitarian errors. (For Origen, see above, pages {23–29}.) {In} 393, Palestinian monks—the severe ones—start a great storm over Origen. They present themselves at the cell of St. Jerome and demand that Origen be condemned. St. Jerome repudiated all taint of Origenist teaching in his own writings, though retaining great respect for Origen. Jerome's friend Rufinus refused to sign up with the attackers of Origen. Then Epiphanius of Salamina[356] came to Jerusalem, and

355. Moses also gives the second conference, on discretion.
356. I.e., the city of Salamis on Cyprus; in Latin the form *Salamina, -ae* was sometimes used in place of *Salamis, -inis*, though *Salamina* is also occasionally found as the accusative form of the latter.

thinking he detected Origenist opinions in the talk of the Bishop of Jerusalem, had a violent argument with him, and went off to St. Jerome, who broke with the Bishop of Jerusalem. Rufinus, Jerome's friend, on the contrary sided with the bishop. Bitter conflict between Rufinus and Jerome {developed}.

The fight soon spread to Egypt, where the Doctors had hitherto been content to pass over Origen's errors in silence, while highlighting the truths taught by him. Among their number was St. Athanasius, for instance. But when the conflict arose, it divided the *contemplatives*—students of Scripture who naturally loved Origen—headed by *Evagrius Ponticus*—against the *actives* who distrusted lofty doctrines which they did not understand and who were looking for an opportunity to get the contemplatives condemned. (For Evagrius, the leading Origenist of the Desert, see above, pages {88–96}.) Some of the monks met by Cassian were of this last party—especially Abbot Abraham, who thinks the reading of Scripture is of little value. The actives, however, had fallen into another heresy—*anthropomorphism*—believing that God had the form of a man, not only in the Incarnation but in His own being.

In 399, after {the} death of Evagrius, Archbishop Theophilus of Alexandria, an Origenist {who} wants to gain control over the desert, sends his paschal letter (announcing the feast—cf. announcement of Easter in our chapter rooms today[357]) and included a condemnation of anthropomorphism to please Origenist monks. Three congregations of Scete declared the bishop heretical and refused to read the pastoral letter. Paphnutius alone held firm. {See the} story of old *Abbot Serapion*, who cannot give up the heresy, until finally convinced by a learned visitor from Cappadocia, he sobs, "They have taken away my God."[358]

---

357. Cf. *Regulations*, 283 (#596): "**Easter Sunday**. After the community have entered Chapter, and before the reading of the Martyrology, the Cantor announces the Paschal solemnity at the desk. He does not read the martyrology (268), but after making a profound bow, returns to his place"; #268 (133): "On Easter Sunday, when the Cantor announces the solemnity in Chapter (596), we uncover, standing turned in choir with the sleeves raised. When he retires, we sit down and cover, and not until then do we salute each other as usual. The Invitator sings the martyrology."

358. *Conf.* 10, c. 3 (col. 824A).

Rioting monks in Alexandria persuaded Theophilus to condemn Origen. He meets them saying, "When I see you, I see the face of God." They reply, "If you believe that, condemn Origen." Thus they got some satisfaction. Having changed his position completely, Theophilus now begins a persecution of the Origenists in the desert, supported by the "actives." The Origenists begin to leave Egypt, either expelled, or departing of their own accord. Theophilus (according to Palladius, pro-Origen) attacked Nitria with soldiers, burnt three cells, books, etc. Theophilus in turn said Origenists fortified Nitria to resist his "visitation." Isidore and the "Tall Brothers" (four leading Origenists) lead a troop of 300 Origenist exiles to Palestine. Leaders go on to Constantinople, to get support of St. Chrysostom.[359]

Was Cassian involved in the Origenist conflict? He himself says nothing directly about his own part.

1. No Origenist heresy in Cassian;

2. But Cassian follows Evagrius, in orthodox Origenist ascetic doctrine;

3. Cassian probably knew Evagrius;

4. Cassian's friends (Paphnutius, etc.) were the Origenists of Nitria;

5. Cassian leaves Egypt at this time and is found at Constantinople where he is ordained around 402.

It is probable that Cassian and Germanus left Egypt with the Origenists, or as a result of the struggle. They were probably involved with the Origenist theologians and probably rated as the frowned-on "foreign element" which Theophilus and the Copts attacked at Nitria (out of political opportunism of course). The golden age of Egyptian monasticism came to its end at the moment when Cassian left Egypt, at the beginning of the fifth century. Now the monastic movement would gain firm foothold in the West, especially in Southern France.

---

359. Merton follows O. Chadwick (35–36) closely here; the reference to Palladius is to *Dialogus de Vita S. Johannis Chrysostomi*, cc. 6–7 (*PG* 47, col. 24).

Cassian in Constantinople

The Origenists fled to Chrysostom because he was an ardent and uncompromising defender of the truth—not a politician or an opportunist. Indeed he was not enough of a diplomat for some: too outspoken; no human respect; above petty squabbles—a holy and objective thinker. Cassian {was} an enthusiastic admirer of Chrysostom, who ordained him deacon. He writes of Chrysostom (in *de Incarnatione*): "Remember John who was so admirable in his faith and purity. Remember John, the great John, who like his namesake the Evangelist lay on the Lord's breast, a disciple of Jesus and an apostle. Remember him, I say, and follow his faith and purity. Meditate on his teaching and his holiness. Always remember him who taught you and nourished you, in whose breast and arms you grew to manhood and the faith [he is addressing the people of Constantinople]. He was alike my master and yours. . . . Read his writings and keep what he has given, take to yourselves his faith and his saintliness. It is a great thing to attain to his stature, but it is hard—nevertheless it is a magnificent thing even to follow him. . . . Keep him always in your thoughts and in your mind, meditate upon him in your heart . . . etc." (cf. Chadwick, p. 38).[360]

St. John Chrysostom was born {in} 347 at Antioch. {He was a} great orator at Antioch {who} pleads the cause of the poor. {In} 398 {he was} consecrated archbishop of Constantinople {and shows} ardent reforming zeal {along with} fearless condemnation of abuses. Cassian considered Chrysostom an ideal bishop and a great saint. He pointed to him as a master. However there is apparently little real influence of Chrysostom in Cassian. (He quotes him once only and the sentence has never been found in Chrysostom's writings![361]) Chrysostom was not an Origenist.

---

360. The translation follows that in O. Chadwick closely but not exactly; the passage is from *De Incarnatione Domini*, 7:31 (*PL* 50, col. 270A), the final chapter of the work.

361. See O. Chadwick, 38; the passage is in *De Incarnatione Domini*, 7:30 (*PL* 50, col. 266A–267A): "*Et illum quem si nuda deitate venisset, non coelum, non terra, non maria, non ulla creatura sustinere potuisset, illaesa Virginis viscera portaverunt.*" ("The pure womb of the Virgin carried him whom neither the heaven nor the earth nor the seas nor any created thing could have borne if he had come in unveiled divinity.")

But he took the Origenists under his patronage. This contributed to his downfall.

Chrysostom was so outspoken that he had many enemies (especially the Empress Eudoxia) and a party was formed to throw him out of Constantinople. This party was headed by Theophilus, Patriarch of Antioch. Rancor grew when Chrysostom began to give preference to exiles from Egypt, not to local talent in the clergy. (Palladius was consecrated bishop by St. Chrysostom; Cassian was placed in charge of the Cathedral treasury.[362]) Chrysostom himself could not be accused of Origenism, but he was vulnerable through the Origenism of his proteges. Riots and trouble {erupted}: Chrysostom {was} deposed in 404, {his} cathedral burned to the ground; Cassian, Germanus, Palladius etc. move on to Italy. Chrysostom was exiled to Armenia, then to the Black Sea. Brutally treated by guards on the journey, he died on September 14, 407. {He is} patron of all preachers of the Word of God.

Cassian in Gaul

From Constantinople, Cassian went to Rome where he met and made friends with St. Leo the Great, not yet Pope. (Some think he met Pelagius at Rome at this time.) Legend says that in his contact with Cassian, St. Leo wanted to go off and be a hermit but was forbidden by Pope Innocent I.[363] In 410—Alaric and the Goths invade Italy. Cassian leaves about this time. {He} goes to Marseilles—where the bishop is a friend of St. Jerome and St. Honoratus[364] and a patron of the monastic movement. Note con-

362. See O. Chadwick, 39–40: "Germanus and Cassian, the one ordained by Chrysostom to the priesthood, the other to the diaconate, were given the care of the cathedral treasury. . . . [After Chrysostom's exile, the] public stature of the two companions had grown: for having executed their trust by depositing with the city magistrates valuables of gold and silver and clothing from the treasury, they carried the receipt and letters from their party leaders to Pope Innocent I at Rome." But in *Cassian the Monk* (New York: Oxford University Press, 1998), Columba Stewart writes, "Some have inferred from this commission that Cassian and Germanus had been in charge of the cathedral treasury at Constantinople; Palladius' text, however, is not so specific" (14).

363. See O. Chadwick, 41, n. 1.

364. See O. Chadwick, 41, n. 2.

nections with Abbey of Lérins (importance of the monasticism of Lérins, the greatest center in the West at this time). Cassian {was} ordained priest by Innocent I or Proculus, Bishop of Marseilles.[365]

Provence was the last refuge of Roman and Christian civilization as the barbarians broke through in the north and in Italy. Refugees came from France and Italy. Many of these refugees, disillusioned with the world, became monks. (On Provence at this period—see Chadwick, *Poetry and Letters in {Early Christian} Gaul*.[366]) {In} 412—Visigoths passed through Provence and unsuccessfully besieged Marseilles. Arles became capital of Gaul.

Monasticism existed in Gaul (St. Martin—St. Honoratus, etc.) but it was still not completely accepted even by Christians—Bishops persecuted the monks, crowds mocked and attacked them. In many places, monks as such were accused of heresy, and Proculus of Marseilles did not have an easy time of it because he liked the monks. His adversaries used this as a weapon against him. Gallic monasticism was also still internally weak:

1. Martin's ideal—the semi-eremitical, was beyond the average man.

2. It depended so far on Egyptian ideals, which were hard to understand and follow in Gaul. They needed adaptation.

St. Martin and Ligugé[367]

Martin introduced monasticism to Gaul in the fourth century. He died {in} 397. He wrote no Rule. His monks simply followed his example and oral teaching. He himself learnt monastic

365. See O. Chadwick, 41.

366. Merton actually calls the book *Poetry and Letters in Fourth Century Gaul*; for good measure, in his first letter to Nora Chadwick, dated May 26, 1964, he writes, "I also used your *Poetry and Letters in Sixth Century Gaul* with [the novices] last year and will, no doubt, use it again" (Thomas Merton, *The School of Charity: Letters on Religious Renewal and Spiritual Direction*, ed. Patrick Hart, ocso [New York: Farrar, Straus, Giroux, 1990], 217; the reference is evidently to the first series of his conferences on Pre-Benedictine Monasticism). In fact the book focuses principally on the fifth century, the final flowering of Gallo-Roman culture in the period of the barbarian invasions. Merton continued to correspond with Chadwick, particularly about her work on Celtic monasticism: see the letters in *The School of Charity*, 228–29, 282–83, 308, 326.

367. N. Chadwick provides an overview of Martin of Tours and of his biography by Sulpicius Severus in the fourth chapter of her *Poetry and Letters*,

life from observation of monks in Italy. After his military service and baptism he went to be trained in asceticism by St. Hilary. Martin then went to Hungary {and} started his first community at Milan. {He} was {a} hermit on an island in {the} Mediterranean (Gallinaria). {He} founded monasteries at Ligugé and Marmoutier, near Tours, of which he became bishop. Even while bishop he lived with the monks at Marmoutier, outside {the} town. With his monks he evangelized the countryside. He maintained perfect poverty even as a bishop—proud to look like a slave. His monks were mostly recruited from the aristocracy. Among them {were} young children of nobles. Rigorous poverty {was required}. Wine {was} not permitted. Fish was eaten on big feasts. They lived in caves and huts.

St. Honoratus had begun to provide a solution with his cenobium of Lérins,[368] but there was still needed a new system, an adaptation, a rule, an ordered way of life. Cassian came to provide it.

Lérins {was} an island monastic settlement like Iona, but in {the} Mediterranean. {Its} islands {were} praised for their beauty. {It was} settled by monks early in {the} fifth century, by St. Honoratus (d. 430). Honoratus had previously been a hermit in the coastal mountains {who} fled to this desert island, infested with snakes and without water. He found water. Honoratus became bishop of Arles {in} 426. Maximin succeeded him as head of Lérins. Many saints of Lérins became bishops: v.g. Maximin, Faustus, Theodore, etc. especially St. Caesarius of Arles and Vincent of Lérins, and Eucherius of Lyons. Caesarius entered Lérins in 489. *Monastic Doctrine*—in the *Instructions* of Faustus[369] (*Sermones*, see *PL* 58:869 ff.)—{included:} stress on active pursuit of perfection; monastery not a refuge for mediocrity; exam-

---

89–121; Merton will discuss Martin in somewhat more detail in "Pre-Benedictine Monasticism," first series, 5–6.

368. For Lérins see N. Chadwick, *Poetry and Letters*, 146–60 and *passim*.

369. Faustus, bishop of Riez, had been abbot of Lérins and returned there to deliver homilies to the monks; for a discussion of his life and thought (which does not include the details mentioned here by Merton) see N. Chadwick, *Poetry and Letters*, 192–207.

ination of conscience cultivated assiduously; special severity towards critical and rebellious monks; love of the monastery of one's profession "as a bird loves its nest";[370] interior mortification of self-love emphasized more than exterior austerity.

St. Caesarius was the first to attempt a formal monastic Rule in the West. Until that time, regularity depended on the relations between the monk and the spiritual father assigned to him by the Abbot. Cassian wrote his *Conferences* primarily for the monks of Lérins[371] and this served them as a kind of Spiritual Directory on which they based their life until St. Caesarius wrote his Rule. Cassian was admirably fitted to make the great synthesis of monastic doctrine and adapt the Eastern tradition to the West:

1. He was an experienced monk himself;
2. He had met and lived with the greatest monks of his time;
3. He knew all the great centers of monasticism;
4. He knew both cenobites and hermits;
5. He was steeped in monastic doctrine;
6. He himself had a high monastic ideal;
7. He had the genius required to make this synthesis.

Cassian arrived at Marseilles about 410. The monastery of Lérins had just been founded. Cassian founds the monastery of St. Victor, on a point across the bay from the city. Here he founds a center for monastic life in southern France. Castor, Bishop of

---

370. *Sermon 7* (*PL* 58, col. 885C).

371. This would seem to be rather an overstatement; the second series of *Conferences* (11–17) are dedicated to Honoratus, the founder of Lérins, and Eucherius, also a well-known monk and writer of Lérins (both of whom went on to become bishops) (col. 844B–845A). But the original series (1–10) was dedicated to Bishop Leontius and Helladius, who are later said to have requested them (col. 1087C), neither of whom was connected to Lérins—the first was related to Bishop Castor of Apt, whose request prompted the composition of the *Institutes* and at least indirectly of the *Conferences*; the second (who later was raised to the episcopacy as well) was himself attracted to the anchoritic life (col. 479A). The third series (18–24) are likewise dedicated to four priests not known to be associated with Lérins (col. 1088C–1089A). Note, however, that according to O. Chadwick, "The *Institutes* and *Conferences* dominated thought at Lérins, . . . and the prestige of Lérins spread the tempered Egyptian ethos northward to the monasteries of central Gaul" (168).

Apt (back in the mountains) asks for some writings on monasticism and Cassian writes the *Instituta* (about 420). The idea {was} to give a basis for *uniform observance* based on the traditions of the East. {The} *Conferences* {were} written 425–428. The influence of his writings dominated Lérins[372]—nursery of bishops, who soon took over great dioceses of France. {This} influence spreads through Italy, Spain, Africa. His influence on St. Benedict made him, in fact, a permanent force in Western monasticism. He died about 433, shortly after being attacked as a semi-pelagian. Local cult {grew}—with feast at Marseilles on July 23—Pope Urban V engraved words *"Sanctus Cassianus"* on {a} silver casket containing his relics.[373] {The} Oriental Church—still celebrates his Feast on February 29. In the *Philokalia* he is included as Saint Cassian the Roman.

III. The Instituta

Title: De Instituta coenobiorum et de octo vitiorum principalium remediis[374] {was} written at the request of Castor, Bishop of Apt, about 417–418. It is ostensibly an account of the observances and ascesis of the Desert Fathers of Egypt but is marked by the desire to make an *adaptation* to the needs of France.

Division: {There are} two parts, {the} first four books and then the final eight books. *Part I*—the four first books treat of the *observances of the Egyptian monks*: Habit (Bk. 1); Canonical Office (Bk. 2 and Bk. 3)—(the night office is according to the Egyptian rite, the day hours according to the rite in Palestine and Mesopotamia); common life and formation of candidates (Bk. 4). *Part II*—Books 5–12, treat of the *eight principal vices*: Bk. 5— Gluttony; 6—Lust; 7—Avarice; 8—Anger; 9—Sadness; 10— Acedia; 11—Vainglory; 12—Pride.

---

372. See O. Chadwick, 168.

373. See O. Chadwick (172), who notes that Urban had been abbot of St. Victor.

374. *Concerning the Institutes of Cenobites and the Remedies for the Eight Principal Vices.*

PART ONE OF THE INSTITUTA—*The Exterior of the Monastic Life*
Book 1—*Of the Habit*

He begins with the habit and with the exterior because he wants his reader first to get a good idea of what a monk looks like, before describing his interior life. So too, necessarily, in monastic formation today: one begins with exterior practices which form an atmosphere in which the interior perfection can grow. The different parts of the habit have a symbolic value (cf. priestly vestments and prayers while vesting):

The Cincture—Because the monk is a soldier of Christ always girt up and ready for battle.

The Robe—To keep the monk warm and to hide his nakedness, not to foster vanity—a purely utilitarian garment. No symbolism? *Haircloth* robes are repudiated as vanity, and as impeding the monk's work, which is necessary to his vocation (66).

The Cowl (hood—*cuculla*)—This garment is not merely utilitarian but adopted for its symbolism also (68). Like our oblate's hood {it} covers only head and shoulders—represents the innocence and humility of childhood—apparently it was a children's garment.

The Colobion—cf. Carthusians today—symbolizes mortification (because made of linen) (69): a robe without sleeves—to permit work.

The Anabolas—cords with which to tie up their robes?? (obscure).

The Mafortes—a kind of small cloak over the shoulders—cheap and common—indicating humility.

For outdoor use:

The *Melotes*—or goatskin overcoat. This symbolized mortification and gravity. They also carried a long walking stick—*baculum*. Sandals {were permitted} for the feet, *when on a journey.*

A final note on the monastic habit: The earliest representations of Christ on the Cross showed Our Savior *living* and dressed in a *colobion*. The *colobion*, a sleeveless or short-sleeved tunic, was worn by the Romans of the Republican era and was later adopted by bishops and monks. Only in the eleventh century did Our

Lord appear naked on the Cross in Christian iconography, at
Byzantium.

Book 2—The Night Office of the Egyptian Monks

Cassian begins by condemning excessive *quantity* in the
psalmody of certain monks (Palestinian). He regards as excessive—eighteen, twenty or thirty Psalms with antiphons and other
things to be sung at {the} night office. There are also differences of
opinion about the day hours, he says—some thought at the third
hour there should be three psalms, at the sixth hour six, at none
nine etc. These he reproves. To settle arguments, he appeals to
the "ancient custom which is observed in all Egypt" (79).

The principle—Psalmody, like everything else in the monastic life, must be regulated not by the inspiration of the individual but by the tradition of the elders. We have not come to the
monastery to do our own will, especially in this matter of prayer.
Obedience is the touchstone of monastic renunciation. Also the
Superior is chosen because, among other things, he has proved
himself perfect in obedience. In this way God's will is done in
the monastery. The Superior obeys the tradition and customs of
the ancients and the monks obey the Superior and nobody in
the monastery does his own will (81).

The practice—in all Egypt, twelve psalms are judged sufficient for the night office. One monk chants the psalm, the others
sit and listen (87). There are two lessons, one from {the} Old Testament and one from {the} New (both from the New Testament
on Sundays). After each psalm, they stand for a moment praying in silence, then prostrate themselves on the ground for a short
time. (If they stay too long they might fall asleep, he laments.)
Read chapter 7.[375] Then one monk recites a short oration and the

375. This chapter, entitled *"De disciplina orandi"* ("On the System of Praying"), contrasts the hastiness of monks in Gaul to complete the office with the
custom of the Egyptian monks, who reflect for a time on the psalm just recited
before kneeling and prostrating themselves, and who remain prostrate only for
a brief time lest they be drawn to wandering thoughts or to sleep; the Egyptian
monks also follow closely the example of their leader in bowing and rising lest
they be thought to pray independently of the group (col. 91A–94A).

next psalm continues. At the end of the Psalmody they sing the Alleluia.

Note that "mental prayer" was thus incorporated in the office itself. This throws light on the Benedictine concept of meditation—not a special exercise. Read {the} *Rule*, chapter 20,[376] and explain in light of this passage from Cassian; also chapter 52 of the Oratory of the Monastery. Admirable simplicity of Benedictine prayer![377]

The discipline of the office:

a) Great silence and attention—no moving around or noise. (Read c. 10.[378])

b) Quantity {is} not the main thing, but *attention* and real prayer: "They consider it more profitable to say short and more frequent prayers [the *orationes* after the psalms] so that by more frequently going to God they may cling more closely to Him"

---

376. "If we wish to prefer a petition to men of high station, we do not presume to do it without humility and respect; how much more ought we to supplicate the Lord God of all things with all humility and pure devotion. And let us be sure that we shall not be heard for our much speaking, but for purity of heart and tears of compunction. Our prayer, therefore, ought to be short and pure, unless it chance to be prolonged by the impulse and inspiration of divine grace. In community, however, let prayer be very short, and when the superior has given the signal let all rise together" (McCann, 69).

377. "Let the oratory be what its name implies, and let nothing else be done or kept there. When the Work of God is finished, let all go out in deep silence, and let reverence for God be observed, so that any brother who may wish to pray privately be not hindered by another's misbehavior. And at other times also, if anyone wish to pray secretly, let him just go in and pray; not in a loud voice, but with tears and fervour of heart. He, therefore, who does not behave so, shall not be permitted to remain in the oratory when the Work of God is ended, lest he should, as we have said, be a hindrance to another" (McCann, 119).

378. This chapter, entitled "*Quanto silentio et brevitate orationes apud Aegyptios colligantur*" ("On the silence and brevity with which collect prayers are made among the Egyptians"), declares that such silence prevails when the Egyptian monks assemble for prayer that one would not know anyone is present other than the one chanting the psalm or offering the prayer; there is no sound other than an occasional involuntary sigh from a monk moved by fervor of spirit. Anyone who does cough, yawn, or make other unseemly noises is doubly blamed for praying carelessly and for disturbing his brothers. To avoid distractions and demonic attacks the monks conclude their prayers quickly, and prefer short and frequent prayers (col. 97B–99A).

(99). *Non enim multitudine versuum, sed mentis intelligentia delectantur* (100).[379]

c) The psalmody is slow—hence the senior bangs on the seat and makes them all rise up for an oration if they start going too fast (101).

After the night office: They work alone in their cells, in the dark (weaving etc. can be done in the dark) because they believe that work is of great value to the life of prayer (102). They do not return to bed, but work and meditate until daybreak. The reason is:

a) so as not to lose the grace and fervor acquired during the psalmody;

b) *so as not to lose the clarity of mind* which is now theirs and which would go away if they fell asleep.

In their work and prayer they remain quiet in their cells and preserve their stability and peace and recollection, avoiding useless and harmful thoughts and guarding their hearts against the attacks of the enemy. They do not waste time talking together, but go at once to their cells to work and pray alone and in complete silence (105). (These are the cenobites, not the hermits.)

Other matters: No one should pray with an excommunicated monk. The bellringers—should be vigilant and observant—know the course of the stars in order to awake the brethren at the right time (109).

Book 3—Day Hours

He says he will deal with Tierce, Sext and None as said in Palestine and Mesopotamia since in Egypt they are recited privately during work and not publicly. The only offices recited publicly in Egypt on weekdays are *Nocturns* and *Vespers*. On Sundays there is also the Eucharist at Tierce. {There is} no mention of Prime and Compline which do not yet exist. Tierce—commemorates the coming of the Holy Spirit; Sext—the Crucifixion of Our Lord; None—the Descent of Christ into hell,

379. "For they are delighted not by the large number of verses but by the comprehension of the mind" (c. 11).

liberating those held captive there. Lauds—was "recently" instituted at Bethlehem to prevent too many monks from returning to bed (c. 4). Chapter 7—penances for those late to Little Hours—{is the} source of St. Benedict's *Rule*, chapter 43.[380]

Book 4—De Institutis Renuntiantium[381]

This book deals with the reception of novices and their formation in preparation for monastic profession (*renuntiatio*). He begins with the *conditions* on which the novices are received. His treatment is based on information from the Egyptian cenobia which he knew and also from Tabenna, which he had not visited. He speaks of Tabenna as a monastery where 5000 monks obey their one abbot with more perfection during their whole lives than one can persuade one monk (in France) to obey for a short time. He also stresses their *perseverance in humility and subjection* all their life long. This is not sufficiently realized by monks: it is a great perfection to retain *all one's life* the humility and docility one had as a novice. The precise point of this book is not merely to describe the observances and methods of formation, but rather more precisely to explain the extraordinary perseverance and humility and obedience of these monks—what formation has made such perfection possible (152). It must indeed be built on a very firm foundation.

Chapter 3—The examination of the candidates. (Read this chapter.[382]) He must wait ten days or more at the gate before even being admitted. This is required as a proof of his serious intention of entering, of his humility and of his patience: some

---

380. This chapter prescribes that any monk arriving at the Night Office "after the *Gloria* of the ninety-fourth psalm, which we wish for this reason to be said very slowly and deliberately," is not to take his proper place but stand apart and do public penance after the completion of the Office; a similar regulation governs anyone arriving after the conclusion of the first psalm for any of the Day Hours (regulations for those arriving late for meals are also found in this chapter) (McCann, 103, 105).

381. "On the Institutes of Those Professing Renunciation."

382. This chapter, entitled "*Quo examine probatur, qui in coenobia suscipiendus est*" ("On the testing which one who is to be received into the monastery undergoes") (col. 154A–156A) is summarized by Merton in the passage that follows.

indication that he has a genuine vocation and will persevere. He is to be spurned by the brethren and treated as if he were coming to the monastery to seek an easy life and evasion of responsibility. Insults will show how he will later stand up under trials. The man who reacts with hostility, becomes mean and revengeful, will not be a truly obedient monk. (Note the great importance, in monastic life, of *really* overcoming and sacrificing our touchiness, our demands for affection and consideration, so that we may be able to get along without the consolations required by a child.) It is to be carefully ascertained whether he has really renounced all that he possesses, for if he still retains something, even a small coin, he cannot be admitted (155). For in time of trial he will fall back on what he possesses and leave the monastery. It is important to determine whether the postulant really seeks to cast himself entirely on the care of God— burning all his bridges behind him. (Note differences in modern discipline: cf. Canon Law, etc.[383])

Chapter 4—The monastery refuses to take any money from the postulant—to prevent him from thinking the monks indebted to him, or thinking himself important or necessary to the monastery (cf. St. Benedict[384]); to prevent also a spirit of pride which would drive him to "sacrilege" in seeking to take back what he had given (157).

Chapter 5—(Read.)[385] Hence the candidate is stripped of everything, even of his clothes, in the presence of the brethren. (NOTE—this throws light on our ceremony for the novice-habit.[386])

383. Cf. Canons 538–86, "Admission into a Religious Institute," of the 1917 Code of Canon Law, in John A. Abbo and Jerome D. Hannan, eds., *The Sacred Canons: A Concise Presentation of the Current Disciplinary Norms of the Church*, 2 vols., 2nd revised ed. (St. Louis: Herder, 1960), 1:534-602.

384. Benedict has a different attitude toward this matter; cf. c. 58: "If he possess any property, let him either give it beforehand to the poor, or make a formal donation bestowing it on the monastery" (McCann, 133).

385. This chapter, entitled *"Cur hi, qui renuntiant, suscepti in monasteriis propria vestimenta deponant, et ab abbate aliis induantur"* ("Why those who are making renunciation put aside their own clothes upon being received into monasteries, and are clothed by the abbot in other garb") (col. 158A–159A), is summarized and quoted by Merton in the passage that follows.

386. See *Regulations*, 4–5 (nn. 8–10): "On the day when a postulant is to receive the holy habit, the wardrobe-keeper takes the habit to the Chapter room

By this he shall know not only that he is stripped of all he used to possess, but that he has put aside all the pomp of the world and has *descended to the poverty and indigence of Christ . . . to be supported by the holy and loving gifts of the monastery,* in order to carry on his campaign for sanctity, *knowing that he has nothing, but will be fed and clothed by the community.* And he should take no care for the morrow, nor should he blush to be numbered among the poor, that is to say, joined to the body of the brethren, whom Christ deigned to number among His brothers and indeed whom He joined as their servant (159).

{Here is} a rich text for meditation: humility, poverty, dependence, supernaturalized by union with Christ in the mystery of His Incarnation.

Chapter 6—His former garments are kept by the cellarer during the time of his probation. If he perseveres in his first fervor, his clothes are given to the poor. But it is to be carefully observed whether he has the right spirit—*He does not have it if he is a murmurer or if he commits the slightest fault against obedience.* In these cases the postulant is immediately dismissed. This provides the background for St. Benedict's *Rule,* chapter 58, lines 10–13.[387]

Chapter 7—Postulancy—He is not immediately united to the community, but turned over to a "senior" living outside the gate. He receives his formation for a year in the guest house.

---

and places it on a table between the Abbot's seat and that of the Prior. . . . The Abbot puts on a white stole and blesses the habit. The postulant, meanwhile, at a sign from the Father-Master, kneels down, and after the blessing of the habit, goes and kneels before the Superior, who, being seated and uncovered, clothes him, assisted by the Father-Master and the wardrobe-keeper. . . . When the postulant's secular clothes are being taken off, the Cantor intones the Canticle "**Benedictus**" on the sixth solemn tone, and the two choirs continue it alternately. . . . If several postulants are receiving the habit, the **Benedictus** is sung more slowly, so that the **Gloria Patri** is not said until the end of the clothing."

387. "Let him be addressed thus: 'Behold the law under which you wish to serve; if you can observe it, enter; if you cannot, freely depart.' If he still abide, then let him be led back into the aforesaid noviciate and again tested in all patience. After the lapse of six months let the Rule be read to him so that he may know on what he is entering. And, if he still abide, after four months let the Rule be read to him again" (McCann, 131).

After that he enters the community and is placed under one of the deans (160).

The spiritual formation of the novice. (Read c. 8.[388]) Chapter 8 says that the principal concern of the spiritual father and the basis of his instruction (*sollicitudo et eruditio principalis*[389]) is to lay a solid foundation for a perfect life. And this solid foundation is TO TEACH THE NOVICE TO OVERCOME HIS OWN WILL IN ALL THINGS (*ut doceat eum primitus suas vincere voluntates*) (160). This is described as the "alphabet of religious perfection." Note the novice does not merely passively abandon his own will but he actively *overcomes* it by a higher principle within himself, that is to say by the action of his will subjected to and united with the Holy Spirit. It is a free constructive action, by which he actively does the will of his spiritual father. How is this done? The spiritual father procures as many occasions as possible for the novice to give up his own will and practice obedience. . . . *haec illi semper de industria imperare procurabit, quae senserit animo ejus esse contraria.*[390]

What is the reason for this? Simply to "break" the will of the junior and make him passive and inert? Not at all. It is to give his will strength in overcoming his passions. For the passions gained control of man's reason through the disobedience of Adam to God. As regards the "judgement"—the young monk must learn that when he is not able to see things in any other way than *his* way, he is seriously handicapped. One who can only see things his own way is not really capable of being a monk, because he is not capable of genuine obedience. The purpose of obedience to a Spiritual Father is to retrain our will and our spirit, subjecting them to grace, so that we in our turn may gain control of our baser passions. *Multis quidem experimentis edocti tradunt, monachum, et maxime juniores, ne voluptatem quidem con-*

---

388. This chapter, entitled "*Quibus primum institutis juniores exerceantur, ut ad superandas omnes concupiscentias proficiant*" ("On the customs by which the juniors are initially trained so that they may become proficient in overcoming all sinful desires") (col. 160B–161A), is summarized and quoted by Merton in the passage that follows.

389. Col. 160B.

390. Col. 160C (which reads ". . . *semper imperare de industria* . . ."): "[the spiritual father] will always purposely take care to order [the novice] to do things that he considers to be opposed to [the novice's] way of thinking."

cupiscentiae suae refraenare posse, nisi prius mortificare per obedientiam suas didicerint voluntates (160–161).[391]

Note that this primacy given to obedience makes the ascetic life more objective and our asceticism more *sane* and *effective*. Instead of battling with our will to dominate each feeling and passion that arises within us, we submit our will to the will of God expressed by another man, and in renouncing our self-love *we renounce all our evil desires at once in their cause and root*. Instinctual movements will still arise but they are indifferent and harmless in themselves.

Everything then depends on our ability to overcome our own will by obedience—not only chastity, but also our conquest of the other vices, our perseverance in the monastic life, our acquisition of true humility: "Therefore they [the Fathers] declare that it is impossible to overcome anger, or spiritual sadness, or the spirit of fornication, and that one can neither preserve true humility or firm and lasting concord with the brethren, nor can one remain long in the monastery, if one has not first learned to overcome his own will" (161). Hence the tremendous importance of obedience in the *Rule* of St. Benedict.[392] Without obedience one can not only not be a true monk, but one cannot even acquire any other solid virtue. The apparent virtues of the disobedient are unsubstantial and illusory and this is proved in the long run. The root of all sin is still alive and strong in their self-will. Whether artificial humiliations and contradictions are always and in all circumstances to be "procured" is another matter, but inevitably the novice will have to obey in things he does not like, and if he cannot overcome his own will in these things he had better recognize the fact that he has no vocation, since, as St. Benedict says, zeal for obedience is one of the signs of a true vocation.[393]

391. "For taught by many experiences, they maintain that a monk, and particularly younger monks, are unable to rein in even the enjoyment of their own desires unless they have first learned through obedience to mortify their own wills" (text reads *"siquidem"* for *"quidem"*).

392. See c. 5 ("Of Obedience"); c. 68 ("If a Brother be Commanded to Do Impossible Things"); c. 71 ("That the Brothers Be Obedient to One Another") (McCann, 33, 35; 155; 159).

393. Chapter 58, on "The Order of Reception of Brethren," specifies that the novice is to be examined to discover "whether he is zealous for the Work of God, for obedience, and for humiliation" (McCann, 131).

Chapter 9—Openness with the Spiritual Father. This is pre-scribed as *a test of true humility.* False and imaginary humility, says Cassian, is a humility without openness, which shrinks from humiliating self-revelation. Also remark that it is con-nected with obedience—so that one withholds nothing however intimate and private, under one's own uncontrolled dominion, even one's thoughts. One obeys even in thought. This must be properly understood. The openness demanded by Cassian has two aspects:

1. The revelation of all "evil thoughts" as soon as they pre-sent themselves—nullas penitus cogitationes prurientes in corde perniciosa confusione celare, *sed confestim ut exortae fuerint, eas suo patefacere seniori. . . .*[394]

2. The docile acceptance of his judgement in their regard—*nec super earum judicio quidquam suae discretioni committere, sed illud credere malum vel bonum quod discusserit ac pronuntiaverit senioris examen.*[395]

If these two are faithfully kept, the devil has no chance to de-lude the young monk. "The devil can not otherwise delude and overcome the young monk, except by leading him, through arro-gance or shame, to hide his thoughts. IT IS INDEED A GENERAL AND EVIDENT INDICATION THAT A THOUGHT COMES FROM THE DEVIL IF WE ARE RELUCTANT TO REVEAL IT TO OUR SPIRITUAL FATHER" (162). Cass-ian stresses the importance of making known all our evil tenden-cies. He anticipates the modern awareness of {the} therapeutic value of getting things out. Certain directors harm souls by *sever-ity* in dealing with mere tendencies. Indeed gentleness and understanding are most helpful and a wise father will always display these qualities. The devil often makes us fear *severity* without cause, to deprive us of *mercy*. Behind Cassian's doctrine is the belief that if in our thoughts we do not obey the Spiritual

394. Col. 101B: "not to conceal deep within their heart any impure thoughts out of a harmful embarrassment, but immediately, as soon as they have arisen, to make them known to the elder . . ."
395. Col. 101B: "and in making a judgement on such things not to entrust anything to their own discretion, but to believe that to be bad or good which the examination of the elder has probed and evaluated."

Father then we are in danger of obeying an evil spirit. What choice is to be made in such a situation?

Chapter 10—Obedience in all things:

a) The junior does not even go out of the cell without permission of the Father—nor satisfy the needs of nature.

b) All that is commanded the junior hastens to fulfil as if it came from God Himself.

c) The junior even attempts to do the impossible, when it is commanded by the Father, rather than doubt his command.

d) Clothing is changed when the Senior, seeing they need clean clothes, gives out a change of garments. Reference is made to their sparing diet (c. 11).

e) Promptitude in obeying the first signal to go to prayer, so that if one is writing and he hears the signal, he stops in the middle of a character he is tracing.

"They believe that obedience is more important not only than manual labor, or reading, or silence in the cell, but also prefer it to all other virtues, so that they believe *that all else is to be placed after obedience*, and they are willing to suffer any other loss rather than risk the slightest trace of violation in this regard" (166). Note the emphasis is always on obedience to a living and concrete *man* rather than to an abstract *rule*.

Chapter 14—Poverty—They cannot call anything their own. The few things that they have for their use, are given them by the monastery. Each monk has "*colobion, mafortes*, sandals, *melotes* and a rush-mat, or *psiathium*," corresponding to the *matta* of St. Benedict, chapter 55 (used to *sit on* in meditation, or to sleep on).[396] The proceeds from their work go to the monastery and no one desires to have more than the daily ration of two small loaves, on account of his greater earnings. "Thus they consider themselves strangers and as it were pilgrims, guests and servants of the monastery *rather than masters of anything*" (170). Essence of poverty {is} renunciation of *dominium*.[397] Cassian here comments on the lack of poverty in French monasteries—(c. 15): "each

---

396. *Rule*, c. 55: "For bedding, let this suffice: a mattress [*matta*], a blanket, a coverlet, and a pillow" (McCann, 127).

397. "lordship, mastery, control."

one carrying around his own keys," with rings for sealing private documents. "We need not only a small box or basket, but crates and trunks to contain the things we have brought with us from the world." The French monks "shake with indignation" if another so much as touches the things given them for their use (171).

Chapter 16—Penances {include} public accusation for breaking even smallest objects; full prostration for coming late to office, or giving out a psalm wrongly. Penances also for: murmuring, being slow to obey, slow to return to cell after prayer, holding hands with a brother, talking with one who does not live in {the} same cell, laziness at work through preference for reading, writing notes without permission—not to mention far worse faults ("seldom committed in Egypt"[398]) of quarreling, familiarity with woman, avarice, eating between meals, etc.

Chapter 17—Origin of Reading in Refectory. Reading in refectory did not originate in Egypt, says Cassian. The silence of the Egyptian monks at table was perfect. (This eating in silence is regarded by him as the ideal.) Reading originated among the Cappadocians, not so much for the sake of giving good spiritual ideas as for the sake of preventing worse things from happening— "to prevent useless and idle talk and above all to put a stop to arguments which so easily arise when people are eating together."[399] He says the Cappadocians found no other remedy than to introduce reading. He adds that the Egyptians eat in great recollection with their cowls pulled down so low over their eyes that they see no one else.

Chapter 18—The Egyptians, he avers, thought it a sacrilege to eat (between meals) an apple fallen from a tree in the orchard— not only because of gluttony but because of the religious principle that the monk receives everything from God through his superiors. This principle of faith is uppermost (178).

Chapter 19—How the servants of the refectory succeed each other weekly—the care they take of the vessels in their charge, etc. They also take great care in their charity to prepare the food well for the brethren ({cf. the} story {in} c. 21 of Palestinian monks

---

398. This phrase is not found in chapter 16.
399. Col. 175A.

going far into the wasteland to find wood for kitchen fire when none was available[400]).

Read—*Chapter 20*[401]—great attention to the smallest things— out of faith—but avoid a pharisaical and scrupulous attitude. Keep sense of perspective.

Chapters 23 ff.—edifying stories of obedience and humility: Abbot John received the gift of prophecy in reward for his perfect obedience. He served his Spiritual Father faithfully from youth to mature age, so that the Father was in "stupor" at his obedience. He is the one who watered the dry stick. (Carried the water 2 miles each day!?) Dispositions with which he obeyed: "*sine ulla permutatione vultus, vel rationis discussione*";[402] after a year, the Father said, "Well, has that stick taken root yet?"[403] John said he didn't know. Father kicked it over and that was the end.

Chapters 30 and 31 relate the humility of Abbot Pinufius, who fled to Tabenna where he was not recognized and was admitted as the least of the novices, an old man of the world who had embraced the monastic life "when he could no longer gratify his passions."[404] {N.B.} his great meekness, working in the garden under the command of a junior brother, the consternation of the monks when his true identity is revealed (for his name is famous) {and} his subsequent flight to Palestine, again in the desire to be unknown and the last of all.

Chapters 32 ff.—*The Address of Abbot Pinufius to a novice receiving the habit.* Summary of his points:

1. Great glory is given to those who are faithful in the monastery but those who are tepid will be punished, so that it is better

400. Col. 181A–182A.
401. This chapter tells the story of a monk who inadvertently dropped three lentils on the ground when he was on kitchen duty; the lentils were found by the monastery steward, who reported the monk's carelessness to the abbot, and the monk was given a public penance. The point of the story is that even the most insignificant things in the monastery are considered to belong to the Lord, and therefore are to be treated with the greatest care and reverence.
402. Col. 184C: "without any alteration of expression or discussion of the purpose of it."
403. Col. 184C.
404. Col. 191B.

to stay in the world than to lead a mediocre life in the monastery. It is therefore a great responsibility to *admit* one to the monastery not being sure if he is really serious.

2. Hence the monk must consider carefully why he has left the world. He must consider what is the nature of renunciation, and the means to renounce himself.

3. Renunciation *"nihil aliud est quam crucis ac mortificationis indicium."*[405] (*Read* chapter 34.[406]) Renunciation here means monastic profession and all the sacrifice it implies. To live in the monastery is then to live crucified to the world—*"sub crucis sacramento"*[407] (195). But how can one live "constantly crucified"? What does this *mean?* (*Read* chapter 35.[408])

4. This "sacrament" is made effective in our lives by the fear of God. *"Crux nostra timor Domini est."*[409] And he continues, "Just as one crucified no longer has the power to move his limbs where he wills, so too we are no longer able to move our wills and desires to what pleases and attracts us, but only according to the will and law of God."[410]

5. As one dying on the Cross has his eyes fixed on death which will end his torments, so we in the monastery have our eyes fixed on heaven which will be our reward.

6. We must therefore take care that we do not return, with our desires, to the things that we have left, to the cares of the world and to attachment to our family, etc. And in order to crush the serpent's head and live in the poverty and humility of Christ

405. Col. 194B (which reads ". . . *est aliud* . . ."): "is nothing else than the outward sign of the cross and of mortification."

406. Col. 194B–195B: The rest of chapter 34 emphasizes that the life of monastic renunciation is a participation in Christ's passion, dying to this world and to sinful desires in conformity with Paul's call in Galatians to be crucified to the world (6:14) and with his assertion that "it is no longer I who live but Christ who lives in me" (2:20), and in obedience to Christ's call to take up one's cross and follow Him.

407. "beneath the sacrament of the cross."

408. This chapter, entitled *"Quod crux nostra timor Domini sit"* ("That the fear of the Lord is our cross") (col. 195B–196B) has been translated above (p. 122, n. 326), and is summarized and partially translated by Merton in the following passage.

409. Col. 195B: "The fear of the Lord is our cross."

410. Col. 195B–196A.

we must observe those first movements of evil desire and make them known to the Spiritual Father.

7. "Therefore, going forth to serve the Lord, prepare thy soul not for rest, not for security, not for delights, but for temptations and anguish."[411] When one has contempt for the world, he does not fear the loss of anything. Then he is truly *humble* and his humility is proved by the following *signs.*

8. The degrees of humility are as follows:

a) The mortification of all our desires;

b) The manifestation of all our acts and thoughts to the Spiritual Father;

c) To do nothing by our own judgement but in all to submit our judgement to the Spiritual Father;

d) In all things to be obedient and meek and constant in patience;

e) Do no injury to anyone and to accept injuries without sadness;

f) To do nothing that is not indicated by the common rule or the examples of the seniors (same wording as St. Benedict[412]);

g) To be content with everything that is lowest (*omni vilitate*)[413] and to do what one is commanded considering himself an unworthy and useless servant;

h) Not only to call oneself the worst of all but to believe in one's inmost heart that it is so (same wording as St. Benedict[414]);

i) To restrain one's tongue and not to be a loud-speaker;

j) Not to be *facilis et promptus in risu*[415] (cf. St. Benedict[416]). Ten degrees in all. And he adds that when one has ascended these ten one arrives at the charity of God which casts out fear. Obviously St. Benedict modeled himself on this in Chapter 7.

9. The monk must seek his counsel and model not in many but in few or one only.

---

411. Col. 198A (c. 38, citing Ecclesiasticus 2:1).

412. Eighth degree: "*si nihil agat monachus nisi quod communis monasterii regula vel majorum cohortantur exempla*" (McCann, 46).

413. Col. 199A: "for every lowliness."

414. Seventh degree: "*si omnibus se inferiorem et viliorem non solum sua lingua pronuntiat, sed etiam intimo cordis credat affectu . . .*" (McCann, 44).

415. Col. 199B: "quick and ready for laughter."

416. Tenth degree (McCann, 46).

10. Three counsels for perfection (chapter 41—evidently influenced St. John of the Cross in his *Cautions and Counsels*[417]).

a) To be blind and deaf to everything that does not edify—just not to see it;

b) To receive injuries and insults without replying;

c) Never to criticize or to analyze the commands of superiors but to carry them out in simplicity knowing that this is good for you.

11. Finally the monk must never make his perseverance depend on others—for instance it is not enough merely to persevere if he is not troubled by others—he must not depend on "not being troubled"[418] (outside) but on the virtue of patience (within himself).

12. The summary of the way of perfection (c. 43) has already been given above, in the narrative of Cassian's life (page {122–23}).

Instituta Book 5—De Spiritu Gastrimargiae (The Spirit of Gluttony)

{This is} the first of the books treating of the struggle against the eight principal vices. In exploring these vices he seeks first of all to know their *nature*, then their *causes*, and finally the *remedies* for them—a very logical approach, though Cassian is not strictly systematic. Too often in our struggle for virtue, we pay no attention to the hidden causes of vice: we simply oppose passion as passion, and ignore the roots of deordination which makes our passion become sinful. The knowledge of self and of the remedies for sin was one of the keystones of the asceticism of the Desert. Ascetic practice was of no value unless it was based on a genuine knowledge of the state of affairs—not just on vague feelings and premonitions of guilt. Note also that this knowledge had to be applied by a Spiritual Father; no one presumed to be his own director. When one was mature in the spiritual life, when the eight vices had been brought under complete con-

417. For the first counsel, see the *Caution* 3 against the world, and *Counsels*, 2 (*Complete Works*, III:201–202, 207); for the second, see the *Caution* 1 against the flesh, and *Counsels*, 3 (204, 208); for the third, see *Caution* 2 against the devil (203). N.B. there is some similarity here but it is not so strong as to demonstrate clearly a dependence upon Cassian.

418. Col. 201 (c. 42).

trol, then one would be directed by the Holy Ghost. He who is not directed by the Holy Ghost or by a Spiritual Father will *necessarily* be at the mercy of his vices, and of the evil spirits, Cassian thought. The inordinate passions exercise a veritable tyranny over the soul as long as we do not know their hidden causes in ourselves. Hence the first thing is, with the help of God's light, to *dispel the ignorance* which leaves us at their mercy (c. 2; col. 204). Note the tremendous importance of insight, self-knowledge. Good will, without knowledge, leads to disaster.

Cassian explains his aim: "We wish to penetrate the abysmal darkness of vice with the pure eyes of the soul, and lay this darkness bare and bring forth the vices to light. We wish to make known their causes and nature to those who are still bound by them as well as to those who have them not. And thus, according to the prophet, we will pass through the fires of vice which most dreadfully burn our souls, and enter immediately into the waters of virtue which extinguish those fires, and thus pass on unharmed, refreshed by spiritual remedies, and merit to be brought at last by purity of heart to the delights of perfection" (204).

Cassian *begins with fasting.* Start with control of the belly— the earliest, most obvious and most elementary passion. The passion of infancy! Today we have lost a real sense of the importance of fasting. If we do not know how to fast, according to our strength, we will *lack a realistic spiritual life* right from the start. Interior mortification is not the whole story, however; discretion is also necessary.

Chapter 4—The proximate preparation for the treatment of gluttony: *discretion in imitating the example of others*. It is true that St. Anthony imitated the good he saw in all the other ascetes, when he began his ascetic life. This venerable tradition is quoted with approval (207–208). Yet nevertheless, in the Mystical Body of Christ all do not have the same part to play and the same function. There is one end for all who consecrate themselves to God (*unus religionis nostrae finis*) but there are different ways to that end (*professiones diversae quibus ad Deum tendimus*)[419]—respect

---

419. Col. 209A: "*Quia licet unus religionis nostrae sit finis, professiones tamen diversae quibus ad Deum tendimus.*" ("Granted that there is a single goal of our religious life, there are nevertheless various paths by which we draw near to God.")

for individual needs and attractions and abilities. Hence what
each monk must do is this:

a) He must note those in whom THE VIRTUES OF DISCRETION
AND CONTINENCY ARE OVERFLOWING MOST COPIOUSLY BY THE GRACE
OF THE HOLY SPIRIT.

b) He must not expect to possess in perfection the virtues
of all, but he must strive as far as he can to imitate the good that
is *possible to himself.*

c) And therefore he must strive particularly to imitate those
who possess in high degree *those particular virtues which he himself needs for the fulfillment* of his own vocation (209).
But note the danger—those with misguided zeal and disguised
natural ambitions tend to imitate those with the same fault and
much harm is done by this—hence, be guided by direction!

Chapter 5—APPLICATION—All cannot keep the same rule of
fasting—some are capable of more, others of less (c. 5—see
mimeographed translation[420]). *"Nec robur unum cunctis corporibus
inest."*[421] There must therefore be a different standard as to the
time of eating and the quantity of food, depending on the
strength of each class or even of the individual. *But all must follow a rule of fasting and continency.* He remarks indulgently that
not all can fast for a week, or for three days, or even for two days,
and some, worn out by sickness and old age, are scarcely able to
hold out until sunset before breaking their fast! "Not all are suited
by an insipid dish of watery vegetables, nor are all able to re-
strict themselves to raw herbs. And still others are unable to fast
on dry bread."[422] Some are not filled with two pounds of bread,
others are stuffed when they have eaten a pound or even six
ounces (212–213). But in all of them, there is one standard: they
should not eat so much that they feel that their stomach is stuffed:
in other words, *not to eat to their full capacity* (213). Reason for
fasting and mortification of appetite for food: both the *quality*

---

420. Merton is evidently referring to the translation of selections from Cassian by Augustine Wulff, ocso, of Gethsemani, which includes *Institutes*, Books
2 (cc. 10–14), 4–5 (excerpts), 10 (complete), 11–12 (excerpts); *Conferences*, 1–2
(complete), 5, 9, 10 (excerpts), 14 (complete), 19 (excerpts).
421. Col. 210A: "the same strength is not present in all bodies."
422. Col. 211A–212A.

and the *quantity* of food, when inordinate, tend to blind the heart and dull the spirit, and while fattening the flesh, enkindle the fires of vice (215–216). When the body is too well fed, it cannot be governed by discretion of the mind (217; c. 6). It disturbs the spirit of contemplation, weakens the will and makes the soul vacillating and inconstant. Hence—let us return to the principle— we must eat and drink only what the body *requires for nourishment, and not what the desires of our appetite prompt us to eat, for our own satisfaction.*

Chapter 7—An important chapter for our day: if the weakness of the body requires that we eat more or better food, this is no obstacle to purity of heart, provided that we stick to our principle of not eating merely to satisfy our taste and desire for more and more food. *INFIRMITAS CARNIS AD PURITATEM CORDIS NON OF-FICIT SI HAEC TANTUMMODO QUAE FRAGILITAS CARNIS, NON QUAE VOLUP-TAS EXIGIT, USURPENTUR* (222).[423] Then he adds an important note: many who abstain from solid and good foods, or who try to abstain from food almost entirely, *are more easily overcome by temptation and fall into sin* than those, who taking into account the needs of their body, allow themselves moderate and sufficient nourishment (223). It is therefore not against ascetic principles to eat sufficient good food, and a sufficient quantity, to preserve our bodily health. For what is thus eaten is consumed for the support of the body and does not nourish vice. How are we to be guided in the satisfaction of appetite? He repeats his principle—eat what is sufficient for health, but do not eat to the full satisfaction of your desire for food. (In practice, for the novice, if under obedience he eats everything set before him, he is not "eating according to his own desire" and he fulfils the requirements, but no one should be forced by obedience to stuff himself. In particular cases, it is better to have a better quality, in small quantity, than to stuff with potatoes and bread.)

Chapter 9—The rule of fasting then *depends on each one's conscience*—(of course under *obedience*). He notes that the custom of heavy eating after a long fast does nothing to promote purity of

---

423. Col. 221A–222A: "Bodily weakness does not interfere with purity of heart if only as much food is consumed as bodily weakness, not pleasure, requires."

heart, but only brings on torpor of spirit. It is merely another form of gluttony. MELIOR EST RATIONABILIS CUM MODERATIONE QUOTIDIANA REFECTIO, QUAM PER INTERVALLA ARDUUM LONGUMQUE JEJUNIUM.[424]

Chapter 10—Fasting must be supported by interior virtue, especially by *humility, obedience, compunction,* poverty of spirit that desires no possessions, meekness. We must overcome sadness, vanity and pride. We must keep our hearts free from vain imaginings and think of the presence of God.

Chapter 11—All the vices are interconnected, so that if one does not overcome anger, pride, etc. he cannot overcome lust; so too with gluttony. *It is necessary to overcome gluttony in order to be safe against lust.* This is a familiar truth. (The interconnection of the vices and of the virtues is a familiar theme with Cassian—and one may conclude that though a person may overcome gluttony in eating, the same instinct will very easily satisfy itself in some other vice if he does not at the same time overcome *all* the vices.)

Chapter 13—However, the beginning of the struggle is to overcome the vices of the flesh after which one may go on to conquer those of the spirit. *Oportet nos primum libertatem nostram carnis subjectione monstrare* (228).[425] The man with a full stomach cannot face the battle with interior and more spiritual vices.

Chapter 14—Fasting must be supported at the same time by vigils, holy reading and compunction of heart and interior meditation. Otherwise fasting itself does not become a positive and spiritual value, but remains only negative and relatively sterile. "We will never be able to despise the pleasure of food unless our minds, rooted in divine contemplation, take greater delight in the love of virtue and the beauty of heavenly things" (230). (Note—it is clear from Cassian that our fasting must have a solid positive foundation. It must not be based on a neurotic fantasy or compulsive urges or human respect—a mere desire to compensate for feelings of unworthiness or inferiority in ourselves. Such fasting is not based on virtue and strength but on weakness and dis-

424. Col. 224B–225A: "A reasonable daily allowance of food, taken in moderation, is better than an occasional long and demanding fast."
425. Col. 228B (which reads ". . . *nos quoque primum* . . ."): "We should first demonstrate our freedom by control of the flesh."

guised vice, and it ends in trouble. It must be based on love for God and on a valid estimate of our real condition. Fasting in a word is not to be undertaken by a soul that is imperfectly adapted to reality. One must be able to recognize objectively what he really needs, or else obey a director in this matter.)

Chapter 20—Practical Hints:

1. The first practical rule—the monk sets a time when he shall eat (or the time is set for him by the Rule) and *he takes no food or drink between meals.* A valid practice for us—not drinking between meals, unless there is a real necessity.

2. Fast of the body must be coupled with fast of the soul— fasting from the evil food of anger, detraction, envy. (St. Bernard took this up also.[426]) (See c. 21; 238.) He says, "by detraction we devour our brother" (240)—repeating a thought from the *Verba Seniorum.*[427]

3. Remember that our enemy is not food, which is outside, but self-love which is within us.

4. We must avoid filling our stomach to satiety when eating —but eat enough to sustain our health.

5. We must resist the desire for special and more succulent foods.

6. To presume to fast openly more than custom or tradition indicates, is a sign of vanity and ostentation; so also to neglect common foods and eat other extraordinary things. (Stick to bread, says Cassian.)

7. Charity comes before fasting. The Desert Fathers always broke their fast to entertain a guest (i.e., ate earlier). ({Cf.} c. 25— the hermit who ate six times a day with guests, but took so little

426. See "*Sermo II in Capite Jejunii*" (*PL* 183, col. 173B): "*jujunandum est longe amplius a vitiis, quam a cibis*" ("Fasting should be far more from vices than from food").

427. See *PL* 73, col. 870D (*Verba*, 4:51): "*Dixit* [*Abbas Hyperichius*] *iterum: Bonum est manducare carnem et bibere vinum, quam manducare in obtrectatione carnes fratrum.*" ("Abbot Hyperichius also said: It is better to eat meat and drink wine than to eat the flesh of one's brothers by detraction.") The same saying, with slightly different wording, is also found in another collection included in Rosweyde's *Vitae Patrum* (*PL* 73, col. 786BC), and in the Greek alphabetical collection in *PG* 65, col. 429/430C (Hyperichius 4).

that he was still hungry.) Chapter {27} {relates} the story of the two hermits—one says, "The sun has never seen me eat"; other replies, "It has never seen me angry"[428] (implication).

Chapter 25—Begins a series of chapters with miscellaneous affairs, stories, etc.—some very interesting.

Chapter 29—Abbot Machete—who had obtained by grace the prayer never to fall asleep during spiritual conferences, but as soon as anyone began to detract or speak of vain and worldly things, he immediately fell into a deep slumber.

Chapter 30—Abbot Machete explains his conviction that monks who judge others will certainly fall into the same faults which they have judged in others.

Chapters 33–34—Abbot Theodore—tells them that the way to arrive at the understanding of Scripture is to ignore the commentaries and overcome the vices of the flesh (example of a statement that must be accepted with qualifications!!)

Chapter 35—Abbot Theodore comes to Cassian's cell in the evening and finds him asleep; rebukes him saying "How many there are who remain awake in prayer and embrace God in their hearts, and here you are sleeping."[429]

Chapter 36—The hermits on the sand bars of Diolcos. They visit Diolcos, and Abbot Archebius, in his charity, moves out of his cell and gives it to them and builds himself another one. Later more guests arrive and he does the same for them (c. 37).

Chapter 39—Abbot Simeon, from Italy, came to Diolcos. He did not know the language and could do no work—in good faith. A neighbor, in order to get him busy, pretends to have {a} brother in {the} army who needs to read the Bible in Italian—copies Bible in Italian—year's work—gets food etc. and his vocation is saved.

Chapter 40—The two boys who died in the desert rather than eat figs which they were carrying to a sick hermit. Again, an exaggeration which is not true virtue.

---

428. Col. 245BC; Merton cites c. 26.
429. Col. 254A.

Instituta Book 6—DE SPIRITU FORNICATIONIS[430]
(This book is not translated in the *Nicene and Post-Nicene Fathers*.[431])

Chapter 1—The second struggle is that against the spirit of fornication, the longest struggle of all: . . . *longum prae caeteris ac diuturnum* (266).[432] It is a frightful war (*immane bellum*)[433] which by few is finally brought to the state of complete and perfect victory. It starts in man's youth and lasts until all the other virtues are acquired. It is closely connected with gluttony, and the Fathers stress this connection. It attacks on two fronts: (a) in the body; (b) in the mind. On both these fronts it must be met—by fasting and mortification, by *contrition* and *prayer*, by meditation on the Scriptures, combined with *scientia spiritualis* (understanding of mystical sense), by manual labor, all of which must be founded on TRUE HUMILITY—. . . *humilitas vera, sine qua nullius penitus vitii poterit triumphus acquiri* (269).[434]

Chapter 2—The chief remedy against lust: *CUSTODIA CORDIS*.[435] "From the heart proceed adulteries" (Matt. 15). If we guard our heart, we prevent the beginnings from arising. We must indeed fast, he says, but if we place all our hope in fasting and neglect interior custody and do not meditate we cannot be pure. Therefore we must, he says, purify the interior of the dish and cup, so that the exterior may be pure also.

Chapter 3—Another remedy—*solitude: "quies ac solitudo"* (270).[436] Other vices are cured by living with other men in society —for instance our falls into anger, sadness and impatience are, he says, humiliating in society and we are stimulated to rise again more rapidly. But lust may find incentives in social life itself. The purpose of solitude in this connection is to make the

430. "On the Spirit of Fornication."
431. *The Works of John Cassian*, trans. Edgar C. S. Gibson, in Philip Schaff, ed., *A Select Library of the Nicene and Post-Nicene Fathers*, 2nd series, vol. 11 (New York: Christian Literature Co., 1894).
432. "lasting beyond the rest, and ongoing."
433. Col. 267A.
434. ". . . genuine humility, without which absolutely no victory over any vice can ever be gained" (text reads ". . . *poterit umquam* . . .").
435. "guarding of the heart": cf. col. 269A: "*Omni custodia serva cor tuum*" ("Keep your heart under every guard," quoted from Prov. 4:23).
436. "calm and solitude."

mind tranquil and quiet and deliver it from images which incite to passion. Note however that some souls in solitude find that their imagination runs riot, and are better under control in a social life where there is some activity to keep them occupied. (Cassian does not make this last point, however.)

Chapter 4—Continency and chastity: Social life, says Cassian, promotes the virtue of continency. Perfect chastity is more a matter for solitaries. *Chastity*, according to him, is perfect virginity of spirit in which one has gone beyond all impulsions of the flesh, all imaginations and all incentives to sin. Examples—St. John {the} Baptist, St. John {the} Evangelist, Elias, Jeremias, Daniel. One can attain to this virginity of spirit, after having been a sinner, but it is extremely laborious (271). He says that this perfect chastity is very difficult if not impossible when living with other men. *Continency*—is the virtue of those who, though feeling first movements and incentives to sin, resist temptation and do not sin. They conquer, but they are disturbed by the smoke and turmoil of the battle. Main sources of strength for the continent: desire of heaven or fear of hell.

Chapter 5—The necessity of grace. The combat will always be hot and difficult as long as we rely explicitly or implicitly in our own powers. We must trust and hope entirely in the grace of God, while making all the efforts we can ourselves. We cannot overcome without grace.

Chapter 6—But the perfection of chastity is *a very special gift and grace* of God. *Peculiare beneficium Dei ac speciale donum.*[437] "It is beyond the limits of nature not to feel the sting of fleshly infirmity" (275). This special grace makes man most like unto the angels, and true citizens of heaven. The monks especially sought this heavenly liberty and peace.

Chapters 7 ff.—The battle for continency. As athletes in training are not allowed to satisfy their desires, so the man who desires to overcome the lusts of the flesh must mortify all his appetites (cc. 7-8). Above all must we practice interior mortification to preserve *purity of heart* (c. 9). To do this, we must remember how our thoughts are clearly seen by God and His

---

437. Col. 272B–273A: "a particular benefit and special gift of God."

angels (278). Perfect purity of heart is found in those who do not even suffer any movements of concupiscence or see any images in sleep when a pollution occurs. (Pollution occuring in sleep is of course no sin, he declares.) See *Conference* 22 for further information. We must therefore guard our eyes (c. 12) and above all our thoughts (c. 13). He is extremely strict about any thought of woman—even of one's own mother or holy women: these lead quickly to thoughts of others which incite to lust. We must dash all such thoughts against the stones—that is to say stamp them out in their first beginnings. One of the chief means for doing this is to *fill our minds with the Scriptures and arm our wills with the fear of God.* The Fathers are very strict about immediate resistance to the first sign of an impure thought, or of anything that could lead to one.

Chapters 14 ff.—Perfect chastity:

a) The authority of the Apostle praising perfect chastity— "This is the will of God, your sanctification, etc." (I Thess. 4). Other texts from the Apostle showing that the impure cannot see God (c. 16).[438]

b) The more sublime the virtue of perfect chastity, the more difficult to achieve and the greater the obstacles. What we must do—first of all keep continency; then have contrition of heart; prayer with groanings, "that the dew of the Holy Spirit may descend into our hearts and extinguish the furnace which the King of Babylon does not cease to stoke up with carnal suggestions" (288). HUMILITY is the foundation of true chastity (c. 18). "*Spiritualis Scientia*"[439] (contemplation through Scripture) is the reward of perfect chastity.

c) When the soul is perfectly chaste, then, even though pollutions may occur at night, they do so without any dreams or feelings or awareness.

d) To preserve this condition—we must keep up an "*aequale moderatumque jejunium*"[440]—that is to say a fast that is moderate,

438. Actually only one other text, Hebrews 12:14 (col. 287A).
439. Col. 288A, which reads "*scientiam spiritalem*" ("spiritual knowledge"); "*spiritalis*" rather than "*spiritualis*" is the usual reading in Cassian.
440. Col. 292A: "*aequale moderatumque semper tenendum est jejunium*" ("a balanced and moderate fast must be maintained at all times").

but constant: *no extremes*. Extremes and violence in our asceticism perturb the soul and stir up the flesh. Also we must remain
always *humble* and *patient*, and *resist anger*. For the passions are
so connected together that when one is stirred up it arouses the
others. *Ubi enim furoris insidet virus, libidinis quoque necesse est in-
cendium penetrare.*[441] Finally, he concludes that nocturnal vigils
are also very favorable to perfect chastity (292).

Book 7—THE SPIRIT OF AVARICE (*Philargyria*—term taken from
St. Paul[442] and left in the Greek as being stronger.)

He starts out immediately by stating the nature and causes
of avarice. This is one of the texts where Cassian excels in psychological analysis. Its nature—"*amorem pecuniarum*"[443]—love
of money and of possessions in general. "*Pecunia*"—trace origin
of the word—"*Pecunia*" comes from the Latin "*pecus*" meaning
cattle. This sign was the first one used for money in the Roman
Empire. It is an "unnatural vice," because by it a man submits
himself to material and inanimate things which are outside himself and below him. *Peregrinum bellum et extra naturam* (291).[444]
What is its source? *corruptae ac torpidae mentis ignavia*[445]—the low-
ness, smallness, narrowness of a corrupt and inert mind—in fact,
cowardice. The love of possessions {is} a confession of our own
inadequacy—there is nothing in us to be a source of peace and
strength—we place our hope in things outside ourselves—no
courage. {N.B.} importance and depth of this analysis—which has
become almost incomprehensible in our age. Is our materialistic
society one of weak and degenerate souls that have no inner spiritual resources? Perhaps more so than we think. In contemplative
monasteries—when we start going out of ourselves to place our
hope in things that can be bought and sold, we are confessing the
inanity of our interior life. *Si ergo, fratres charissimi, esse divites cupi-
tis, veras divitias amate* (St. Gregory, Office of Sexagesima[446]). An-

441. Col. 292A: "For when the poison of anger takes hold, the fire of lust inevitably enters in as well."
442. I Timothy 6:10.
443. Col. 291C.
444. "a foreign war, outside the natural state."
445. Col. 294C: "the qualms of a corrupt and sluggish mind."
446. *Breviarium Cisterciense* (*Hiems*), 446: "Homily 15 on the Gospels" ("And
so, dearest brothers, if you desire to be rich, love genuine riches").

other important factor—*initio abrenuntiationis male abrepto*:[447] starting off with a "conversion" or gift of self that is not complete —leaving the world without burning all our boats behind us, entering the monastery with conditions. Perhaps the most important factor of all—*erga Deum tepidus amor*.[448] Love of material goods proves lack of love for God. That is why St. Paul compares love of riches to idolatry. See his teaching on labor and poverty. "For we brought nothing into the world, and certainly we can take nothing out; but having food and sufficient clothing, with these let us be content. But those who seek to become rich fall into temptation and a snare and into many useless and harmful desires, which plunge men into destruction and damnation. For covetousness is the root of all evils, and some in their eagerness to get rich have strayed from the faith and have involved themselves in many troubles" (I Tim. 6:7-11). The early Fathers fully realized the seriousness of Christ's teaching on detachment and poverty of spirit. Because property is *legitimate* and even to some extent *necessary* we tend to forget that it can also be dangerous. Is it not true to say that the average American Christian has no longer any consciousness that his love of money and possessions may involve him in serious temptations?

Chapter 2—This vice in itself *is easy to resist* because the seeds of it are not in our nature itself, as for instance gluttony and lust. But unfortunately, once it has been admitted into our souls, it takes a firm hold on them, for the *neglect* to resist it when the struggle is easy makes the difficulty all the greater when it finally takes hold. And when it does take hold on us it becomes a root principle for all other vices—*malorum omnium efficitur radix, multiplices fructificans fomites vitiorum*.[449]

Chapter 3—interesting psychologically. He speaks of the other vices which have their root in a *naturally good instinct*:

447. Col. 292C: "by the beginning of a life of renunciation having been carried out poorly."
448. Col. 292C: "*et erga Deum tepido amore fundato*" ("and by a love of God lukewarm from the start").
449. Col. 293A (which reads "*Malorum namque omnium . . .*"): "For it becomes the root of all evils, producing multiple incitements to vice."

a) Lust—rooted in a good instinct, by which the race is pro-created. And he also observes that infants with no reason and no capacity for lust as we understand it, manifest movements of carnality in this regard—this point has become very important in modern psychiatry.

b) Anger also {is} a good instinct in itself. Even sorrow has a good natural use, and so has fear. So the irascible and concupiscible appetites are necessary to our nature and good. It is not surprising that vices arising from these will be hard to curb.

The general principle (c. 4) is that these appetites are not to be considered as seeds of sin planted in us by God, but as good gifts given us to serve Him with, and which, as the result of the fall, we misuse and turn against Him (294).

Chapter 5—After considering the deviation of good instincts, he turns to the vices which are without root in any good natural appetite but have their origin in the corruption of our will—*solius corruptae ac malae voluntatis arbitrio* (295).[450] These are especially envy and avarice. He repeats that since these are easy to resist in their beginnings, we are all the more enslaved to them if we allow them by our neglect to take possession of our souls. Once we have contracted avarice, he says, the cure is almost impossible. This ought to give us food for thought! It is a hard saying.

Chapter 7—The growth of avarice—(note this does not apply so much in the context of modern religious poverty.)

1. It gains possession of the "slack and tepid soul of the monk."[451] In other words, to resist the beginnings we have to resist negligence, tepidity, and the "natural spirit." In other words, a moderate and alert discipline is sufficient to guard against the beginnings.

2. The first faults—keeping back small sums of money for a "reasonable" cause. (Note the real fault here—substituting our own Providence for God's, lack of spirit of faith and trust, beginning to take care of ourselves—the root-fault which undermines monastic vocations.) The monk argues with himself that *what is given by the monastery is not sufficient*, and that in the fu-

---

450. "by the decision of a corrupt and evil will alone."
451. Col. 296A.

ture, when his health declines, it will be altogether inadequate, above all since the care of the sick in the monastery is very deficient, he thinks.

{3.} The next step—since he will not be taken care of in this monastery, and he cannot fully care for himself, he must provide means to go elsewhere. Thus his mind becomes *ensnared in thoughts* of things that "might happen" and that must be guarded against, and with these thoughts he becomes preoccupied with every possible source of gain—wherever he can get another penny.

4. *Opus peculiare*[452] (cf. *Rule* of St. Benedict, c. 55). The next step after this explains a mysterious term in the *Rule* of St. Benedict—where the Abbot must search the dormitory for *"opus peculiare."* Usual translations of the *Rule* say something vague about "private property."[453] Actually it is something more precise —private *work*, a job undertaken by the monk, without knowledge of the Abbot, to provide for himself money to go elsewhere. State of mind of the monk engaged in this: *He is haunted by worries and distractions*—how to make more money—how to sell his products secretly—where to keep the money safely, etc., etc.— thoughts of investments and speculation (buying something else and selling at a higher price).

5. He is then completely possessed by the *hunger for gold*: the *rabies pecuniae* (297). Cassian compares his soul to a victim in the coils of a serpent. When the sin has him at its mercy, there is nothing he will stop at—he will lie, perjure himself, steal, break promises, give in to anger and hatred—will not stop at any bounds of decency and humility. Gold has become his god, his idol, and he throws everything aside to serve it. (Note, at the present day, in strict monasteries, this would not be altogether possible, literally. But the spirit can easily take possession of a soul—he may not engage directly in clandestine business, but he may be engaged in stealing, in dishonest and irregular communications with friends supposed to help him, etc. The mentality

452. Col. 297A.
453. So McCann, 127, though in his note on this term he writes, after making reference to this passage in Cassian: "Originally it appears to have meant a 'special job of work', by means of which you were able to earn a little money for yourself. From that meaning it passed on to signify the personal property so acquired and to stand for 'private property' or 'private ownership'" (193–94).

is the same, its expression a little different, as our legislation is more strict and precise.)

Chapter 8—Having sunk to these depths, no virtue is any longer possible for the monk—no obedience, charity, humility, etc.

Chapter 9—Cassian asserts that the monk who has money of his own cannot remain in the monastery. He will surely leave. On all sides he is seeking pretexts to justify his departure—he is unjustly treated, if clothes come too slow from the vestiary—the work is badly arranged, and everything that is done is wrong. In the end, he also tries to persuade others to leave with him.

Chapter 10—By this means, the devil separates him from the flock and makes ready to devour him. Ironically, now the one who refused to do even light work for the monastery is giving himself day and night to immense labors for his own profit. Prayer, fasting and everything else is set aside in order to make money.

Chapter 11—Oftentimes, they become involved with women in their business dealings and this makes their fall all the more certain.

Chapter 14—Having exhaustively discussed the causes and the psychology of the spirit of avarice, which is fundamentally rooted in cowardice of soul which cannot abandon itself to God and leave Him to care for it, he now goes on to discuss various kinds of avarice.

1. Those who entered the monastery with little or nothing, learn in the monastery to acquire wealth and possessions which they never knew before—like Giezi, the servant of Eliseus.

2. Those who having renounced all, turn back and desire to recover what they have given up—like Judas.

3. Those who in the very beginning are deceitful, and do not renounce all but keep some back, like Ananias and Sapphira. (Note that in each instance the culprit "lies to the Holy Ghost."[454])

Chapter 15—Scripture—an illustration from Deuteronomy 20:8—before a battle, the scribes of Israel were to proclaim that certain categories were to withdraw—the man who was build-

454. Peter's words to Ananias in Acts 5:3, but not used by Cassian.

ing a new house, a man who had just planted a vineyard, a man about to be married, and the man who is afraid. "If there is one among you who is frightened and has panic in his heart, let him return and go back into his house, lest he cause his brothers to grow faint as he himself is faint with fear." Cassian's application: it is better not to attempt renunciation of all, frankly admitting one does not mean business, than to take back what one has given—(as someone else has said—to place the victim on the altar and then weep when it is consumed). It is better not to make a vow than to make one, then infect others with faintheartedness and tepidity, withdrawing also the substance of *their* gift from the altar. Throughout one's whole religious life one must firmly cling to a spirit of simple faith and avoid hesitation, double-mindedness and fear—we cannot serve God and Mammon (Matt. 6), and the "double-minded man is inconstant in all his ways" (James 1). {N.B.} importance of this principle, from the psychological point of view. So much trouble, in religious orders, comes from this unconscious duplicity, which makes our life a pretense and a sham, although we manage to salve our conscience and create for ourselves a multitude of pretexts for evading our gift of self. Note, the way in which we create alibis for ourselves—is not merely by glossing over weakness with excuses, but also by living in such a way that there is much *apparent zeal* and generosity, directed however to something that does not matter while the really important things are forgotten. Our zeal for the non-essential is thought to justify our lives, and to excuse the evasion of the essential. Cassian goes on to give examples of those who pervert the Scriptures to justify their avarice. "It is more blessed to give than to receive"—therefore one must possess money, etc.

Chapter 17—Our models—the Apostles, and especially Paul. . . . *pro Christo gloriosam cum Apostolo suscipere nuditatem* (308).[455] The Apostles did not have riches to share with the poor. They worked for their own living and then, in addition, asked the faithful to send money to the poor in Jerusalem. They did

---

455. "for the sake of Christ to undergo with the Apostle a praiseworthy nakedness." (This passage actually comes at the end of c. 16.)

not have any surplus to share themselves. How are we to imitate them?

Chapter 18—"Let us not rest in our own judgements and decisions, promising ourselves that by our tepid and miserable condition we shall reach evangelical perfection: but let us follow the footsteps of the apostles, and let us not in the least deceive ourselves but let us all together seek to observe the discipline and the rules of the monastery so as thereby to renounce this world in truth. Let not lack of faith lead us to retain any of those things which we have despised. Rather let us gain our living not by hidden funds but by our own labor" (312).

Chapter 19—St. Basil's remark to Syncleticus, the Senator,[456] who left the world but kept some funds to live on. *Senatorem perdidisti et monachum non fecisti* (312).[457]

The struggle for poverty (cc. 20 ff.):

1. The monk must *not possess* the smallest piece of money. (Note that Cassian is speaking here always against money first of all—against possessions that can be made "liquid" rather than goods that can be consumed.) (Money is the blood of that mystical person, the world.)

2. The monk must also get rid *of all interior desire* to have any money.

3. In order to overcome the spirit of avarice and desire of money, the monk renounces *all possessions* and embraces "nudity." This is interesting, a point we overlook in our day. The end—purity of heart which has no stain of desire for money, which is essential to the worldly spirit. The means—renouncing all possessions and being content with nothing, or with the poorest of all things given for our use. But this is not poverty in itself.

4. Faith and resolute determination to go forward trusting in God to take care of us: refusal to look back, or to allow fear for our future to weaken our spirit of trust. These are essential

456. O. Chadwick ([1968], 45) suspects that this is an interpolation, since "syncleticus" is not a proper name but the Greek term for "senator," a mistake Cassian himself would not have made.

457. "*Et senatorem, inquit, perdidisti, et monachum non fecisti.*" ("'You have lost the role of senator,' he said, 'but have not gained that of monk.'")

to the perfect spirit and practice of poverty—they are at once the best means and the fruit of poverty.

5. Fear the punishment given to prevaricators—Ananias and Sapphira, Judas.

6. Practice perfect patience, based on humility. Without this patience, poverty is insupportable. Note again the radical importance of humility. Everything depends on it (c. 31).

7. The norm of monastic poverty: to be content with enough food to live on and enough clothing to cover our nakedness (cf. II Tim. 6).

Instituta 8—On the Spirit of Anger

Anger is a deadly poison that must be drawn out completely from the inmost recesses of our soul (c.1; 322). Cassian's emphasis is on the *completeness* with which we must overcome anger. It lurks like a murderer in the depths of our heart, blinding our reason with evil darkness.

Its effects (c. 1; 323):

a) Makes it impossible for us to gain judgement and discretion;

b) Makes purity of heart and contemplation impossible (as do all the vices);

c) Prevents us from possessing maturity of counsel;

d) Makes us incapable of true spiritual life, of justice, and of seeing the true light of God;

e) It debars us from eternal life;

f) But it also deprives us of natural social graces, makes us boorish and rough;

g) The angry man can have no peace;

h) He will scarcely ever be free from sin.

Chapter 2—Against those who say anger is justified, and that we must exercise wrath against tepid and irregular brethren in order to correct them. They quote Scripture to show that in this man can be like God, Who vents His wrath upon sinners. In arguing thus, Cassian says, "These men do not understand that while they are opening the way for men to practice a detestable vice they are at the same time blaspheming the immensity of

God, the Fount of all purity, by defiling Him with carnal passion" (325).[458] An important point: monks are prone to bitter zeal, as St. Benedict saw (*Rule*, c. 72[459]) and they unconsciously imagine that God is like themselves—angry in the same way, with the same imperfection. They have made for themselves a God in their own image, to justify their own imperfection. Note that the Desert Fathers were prone to anthropomorphism.

Chapter 3—Scripture is not to be taken literally when it speaks of God as angry, any more then when it says He sleeps, or stands, or sits, or walks, etc.—or when it says that He forgets, or does not know certain things.

Chapter 4—So God is not angry in the sense of being moved by passion. *Digne Deo, qui ab omni perturbatione alienus est, sentire debemus* (329).[460] When we speak of God "being angry" we are speaking of the effects of sin, and of the disaster which befalls *us* when we go against His will. But God is not moved to anger within Himself.

Chapter 5—*The meekness necessary for monastic perfection.* St. Paul (Ephesians 4:31: "Let all bitterness, and wrath, and indignation, and clamor, and reviling, be removed from you, along with all malice") proves that Christian perfection demands freedom from anger and impatience. The monk who sincerely desires perfection, says Cassian (330), and who enters with all his heart into the spiritual warfare, must then overcome all anger. *All*—that is to say that *no anger is allowed or excused as justifiable for a monk*. If we correct a brother, we must do so with gentleness and charity, "lest hastening to bring medicine to one with a slight disease, we ourselves become infected with a far worse sickness, becoming blinded by our anger" (333). It is necessary for one who wishes to cure another to be himself free from every sickness (a basic axiom of the Desert Fathers).

458. Col. 325AB.

459. He contrasts "an evil zeal of bitterness which separates from God and leads to hell" with "a good zeal which separates from evil and leads to God and life everlasting," and warns, "Let monks, therefore, exercise this zeal with the most fervent love" (McCann, 159).

460. "We should think of it in a way worthy of God, who is far removed from all emotional upheaval."

Chapter 6—He insists that it does not matter whether our anger has a just cause or not: from the moment we give in to the passion our soul is blinded and it cannot see the light of God. *Is anger ever virtuous?* (c. 7). Since the Psalm says, *irascimini et nolite peccare*,[461] there is a virtuous anger. This is the anger with which we extinguish the movements of concupiscence in our own souls. An example: the holy indignation with which David rebuked his followers when they wanted to kill Semei for cursing him. Anger here {is} used as an instrument of meekness and humility. Read: II Kings 16:4-12. Note the dispositions of David: perhaps not perfect, but at least they look good. Then Read II Kings 19:18-23. However this was not real kindness but only a sort of superstition. Semei is finally killed by Solomon (III Kings 1:8-9, 36-46). Hence God wills anger, when it is directed against ourselves and our passions. The effect of this anger is the avoidance of sin. Traditionally, we may not be able to get rid of anger at once, but *at least before the end of the day* (c. 10).

Hidden anger is also a sin (c. 12). There are some who restrain their anger not because they are meek and virtuous, but because they are afraid to put it into effect—*non appetitu placiditatis, sed inopia ultionis* (341).[462] They do not burst out into open anger, but treat the ones who offend them with coldness and rudeness, denying them the usual affability. But this is not virtue. It is also sin. It is not enough to reduce our anger to a cold, nonviolent form of expression. We must get rid of it, and replace it by charity. Cassian says: "The fury that is held back and pent up under a calm exterior may not offend the men around us but it certainly offends the Holy Spirit" (341). It "excludes the splendor and radiance"[463] of the Holy Spirit. It is very important for monks to realize that in "punishing" their brethren with sour looks and refusing to be polite or kind to them, they are victims of their vice of anger. They restrain their hostility and do not give it open expression not because they do not want to hate, but because they do not want their sin to be observed and manifest. Hence there is in this a kind of hypocrisy—especially when

461. Col. 355A: "Be angry and sin not" (Ps. 4:5).
462. "not from a desire for calmness, but due to lack of ability to avenge."
463. Col. 341B.

this severity towards others is accompanied with righteous feelings of self-complacency and self-congratulation.

On bearing grudges (c. 13). Our Lord does not accept the sacrifice of our prayers if we bear a grudge in our heart. Read Matthew 5:21-26:

> You have heard that it was said to the ancients, "Thou shalt not kill"; and that whoever shall murder shall be liable to judgement. But I say to you that everyone who is angry with his brother shall be liable to judgement; and whoever says to his brother, "Raca," shall be liable to the Sanhedrin; and whoever says, "Thou fool" shall be liable to the fire of Gehenna. Therefore, if thou art offering thy gift at the altar, and there rememberest that thy brother has anything against thee, leave thy gift before the altar and go first to be reconciled to thy brother, and then come and offer thy gift. Come to terms with thy opponent quickly while thou art with him on the way; lest thy opponent deliver thee to the judge, and the judge to the officer, and thou be cast into prison. Amen I say to thee, thou wilt not come out from it until thou hast paid the last penny.

(Very important for *all* Christians, not just monks.)

Chapter 13 has some fine psychology in it. Cassian shows how when we have offended another, instead of admitting our fault we despise and hate him for being offended at us, and blame *him* as if he had done wrong in taking our actions amiss. That is why Jesus commands us to be reconciled if our brother is offended *with us*—and not only that we should pardon those who have offended us. Hence it is necessary that we be reconciled with one another before we go to prayer together, since "The Lord is not pleased by our common prayers if what He gains in one of us He loses in another, who is dominated by sorrow" (343). {N.B. the} importance of the *Pax* before Holy Communion. Hence if our brother has something against us our prayer is of little worth, just as if we ourselves were angry with him.

Projection (c. 14): here again Cassian manifests his psychological finesse. He discovers the mechanism of "projection" by which we place on others the blame for our own faults, impatience, etc. in order to rationalize these faults and overlook them.

We blame our defects on the vices of others, and thus prevent ourselves from making any progress in virtue—a most important observation. Hence, as a remedy, he says (c. 16) that our virtue must depend on our own efforts and not on the virtues of others, for the souls of others are not under our control. But our own souls are in our own power, and we ought to do something about controlling them!

True and false love of solitude. This leads naturally to the delusion of those who want to change their Order or go into solitude, as a result of their projection of their own weaknesses upon the community or the brethren. Far from being ready for solitude, such souls are weak in virtue. Only the perfect can rest assured that their desire of solitude is based on a true love of contemplation rather than on pusillanimity. For those who go into solitude without being perfect not only do not get away from their vices, but become more deeply enmeshed in them (345). It is an illusion to think oneself patient and meek when he is not tried by any adversity. Such men, as long as they are alone, behave themselves. But as soon as they have the slightest occasion, and find themselves with others, they break out in ferocity (c. 18). Cassian then speaks of hermits flying into a rage with their pen, or their knife, or with the flint that does not immediately produce a spark when they want to read after their night vigils (346).

The struggle against anger (cc. 19 ff.):

1. We must have the right aim: to get anger out of the inmost recesses of our hearts (348). It is not enough to destroy the fruits of anger, we must pull out the roots. For "he who is angry with his brother is a murderer."[464]

2. In order to do this, we must get rid of the idea that there are just causes for anger against the *person* of our brother. Patience does not consist in avoiding unjust anger but in avoiding all anger (351).

3. If we go by these principles, the light of our conscience will not be obscured by the fumes of anger and we will see better

464. Merton actually conflates two scripture verses quoted by Cassian in chapter 19 (col. 348B–349A): "he who is angry with his brother is liable to judgement" (Mt. 5:22) and "anyone who hates his brother is a murderer" (1 John 3:15).

how to avoid it. But we must remember that if we give in to anger, even under {the} guise of justice, we will lose our judgement and will fall into sin.

4. We must never go to prayer without forgiving our brothers from our heart and casting out all rancor, and seeking to be reconciled with those we have offended.

5. We should keep in mind the fact that we may die at any moment and that if we drop dead with a sin of anger on our soul, all our labors, fastings, vigils, and other works will be of no use to us whatever. Read chapter 22:[465] the resolution to root out the vice of anger—not only not being angry "without cause" but not being angry at all.

Instituta 9—ON THE SPIRIT OF SADNESS

Note the intimate but hidden relationship between sadness and anger. What is sadness? What causes it? It is certainly a *sin*. See Clement of Alexandria (*Pedagogue* 1:13:101): "Sadness is a cramping of the soul which disobeys the Logos."[466] The soul closes in on itself and refuses grace and instruction from God. Cassian says sadness "eats out the heart of the monk" (*edax tristitia*) (351)[467]—like a worm in an apple.

Effects (c. 1):

1. If we allow sadness to get the better of us, contemplation and purity of heart become impossible.

2. We may still be able to pray, but only very weakly and ineffectually.

465. This final chapter is numbered 21 in *PL* but 22 in the Petschenig edition (Corpus Scriptorum Ecclesiasticorum Latinorum, vol. 17 [Vienna: Tempsky, 1888]) used in the *Nicene and Post-Nicene Fathers* translation; it is entitled "*Remedia quibus iram de cordibus nostris eradicare possimus*" ("Remedies by which we can root anger out of our hearts") (col. 351A–352B): it notes that anger, whether righteous or not, results in lack of discernment and clear thinking, keeps the soul from being a proper temple for the Holy Spirit, and is an inappropriate state for approaching God in prayer. Anger can make all the efforts of chastity and poverty, fasting and vigils ultimately of no value.

466. This is translated by Wood as "grief, depression of mind disobedient to reason" in *Christ the Educator*, 89; the source of Merton's translation is unlocated.

467. Col. 351B–352B: "*Quinto nobis certamine edacis tristitiae stimuli retundendi sunt*" ("In the fifth contest we must blunt the pang of ravenous sadness").

3. We can no longer apply ourselves to reading. Our sorrow takes up the best of our energy and attention. (Conversely—reading helps to overcome sadness.)

4. We find it difficult, when we are sad, to be pleasant and charitable with our brothers.

5. We frequently offend against patience.

6. We are tepid and murmur when we perform our duties in the monastery.

7. But the chief effect of sadness is that it makes a monk weak and unstable, deprives him of sane judgement, so that he cannot make a decision and stick to it; it drives him to and fro like a drunkard, and in the end brings him to the abyss of despair. He quotes Proverbs 25:20: "As vinegar upon nitre so is he that sings songs to a very evil heart. As a moth doth by a garment, and a worm by the wood, so the sadness of a man consumeth the heart."[468] Hence we must be persuaded that the *struggle against sadness is an essential part of the ascetic life* (353).

Modern ascetic treatises do not bring this out so forcefully. We think sadness is a mood, an emotion, rather than a passion which easily leads to sin. There is a *sin* of sadness. Sometimes instead of trying to react against sadness, we submit passively to it, saying "it is a cross—God wants us to feel that way." No, God does not want us to submit to the sadness which eats the heart out of our virtues and of our interior life. This is a sin. It is a great self-deception to submit to this sadness and feel virtuous over our self-pity. In this sin of sadness lies the mystery that our soul inwardly *desires to feel sad* (even though the sadness is painful and depressing) but we *prefer* the sadness with all its effects, rather than make the constructive efforts that are demanded of us by God. Sadness in the spiritual life comes from preferring what is destructive and negative, and refusing to take positive steps to be constructively good. It is most often generated without any fault on our part, by an unbalanced and defective spirituality—negative sentimentalism and self-pity—a cult of "dolorism"—suffering for its own sake, etc., etc. Above all, then, we must avoid a false and destructive spirituality. Just as moths

468. Col. 353B–354A.

make a garment totally useless, so sadness ruins our spiritual life (c. 3). If we are to build a spiritual temple for the Holy Ghost, we must not use worm-eaten beams and timbers (355).

Causes of Sadness (cc. 4 ff.):

1. As an after-effect of anger. We become sad and discouraged after we have exhibited our temper.

2. As an after-effect of lust or desire for possessions—especially when a vain hope of pleasure or profit has been exploded for us, and we fall back into the poverty and monotony of our miserable little life, which we had hoped to escape from for a moment. (Note this matter of *vain hope* for escape, for "distraction" in Pascal's sense, is at the root of most of our sadness.)

3. The sudden work of the devil, bringing on sadness in a flash without any apparent reason for it. Cassian describes this sadness which we feel when we ought normally to be consoled by the presence of our friends: "By the action of the cunning enemy we are suddenly depressed by so great a sorrow that not even the arrival of our dear ones and those closest to us can inspire us to receive them with our usual affability. The things that arise in the friendly conversation, far from consoling and cheering us, seem to us to be stupid and out of place, and we are absolutely incapable of giving a civil answer, our hearts being filled, even to the most remote corners, with the gall of bitterness" (355). This is a particularly painful form of sadness, in which we feel we are hurting those we love, and seem incapable of doing otherwise. Is the devil the sole cause? Modern psychology would probably find causes within our own nature—a kind of unconscious self-hate, expressing a desire to enjoy perverse suffering or to inflict it on others. Yet at the same time this can clearly be a matter of purification which shows that one is more and more alienated from what used to give consolation. A *division* is set up in the soul. When this division is salutary then sadness is a sign of growth. When division is morbid, then sadness is a vice and an obstacle. Salutary division—separation from what used to please and delight us. Morbid division—rebellion against the reality of our life or its obligations.

4. *The causes of our sadness are not to be sought for in other people, but in ourselves.* Cassian says very graphically: "We have in our-

selves the causes of sin and the seeds of vice, and when the rain of temptation falls upon our souls, these seeds germinate and bring forth immediate fruit" (355; c. 5).

5. Again, the vices of others would not be sufficient cause to produce sadness in us if the seeds of vice were not present in us (c. 6). Therefore we must refuse ourselves the luxury of blaming others for our sadness, and projecting on to them the vices which are in our own soul. This is a luxury because in fact it makes it easier for us to bear our own misery, since we convince ourselves that others are at fault. *It takes real courage to recognize that we ourselves are the cause of our own unhappiness.* And that means that we must make ourselves responsible for changing the sad state of affairs—which is difficult and arduous work. And it takes time.

How to get along with others. Note: today there is an exaggerated preoccupation with "getting along" and "adapting" to common life. People make too much of this, as if we had to be constantly amusing and placating one another. This is not Cassian's attitude. He is simpler and more sane. Cassian now shows that this question of sadness is a matter of social adaptation. The man who cannot get along with others is sad and antisocial. He may rationalize this fault of character as a "virtue" ("love of solitude") but he will do so to his own cost. He must, on the contrary, conquer sadness by learning to get along charitably with other people. Hence the vice of sadness should never lead any one to embrace the life of a hermit (c. 7); this would not be a true solitary vocation.

1. One must firmly make up his mind to get along with others, and realize it is God's will. It is an obligation that cannot be escaped. God has decreed that happiness must depend not on separation from men, but on patience, self-sacrifice in getting along with others; therefore we must fully accept this ordinance of God (359).

2. We must not allow ourselves to be scandalized by frictions and dissentions. When these arise, we must not try to change the exterior situation, but to change our own interior by patience, long-suffering, meekness and peace.

3. Cassian holds as certain that the monk who controls his own emotions and overcomes his passions can live peaceably not only with men but with wild beasts. Hence the obvious importance of overcoming ourselves before we can hope to live in the desert, among wild animals! (c. 8; 357). Note in all this the implicit orientation to an *eventual life of solitude* and not mere "social adjustment."

The worst kind of sadness: A special, and very evil form of sadness is the despair into which we fall if we have committed a sin or a serious fault. This sadness is not only useless but most sinful and displeasing to God—it is the despair of Judas or of Cain (357).

A good form of sadness is contrition of heart after sin—it is the sadness mixed with hope that moves us to change our lives and turn to God, not the death-bringing sadness of the world (II Cor. 7).

How to tell the difference between these two kinds of sadness (c. 11; 358-59). Spiritual sorrow has the following qualities:

1. It produces true penance and firm stability in the interior life.

2. It is obedient.

3. It is affable (cheerful with others, not mad at *them*).

4. {It is} humble (not based on rage against self).

5. It is meek, sweet and patient, impregnated with the charity of God.

6. It seeks hard and painful things for the body and the soul out of love of penance.

7. It is full of joy and hope, and contains within itself all the fruits of the Holy Spirit (Gal. 5).

Worldly sorrow, on the contrary, is:

1. Impatient (cannot stand the humiliation of self).

2. Hard.

3. Full of rancor (resentment, spirit of revenge and bitterness).

4. Full of fruitless sorrow and despair, meriting punishment.

5. It robs us of all energy to work and do penance for our salvation.

6. It is irrational and makes it impossible to pray.

7. It destroys all the fruits of prayer and of the Holy Spirit.

The basic principle, and remedies (cc. 12, 13)—we must first of all embrace the basic principle of Cassian. *Sadness is a sin,* and it is to be resisted at all costs. We cannot passively "undergo" the motions of evil sorrow, under pretext that we are helpless and cannot resist—that it is "not our fault." He says: "The sadness of the world, which brings death to the soul, is to BE RESISTED JUST AS MUCH AS THE SPIRIT OF FORNICATION OR OF AVARICE OR OF ANGER, AND MUST BE COMPLETELY ROOTED OUT OF OUR SOULS" (360). Means of resisting—remedies against sadness:

1. Meditation on the promised reward of heaven.

2. Resisting vain and worldly hopes with firm hope for things that cannot be seen.

3. Patience in all adversity, and generous use of the occasions presented by the common life.

We now come to the important conference on *Acedia*. Why *two* conferences on sadness? Is there a difference between these two? *Tristitia* seems to be a sadness caused by adversity and trial in social life. {It} comes from lack of peace *with others. Acedia* is rather the sadness, the disgust with life, which comes from a much deeper source—our inability to get along *with ourselves,* our disunion *with God.* Other monastic writers also distinguish *Acedia* and *Tristitia* (v.g. Palladius,[469] Evagrius,[470] St. Athanasius,[471] St. Isidore[472]). But St. Gregory the Great does not distinguish: he

469. See Palladius, *Dialogue,* 138: "To each one of these vices God has assigned its contrary virtue. Thus self-control is opposed to lust, . . . joy to sorrow, . . . patience to accidie, . . ." (c. 20).

470. See *Praktikos,* 6, 10, 12, in *The Praktikos; Chapters on Prayer,* 16–18; Bamberger notes that this section on the eight capital vices appears in *PG* [vol. 40] as a separate work, but should be included as an integral section of the *Praktikos* (16, n. 24).

471. See *Life of St. Anthony,* c. 36: "From this there follows immediately apprehension of soul, confusion and disorder of thought, dejection, hatred toward ascetics, spiritual sloth, . . ." (168; "dejection" is κατηφεια; "spiritual sloth" is ακηδια—see *PG* 26, col. 896).

472. *Sententiae,* 2:37 (*PL* 83, col. 638C): "*tristitiae quoque gaudium, accidiae fortitudo . . . opponenda est*" ("joy should be set against sadness, and fortitude against acedia").

treats the two as one, and hence has only seven capital sins.[473] St. Thomas follows St. Gregory.[474]

Instituta 10—THE SPIRIT OF BOREDOM (ACEDIA)

Acedia, or accidie, is a technical term which may be roughly rendered as the "spirit of apathy and boredom." Book Ten should be read in {its} entirety, as a text of special importance for all monastic and medieval spirituality.

Background: The term ἀκηδια is used in the Septuagint for negligence, says Bardy,[475] citing Isaias 61:3—but our translations speak rather of grief and mourning. Bardy cites a homily of Antiochus of Saint Sabas in which he depicts the *acediosus* as unable to be interested in anything—except meals. He cannot read—he opens and closes the book without fixing his attention on it. He wastes his time in gossip. Elsewhere (*Conference* 5),[476] Cassian speaks of two kinds of acedia:

1. a sadness expressed in torpor and sleep;
2. a sadness driving one to instability and wandering.

The remedy is healthy mental and physical activity, combination of work and prayer. *St. Gregory the Great* says that the remedy is to "think of the joys of heaven."[477] *St. John Climacus* treats

---

473. *Moralia* 31:45 (*PL* 76, col. 621A); it should be noted that the lists in Cassian and Gregory have other differences: Gregory omits pride as being in its own category as the root source of all sin, and adds envy (*invidia*).

474. *Summa* I–II, Q. 84, art. 4 (ed. Gilby, 26:73-79); Thomas' list is identical to Gregory's.

475. G. Bardy, "Acedia," *Dictionnaire de Spiritualité*, ed. F. Cavallera *et al.*, 17 vols. (Paris: Beauchesne, 1932–1995), 1:166-69; the first reference is found in col. 166, the second in col. 167 (citing Homily 26 [*PG* 89, cols. 1513–1516]).

476. Col. 627A (c. 11).

477. St. Gregory the Great, *Pastoral Care*, trans. Henry Davis, SJ, Ancient Christian Writers, vol. 11 (Westminster, MD: Newman, 1950), 95–96: "The joyful are to be admonished in one way, the sad in another. Thus to the joyful are to be displayed the sad things that accompany punishment, but to the sad, the glad promises of the Kingdom. The joyful should learn by severe warnings what to fear, the sad should be told of the rewards to which they may look forward. It is to the former that it is said: *Woe to you that now laugh, for you shall weep*; but the sad should be told the same Master's teaching: *I will see you again, and your heart shall rejoice, and your joy no man shall take from you*" (Part II, c. 3 [*PL* 77, col. 53]).

it as a "child of talkativeness."[478] He calls it a "slackness of soul, a weakening of the mind, a neglect of asceticism, hatred of the vows."[479] It is a "general death for the monk" (Step 13).[480] Read *Ladder*, p. 138 ff.[481] Remedies: true obedience and manual labor, thought of death and joys to come, psalmody.

Definition of Acedia—some synonyms: languor, torpor, spiritual gloom, depression, discouragement, indifference to salvation. This is a subtle and somewhat difficult matter. It is more than just sloth in the sense of a laziness that shirks duty or avoids work. It is an interior and spiritual sloth that seems, at times, to shirk the obligation of living. It is a weariness of life itself, *taedium vitae*, a disgust with *everything* which modern psychology might in most cases trace to a kind of neurotic depression. It certainly implies discouragement—and to some extent a kind of *abulia*—a paralysis of the spirit combined with restlessness and indecision. Acedia is in fact one of the great spiritual diseases of our time. In a sense it is a disease of the best minds. The intellectual elite is faced with despair because it sees the utter hollowness of the world that man has made for himself, and sees no hope for an improvement. (Less gifted minds are able to delude themselves with a false optimism, hopes for a better future in the natural order etc.) Acedia is the disease which afflicts the whole world, especially the unbelieving world. A Christian knows how to face

478. *Ladder* 13:1:"one of the branches of talkativeness, and its first child" (138).

479. *Ladder* 13:2 (138).

480. *Ladder* 13:3: "for the monk [it] is a general death" (139).

481. This section points out that despondency (*acedia*) is more characteristic of the eremitic than of the cenobitic life ("a constant companion of the hermit"); that it comes at noonday; that it incites pretexts for hospitality and visiting; that it can induce physical illness; that the battle with despondency, the "gravest" of the eight capital vices, produces spiritual horror; that the spirit of despondency engages in conflict only with those who struggle against it—otherwise it encourages relaxation; that it is resisted by recollection of sin and by manual labor. The section concludes with a dialogue between the monk and despondency: "'Tell me you worthless, shuffling fellow, who viciously spawned you? . . .' 'I have many mothers; sometimes insensibility of soul, sometimes forgetfulness of things divine, sometimes excessive troubles. . . . What completely mortifies me is prayer with firm hope of future blessings . . .'" Climacus concludes: "This is the thirteenth victory. He who has really gained it has become experienced in all good."

the disastrous conditions of the world today with sobriety, compassion, without false and shallow exuberance, but with theological hope. In order to do so he must resist the temptation to acedia which has infiltrated even into the heart of man's spirit and of his intellectual life (viz. existentialism).

How does Cassian define Acedia?

1. It is *taedium seu anxietas cordis*.[482] It is the effect of finding experience *wearying* and *narrowing*. It is the fruit of a lessening of psychic energy, and of euphoria, with a resulting sense of poverty, helplessness, discomfort, lack of resources, lack of ambition, lack of desire for good. "*Acediosus ex nimia tristitia torpescit*" (St. Thomas, II–II, Q. 35, a. 1).[483] *Dormitavit anima mea prae taedio*[484]—Psalm 118 (in Greek: *ap'akedias*). "Acedia" as a *passion*—impedes all man's actions, but especially that of his voice so that he becomes silent and morose, doesn't want to speak (St. Thomas).[485] This would apply also in choir—a great center of acedia! As a *vice*—{it} is an *inhibition of the will* so that the will grows cold and powerless to do good or resist evil. In particular, it is the spiritual distaste of the will for the good connected with charity—so that the will remains inert, and does not move itself to avoid evil that is opposed to charity, or to do the good which will obtain greater charity. Thus, under the effect of acedia, *charity grows cold*. Acedia sees this and accepts it with indifference. Then it is a real sin. The Fathers generally take acedia in a broad sense as the disinclination of the will to do good and resist evil—a kind of neglect that flows from tediousness, anxiety, pusillanimity, etc.

2. Cassian points out that it most affects certain classes of monks: (a) the hermits; (b) the wandering monks. (Presumably

---

482. Col. 360C: "*taedium sive anxietatem cordis*" ("weariness or anxiety of heart").

483. "The one afflicted with acedia is sluggish from too much sadness." N.B. that this is not a direct quotation from Thomas but a summary by Gazaeus (col. 360D) of Thomas' teaching in this section (ed. Gilby, 35:21-25).

484. Col. 369A (c. 4): "My soul slept from weariness" (Ps. 118:28).

485. I–II, Q. 35, art. 8 (ed. Gilby, 20:107): "The reason why special mention is made of torpor's depriving one of speech is that, of all outward movements, the voice best expresses inward thought and feeling."

Tristitia afflicts the cenobites.) He says some of the Desert Fathers thought that acedia was the "noonday demon"[486] of Psalm 90, because it was worst around Sext when the hermit was hot, bored, and hungry, worn out and disgusted with life and yearning for a bite of food. Here acedia is purely and simply a passion. To *feel* this is no sin, if we do not consent. Note {the} possibility of material sin, however.

Before we proceed any further, it may be well to remark that souls that are severely afflicted with this passion in the very beginning of their religious life, who in addition have *never* experienced any consolation in the monastery and have *never* known anything but acedia, repugnance, disgust etc., and who in addition are seriously doubtful about their vocation, almost certainly lack the aptitude for our life. This is probably much more than a mere passing trial. However, care must be taken to see that their vocation is indeed well tested—say for about a year. If after that they continue to drag along without hope, they should not stay in the monastery. When they really lack vocation, they will usually leave before this. It is probably not an infidelity on their part, but a mere lack of aptitude for which they are not responsible. It should be accepted and dealt with frankly.

The action and effects of acedia (c. 2):

1. It can become a kind of obsession (*obsederit mentem*).[487]

2. It then produces *horror loci, fastidium cellae, fratrum aspernatio, desidia et inertia in operibus.*[488]

Disgust for the place—(the section of the desert where one is living, in our case the monastery, or the Order); *disgust for solitude—"cella"* means not just the cell as a physical building, but the obligation to remain there in prayer and recollection. *Note that acedia can often be brought about by strain and imprudent efforts to remain recollected.* Acedia is very often the punishment

486. Col. 364A–365A.
487. Col. 365A: "it besieges the mind."
488. Col. 365A–366A: "*horrorem loci, fastidium cellae, fratrum . . . aspernationem gignit atque contemptum. Ad omne quoque opus quod intra septa sui cubilis est, facit desidem et inertem.*" ("It causes disgust for the place, repulsion for the cell, scorn and contempt for the brothers. It makes one lazy and sluggish toward every task there is within the enclosure of his chamber.")

for angelism—for an unrealistic view of our nature—dividing man against himself as if the spiritual life were the life of the spirit alone. The body must have its share, or disaster will result. *Contempt for the brethren*—this contempt manifests itself by projection and rationalization—the brethren are regarded as "bad monks." Thus the ego of the *acediosus* is spared the humiliating truth that he himself has lost his fervor. He is enabled to go on being spiritually slothful while accusing everybody else of being tepid. He thinks himself fervent because he can see faults in the others and criticizes them. This is very common in the monastic life, alas! There remains the telling fact that he is slack and negligent in his duties. Note however, Cassian makes a very important qualification: he is lazy and slow "regarding any job which he has within the confines of his hut,"[489] that is—anything that falls under the duty of his solitary and enclosed life. But he is eager for other jobs outside the cell and far afield—and zealous in carrying them out. He applies the text of the psalmist *dormitavit anima mea prae tristitia*. Read: Chapters 4 and 5.[490]

3. It begets illusory desires for the active life and for a "fruitful apostolate." The monk complains that he is wasting his time here with these useless solitaries and ought to be out edifying others with his virtues and his preaching. He is so full of rich doctrine, needed by the Church! This temptation is less dangerous in novices than in priests who, after several years of profession, cannot get the job they like in the monastery and are

489. See previous note.
490. Chapter 4 (col. 569A), which is entitled *"Quod acedia excaecat mentem ab omni contemplatione virtutum"* ("That acedia blinds the mind from all contemplation of the virtues"), reads: "The blessed David distinctly summed up all the inconveniences of this sickness in one verse, saying, 'My soul slept from weariness' [Ps. 118], that is, from acedia. Rightly enough, he did not say that his body had slept, but his soul. For the soul that has been wounded by the dart of this passion truly sleeps, away from all contemplation of the virtues and insight of the spiritual senses." Chapter 5 (col. 569B–570A), which is entitled *"Quod duplex acedia sit in pugna"* ("That acedia is twofold in battle"), reads: "Therefore let the true athlete of Christ, who desires to struggle lawfully in the contest of perfection, hasten to expel this disease from the hiding places of his soul; and let him contend against this most wicked spirit of acedia on both sides, so that he may neither perish, struck down by the dart of sleep, nor withdraw, driven from the cloister of the monastery as a fugitive, even if under the pretext of some pious excuse."

relegated to the ranks. They chafe under the yoke of the common life—which is indeed not an easy one to bear. But anyone who makes profession in a contemplative monastery must be willing and ready to bear it.

4. Desires to transfer to other monasteries. "The grass is always greener on the other side of the fence"—imagining all the perfections and advantages of other communities, seeing the drawbacks and deficiencies of our own vocation (367).

5. Read the description, in the translation, of the *acediosus* weary with hunger about noon time.[491] He finally trumps up pretexts for visiting pious women and giving them spiritual direction. False charity comes in here—to enable him to elude his obligations.

6. Habitual sleeping—is another psychological escape of the *acediosus*, or conversations with others (c. 3; 368). This sleep is not only bodily but physical {*sic*} (*Dormitavit anima mea prae taedio*—quoted here—c. 4; 369). The soul has closed its eyes to contemplation and virtue and sees nothing any more of the spiritual life. The "spiritual senses" are completely deadened, anesthetized.

7. Actual instability (not only a roving mind) is an inevitable fruit of real acedia (c. 6; 370).

8. Gluttony and the love of the company of tepid monks—flow from acedia (c. 6).

St. Paul's description of Acedia—Cassian then goes on to exegete a famous passage from the Epistles of St. Paul to the Thessalonians, in which the nature of acedia and its relation with false mysticism is discussed, and the Apostle gives the true remedy—a life of simplicity and *zeal for manual labor*. Cassian goes into detail describing the Apostle's approach to the problem—how he first praises the Thessalonians, and gains their sympathetic attention before pointing to the evil that is in their midst.

St. Paul's remedies for Acedia (see I Thess. 4:11):

1. *Ut quieti sitis*[492]—the avoidance of agitation, excitements, curiosities, distractions, vain opinions—(the Thessalonians were

491. Col. 367B (c. 2); the reference is again apparently to the mimeographed Wulff translation.
492. Col. 373A: "that you should be calm."

stirred up by vain prophecies of the Parousia—note how this
spirit of restlessness infects Christians today. It is not a sign of
true faith, but merely of spiritual shallowness)—avoidance of
rumors and *gossip*, and of those who are given to such things.

2. *Ut vestra negotia agatis*[493]—Mind your own business, *age
quod agis*. The *acediosus* cannot do this because he is not at peace
with himself and this is the source of his acedia. He is restless
when alone and unoccupied, and seeks at all costs to flee from
solitude in which he too keenly feels his own deficiency and
poverty of soul.

3. *Work with your hands*—manual labor goes with the
above. Paul does not prescribe idleness and spiritual "void,"
but a reasonable activity which is productive and pacifying. The
lazy man sometimes seeks to escape the humble, profitable round
of daily work by trying to do more numerous and more exalted
tasks of which he is not capable.

4. *To be decent and reserved in relations with outsiders*—not
thrusting oneself upon them, seeking novelties and flattery—
note this temptation of monks. It is so easy to seek out occasions
to be with seculars and to hear the news of the world, while
being admired and praised by them—taking to oneself all the
credit that belongs to the whole monastery. However to be simple
and honest with all men, in sincerity and peace—this bears witness to Christ.

5. *Not to desire the goods of others*—again, not looking at the
benefits and gifts which others seem to enjoy, and not trying to
reach out for them, discontent with what we have ourselves.
Nothing is lacking to us. (In the Second Epistle, he continues—
see II Thessalonians 3:7-18.)

6. The drastic remedy—excommunication—or rather the
brethren are warned not to associate with an *acediosus* (375). However they are to be cared for and treated charitably (c. 15) and
only rebuked out of charity (c. 16).

7. Another important remedy—prayer (c. 14).

The rest of the Book is taken up with examples of industri-
ousness and labor, especially the Apostles (cc. 8–18) and the

493. Col. 373A: "that you should mind your own business" (*"age quod agis"*
means "do what you are doing").

Desert Fathers (22–25) {and} FINALLY—THE IMPORTANCE OF OPEN RESISTANCE, RATHER THAN FLIGHT (c. 25).

Instituta 11—THE SPIRIT OF VAINGLORY (De Spiritu Cenodoxiae)

Definition: Vain glory is "empty glory"—that is to say the desire for empty glory—the need to be praised and admired by men, and to take complacency in ourselves—narcissism (cf. the legend of Narcissus). Vainglory is the passion to take pleasure in our own qualities: real or imagined. Cassian stresses the *subtlety* of this vice. It is *very hard to detect* except in its crass forms. It almost invariably is one of the chief vices of those inordinately attached to their own virtues and perfection in the spiritual life. These "worry about" vanity, but they indulge it in many forms unknown to themselves, and their anxious self-examinations do not help them to overcome it because their very self-examination is prompted by vanity—by the fear of "looking bad," and by the desire to have virtues for which they can be approved or praised. In summary—vanity is the passionate desire to look good, and the fear of being disesteemed. *It is a spiritual vice*—that is to say, like Pride, it attacks most violently the spiritual part of man, while the other vices work principally on the flesh.

Its many forms—A notable characteristic of vanity is that it takes innumerable forms, and that is why it is so hard to detect. It lies in wait for us everywhere, "in our clothes, in the way we walk, in our voice, in our work, in our vigils, in our fasts, in prayers, in solitude, in reading, in knowledge, in silence, in obedience, in humility, in patience it tries to wound the soldier of Christ. . . ." (c. 3; 402). It is like a hidden reef that wrecks the ship of our vocation when we think things are going well. It attacks from opposite sides—we can be just as vain about rags and poverty as we can about our fine clothes and riches. Vanity exists wherever there is something esteemed. Vanity can thrive in a monastery where virtue is esteemed and practiced. Indeed it thrives *more particularly* there. *It grows strongest where there is most virtue*; far from being diminished in solitude it is even worse there, even though there is no one to admire us. For the solitary is capable of getting along with his own admiration of himself and is that much worse off for not needing the admiration of others. When we overcome it in single victories, it rises again all the more strong to combat us. Unlike other vices which diminish with age, this grows stronger as we grow older. In its essence, *vanity* is *a blindness to God which springs from fascination with ourselves* (cf. Scriptural examples, 409–410).[494]

(Cassian does not say so, but one of the only effective ways to fight vanity is to *admit* it and face it squarely, instead of trying to keep it hidden by vain efforts to eradicate it, when these efforts are themselves prompted by vanity. The enemy to look out for is that false desire of perfection which cannot abide a fault in ourselves, which out of real vanity seeks to be spotless, and which is agitated when the slightest spot appears. To fight vanity we must be content to have faults, so long as we do not willingly indulge them. If a man is really vain [and we all are more or less] his whole desire for perfection is in reality inspired by vanity, that is to say by the need to be esteemed and to take complacency in self. Hence it is clear that it is much better to be imperfect in many things, as long as these imperfections spring only from weakness and do not imply a lack of zeal for the spiritual life, than to be perfect and at the same time vain of our perfection. If our imperfections lead us to trust fully and wholeheartedly in the mercy of God, then they are of great benefit to our souls. To be without vanity is to see oneself as an imperfect and sinful creature without feeling undue anxiety or shame, without fighting reality, without losing our peace, but trusting in God. It means accepting oneself as he really is. *The vain man cannot do this.* His passion is for a *false* glory in qualities that he only imagines, or that he exaggerates in some way, and attributes to himself implicitly. He cannot glory solely in the mercy of God.) Cassian concludes, following John 5 (411), that vanity makes a true life of faith impossible.

Forms of vainglory in the Monastic life:

a) The vanity of the *beginner* (c. 13)—Those who have little knowledge or virtue, says Cassian, glory in the sound of their

---

494. Cassian refers to 4 Kings [2 Kings] 20 (Hezekiah) and 2 Paralipomenon [2 Chronicles] 26 (Uzziah).

voice, or in their psalmody, or in the thinness of their bodies; or else they glory in their noble birth or the fact that they have spurned great honors in the world. Beginners also *daydream* about themselves rejecting great titles and fortunes, which in reality they never had a chance to acquire. They delude themselves that they have made heroic sacrifices to come to the monastery and take complacency in this idea.

b) The *progressive*, says Cassian, is tempted by desire for Holy Orders. This is an interesting passage historically (c. 14). He depicts the monk day-dreaming about the sanctity with which he would fulfil the sacred functions and outshine all other priests. Or the hermit dreams of giving spiritual direction and visiting holy women. Souls deluded by these fantasies, says Cassian, lose all contact with reality (415). (Note—it is possible to squander valuable opportunities in the monastic life by wasting our meditations in daydreams. In most souls this is quite instinctive, and in many, especially the young, nothing can be done about it by direct resistance. Violent efforts would only be harmful. We should accept ourselves, laugh at our own weakness, and turn our minds to something better by using a good book, or thinking about something more profitable, and more practical. The soul who really and culpably indulges vanity like this is generally one who is too proud to be ordinary and normal, too puffed up to descend to simple and ordinary means for avoiding these fantasies. Such ones are really badly infected. But the man who is humble enough to be ordinary and to work at his perfection with humble and ordinary means, will not be harmed by the inevitable fantasies of his imagination.) Cassian tells the story of the hermit "inebriated by vanity" who was "saying Mass and preaching" in his cell all alone, when a visitor came and caught him at it (c. 15; 416).

The Cure of Vanity:

a) It is essential to get to the *roots*. Find the deep causes of the vice.

b) Then to prevent these causes from acting—true solitude is a great help. "Avoid women and bishops," says Cassian in a famous remark (418). But give yourself quietly to contemplation in solitude.

c) Never permit ourselves *to do anything for the sake of getting praise or admiration or self-satisfaction alone*. {It is essential} to keep our intention pure in all that we do (and one might add—not to expect it to be spotless—{we} must accept our limitations). Note: distinguish acts performed with the formal intention of being praised, acts which *by their very nature and character* draw special attention to ourselves—showy ways of doing things, affected bearing, affectation in singing, ways in which we evidently place ourselves in the limelight—for instance, always ready with a smart comment, or a story or statement about ourselves. The person who is afraid of public actions may well be vain in the sense that he *fears failure and disgrace* too much. Angry and critical persons are often unconsciously trying "to save face"—or to get revenge for not receiving attention they desire.

d) AVOID SINGULARITY. This is very important. The things that we do that are singular or unusual, even though we may think our intention is pure, by their very nature tend to make us stand out; they draw attention to self. Things of this kind should be automatically avoided. They are fertile sources of unconscious vanity.

e) Meditate on the fact that by vainglory we lose the merit of our actions before God.

Instituta 12—THE SPIRIT OF PRIDE

The fight against pride is the "supreme struggle"—the last and most difficult of all because pride is the original vice from which all others spring and is at the same time the most savage and pernicious of them all. It is the last to be overcome and indeed most monks never finally get around to facing it squarely. "The last of the vices we have to fight and last on the list, it is nevertheless the first in order of origin and of time; a most savage beast and more terrible than all the others we have enumerated, *it attacks the perfect most of all* and devours with a more terrible bite those who are nearing the peak of virtue" (c. 1; col. 422). Later on (c. 24; col. 461), he will say that *spiritual pride* is unknown to most men because it is only apparent in a soul that has overcome the other vices. It only makes itself felt when the other "spirits" have been conquered.

Two kinds of Pride:

a) *Carnal Pride*—attacks beginners and progressives.

b) *Spiritual Pride*—may exist in all but does not become a true problem except in the really perfect. Therefore what may appear to be spiritual pride in a less perfect monk would, according to Cassian, be only a form of carnal pride.

Difference between the two? First of all, remember pride is not vanity, not desire to be admired and praised. Pride is the sin of Lucifer who set himself up in the place of God. It is an act of aggression against God and men, a lifting up of our whole being, a usurpation of a place that does not belong to us, over the heads of others. However, there is a difference: *carnal* pride elevates us above both God and man, but the emphasis is on elevation above other men; *spiritual* pride elevates us above God and man, but it makes us think (at least implicitly) that we can do without God. (Difficulty—one might ask if atheists and communists were not guilty of spiritual pride by this definition—not exactly, according to Cassian. There is latent in them a deep spiritual pride, indeed, but it does not come out fully developed in Cassian's sense because they do not really know anything about God and cannot therefore be guilty of this pride in the strict sense.)

1—SPIRITUAL PRIDE

The Sin of Lucifer (c. 4): Lucifer was the most beautiful and gifted of all the angels. He was above all the others. By pride he fell from the height of heaven into the depths of hell. Hence, Cassian says, if we wish to understand the true nature of pride we should study the fall of Lucifer. How did Lucifer sin?

a) He attributed his supreme gifts to himself and his own excellence and did not recognize them as gifts of God's mercy. In other words he acted as if they were due to him in strict justice.

b) He then went on to trust in his own free will, and believing himself like unto God he assumed that, like God, *it was sufficient for him to will and all he willed would bring him beatitude*—in other words he acted as if the *fulfillment of his own will* were sufficient to make him happy, merely because it was *his* will (problem today). (This can be true of God alone Who is

infinitely above any notion we may have of a contingent will—
whose will is His infinite Being itself—Whose Freedom is His
own beatitude—Who needs nothing outside Himself to make
Him happy. But every created being is contingent, and the exercise of his freedom depends on certain objective norms—it must
correspond with reality—it is not enough for a creature merely
to act freely in order to be happy. On the contrary, as Cassian
wisely points out, the created will that tries to be its own norm
and its own "god" immediately becomes the prisoner of the
worst of tyrants—spiritual pride.)

c) God then left Lucifer to himself. Deserted by God, Lucifer
was allowed to live by his own will. That is his punishment and
his hell. He got what he wanted. Everlastingly he stands in con-
tradiction to himself, with a lawless freedom that can do everything except good, and can be everything except happy,
blessed, peaceful. Hence he is the prisoner of his own will and
of his own despair.

The Special Evil of Pride—opposed to everything that is good.
Pride is especially evil because it destroys not only one contrary
virtue (humility) but *all the virtues at once*, the whole spiritual
life. It is opposed not to a particular moral good but to all good
in our souls. Furthermore (c. 7; col. 434) it is opposed not only
to all virtue and all moral good, but it *is directly opposed to God
Himself* (cf. St. Bernard).[495] However, if pride is not opposed to
humility alone, that does not mean that humility is not the chief
remedy for pride. It is the God-given remedy. Cassian quotes
passages illustrating the *humility of Jesus* by which God over-
came the pride of Lucifer (col. 436–437).

---

495. See *Sermones in Nativitate Domini* 4 (*PL* 183, col. 127B): "*Itaque qui forni-
catur, peccat in corpus suum; qui injuriosus est, in proximum; qui extollitur et inflatur,
in Deum. Fornicator semetipsum dehonestat; injuriosus molestat proximum; elatus,
quod in se est, Deum inhonorat. Gloriam meam, Dominus ait, alteri non dabo (Isai XLII,
8). Et superbus: Ego, inquit, mihi eam, licet no dederis, usurpabo.*" ("For one who for-
nicates sins against his own body, one who does injury, against his neighbor, one
who exalts and inflates himself, against God. For the fornicator defiles himself;
the harmful man injures his neighbor; the self-exalted man, because he is filled
with himself, dishonors God. The Lord says, 'I will not give my glory to another'
[Is. 42:8], but the proud man says, 'Even if you will not give it, I will usurp it for
myself.'")

The struggle against Spiritual Pride. The only way to overcome pride is to have in our hearts the humility of Jesus:

1. Cassian gives us Scriptural texts which we should constantly repeat and meditate until we make them part of ourselves and of our very life: "Of myself I can do nothing, the Father in me He performs the work" (John 5);[496] "By the grace of God I am what I am" (I Cor. 15);[497] "Without me [Jesus] you [monks] can do nothing" (John 15);[498] "Unless the Lord build the house they labor in vain who build it" (Psalm 126);[499] "What hast thou that thou hast not received?" (I Cor. 4).[500]

2. Cassian points out[501] that no human effort is able to attain beatitude—examples of David and the good thief who entered heaven by humble prayer and compunction and trust in the Lord.

3. Cassian quotes[502] the tradition of the Desert Fathers who assert that one's ascetic life is worthless unless one realizes that purity of heart is a gift of God and not the reward of our efforts alone—but that God graciously gives fruit to our lives when zealous efforts show that we try to correspond with grace. Grace is what brings the fruit, not our human efforts, however.

4. Furthermore, in order to avoid pride in our monastic life, we must be humble enough to learn the way to purity of heart from an experienced master who is himself humble and versed in the ways of God—not from those who have nothing to recommend them but vain words. Pride instinctively seeks the "show" of spiritual learning and apparent virtues (449). Above all, the Spiritual Father should be a *man of faith*, and deeply conscious of his own unworthiness and faults. Thus the master is only worthwhile if he knows from experience that all in the spiritual life is to be attributed to the grace of God. (Note—how St. Benedict fulfils this requirement in his *Rule*.[503])

496. Col. 436A (c. 8) (actually a conflation of Jn. 5:30 and 14:10).
497. Col. 437A (c. 9).
498. Col. 437A (c. 9).
499. Col. 437A (c. 9).
500. Col. 438AB (c. 10); these are actually among the more than twenty scriptural passages cited by Cassian in these chapters.
501. Col. 439A–440A (c. 11).
502. Col. 442A–443A (c. 13).
503. See the Prologue where Benedict encourages his readers, "let us ask

5. Remember the punishments of pride: for instance vile temptations and even diabolical possession (c. 20; 457) or also examples from the Old Testament—downfall of Joas (II Par. 24).

Conclusion: EVIDENTER IGITUR MONSTRATUR NON POSSE QUEMQUAM PERFECTIONIS FINEM AC PURITATIS ATTINGERE, NISI PER HUMILITATEM VERAM, QUAM PRIMITUS FRATRIBUS REDDENS, DEO QUOQUE IN CORDIS PENETRALIBUS EXHIBEAT, . . . (c. 23; 460).[504] Summary—humility toward God and brethren, exterior and interior.

2—CARNAL PRIDE

Spiritual pride is known to very few because very few are near enough to perfection to be tempted by it. The majority suffer from carnal pride (461).

Description of Carnal Pride (c. 25):

1. It affects the beginner, or those who have made a bad beginning and never recovered.

2. It makes the monk unable to get rid of the pride of the world, and worldly attitude.

3. He is unwilling to submit, because this carnal pride makes obedience difficult and unpleasant.

4. He is unwilling to live the common life and regard himself as on a level with all the other monks. Nor does he find it possible to be always nice to them.

5. He is unwilling to embrace perfect poverty, but must retain something for himself. He lacks confidence in God, flees sufferings and hopes for a long life.

6. It destroys the spirit of faith, and makes the religious life tepid since the monk begins at once to take care of himself.

7. The foundations of the spiritual life being thus ruined, the monk is a monk in name only and he has built an edifice of vice upon the foundation of pride. Chapter 27 gives a list of vices

---

God that he be pleased, where our nature is powerless, to give us the help of his grace" (McCann, 11, 13).

504. Col. 460B–461A (which reads "*Evidenter itaque . . . in penetralibus cordis exhibeat, . . .*"): "Therefore it is clearly shown that no one can attain the goal of perfection and purity except through genuine humility, which one first shows to his brothers, and also reveals to God in the innermost reaches of his heart."

that flow from pride: it is a repetition of all we have already seen, on avarice, acedia, but also some special traits:

> His eyes rove here and there, vacant and stupid. Instead of salutary sighs, he hacks up phlegm from his throat continually; his fingers are never still, but fly hither and thither like those of a scribe or a painter. . . . While he sits in the spiritual conference he cannot be still; one would think he were sitting on busy worms or sharp thorns; whatever is said in the conference for the edification of all, he takes to be directed in particular to himself, etc.[505]

He is suspicious, always thinking up arguments and self-justification in his heart, obstinate, harsh in speech, hates silence, loud laughter, quick to anger, hurts others and never says he is sorry, etc.

Signs of Carnal Pride (c. 29; 470) (more or less repeats the above): *clamor in loquela—in taciturnitate amaritudo—excelsus et effusus risus—irrationabilis tristitia—in responsione rancor—facilitas in sermone—expers patientiae—caritas aliena [superbia est]—ad tolerandum injurias pusillanimis—ad obediendum difficilis—ad recipiendam exhortationem implacabilis—semper suas definitiones statuere contendens—in omnibus suo potius quam seniorum credit judicio.*[506]

Chapter 30—Some effects of Pride—or rather some characteristic expressions of interior pride: the monk is discontent with the community and wants to live by himself. He thinks he desires greater perfection but actually his pride is driving him to escape the subjection and discipline of the monastery (472).

Chapters 31 ff.—The Battle Against Carnal Pride—Principle: if we wish to reach the highest perfection, we must lay a solid

---

505. Col. 469AC.

506. Col. 471: "*in loquela ejus clamor, in taciturnitate amaritudo, excelsus et effusus in laetitia risus, irrationabilis in serietate tristitia, in responsione rancor, facilitas in sermone, ... Expers patientiae est, charitatis aliena, . . . ad tolerandas [contumelias] pusillanimis, ad obediendum difficilis, . . . ad recipiendam exhortationem implacabilis, . . . semperque suas definitiones statuere contendens, . . . in omnibus suo potius quam seniorum credat judicio.*" ("Loudness in his conversation, bitterness in his silence, excessive and overdone laughter in joy, irrational sadness in seriousness, hostility in answering, superficiality in speech, . . . [Pride] is lacking in patience, estranged from charity, cowardly in enduring insults, prickly about obedience, . . . sullen in accepting advice, . . . always striving to make its own points, . . . in all things relying on its own judgement rather than that of the elders.")

foundation, not of our own will but of Evangelical discipline, self-renunciation: *fundamenta [aedificii spritualis] non secundum nostrae libidinis voluntatem, sed secundum districtionis Evangelicae disciplinam jacere festinemus.*[507] The root of pride being self-complacency, we must renounce self and build on the foundation of the Gospel, seeking perfection not for ourselves but to please God alone. How? Fear of God—humility—meekness—simplicity of heart. Without these virtues, pride will ruin our spiritual life. These virtues in turn depend in large measure upon:

a) Poverty: *Humilitas nullatenus poterit absque nuditate conquiri.*[508]

b) Also depending on poverty, but necessary for the rest of the spiritual life—obedience, charity. For the Holy Spirit comes to rest only upon the meek and contrite man (Isa. 66). Humility—the "athlete of Christ" (*athleta Christi*)[509] will then join battle with this "most ferocious beast"[510] of pride, convinced that no real virtue is possible where pride lurks in the heart.

What to do?

1. Be very humble toward the brethren—be careful never to offend others or to hurt them—*in nullo acquiescentes eos contristare.*[511]

2. In order to do this, we must renounce all our attachments to comforts, privileges, possessions, and our own desires: by these things we come in conflict with others. As long as we cling to our own will and our own way, we will necessarily hurt others, and will refuse to give in to them. This *abrenuntiatio et nuditas*[512] must be based on love of Christ.

507. Col. 473A: "Let us hasten to lay its foundation not according to the will of our own sinful desire but according to the discipline of evangelical rigorousness."
508. Col. 473A (which reads "*Humilitas vero nullatenus . . .*"): "Humility can by no means be acquired without stripping oneself of everything."
509. Col. 474A (c. 32).
510. Col. 474A.
511. Col. 475A (which reads "*in nullo scilicet . . .*"): "certainly going along with nothing that would make them sad."
512. Col. 475A: "*abrenuntiatio vera, quae in exspoliatione omnium facultatum ac nuditate consistit*" ("genuine renunciation, which consists in the ruthless stripping away of all our resources").

3. Again, we must be careful about real and not just exterior obedience. We must really do nothing except what the Abbot desires us to do—*ut, praeter abbatis mandatum, nulla penitus voluntas vivat in nobis.*[513] As long as we oppose our superiors, even interiorly, pride has a firm foothold in our souls and we will never be able to get rid of it. Notice that it is here in the struggle against the *last* vice that Cassian really puts the emphasis on obedience. One would imagine that obedience were a matter for beginners. Here he reminds us that obedience is really difficult, and really heroic, when one has reached a high degree of development, because then one is apt to be confident in his own virtue and trust in his own judgement. And this may be the fatal mistake that debars one from sanctity—it may even wreck the whole edifice of the spiritual life.

4. In order to be thus obedient, we must really *die to the world.* The worldly spirit of self-assurance and self-exaltation makes us believe that we are always right, and enables us to look down on others, to judge our superiors, and to pick and choose among the things commanded of us.

5. If we are to overcome pride, we must *give up attachment to our own judgement* and think of ourselves as foolish and unwise persons. A little attention to our mistakes and faults ought to convince us of this, but we train ourselves not to see our own weaknesses.

6. Real supernatural faith towards superiors—rejecting one's own desires one accepts the will of the Superiors and seniors in the monastery as the holy will of God—with reverence and eagerness, and without any discussion, even interior (c. 32; 475).

7. From these beginnings we can pass on to that deep humility which, in perfect peace of soul, accepts injuries and wrongs with exemplary patience. We must judge ourselves inferior to all; cf. quote from Chrysostom, *Homily 33 in Genesis* (Martène).[514]

---

513. Col. 475A: "so that no will is alive within us except for the command of the abbot."

514. Col. 476C: "Let us not show honor only to those who are older in age than ourselves, or the same age as we are. For what you must of necessity do is not humility. True humility is, rather, when we defer to those who seem to be less than ourselves, and show reverence to those who seem to us to be less worthy than we. If we understand these things rightly, we will judge no one to be

And in this we must meditate on the sufferings of Jesus and of His saints, and realize how small are the things we have to suffer, by comparison. Monks indeed sometimes have a tendency to exaggerate beyond measure their tiny difficulties. We should also meditate that we will soon die, and meet our Judge, and so look at trials in the light of eternity. Finally, he repeats, we must above all believe and realize that we have no hope of practicing any real virtue by our own power, without the grace and the mercy of God. Chapter 33 is evidently one of the sources for St. Benedict's fourth degree of humility. (Read the fourth degree and comment.[515])

---

inferior to us, but we will say that we are excelled by all people. I say this not about myself, who am immersed in countless sins; rather, even if anyone is aware of many deeds well done, unless he feels within himself that he is the last of all, there will be no benefit for him from all his good deeds." The reference to Martène is to Dom Edmond Martène, OSB (1654–1739), prolific collector and editor of early Christian materials; see Joseph Daoust, *Dom Martène: Un Géant de l'Erudition Bénédictine* (Abbaye S. Wandrille: Editions de Fontenelle, 1947); for Merton's interest in Martène see Thomas Merton, *Entering the Silence: Becoming a Monk and Writer—Journals Volume 2: 1941–1952*, edited by Jonathan Montaldo (San Francisco: HarperCollins, 1996), 47, and the headnote to his prose-poem "Rites for the Extrusion of a Leper" in Thomas Merton, *Collected Poems* (New York: New Directions, 1977), 655; the reference may be a mistake on Merton's part: Martène's commentary on the *Rule* of St. Benedict is included with the text of the *Rule* in Migne [*PL* 66, cols. 215–932]; the commentary of Gazaeus on Cassian includes this quotation from Chrysostom as a note to this passage, and Merton may have inadvertently written "Martène" as part of this marginal note when he actually meant Gazaeus.

515. "The fourth degree of humility is that, meeting in this obedience with difficulties and contradictions and even injustice, he should with a quiet mind hold fast to patience, and enduring neither tire nor run away; for the Scripture saith: *He that shall persevere to the end shall be saved*; and again: *Let thy heart take courage, and wait thou for the Lord*. And showing how the true disciple ought to endure all things, however contrary, for the Lord, it saith in the person of sufferers: *For thy sake we face death at every moment. We are reckoned no better than sheep marked down for slaughter*. Then, confident in their hope of the divine reward, they go on with joy to declare: *But in all these things we overcome, through him that has loved us*. And again in another place the Scripture saith: *Thou, O God, hast put us to the proof; thou hast tested us as men test silver in the fire. Thou hast led us into a snare: thou hast bowed our backs with trouble*. And to show that we ought to be under a superior, it goeth on to say: *Thou has set men over our heads*. Moreover, in adversities and injuries they patiently fulfil the Lord's commands; when struck on one cheek they offer the other, when robbed of their tunic they surrender also their cloak, when forced to go a mile they go two, with the apostle

{*IV.*} *The* CONFERENCES *of Cassian*

There are twenty-four conferences. This whole group is divided into three parts. Part I {consists of} ten conferences of Hermits in Scete: Abba Moyses on the essence of the Monastic Life and on Discretion; Abba Paphnutius on the Triple Renunciation; Abba Daniel on concupiscence and conflict of flesh and spirit; Abba Serapion on the Eight Principal Vices (cf. *Instituta*); Abba Theodorus {on} why God permits the saints to be killed; Abba Serenus: two on Distractions, Devils and Temptations; Abba Isaac: two on prayer. This part contains the best and most important of the conferences and we will do well to concentrate on these *decem collationes summorum Patrum, id est, anachoretarum*.[516]

The *Prologue* to the First Part {is} addressed to Bishop Leontius and to "Brother Helladius" (the latter evidently a hermit in France). Cassian, writing in retirement in his monastery (*in portu silentii*[517]), will look out upon the "vast sea" of doctrine of these Fathers of Scete, awed by the fact that here is the wisdom of great solitaries and contemplatives, elevated far above the *anachoresis* of cenobites. The difference between the *Instituta* (for cenobites) and the *Conferences* (for hermits) lies in the fact that the *Instituta* deal with *observances, liturgy* and *asceticism*, the *Conferences* with "the invisible state [*habitus*] of the interior man,"[518] with *perpetual prayer* and contemplation. He warns the reader not to be upset at the loftiness and difficulty of the ideals proposed and *not to judge them by his own state and vocation* (presumably if he is a cenobite) because he does not have the wherewithal to make a right judgement. One cannot fully appreciate these doctrines, says Cassian, unless one has lived in the desert and experienced the illumination of mind which comes from dwelling alone in the vast emptiness of total solitude.

Undoubtedly the first two conferences are among the most important of all Cassian's writings. They are absolutely

---

Paul they bear with false brethren, and they bless those that curse them" (McCann, 43, 45).

516. Col. 478A–479A (Preface to *Conferences* 1–10): "Ten conferences of the greatest Fathers, that is, the anchorites."

517. Col. 479B: "in the harbor of silence."

518. Col. 480A.

fundamental and without a knowledge of his doctrine on purity of heart and discretion, we would fail to understand the
true monastic attitude and miss the whole purpose of the monastic life. They show us that contemplation does not consist
exclusively in solitude and silence and renunciation but that
these are only means to purity of heart. Aspirations to a "more
perfect life" are to be interpreted by us as inspirations to seek a
greater interior perfection.

Conference 1—DE MONACHI INTENTIONE ET FINE[519]

What is the purpose and end of the monastic life? This is
the great and all-important question to which we must always
return. Why have we left the world? The answer is given by
Abbot Moses, a hermit of Scete. *We have come to the desert*, he
says, *to seek the Kingdom of God, and the way to enter the Kingdom
is by achieving purity of heart*. To begin with, Cassian shows us
the modesty of Abbot Moses, and his great hesitation to embark
on a spiritual discourse. The Desert Fathers lived in the true spirit
of silence, and were not given to much talking, or indiscrimi-
nate talking even about spiritual things (c. 1; col. 483). Hence
Moses has to be begged "with tears" to tell them something. It
would be wrong to reveal the secrets of the spiritual life to the
curious or the indifferent.

What is the purpose of the monastic life? The *skopos* and the
telos—the immediate objective and the final end. This distinction must be made first of all. The monastic life, being an "art,"
has these two distinct aims—one immediate, the other ultimate.
When the farmer clears the ground and ploughs, it is to prepare
it for seeding: this preparation is the *skopos*. The *telos* is the har-
vest. In the monastic life we have a *skopos* and a *telos*, and for
these we undergo all our labors and hardships. We know what
we seek, and this is sufficient to make every sacrifice worth while.
If you do not know what you are after, it is much harder, in fact
almost impossible, to apply yourself to the search.

Moses asks them why they have undertaken their long journey and their sojourn in the desert. They answer—"For the King-

519. "On the Purpose and Goal of the Monk."

dom of God"[520] and this he says is the right answer—this is the *telos*. But what is the *immediate objective*—the *skopos*? (Note the practical importance of this. In order to act prudently we must take into account not only what is general and universal, but above all what is particular and concrete. I must not only do "good" in a big, general way, but there is a particular good that must be done here and now. If I do not see it, I will not act rightly. Hence {the} importance of having a clear immediate aim even in small things: {to} know what we are doing—not confine ourselves to big universal aims—in the particular case their power to move us may be very weak, v.g. in meditation—better to have a precise aim, not just "union with God.")

Cassian and Germanus confess that they do not know what is the immediate objective of the monastic life and many monks today are in the same predicament. Hence Abbot Moses says definitely: "*In omni arte praecedit scopos, id est, animae destinatio sive incessabilis mentis intentio, quam nisi* quis omni studio perseverantiaque servaverit, *nec ad finem desiderati fructus poterit pervenire*" (c. 4; col. 485).[521] The *skopos* has a certain *primacy*—hence importance. It must be seen and kept in mind *with perseverance and care*. It is the "*mentis intentio*"[522]—the *what* and the *how* and the *why* of our conduct. Without it, our activity is wasted and gets nowhere. "Those who proceed without a road to follow have labor and not advantage for their journey" (*id.*).

The scopos is purity of heart. Destinatio vero nostra, id est, scopos, puritas est cordis, sine qua ad illum finem impossibile est quempiam pervenire (id.; col. 486).[523] Hence, if we are to make a success of the monastic life, *we must turn all our attention and all our efforts to gaining purity of heart*—that is the ability to love God purely and to do His will for love's sake alone—disinterested love. This

---

520. Col. 483A (c. 3).

521. Text reads: "*In omni, ut dixi, arte ac disciplina praecedit quidam scopos . . .*" ("As I have said, in every art and discipline a particular target is paramount: that is, an end point for the soul, a constant intention for the mind, for no one will be able to reach the objective of a desired goal unless he keeps this target in focus with complete attentiveness and perseverance.")

522. Col. 485B: "intention of the mind."

523. "Indeed our aim, that is, the target, is purity of heart, without which it is impossible for anyone to reach the ultimate goal."

apparently simple little principle, which we all take more or less for granted once we hear it, is one that has had a profound effect on all monastic spirituality. St. Benedict is based on it,[524] and St. Bernard's mystical theology is built on it as on a cornerstone as Gilson points out.[525] Note: the Neo-Pythagoreans who flourished at Alexandria especially made "purity of soul" a central purpose of their ascetic life, with a view to union with the gods.[526]

Hence, a second practical principle of great importance: QUIDQUID ERGO NOS AD HUNC SCOPON, ID EST, PURITATEM CORDIS POTEST DIRIGERE, TOTA VIRTUTE SECTANDUM EST; QUIDQUID AB HAC RETRAHIT, UT PERNICIOSUM AC NOXIUM DEVITANDUM (c. 5; col. 487).[527] What is good for us? Everything that helps us gain purity of heart. What is bad for us? Everything that prevents us from purifying our hearts. "For this we do and suffer all, for this we have left our families, our dignities, riches, pleasures, etc."[528]

Applications and illustrations:

1. It is useless to leave great riches in the world and become attached to a pen or a needle in the desert—the heart is not

524. See the conclusion of chapter 7: "Then, when all these degrees of humility have been climbed, the monk will presently come to that perfect love of God which casts out all fear; whereby he will begin to observe without labour, as though naturally and by habit, all those precepts which formerly he did not observe without fear: no longer for fear of hell, but for love of Christ and through good habit and delight in virtue" (McCann, 49).

525. See his discussion of "pure love" (140–49), an analysis particularly of Sermon 83 on the Songs of Songs.

526. See for example the saying of Clitarchus (n. 17): ψυχή καθαίρεται ἐννοίᾳ θεοῦ ("The soul is purified by the recollection of God") in Henry Chadwick, *The Sentences of Sextus: A Contribution to the History of Early Christian Ethics* (Cambridge: Cambridge University Press, 1959), 77; the later, Christianized version of Sextus (n. 97) reads φωτίςεται ("is enlightened") (24) for καθαίρεται; but see also Saying 24 of Sextus: ψυχὴ καθαίρεται λογῳ θεοῦ ὑπὸ σοφοῦ ("The soul is purified by the word of God through wisdom") (14). In *An Introduction to the Pythagorean Writings of the Hellenistic Period* (Äbo: Äbo Akademi, 1961), Holger Thesleff questions the traditional ascription of the neo-Pythagorean writings to an Alexandrian provenance (46–50).

527. Text reads: ". . . *quidquid autem ab hac* . . ." ("Therefore whatever can direct us toward this target, that is, purity of heart, should be followed with absolute commitment; but whatever pulls us away from it, should be shunned as dangerous and poisonous.")

528. Col. 487B.

pure, because the monk has not kept his objective in view. His eye has wandered and become ensnared by a trifling possession (this then has become his *skopos*) (c. 6; 488). He speaks of one being so attached to a book that he will not even let another touch it or look at it. We remember that a regular war was precipitated among the early Irish monks over a psalter.[529]

2. *But purity of heart is equated with perfect charity.* "If I should give my goods to feed the poor and have not charity . . . it profiteth me nothing."[530] Hence, purity of heart is not the mere external act of renunciation and emptying one's hands. The heart must be emptied of love for creatures and open itself entirely to the love of God. Applying this principle to our own monastic life: we must be careful not to lose sight of our true goal; if we turn aside from it, we will immediately make something else our objective—liturgy, chant, farm work, study, a job, an avocation. These things should be *means* and not *ends*. *Caritas* [apostolica] *in sola puritate cordis consistit* (488).[531] Hence, further important details: purity of heart means—no jealousy, no vanity, no pride, no rivalry, anger, selfishness, no rejoicing in the evil that befalls others, not thinking evil thoughts of them—all this is to offer a pure heart to God: COR PERFECTUM AC MUNDISSIMUM DEO OFFERRE, ET INTACTUM A CUNCTIS PERTURBATIONIS CUSTODIRE (488).[532] It is the ideal of *apatheia* (freedom from passion)—the crown of the "active life."

529. The reference is to the Battle of Culdrevney (461), which according to later sources led to the exile of St. Columba from Ireland and the founding of the monastery of Iona. See John McNeill, *The Celtic Churches: A History, A.D. 200 to 1200* (Chicago: University of Chicago Press, 1974), 89: "Eager for scriptural knowledge and for the best Bible text, Columba is said to have copied without permission a manuscript of Jerome's text of the Psalter and Gospels which Finnian [of Moville] brought from Rome." Finnian, learning of this, was bitterly angry and demanded the copy: when Columba refused an appeal was made to the high king, who ruled against Columba, who then roused his clansmen against the high king. As a penance St. Molaise, Columba's "soul-friend," sent him into exile to convert as many souls to Christianity as were killed in the battle. (McNeill questions the historicity of the details of the story, though the battle definitely did take place and Columba may have had some involvement with it.)

530. Col. 488B (a quotation from I Cor. 13:3).

531. The text reads: "*charitas illa, . . . quae in sola cordis puritate consistit*" ("that love, . . . which consists in purity of heart alone").

532. The text reads: ". . . *semper offerre, . . .*" ("always to offer God a perfect and most clean heart, and to guard it intact from all disturbances").

3. It is for the sake of purity of heart that we do everything we do in the monastic life: OMNIA IGITUR HUJUS GRATIA GERENDA APPETENDAQUE SUNT NOBIS: PRO HAC SOLITUDO SECTANDA EST, PRO HAC JEJUNIUM, etc. (c. 7; 489).[533] *Read* chapter 7.[534] Each monastic observance, fasting, silence, reading, labor, etc., has as its function *to purify the heart of vices and self-love,* to free it from passion, and to *raise us to the perfection of charity,* "ab universis passionibus illaesum parare cor nostrum . . . et ad perfectionem caritatis istis gradibus ascendere" (id.; 489).[535]

4. If on the other hand, we fall into sadness or disquiet when we have to omit one or other of these observances for the sake of something higher (v.g.—to forego fasting in order to entertain a guest) then it shows that the observance is not serving its purpose. For the very purpose of these observances is to purify our souls of anger and sadness and the other vices.

5. It must be understood that if our observances are not working for purity of heart then they will work against it (that is, if we are attached to them out of motives of self-love). "The profit of fasting is not as great as the loss we suffer through anger, and the fruit we gather through reading is less than the harm we incur through despising a brother."[536]

6. "THOSE THINGS WHICH ARE SECONDARY (which "follow" in order of importance after the *skopos*—purity of heart) SUCH AS FASTING, VIGILS, THE SOLITARY LIFE, MEDITATION OF THE SCRIPTURES, OUGHT TO BE PRACTICED WITH A VIEW TO THE IMMEDIATE END: PURITY OF HEART WHICH IS CHARITY" (c. 7; 489). "And we should not on

---

533. The text reads ". . . *jejunia,* . . ." ("Therefore we should do and seek everything for the sake of this: for this solitude should be pursued, for this fasting" etc.)

534. Col. 489A–490B: the rest of chapter 7, as Merton himself will summarize it in the discussion that follows, stresses that the various practices and disciplines of the monastic life are means to the end of purity of heart, which is equated with love, and that to be so concerned with these means that one becomes upset and angry when they are not able to be carried out according to the regular plan is to frustrate the true purpose of these exercises. They are tools, aids to perfection, not perfection itself.

535. The text reads: ". . . *passionibus noxiis . . . istis gradibus innitendo conscendere,* . . ." ("to make ready our heart, unharmed by all noxious passions, . . . by depending on these steps to rise to the perfection of love").

536. Col. 489AB.

their account turn upside down this most important of virtues" (*id.*). He continues (Read text[537]) that as long as purity of heart and charity is inviolate in our heart we will be making progress and no harm will come from omitting these secondary things for a serious motive. And he adds that it is a *hindrance to perfection* to practice any secondary observance in such a way that it blocks our charity and purity of heart and serves our self-love.

7. *Conclusion*: he clearly states the great distinction between ENDS AND MEANS. Fasting etc. are means, *instrumenta*. Charity is the end. Perfection does not lie in the means, but in the end attained by them (*id.*; 490). This cardinal principle of the monastic life must never be forgotten. If we remember it, we should logically make a generous and perfect use of the means, and thus attain our end. If we forget it, we will inevitably waste our efforts and our monastic life will end in frustration, even perhaps in sheer illusion. "One who is satisfied with [the means] as if they were the chief good, and limits the strivings of his heart to this alone and does not apply all his energies to achieving the end . . . will undertake all these exercises fruitlessly" (*id.*; 490). *QUIDQUID IGITUR POTEST ISTAM MENTIS NOSTRAE PURITATEM TRANQUILLITATEMQUE TURBARE, QUAMVIS UTILE AC NECESSARIUM VIDEATUR, UT NOXIUM DEVITANDUM EST (id.; 490).*[538]

In meditating on this, we should remember what he means by peace of heart, which he here identifies with purity and charity. It is not just a negative and natural peace which consists in remaining undisturbed in our own will. This is altogether false peace, and all the monastic observances arm us against it. The

---

537. Col. 489B: "*Ea igitur quae sequentia sunt, id est, jejunia, vigiliae, anachoresis, meditatio Scripturarum, propter principalem scopon, id est, puritatem cordis, quod est charitas, nos convenit exercere, et non propter illa principalem hanc perturbare virtutem; qua in nobis integra, illaesaque durante, nihil oberit, si aliquid eorum quae sequentia sunt, pro necessitate fuerit praetermissum.*" ("Therefore it is proper for us to practice those things which follow after, such as fasts, vigils, solitude, meditation on the scriptures, for the sake of the main goal, purity of heart, which is charity, and not to disturb this main virtue on their account; so long as this is whole in us, and endures unhurt, it will do no harm if some of these secondary practices should be omitted out of necessity.")

538. "Therefore, whatever can disturb that purity and tranquillity of our mind, however useful and necessary it may seem, should be avoided as harmful."

true peace is rooted in renunciation of our own will. This is the peace we must seek and follow with all our heart, not the other.

The Active and Contemplative Lives: Peace, tranquillity, purity of heart in perfect love, this is the summit of the monastic life: it is the life of contemplation, which the monk leads alone with God. Here Cassian simply repeats what has been said, and makes clear that contemplative life on earth is the *skopos* which we must seek by active asceticism. Cassian begins chapter 8 by asserting that the peace of contemplation is the object of the monk's strivings—in so far as it is identified with charity and purity of heart. Here again, we see one of the main sources of the doctrine of our Father St. Bernard who teaches that since "pure love" brings us to the perfection of union with God, in which we contemplate Him and are transformed in Him, this purity of contemplation is to be sought as the summit of the interior life.[539] (The Fathers do not say explicitly whether they are talking about "mystical contemplation" and identifying this with perfect charity—hence there is still room for argument on {the} theoretical question whether perfection implies contemplation.)

Cassian says: *HIC NOBIS PRINCIPALIS DEBET ESSE CONATUS, HAEC IMMOBILIS CORDIS DESTINATIO JUGITUR AFFECTANDA, UT DIVINIS REBUS AC DEO MENS SEMPER INHAEREAT . . .* (c. 8; 491);[540] (Cf. St. Thomas on perfect charity—"*inquantum ab affectu hominis excludatur omne illud quod impedit ne affectus mentis totaliter dirigatur in Deum*" [II–II, Q. 184. a.{2}].[541] Here he is talking about the religious life and evidently the "active" union with God arrived at by the practice of virtues and self-abandonment to Him, rather than mystical union.) Cassian adds—"Whatever differs from this, however great it may be, is to be rated as secondary, or indeed as trifling

---

539. See Bernard's discussion of contemplation as the third and highest degree of truth *in The Steps of Humility and Pride*, trans. M. Ambrose Conway, OCSO, Treatises II, CF 13 (Washington, DC: Cistercian Publications, 1973), nn. 4–5, 19–23 (32–34, 46–53), and Gilson's commentary on this text, 104–18.

540. Col. 490B, which reads: "*Hic ergo nobis . . . destinatio cordis . . .*" ("Therefore this should be our main effort, this unwavering purpose should be unceasingly aspired to: that our mind always cling to God and to divine things.")

541. "so far as the will of a man regards . . . even that which would prevent the affection of the soul from being directed totally to God" (ed. Gilby, 47:24/25) (erroneously reading "a. 4" in Merton's text).

if not actually harmful" (*id.*; 491). He then goes on to speak of Martha and Mary in the Gospel (Luke 10). In Cassian's use of the story here, Martha represents the active life in the ancient sense of the practice of virtue, the *bios praktikos*, which leads to *apatheia*, and thence to *theoria* (contemplation). He is not at all speaking of the apostolic life or preaching as contrasted with the enclosed life of the monk. The works of Martha, practicing the virtues and following out the observances which form us to the life of virtue, is indeed not a "*vile opus*"[542] but a *laudabile ministerium.*[543] Hers is a *pia sollicitudo*[544] and her virtues are necessary and useful.

Note—Elsewhere, Cassian speaks of *two kinds of active life open to the monk*:

1. The Active Life of asceticism, in solitude, to prepare for contemplation and purity of heart;

2. The Active Life of service of the brethren which does not lead directly to purity of heart and contemplation, but is meritorious and will enjoy contemplation in heaven (cf. *Conf.* 14, c. 4, & 23, c. 3).[545] All the Desert Fathers agree that there is also an illusory "active life" or a temptation to activism in which the monk indulges in *unnecessary activity* (trumped up with false pretexts) in order to avoid being alone with himself before God.

But the active life of virtue, however necessary, is not in itself perfection. It is still complex and multiple, while perfection is simple (*unum est necessarium*[546]) and in it the chief good, contemplation (i.e. by purity of heart and charity) is found, containing in itself all the others in an eminent degree.

Cassian concludes: *VIDETIS ERGO PRINCIPALE BONUM IN THEORIA SOLA, ID EST, IN CONTEMPLATIONE DIVINA DOMINUM POSUISSE* (*id.*; 492).[547] This primacy of contemplation is due not to the fact that

542. Col. 491B: "a worthless work."
543. Col. 491B: "a praiseworthy ministry."
544. Col. 491A (which reads "*pia sollicitudine*"): "pious care".
545. Col. 956B–959A; col. 1246B–1248A.
546. "There is one thing necessary": this is the standard Vulgate translation of Luke 10:42, as cited in the notes of Gazaeus (col. 491D); Cassian's text reads: "*Paucis vero opus est, aut etiam uno*" ("Indeed few things are needed, in fact only one").
547. "Thus you see that the Lord has placed the chief good in *theoria* alone, that is, in contemplation of divine things."

it excludes or negates the virtues of the active life, but because it is their fruit and their end: *universae hujus unius parantur obtentu (id.).*[548] Martha is not blamed by the fact that Mary is praised: but Mary retains the first place, the primacy in the hierarchy of value. Note of course that he is speaking of active and contemplative lives united *in the same individual.*

Other Problems:

1. The works of Martha will be "taken away" in eternity—not in the sense that the reward will not remain, but the reward will precisely be the life of a Mary in heaven. Martha's works of mercy are necessary in the present life because of the inequality and impurity of heart and selfishness that divide men. We must deny ourselves in order to give to others. Note here a doctrine which influenced St. Bernard and the Cistercians[549] (c. 10; 495). Charity on the other hand will be much more perfect in the next life and will unite us more closely to God.

2. The problem of distracting activities. Germanus then somewhat querulously complains that "we cannot be contemplating all the time—we have to eat, we have to entertain visitors etc." (c. 12; 497). Moses replies:

a) Continual actual contemplation of God is impossible in this life (because of the frailty of the flesh);

---

548. "Everything else is arranged for the sake of obtaining this one thing."

549. See Sermon 40 on the Song of Songs, n. 3: "to give one's attention to something other than God, although for God's sake, means to embark on Martha's busy life rather than Mary's way of contemplation. I do not say that this soul is deformed, but it has not attained to perfect beauty, for it worries and frets about so many things, and is bound to be stained to some degree with the grime of worldly affairs. This however is quickly and easily cleansed at the hour of a death made holy by the grace of a pure intention and a good conscience" (Bernard of Clairvaux, *On the Song of Songs II*, trans. Kilian Walsh, OCSO, CF 7 [Kalamazoo, MI: Cistercian Publications, 1976], 201). See also *Sermones de Diversis 9 (PL* 183, col. 566D): *"Verumtamen optimam partem elegit Maria, licet non minoris fortasse meriti sit apud Deum humilis conversatio Marthae: sed de electione Maria laudatur (Luc. X, 42), quoniam illa quidem omnino, quod ad nos spectat, eligenda; haec vero, si injungitur, patienter est toleranda."* ("Truly Mary has chosen the best part, but perhaps the humble service of Martha is no less meritorious with God. Mary is praised for her choice, because of all the roles that are shown to us, that one should certainly be preferred; but if this role of service is imposed upon us, it should be patiently undertaken.")

b) But it is possible to have a fixed target to which we constantly return with our minds, renewing our aim after we have been distracted from it, "judging even a momentary departure from the contemplation of Christ to be fornication" (497).

Note—this must be properly understood. First of all, we cannot get the right meaning if we have a pathological horror for the physical aspects of human love, for that will color the image with frightening implications and fill us with agitation and scruples about unavoidable distractions. He reproves a fully voluntary change of aim, a new "target"—a new *skopos*—some other intermediate end that is not pure love for God. In this sense Cassian considered voluntary departure from the contemplation of God and the things of God to be like an infidelity and an impurity for the soul—for by the eyes of our mind and our desire the soul unites itself most intimately with the things it contemplates, and if *we give ourselves that fully* to anyone but God, it is like the sin of adultery. But this does not mean that it is a sacrilege to think of anything or anyone but God, because after all it is His will that we think about many of His creatures, persons and things with whom we deal in carrying out His will, but we must be reserved and cautious. The Desert Fathers believed that dangerous and distracting thoughts were placed in our minds by the devil, and to take complacency in these would be a way of loving them rather than God. Hence we should love God in all things and go through all things to Him. We must not *stop at* the creature. The creature does not become *skopos*.

Cassian's intent here is *not to make us believe that every slight distraction is a mortal sin*, but only to put us on our guard, to show us that selfish and self-seeking thoughts of creatures render our hearts in a sense "impure" and that *we ought immediately to turn to God when we notice our love straying from Him towards other beings*. This applies, incidentally, to anything, no matter how useful in appearance, that really draws us away from God—hence, love for our own virtues for instance. Anything that tends to become an end in itself and is not sought for God is an "impurity" in the heart. To abide in the Kingdom of God is to abide in peace and purity of heart; hence peace and gladness of heart go with purity of heart and charity, which is filled with the joy of the

Holy Ghost. We may say that *peace* is the *skopos*. Discord, turmoil, sadness, bitterness are the kingdom of the devil. Note here his quotations from Isaias on the Messianic Kingdom, interpreted as referring to the joy of the saints in the heavenly Jerusalem (col. 498). They reign with Christ who is "all in all." Moses then goes off into a long disquisition on the nature and immortality of the soul, which we can skip (c. 14).

3. *Contemplation of God* (c. 15): Here Cassian does not go into the very essence of contemplation, but simply lists some of the ways in which we truly know God in contemplation—that is to say the way His various attributes are brought home to us by graces of prayer:

a) He is really talking of "graces of prayer," of lights which come from God, beyond any initiative of ours, but depending in large measure on the purity of our heart and the sanctity of our life: *quae pro qualitate et puritate cordis* in nostris sensibus oriuntur (505).[550] They "arise" or appear to make themselves known as it were spontaneously, by the inspirations of grace, in our hearts (spiritual senses suggested by the term *sensibus*). The notes of Gazaeus on this passage are totally inadequate. He thinks Cassian is listing "subjects for meditation"—"*varii de Deo conceptus et meditandi modi.*"[551] On the contrary, these are *inspirationes* which give us a kind of "experience" of divine things— *quibus Deus vel videtur mundis obtutibus vel tenetur.*[552] "Seen"— the word is not to be taken literally, but it means really "experienced"; God is known by the loving knowledge that comes from union with Him in the depths of our soul, the embrace of pure love (*tenetur*). This experience of God, Cassian explains, is not granted to those who live by their carnal affections or are attached to the things of the world.

b) What are these "lights"?

i) *Admiratio* of His "incomprehensible substance"[553] grasped in the obscurity of hope. This would seem to indicate

---

550. Col. 506A, which reads, "*quae pro qualitate vitae . . .*" ("which arise in our senses according to the quality of our life and the purity of our heart").

551. Col. 505C: "various ideas about God and ways of meditating."

552. Col 506A: "by which God is either seen in a pure gaze or embraced."

553. Col. 505A (c. 15).

the highest kind of contemplation, the mystical knowledge of God in Himself, obscurely.

ii) The other *"contemplationes"* which he lists seem to fall under the heading of *theoria physica*, mystical knowledge of God not in Himself but in His creatures and His actions in the created world. Whereas he says God is "known" in His ineffable substance by hope (raised to the mystical level) here he says God is "glimpsed" *(pervidetur)*[554] through creatures etc.: (a) in the greatness of creation; (b) in the mystery of His judgements; (c) in the mystery of His Providence governing all things. Cassian then lists such things as—the awareness of God's omniscience, seeing into the inmost depths of all beings—His mercy and long-suffering while innumerable sins are committed daily in His sight—the mystery of our own vocation—the Incarnation and the spread of the faith to all parts of the world. In all these things, grace opens up our heart to *wonder and adoration* of the God whose greatness and power we somehow experience, on a level which transcends that of merely natural investigation and understanding. This implies a quasi-experience, an inner, intimate *realization* that goes beyond conceptual knowledge. Note importance of wonder in the contemplative life—part of childlikeness.

4. *The Problem of Distractions*: Germanus breaks in with a question—can the mind ever be altogether free from distractions at prayer? Abbot Moses (c. 17) lays down his principle: MENTEM QUIDEM NON INTERPELLARI, COGITATIONIBUS IMPOSSIBILE EST: SUSCIPERE VERO EAS, SIVE RESPUERE OMNI STUDENTI POSSIBILE EST (506).[555] It is impossible for the mind not to be solicited by distracting thoughts. Involuntary distractions, to some degree, are inevitable. But it is possible for everyone to *reject distractions*. Voluntary distractions can be avoided, but only by those who make efforts—*studenti*. Those who do not make efforts, accept the suggested thoughts and the distractions are then at least semi-voluntary. Note that the grace of God is necessary to help us reject distractions—this is *added* in some manuscripts[556] (to defend

---

554. Col. 505A.

555. "It is impossible for the mind not to be disturbed by thoughts, but it is possible for every earnest person either to accept or to reject them."

556. See the bracketed note at col. 506B: "*studenti per gratiam Dei possibile est*" ("it is possible to the earnest person through the grace of God").

Cassian against semi-pelagianism?). Moses explains: *Ortus earum non omnino pendet a nobis, probatio vel electio consistit in nobis* (507).[557] Also he adds that the nature of our distractions in prayer depends on the general tenor of our life. If prayer is regarded as secondary . . . etc.[558]

The combat against distractions (507) is largely a matter of filling our minds with good thoughts outside the time of prayer. The sluggish and lazy mind, which allows itself to wander everywhere, and does not apply itself to spiritual things, will be more easily distracted and the nature of the distractions will be lower and more reprehensible. To fill our minds with good thoughts, the monastic life enjoins upon us:

1. *Frequens lectio et jugis meditatio scripturarum*—resulting in *spiritualis memoria.*[559]

2. *Decantatio crebra psalmorum*—resulting in *compunctio.*[560]

3. Vigils, fasts, prayer—"*ut extenuata mens non terrena sapiat, sed celestia contempletur.*"[561]

Note however that it is often when the mind is exhausted by imprudent zeal and wrongly applied efforts that distractions can become obsessions. Measure and prudence are necessary here above all. It is useless to try to conquer distractions by violence, especially where there is impatience and pride and the refusal to accept our limitations.

A comparison (c. 18): Abbot Moses then compares the mind to a pair of millstones—these are always turning and they must grind on *something*. Put in something good—the mind cannot

---

557. Col. 506C–507A, which reads, ". . . *nobis, ita . . .*" ("their arising does not depend completely on ourselves; approving or choosing them does depend on us").

558. Col. 507B: "*Quibus rursum negligentia irrepente cessantibus, necesse est ut mens vitiorum squalore concreta in carnalem partem mox inclinetur et corruat.*" ("On the other hand if these practices are stopped because of the onset of negligence, it is inevitable that the mind, hardened by the filth of its vices, will soon be drawn toward the side of the flesh and will fall away.")

559. Col. 507A, which reads, "*spiritalis memoriae*": "frequent reading and constant meditation on the scriptures"; "spiritual recollection."

560. Col. 507A: "frequent chanting of psalms"; "compunction; sorrow for sin."

561. Col. 507AB: "so that the mind, emptied out, may not find enjoyment in earthly things, but contemplate heavenly realities."

be long empty of all thoughts. If it does not have good ones, it will have bad thoughts. *The main sources of distraction are—negligence—vain and worldly conversations—worldly cares* and *solicitude* about useless things (508).

Where do our thoughts come from? (c. 19): from God—from the devil—from ourselves (508). Examples of thoughts coming from God—Assuerus calling for the annals, when he could not sleep (Esther 6); the angel speaking in the prophet's heart (Zacharias 1); Jesus promising to come and dwell with the Father in the heart of those who do His will (John 14:23). Thoughts coming from the devil—example of Judas. See also the devil speaking through false prophets (III Kings 22).

The Discernment of spirits (c. 20): We have to be like smart money-changers, examining gold coins and testing them to see what is pure gold and what a base alloy, to weigh, to judge the coins that have been stamped by counterfeiters. Note—this expression became famous when St. Denis, Bishop of Alexandria, told of his vision in which God told him to use pagan authors and sift them, taking what was good and using it in the School of Alexandria[562]—where he came after Origen. This had been, since Clement, the policy of the Fathers of Alexandria. We must test the spirits—we must judge whether our thoughts are from God, or inspired by worldly philosophy, or Jewish superstitions (513). Here it would seem that a knowledge of theology is implied, for the thoughts he discusses here would have to be judged by their doctrinal content. He speaks especially of monks who let themselves be deceived by the specious teaching of heretics, what *appears to be spiritual* and holy, and he makes the important point that a vocation that is not built on sound doctrine will end in ruin. We must also, he says, be careful of false interpretations of Scripture (515). These are like counterfeit coins, but they do not bear the true image of tradition; they are exaggerations and falsifications of the teaching of the Fathers. They lead us, he says (516), "to perform pious works which since they do not bear the stamp of obedience and the approval of superiors, under pretext

562. Letter to Philemon, quoted in Eusebius, *Historia Ecclesiastica*, Book VII, c. 7 (*PG* 20:647C), where the saying "Prove yourselves sound bankers," described as an apostolic precept, refers particularly to heretics rather than to pagans.

of virtue lead us into vice, and deceive us by immoderate or un-suitable fasts or excessive vigils, or reading that is not proper for monks. All these bring the monk to a bad end." Other temp-tations—to leave the monastery and preach, to direct pious women, to receive holy orders etc. (See the *Instituta*, Bk. 11 on Vanity.) Read chapter 21 on the Illusion of Abbot John—deceived by the devil to undertake an inordinate fast.[563]

Summary—Rules for Discretion (518–519):

1. Careful examination of "inspirations";

2. To see if they are in accord with the teaching of the Church;

3. To beware of false inspirations to "do better," which may be temptations in disguise;

4. Beware of secret vanity;

5. See if they are characterized by HONESTAS COMMUNIS and TIMOR DEI:[564] fear of God—they must be good actions; "*honestas communis*"—ordinary decency and restraint, not exaggerated or odd or eccentric or beyond the usual norms of monks—very important;

6. Avoid everything that savors of *ostentation, novelty,* or *presumption;*

7. Compare with the teachings of the Apostles and Proph-ets. (Since he is talking for hermits, there is not a *senior spiritu-alis*[565] easily available.) Note that it is one of the hallmarks of false sanctity that it is odd and weird and in some sense repul-sive—cf. the convulsionaries of St. Médard.[566]

---

563. Col. 518A–519A: this chapter tells of John of Lycopolis who after fast-ing for two extra days encounters the devil, who falls at his feet and asks par-don for inspiring the fast; at this John realizes that the fast, which weakened his body and wearied his spirit, was like a counterfeit coin, which had the right image on it but was itself falsely made. Cassian draws the lesson of the neces-sity for discernment to determine both motivation for spiritual exercises and their appropriateness at a particular time.

564. Col. 518BC, which reads ". . . *honestate communi, an timore Dei . . .*"

565. "elder, spiritual father."

566. Religious enthusiasts in the early 1630s exhibited various bizarre be-haviors including mass convulsions at the tomb of a Jansenist ascetic in the ceme-tery of Saint-Médard in Paris. For a discussion see "The Convulsionaries of Saint-Médard," chapter 16 in Ronald Knox, *Enthusiasm: A Chapter in the History of Religion* (Oxford: Oxford University Press, 1950), 372–88.

More on distractions: How to attain stability of mind in prayer
(*Conf.* 10, cc. 13–14).[567]

The Problem: from a new angle: Germanus, speaking with
Abbot Isaac on prayer, asks how to attain stability of mind. The
problem this time is not so much that of wanton and worldly
distractions, *as superficial and aimless spiritual thinking,* or attention which is not properly fixed on a definite object. What
Germanus complains of as distraction might seem to us at first
as a real spiritual achievement. He says that during the office,
his mind wanders, by association, from one text to another. A
line of the psalms suggests another line of another psalm, thence
he goes to a line of the Gospels or a verse from St. Paul, and so
on. It might seem to us that it is good to compare one Scripture
text with another and that is true, for in our prayer and our spiritual reading, much fruit is often drawn from the correspondence
of texts, and their reaction upon one another. However Germanus
is not here speaking of this fruitful kind of association. He refers
to *merely mechanical wandering from text to text,* mere superficial
associations. The operation takes place without any special initiative or direction on our part and cannot really count as
prayer; it is just wandering of the mind. Let us notice that it is
not just the *material* we think about that constitutes distractions
(as if thoughts holy in themselves were not distractions). If the
thought is not really a thought, if it is just a passing image in a
whole mechanical series of images, the apparent piety of its content does not make it worthwhile. We are not really thinking or
praying. On the other hand, we cannot always be consciously
concentrating on definite thoughts, and it would not do to strain
to produce clear concepts of spiritual things at all times, and try
to squeeze some good out of them. This is not always possible.
Cassian is aiming at a strict discipline, which enables us to hold
on to the sacred text and get its substance (841).

In chapter 14 Abbot Isaac gives his answer—*Discipline in
prayer* (c. 14): *TRIA SUNT QUAE VAGAM MENTEM STABILEM FACIUNT:*

567. Germanus' question actually begins in c. 12 and extends through c. 13
(col. 839B–841B); Abbot Isaac's answer comes in c. 14 (col. 842A–844A), which
concludes the conference.

Vigiliae, Meditatio, Oratio (842).[568] If we apply ourselves with constancy and attention to these, our minds will become disciplined and stable, says Abbot Isaac. He then adds another help: *manual labor*, but distinguished: it must be labor carried out for the common good (*sacris coenobii usibus dedicatum*[569]). It must also be zealous and *"infatigabile"*[570] *and persevering* (842). The effect cannot be attained by work for self-interest, or slothful work. To "pray without ceasing" we must cast aside all the cares of this life. We cannot pray in Church if we do not pray outside of it. QUALES VOLUMUS ORANTES INVENIRI, TALES NOS OPORTET ESSE ANTE TEMPUS ORANDI (843).[571]

Conference 2—DE DISCRETIONE

At the end of the first *Conference*, Abbot Moses observes that they have passed naturally from purity of heart to a new subject—*discretion*. He adds that they have now been up late and talked long. Hence he will break off, and they can get the necessary sleep to refresh body and mind, so that on the next day he may speak to them of discretion after they have first practiced it by moderation in speech and taking the necessary rest (col. 520). He tells them that the subject of discretion is very important, since according to him discretion *holds the first place among the virtues* (col. 520): *"inter cunctas virtutes arcem ac primatum tenet."*[572] (This can be held in the sense in which St. Thomas holds that prudence: (a) disposes the use of means towards attaining the proper end of each moral virtue; (b) by disposing the means properly, it aids us in attaining the proper balance between extremes, which is essential to every moral virtue [II–II, Q. 47, art. 6 and 7].[573] Hence without prudence the other moral virtues will

---

568. "There are three things which stabilize a wandering mind: vigils, meditation, and prayer."

569. Col. 842A: "dedicated to the sacred uses of the monastery."

570. "tireless."

571. The text reads, ". . . *orantes volumus . . . esse oportet . . .*" ("As we wish to be found when praying, so we must be before the time of prayer.")

572. "among all the virtues it holds the summit and first place" (n.b. this statement is found in the last chapter [33] of *Conference* 1).

573. *Summa Theologiae*, ed. Gilby, 36:21-27.

not function properly, and in this sense prudence is the most important of them all.) Cassian's discretion is a special aspect of prudence: prudence in so far as it is *enlightened as to the true motives of our actions*, and disposes means to ends in the light of this knowledge. But it is also more than prudence, it is a work of the Gift of Counsel.

Chapter 1—Abbot Moses begins by stating that the necessity of discretion will be seen from the examples of the many Desert Fathers who fell through lack of it. And this is the sober truth (col. 524). *Plan of the Conference*: he will therefore concentrate first on the *need for discretion*. Then he will go on to discuss the *ways of acquiring and practicing it*. In doing this he will also take into account the *great merit of discretion* and the grace that it brings. All these points are vitally important. The monk must not only be convinced that he needs discretion, but he must be convinced that it is very meritorious, sanctifying and pleasing to God. Very often, confusing discretion with the prudence of the flesh (i.e. a worldly prudence which spares our fallen nature unreasonably) we act as if discretion were something less good which we had to fall back on out of weakness. It seems to be a lower level with which we are obliged to be content because we cannot do more. We must on the contrary be convinced that true supernatural discretion is a *greater good* and *leads to higher sanctity* even though it seems more lowly and pedestrian than the flights to which we imagine ourselves called.

The supernatural character of Discretion. On the contrary, Moses declares that discretion is a *heroic virtue—non mediocris virtus*.[574] He adds that it is *eminently supernatural*, and a true gift of grace: *non potest humana industria comprehendi nisi divino fuerit munere gratiaque collata* (col. 524)[575]—INTER NOBILISSIMA SPIRITUS SANCTI DONA[576] (he quotes I Cor. 12). Here he speaks evidently not only of the infused virtue of prudence but of the charismatic gift of discernment of spirits. Scholastic theology would make clearer

574. Col. 524B: "not an ordinary virtue."
575. The text reads: "*nec quae humana passim valeat industria comprehendi, nisi . . .*" ("not one which human effort is somehow capable of gaining, unless it has been united with the divine gift of grace.")
576. "among the noblest gifts of the Holy Spirit."

distinctions. It is for us to take Cassian as he stands, and not to
demand too great technical precision. Read the end of chapter 1:
"The task assigned to discretion is neither earthly nor small. . . .
The monk must go after it with all his energies . . . *omni intentione.*" Note his description of discretion as a certain knowledge
of the "spirits that arise within us." If not, he will walk in complete darkness, and not only incur grave dangers of complete
spiritual ruin, but meet with many obstacles and difficulties
where the way should be smooth and simple (col. 525).

The Importance of Discretion: Proof from the tradition of the
Desert Fathers, especially *St. Anthony*. Read chapter 2[577]—an account of a discussion of St. Anthony and his disciples, at which
Moses was present as a young monk in the Thebaid. The question
was raised: which is the most important of the virtues (or means
of monastic perfection)? Some said—fasting, vigils; others—
poverty—solitude (*anachoresis*); still others—in the practice of
fraternal charity. St. Anthony having listened to them all, said:
"All these things are necessary and useful—but many who have
practiced them have nevertheless come to ruin. Hence they do
not of themselves bring a monk to sanctity. There must be
something else."[578] He adds that if they study the ruin of great
ascetics and solitaries and find out what was lacking, they will
probably discover the real key to true perfection, *quid princi-
paliter ducat ad Deum.*[579] They fell because they went to excess,
and they did this because they had not been properly instructed
in the ways of monastic perfection and hence *lacked discretion.*
Without discretion their other virtues came to nothing and bore
no fruit. Discretion, avoiding contrary extremes (*praetermittens
utramque nimietatem*[580]) teaches the royal road to God, and this
discretion is what the Gospel calls: "the light of the body which
is the eye, and if the eye be single the whole body is lightsome"
(Matt. 6:23).[581] Discretion is neither carried away by enthusi-

577. Col. 525A–527B: Merton summarizes this chapter in the discussion
that follows.
578. Col. 526AB (a summary rather than a verbatim quotation).
579. Col. 526B: "that which first and foremost leads to God."
580. Col. 526BC.
581. Quoted in col. 526C–527A.

asm, "lifted up" in time of fervor, nor depressed and discouraged in time of trial. After the discussion of some Scripture texts on the necessity of doing all things with wisdom and counsel Abbot Moses concludes that "no virtue can be made perfect or even continue in existence without discretion" (col. 528): discretion leads us *safely* to God; it brings us *more easily* to the heights of perfection, while without it these heights would be impossible to reach at all by most men. Discretion in a word gives *sound judgement* which is absolutely necessary in a solitary. It gives solidity and perseverance to monastic vocation: *fixo gradu intrepidum monachum perducit ad Deum* (528).[582]

Examples of Indiscretion: Saul and Achab (c. 3); Hero (c. 5): following his own will and judgement rather than the monastic traditions, refused to participate in Easter synaxis—deluded by {the} devil, {he} jumped in a well; the two brothers in the desert, one of whom dies of presumption because he wants to be fed by a miracle (c. 6); the monk who tried to sacrifice his son to God (c. 7), deluded after many false visions—his son sees him sharpening up the knife and takes to flight; the monk whose illusory revelations led him to circumcize himself and fall into Judaism (c. 8). In all these examples we have *presumption*, independence, reliance on one's own interior lights, leading to complete lack of contact with reality and gross errors ending in spiritual destruction.

Chapter 10—Acquiring Discretion. Fully convinced by these stories that discretion is absolutely necessary and that all the other virtues depend on it, Germanus asks how it may be acquired and how true and false discretion may be known. Moses answers: *VERA DISCRETIO NON NISI VERA HUMILITATE ACQUIRITUR.*[583] Hence it is obvious that since discretion depends entirely on humility, humility is in fact the true foundation of the monastic life. St. Benedict was therefore very wise in making it the heart of his ascesis and of his *Rule.*[584]

---

582. The text reads "*quae . . . perducat . . .*" ("that leads a monk undisturbed to God by set stages").

583. Col. 537AB, which reads: ". . . *Vera, inquit, discretio . . .*" ("Genuine discretion is not acquired except through genuine humility.")

584. The reference is to chapter 7, "Of Humility" (McCann, 37–49); see Louis

Signs of true humility. Here we recognize the classical teaching of the ancient monks, in points which have already become
familiar to us in our study of the *Institutes*.

a) The first sign of humility is submission to the judgement
of a senior (Spiritual Father), not only in the matter of one's actions but also of all one's judgements. Humility therefore goes
with *docility*, and *obedience*. It is marked by a salutary distrust of
our own judgements, and submission to those who have likewise submitted to those before them. Hence—*sound tradition.*
*Nullatenus enim decipi poterit quisque, si non suo judicio, sed majorum
vivit exemplo* (538)[585] (cf. St. Benedict's eighth degree of humility[586]). This standard is practical only when applied to concrete
monasteries and Spiritual Fathers. It is not merely a matter of
guiding yourself with an approved book, but of following the
customs and traditions of the group to which you belong. If it is
certain that these customs and traditions are not for you, then go
elsewhere. (But even in this one would need to follow the guidance of a Spiritual Father and not one's own judgement.) Hence,
correlatively, a sign of a proud and indiscreet spirit is that he is
guided mostly by his own judgement and usually prefers his own
views to those of the seniors and to the traditions of the community, which he tries to oppose and subvert, or at least to bypass.

b) Together with docility, the other necessary disposition
for acquiring discretion is *openness* with the Spiritual Father. The
enemy cannot deceive one who, *universas cogitationes in corde
nascentes perniciosa verecundia nescit obtegere, sed eas maturo examine seniorum vel reprobat vel admittit* (col. 538).[587] By this we are
protected against our own ignorance and inexperience. Evil or

---

Bouyer, *The Spirituality of the New Testament and the Fathers*, trans. Mary P. Ryan,
History of Christian Spirituality, vol. 1 (New York: Seabury, 1963), 517: "This
primordial importance given to humility is . . . a legacy from Cassian. Benedict's whole doctrine of spiritual progress consists in his teaching on the degrees of humility."

585. "For one cannot possibly be deceived if he lives not according to his
own judgement but in accord with the example of the elders."

586. See McCann, 47: "that a monk do nothing except what is commended
by the common rule of the monastery and the example of his superiors."

587. "has learned not to conceal, out of a dangerous shame, all the thoughts
being produced in his heart, but either rejects or allows them in conformity with
the mature probing of the elders."

indiscreet thoughts often lose their sting as soon as we resolve to manifest them.

Chapter 11—the example of the disciple who was hiding an extra loaf and eating it in the evening—the devil departs from him as soon as he confesses his fault to the Spiritual Father. Conclusion: the devil ruins those who trust in their own judgement and hide their acts and thoughts from their Spiritual Father. *Not all Spiritual Fathers are of equal merit.* Cassian does not believe blindly in manifestation of conscience as a universal remedy for all ills. It can happen that the Father himself is indiscreet. Hence one must make a *wise choice of the senior* to whom one entrusts himself. The mere fact that a monk is old and has grey hair does not mean that we should accept his teaching or follow his example. The Spiritual Father himself is to be chosen for his true discretion—proved by a long life of virtue—and by fidelity to the true monastic tradition, not just adherence to his own will and opinions. {Cf. the} example of an indiscreet spiritual guide: by harshness and rigidity a certain Father drives a young monk to despair and loss of vocation, but the monk is saved by the intervention of Abbot Apollo (c. 13). Lesson: the prudent Father is one who is able to understand and compassionate with human weakness. He must above all understand that it is the grace of God that makes saints (col. 547).

Examples from Scripture—Even the saints are guided by other men. Samuel was sent to Heli for instruction (c. 14); Paul was sent to Ananias (c. 15): "Arise and go into the city and there it shall be told thee what thou art to do . . ." (Acts 9:7). "It is most obviously proved that the Lord does not show the way of perfection to anyone who, when he has a source of instruction available, has disdained the doctrine of the seniors . . ." (col. 549).

Another important principle: in order to acquire humility and discretion, we must studiously *avoid extremes* on the principle that *extremes are equally vicious*—"extremes meet"—*nimietates aequalitates sunt* (col. 549).[588] Extreme fasting is as bad as gluttony. Many have been ruined by inordinate vigils, when they could not be conquered by excessive sleep. Virtue consists in

588. "extremes are equivalent."

following the middle path between extremes. In order to avoid extremes, we must eat and sleep when the time comes, even though we may not feel like it: *Ita est escae somnique refectio hora legitima, etiam si horreat, ingerenda* (col. 550).[589]

What is the proper measure of food? Moses allows two small loaves of bread a day, with water—weight about one pound. This is considered quite easy by Germanus and Cassian, coming from the strict regime of Palestine. Germanus complains that this is more than he can eat, and he does not consider this fasting. Moses insists that regularity in following this diet will in the long run prove more difficult than the occasional use of vegetables and fruit, with less bread (or following the bad example of the monk Benjamin—see chapter 24: instead of two loaves a day, Benjamin would fast every other day and then eat four loaves at his next meal; he left the desert to return to the "vain philosophy of the world"[590]). For the rest, the practical principle is that we should eat what we need but not eat to our fill (col. 554).

The second conference ends without answering the main question which had interested Germanus and Cassian, namely how to overcome distractions and live in a state of continual prayer. This will be treated in *Conferences* 9 and 10 by Abbot Isaac; also in *Conference* 4 of Abbot Daniel, on Temptations, and *Conference* 7 of Abbot Serenus, on "The Instability of the Mind and Evil Spirits."

Conference 4—De Concupiscentia Carnis et Spiritus [591]
by Abba Daniel

Chapter 1—Interesting for details on Abba Daniel, a most humble man. Paphnutius advanced him very young to diaconate and priesthood. Daniel would not officiate as priest but only served Paphnutius as deacon, and instead of succeeding him, as priest of Scete, died before him.

Chapter 2—The question—*Why our thoughts and moods are so mobile and unstable.* Consolation and desolation—fervor and in-

---

589. "Thus the refreshment of food and sleep should be taken at the proper time, even if it is unappealing."
590. Col. 555B.
591. "On the Desire of the Flesh and of the Spirit."

ability to pray—alternate without apparent reason. Text of chapter 2:

> So then we asked this blessed Daniel why it was that as we sat in the cells we were sometimes filled with the utmost gladness of heart, together with inexpressible delight and abundance of the holiest feelings, so that I will not say *speech*, but even *feeling* could not follow it, and pure prayers were readily breathed, and the mind being filled with spiritual fruits, praying to God even in sleep could feel that its petitions rose lightly and powerfully to God: and again, why it was that for no reason we were suddenly filled with the utmost grief, and weighed down with unreasonable depression, so that we not only felt as if we ourselves were overcome with such feelings, but also our cell grew dreadful, reading palled upon us, aye and our very prayers were offered up unsteadily and vaguely, and almost as if we were intoxicated: so that while we were groaning and endeavoring to restore ourselves to our former disposition, our mind was unable to do this, and the more earnestly it sought to fix again its gaze upon God, so was it the more vehemently carried away to wandering thoughts by shifting aberrations and so utterly deprived of all spiritual fruits, as not to be capable of being roused from this deadly slumber even by the desire of the kingdom of heaven, or by the fear of hell held out to it.[592]

Chapter 3—Threefold cause: *Negligentia nostra; Impugnatio diaboli; Dispensatio Domini*[593]—He begins with this one.

Chapter 4—Reasons for our testing by Divine action causing aridity and desolation.

1. To promote humility and self-knowledge, self-distrust, realization of our dependence on grace.

2. To test our perseverance, the seriousness of our will to serve God, and to stimulate us to further effort.

592. *Works*, trans. Gibson, 331.
593. Col. 586B, which reads: "*de negligentia nostra, aut de impugnatione diaboli, aut de dispensatione Domini . . .*" ("from our own negligence, or from the attack of the devil, or from the permission of the Lord").

Chapter 5—We can do nothing without grace, and indeed grace visits us frequently and awakens us from negligence when we have done nothing to deserve it. The text of chapter 5:

> And by this it is clearly shown that God's grace and mercy always work in us what is good, and that when it forsakes us, the efforts of the worker are useless, and that however earnestly a man may strive, he cannot regain his former condition without His help, and that this saying is constantly fulfilled in our case: that it is "not of him that willeth or runneth but of God which hath mercy." And this grace on the other hand sometimes does not refuse to visit with that holy inspiration of which you spoke, and with an abundance of spiritual thoughts, even the careless and indifferent; but inspires the unworthy, arouses the slumberers, and enlightens those who are blinded by ignorance, and mercifully reproves us and chastens us, shedding itself abroad in our hearts, that thus we may be stirred by the compunction which He excites, and impelled to rise from the sleep of sloth. Lastly we are often filled by His sudden visitation with sweet odours, beyond the power of human composition—so that the soul is ravished with these delights, and caught up, as it were, into an ecstasy of spirit, and becomes oblivious of the fact that it is still in the flesh.[594]

Chapters 6–7—The value of trial and temptation—illustrated by texts from Old and New Testaments. The struggle between flesh and spirit is *salutary*, willed for us by God to keep us from a false security and complacent self-satisfaction (*ignava securitas*) (col. 599; c. 12).

{*Chapters*} *10–17—Psychology of Temptation and Conflict:* an examination of the limits of voluntary control, and involuntary activity of the passions; he represents the *will* as situated in between *concupiscentia carnis* and the *concupiscentia spiritus*[595] (cf. Plato)[596]—the latter a desire and appetite for fasting, prayer,

594. *Works*, trans. Gibson, 331–32.
595. "desire of the flesh. . . desire of the spirit".
596. The reference is presumably to the image of the tripartite soul in the *Phaedrus* (246a–256e), in which the rational faculty is depicted as a charioteer that must control its two horses, the spirited and appetitive faculties.

etc. *The will is represented as by nature inclined to compromise,* wanting the fruits of the spirit without renouncing the flesh; hence—*tepid* (Apoc. 3). However there is another aspect. The will is also inclined to *moderation* and should not be drawn away to excess even in the use of spiritual means like fasting and mortification. So the struggle is productive of *balance, aequitas media.*[597] The desires of the flesh remind the will to turn to God for help. Excess of mortification leads to exhaustion and will returns to necessary relaxation of flesh in order to maintain a just equilibrium. In this way purity of heart is acquired by constant struggle *jugi sudore et contritione spiritus.*[598] Thus the soldier of Christ is taught to follow the "Royal Way," the King's highway (*via regia*) which is the middle path of *justa aequilibratio* and *sana et moderata virtus.*[599]

Chapter 13 f.—The demons however try to upset this balance by undue pressure on one side or the other—leading to excess in material things or in spiritual exercises.

Chapter 17—The sad condition of eunuchs who, without salutary trials, vegetate in tepidity. He is a *homo animalis,* and worse than a *homo carnalis.*[600]

Chapter 19—The Three Types of Soul: (cf. William of St. Thierry[601]). A classic division—*carnales, animales, spirituales.*[602]

597. Col. 599C: "balance through moderation."
598. Col. 599B: "by continual effort and contrition of spirit."
599. Col. 600A, which reads *"justa aequilibratio . . . sanam et moderatam inter utramque virtutem viam, itinere regio . . ."* ("a proper balance, . . . the path of health and moderation between the two forces, along the royal way" [n.b. in Cassian's text *"sanam et moderatam"* modifies *"viam"* rather than *"virtutem"* and the phrase for "royal way" is *"iter regium"* rather than *"via regia"*]).
600. Col. 606C: *"Qui status, a carnali qualitate descendens, efficitur animalis, . . ."* ("This state, stemming from their fleshly condition, becomes animal, . . .")
601. In the *Golden Epistle* (*A Letter to the Brethren at Mont Dieu*), trans. Theodore Berkeley, OCSO, CF 12 (Kalamazoo, MI: Cistercian Publications, 1976), William uses the framework of three levels of spiritual development: "there are beginners, those who are making progress and the perfect. The state of beginners may be called 'animal,' the state of those who are making progress 'rational' and the state of the perfect 'spiritual'" (1:12 [25]). This is a somewhat different triad than that of Cassian, as William omits the *carnales* as not yet on the road to spiritual progress, and inserts the *rationales* between the *animales* and the *spirituales.*
602. Col. 605B, which reads *"carnalis, . . . animalis, . . . spiritalis"* ("fleshly, . . . animal, . . . spiritual"); note that "animal" means motivated only by the

He gives it a special treatment however: the *carnalis*—becomes the man of the world tormented by passions; the *animalis*—is the monk in neutral security, vegetating without real virtue. The *homo carnalis* is in a *better state* because he realizes his need for God, and is humble, while the *animalis* thinks himself secure, will not listen to admonitions. So *carnales* can be converted and become deeply spiritual. Such conversions are rare or non-existent among *animales* (background of St. Bernard, Letter {171}[603]).

Chapters 20–21—De Male abrenuntiantibus:[604] false and superficial conversion—a mere external change on entering monastery. Character sketches of types of false monks {are provided} —the unduly serious—the dissipated. (Read from chapter 20.[605]) They have in common *attachment to their own will*, and attachments to petty things in monastic life (see c. 21). *Conference* 4 ends here.

"anima" or mind, rather than by the spirit; Cassian goes on to quote I Cor. 2:14 as exemplifying the "animal" man: *"Animalis autem homo non percipit ea quae sunt spiritus Dei: stultitia enim est illi"* ("The animal man does not perceive those things which are of God's spirit: for they are meaningless to him"): *animalis* is thus the Latin equivalent of Paul's *psychikos*, the "natural" man (see *Golden Epistle*, 25, n. 2).

603. The number of the letter is left blank in Merton's text, but it seems clear that the reference is to Letter 171 (in the numbering of *The Letters of St. Bernard of Clairvaux*, trans. Bruno Scott James [Chicago: Regnery, 1953] [= #96 in the collection in *PL* 182 (col. 229)]), addressed to Abbot Richard of Fountains: "Your progress from good to better is no less wonderful, no less gratifying, than a conversion from evil to good. It is much more easy to find many men of the world who have been converted from evil to good than it is to find one religious who has progressed from good to better. Anyone who has risen even a little above the state he has once attained in religion is a very rare bird indeed" (241).

604. Col. 608A: "On those who have made their renunciation badly" (title of chapter 20).

605. Col. 608A–609B: chapter 20 discusses monks who invent excuses for gathering wealth—whether to support their relatives, or their fellow monks, or projected foundations over which they would preside as abbots—rather than stripping themselves not only of external possessions but of self-will by submitting themselves to the guidance of elders. The root of such behavior is pride, which takes two forms, one of self-satisfied gravity, the other of frivolity; they are equally deficient, but the former is the more dangerous as having the outward appearance of virtue.

Conferences 9 and 10—DE ORATIONE: Conferences of Abbot Isaac on Prayer

Together with the first conference, of which they are a logical continuation, these are the two most important of Cassian's conferences, and the most interesting for contemplative monks. They are the solid foundation of Benedictine prayer. In an interesting unpublished article on "The Traditional Way of Benedictine Prayer," Fr. Paschal Botz, OSB says: "We can call Conferences 1, 9 & 10 the textbook of prayer for St. Benedict."[606] He quotes Dom C. Butler, "The theory and practice of prayer are unfolded in Cassian with a richness, an elevation and a practicality that have never been excelled."[607] Fr. Paschal goes on: "There are many points of direct contact in language and thought between Cassian and St. Benedict so that there can be no doubt that Benedict accepted the *Conferences* as the norm of prayer."

At the end of Abbot Moses' first conference on Purity of Heart, the question of distractions and constant prayer was raised. That led into the topic of discretion in the second conference, but this was a by-path. Not until the ninth conference does Cassian return to the question of the *pure prayer* which must constantly rise from the heart of the monk who is tranquil and purified of his attachments to inordinate passion. *Conference* 9 begins with a resumé of the basic ideas in *Conference* 1, to tie in the subject of pure prayer. It starts with a treatment of the qualities of pure prayer, goes on to talk of the different kinds of prayer and how they are to be used. This is followed by a brief *commentary on the Lord's Prayer*. After this, in chapter 25 Cassian goes on to speak of *mystical prayer* and the *gift of tears*, and returns after that to certain *external conditions for solitary prayer*. *Conference* 10 begins with a couple of brief digressions, on the Egyptian custom for the celebration of Easter and on the anthropomorphite

606. This is a 27-page mimeographed article still preserved at Gethsemani; the relevant sentences (from page 2) read: "The whole vast tradition of prayer from East and West was digested and presented in the *Conferences of Cassian* (especially conf. 1, 9, and 10). We can call these the textbook of prayer for St. Benedict."
607. Cuthbert Butler, *Benedictine Monachism* (London: Longmans, 1924), 62: "The theory and practice of prayer are unfolded with a richness, an elevation, and a practicality that have never been surpassed."

heresy, which leads in to the question of the *humanity of Our Lord and our prayer.* The rest of the conference is taken up with the question of perpetual prayer, and how to avoid distractions. We have already touched upon this in connection with the subject of distractions in the first conference. Let us turn now to *Conference* 9 which is the more important of the two.

Purity of heart and pure prayer. Abbot Isaac takes up the theme of Abbot Moses: purity of heart. Why? because the monk is essentially and above all a man of prayer. *He purifies his heart in order by prayer and contemplation to be as constantly united with God as is possible in the present life.* According to Abbot Isaac, *constant prayer is the reason for our withdrawal from the world, and it is the normal accompaniment of purity of heart.* The two go together. So just as everything in the monastic life tends to produce purity of heart (Abbot Moses) so everything in the monastic life tends to promote *uninterrupted perseverance in prayer, unshaken tranquillity of mind, and perfect purity of heart* (col. 771). {With} constant prayer {there is the} problem: not constant consolation; not constant feeling after prayer; prayer as a virtue, a *habitus,* part of a whole context of virtues. (Read chapter 2 here.[608]) All the virtues of the monk tend to this summit of prayer, but if they do not attain it, they cannot remain stable themselves. All the monastic observances should tend to keep us in constant prayer—for instance, the *balance between bodily and spiritual works*—is designed to promote true prayer (772). (Note the wisdom of the Desert Fathers. A superficial reader of such a text might think the important thing is the perpetual application to prayer and unconsciously think that this would mean perpetual application *of the mind in the same way all the time* to prayer, and this is in fact fatal to the life of prayer. We must wisely preserve a healthy alternation between bodily and spiritual works, so that our faculties and powers apply themselves *in turn* in different ways to prayer, and one rests while the other works. This is the secret of Benedictine balance and sobriety, which we should always try to preserve at all costs because without it perpetual prayer is really impossible.) *All the structure of the virtues tends to*

608. Col. 771A–773A: chapter 2 is summarized by Merton in the passage that follows.

the perfection of prayer. Ad orationis perfectionem omnis tendit structura virtutum (772).[609] Prayer is the soul of the life of virtue. Prayer is the completion of the edifice of virtue. Virtue without prayer is then imperfect, and the most important thing is lacking to a life of virtue if contemplation (in some sense) is absent from it. Isaac even goes further, and adds that unless the organism of virtue is kept alive and integrated by prayer, which is its fulfillment, it will die and disintegrate. *Nisi hujus culmine haec omnia fuerint colligata, NULLO MODO FIRMA POTERUNT VEL STABILIA PERDURARE* (772).[610] Prayer climaxes and "fixes" perfection. At the same time, prayer (contemplation) cannot be acquired without the exercise of all the virtues. Hence there is a vital and essential relationship between prayer and all the virtues in the spiritual life (virtues—"strengths"). Since the life of prayer is built on the foundation of virtues, it is useless to talk about it unless we keep in mind the virtues on which it depends. This is just another way of linking prayer and purity of heart, because the function of all the virtues is to purify the heart and remove those obstacles which make it difficult or impossible to keep recollected and engage ourselves with God alone. The most important virtues for the life of prayer, singled out here for special mention, are (773): simplicity, humility, mortification, faith (in the Gospels). When these four foundation stones are laid at the base of the edifice it cannot be shaken by passions or by the attacks of the enemy. But note—it will indeed be attacked.

Steps to take in the life of virtue to prepare for pure prayer (c. 3)—*Ut eo fervore ac puritate, qua debet, emitti possit oratio:*[611]

a) Get rid of all cares for material things, and for worldly business. A clean sweep must be made of all sources of distraction —i.e., of all avoidable business. The man of prayer must renounce

---

609. Col. 771B–772A, which reads: "*omnium*"; Cassian's text is translated "The structure of all the virtues tends to the perfection of prayer," whereas Merton's version is translated as in the previous sentence: "All the structure of the virtues. . ."

610. The text reads ". . . *colligata atque compacta, nullo modo* . . ." ("Unless all these things have been brought together [and joined] with this as its completion, by no means can they endure in firmness and stability.")

611. Col. 773B: "in order for prayer to be offered with that fervor and purity that is proper."

all concern with secular and material affairs, in so far as it is possible.

b) Purify the memory of all vain talk, distractions, idle jokes, and avoid all conversations where these will be heard; hence serious practice of *silence.*

c) Get rid of temptations to anger, *tristitia*[612] and lust—this most of all by solitude, withdrawal from the world.

d) Lay the foundations of humility really deep in the soul (*profundae humilitatis inconcussa fundamenta*).[613]

e) Then build on humility all the other virtues.

f) Take a special care for *recollection,* outside the time of prayer, lest we bring distractions with us to our prayer. *Quales orantes volumus inveniri, tales nos ante orationis tempus preparare debemus* (773).[614] An interesting expression is used (col. 774, top): *procumbentibus nobis ad pacem*[615]—for "going to pray" or "settling down to prayer": *pax* taken as synonymous for prayer (cf. Byzantine expression *hesychia*); *procumbens*—bodily prostration, to dispose for prayer by signifying humility and total submission to God. Lesson: prayer depends on our submission to God and humility, in which is true peace. A basic principle: remote preparation for prayer—a whole life of virtue; proximate—recollection and the thought of divine things even apart from the time formally devoted to prayer. Thus we can fulfil the command of the Apostle to "pray without ceasing" only if we purify our hearts of all attachments, love virtue with all our might, and devote ourselves totally to seeking the contemplation of God.

The instability of our minds—sources of distraction (cc. 4 ff. —De Mobilitate Animae).

The soul {is} compared to a feather which, if it is dry, will rise up lightly on the slightest breath of wind, but if it is wet it remains on the ground. So our souls if they are "dry" and pure of all concern with things that are not God, will rise up as it were

---

612. Col. 773B: "sadness."

613. Col. 773C: "stable foundations of deep humility."

614. "As we wish to be found when praying, so we must prepare to be before the time of prayer." (See the almost identical statement at col. 843A, the final chapter of *Conference* 10, quoted above on page 220.)

615. "prostrating ourselves for peace."

instinctively, by His grace, to Him. (Read chapter 4 here.[616]) This implies an optimistic view of our souls; they tend spontaneously to God when obstacles are removed, according to Cassian. He speaks of the work of asceticism as RESTORING the *mobilitas naturalis* (775)[617] of the soul, by which it seeks God. This is not necessarily Pelagian. He is probably taking grace into account. He does not belong to the age that made clear technical distinctions between nature and grace. *Amor meus pondus meum.*[618]

Sources of distraction (c. 5). The Lord in the Gospel (Lk. 21:34) does not say that we must take care lest our hearts be weighed down with obvious and terrible sins, like blasphemy, murder, etc., but with surfeiting and drunkenness and the cares of this life. Now as Abbot Isaac says, the monk is far away from opportunities for reveling and surfeiting, but he warns that there is a kind of spiritual gluttony and drunkenness of which he must beware. This is drunkenness that "does not come from wine"[619] but is as the gall of dragons, a diabolical inebriation that comes from *activism*. In a word Abbot Isaac is saying that there may not be much chance of surfeiting and drunkenness for the monk, but he *can* be overwhelmed with cares for temporal things and begin to lose himself entirely in temporalities. *The greatest danger*

616. This chapter (col. 774B–775A) consists in the comparison of the soul to the feather, just summarized by Merton, and includes a quotation from Luke 21:34 about not letting the heart become "weighed down" by earthly pleasures and cares.

617. Col. 774B, which reads *"naturali mobilitate"* ("by its natural motion").

618. Augustine, *Confessions* 13.9 (*PL* 32, col. 849), which reads, *"Pondus meum amor meus"* ("My weight is my love"); see Merton's comments in "The Recovery of Paradise," his part of the dialogue with D. T. Suzuki entitled "Wisdom in Emptiness" that was originally intended as an Introduction to *The Wisdom of the Desert*: "Remember Augustine's dictum, *amor meus, pondus meum*. 'My love is a weight, a gravitational force.' As one loves temporal things, one gains an illusory substantiality and a selfhood which gravitates 'downward,' that is to say acquires a *need* for things lower in the scale of being than itself. It depends on these things for its own self-affirmation. In the end this gravitational pull becomes an enslavement to material and temporal cares, and finally to sin. Yet this weight itself is an illusion, a result of the 'puffing up' of pride, a 'swelling' without reality. The self that appears to be weighted down by its love and carried away to material things is, in fact, an unreal thing" (Thomas Merton, *Zen and the Birds of Appetite* [New York: New Directions, 1968], 127).

619. Col. 776A (quoting Joel 1:5); the reference to "the gall of dragons" comes from Deut. 32:33.

to the monk's life of prayer is the possibility of becoming too attached to his work. In order to avoid this attachment, *work must be kept strictly to the necessary limits.* A monk should mortify the instinct to work overtime or to undertake unnecessary projects. He must see that his jobs do not multiply on all sides. The basic principle: if a monk can support himself on a dollar a day, he should not work for two dollars. *He should work for his bare necessities and no more.* When he has a cell of one or two rooms, he should rest content and not go enlarging everything and creating more work for himself. When he has two good robes, he should not bother about getting more. The restless soul ruins his life of prayer by constantly imagining there are new things that need to be done. All this is *PASSIO LIBIDINIS MUNDIALIS* (777).[620]

Note: At the other extreme are the monks who do not work at all, or rather who have no zeal for the common work. These, if they do not work for the monastery, are often taken up excessively with projects of their own and it is mere hypocrisy on their part to pretend that they can exempt themselves from the common work in order to "pray." But it is the same disease in both cases: the itch of our human will to work and to produce unnecessarily when we cannot bear the spiritual labor of being alone with God and putting up with our own nothingness in His presence.

READ chapter 6[621]—the hermit deluded by the devil and wearing himself out breaking a huge rock with a sledge hammer. *Nota bene.* This example of "sickness of mind"[622] which prevents prayer:

1. The hermit is very busy with something he has convinced himself to be "necessary work."[623] He is building useless additions on to his cell, and going in for useless repair jobs.

2. He is being driven to this work by the tyranny of the devil, who urges him on with a red hot torch. In other words it is a *burning and compulsive need for work* that keeps him from his prayer; he is running away from himself and from God. Excessive work is his means of doing so.

620. The text reads "*passionem libidinis mundialis*" ("the passion of worldly desire").
621. Col. 777A–778C, summarized by Merton in the passage that follows.
622. Col. 777A.
623. The implication of the passage, which says only that it was unnecessary ("*superfluis*") (col. 777A).

3. So powerful is the influence of this "devil" that even natural fatigue cannot persuade him to sit down and rest. The importance of this is evident, because some who are infected with the same sickness interpret their symptoms as "zeal" and "generosity." But if they would listen to the voice of their conscience, and examine themselves with discretion, they would easily tell the difference between this and true zeal and generosity. For the latter is accompanied by peace and emptiness of self and is blessed by true obedience. (Note: The cenobite can always extort permissions or commands to carry out the useless works to which he is attached. Yet in his heart of hearts he can tell that this is not true obedience.)

4. This work of the devil is a mockery of God's image in man—*dira ludificatio.*[624]

Cassian's conclusion: This worldly activism, this "ambition" which seeks to escape the inner solitude of the soul by the mirage of external accomplishments, is therefore *not merely a matter of undertaking works foreign to the monastic state.* (Application to us: we cannot pride ourselves on being free from this vice merely because we are not engaged in preaching or teaching school or running around the neighboring cities.) What matters, says Cassian, is our care in *restraining the need for undue work that is at hand, and tempts us by the appearance of necessity.* In other words, generosity in the contemplative life and true zeal for prayer demands that we mortify the instinctive urge to get into activities which tempt us here and now and appear to be useful and necessary. We have to learn to confine our works within the limits of necessity and obedience, and beyond that to *give our preference to prayer.*

Cassian points out that the activities which are compatible with the monastic state as such, can become distracting and inordinate if they are allowed to take up too great a part of our life and push prayer into the background. In fact they can be *just as distracting* as greater and more ambitious projects belonging to the apostolate or to life in the world. Naturally we should also be detached from purely *recreational* activities. Each one needs work and a certain relaxation of mind, but to avoid disorder, we

624. Col. 777C, which reads "*dira . . . ludificatione*" ("terrible trickery").

must *follow obedience* alone. Useless projects prevent true purity of heart. They prevent the monk from resting in God. They make the soul forget that God is its life and its joy, and they make it turn to other sources of satisfaction. This is in fact a spiritual death. We must be careful to keep our souls delicate and docile, responsive to the invitations of grace, and for this end we must not allow ourselves to be too much carried away with projects and activities which dull the spiritual sensibility of the soul. Work within reason refreshes the soul and helps prayer, but as soon as work becomes an outlet for self-love it ruins purity of heart. Neglect to mortify and control this desire for useless activity is the ruin of many potential contemplatives in our monasteries. But when our hearts are truly pure, then we live among the angels and no matter what we do, whether we work or pray, everything is transformed into pure prayer (778).

The Different Kinds of Prayer (cc. 8 ff.)—Abbot Isaac begins his discussion of the different kinds of prayer with true humility. Unlike the writers of familiar manuals and the readers of them for whom prayer becomes in theory such a clear and simple matter, Abbot Isaac reminds us of the fact that prayer is a mysterious and secret activity of the soul alone with God, and that it is rash to talk too glibly about it, because in fact "It is not possible to understand the various kinds of prayer without tremendous contrition of heart and purity of mind and the illumination of the Holy Ghost" (c. 8; 780).

The first difficulty in explaining the "kinds of prayer" is that there is in reality *an almost infinite variety*. Prayer is always varying. It is a living reality and there are as many kinds of prayer as there are variations of spiritual states in all the different souls of men. The second half of chapter 8 is extremely wise, and Abbot Isaac reminds us that we pray differently under different circumstances, and in "classifying" prayer we must not forget these differences and these potential variations. In other words we must not bind ourselves to pray always in the same way, or expect our prayer to fall always into the same pattern. We must not impose a rigid plan on our prayer life and try to make life conform to an abstract theory of our own, but we must on the contrary let our prayer be living, and let it grow out of our life in union with God. These cautions having been given, Abbot Isaac, following St. Paul, hesitantly suggests a possible division into *four kinds of prayer*, which may or may not cover the whole field of possibilities somehow (c. 9; 780–81). The four kinds of prayer (cf. I Tim. 2:1) are: Supplications, Prayers, Intercessions, Thanksgivings. He will first discuss the nature of each one. Then he will go on to see whether all four kinds belong in the prayer life of each Christian, or whether one form is appropriate to some, others to others, etc.

Supplication (obsecratio): The prayer of an earnest and contrite heart for the forgiveness of sin (783).

Prayers (orationes): Are especially those in which we offer, promise or vow something to God. Here the direction of the heart is to resolve something good and promise its accomplishment while praying for grace to carry it out, and desiring that God may be pleased with the offering, etc. "We pray when we renounce this world and pledge ourselves to die to all mundane acts and styles of living, and set ourselves to serve God with all our heart . . ." etc. (see c. 12; col. 784). The value of this prayer is proportionate to the sincerity of our intention to put into effect our good resolutions.

Intercessions (postulationes): Prayers offered for others in a time of fervor, whether for our own friends and relatives or for the peace of the world—for the good of the whole Church. Here is where Cassian considers the monk's role as intercessor for others, "for all men, for Kings and for those in high positions."[625] Here we have the monk's apostolate of prayer, the monk as the one who brings down grace upon the sinful world by his intercession. {This is} not just {the} official line!

Thanksgiving (gratiarum actio): These prayers well up from the heart which remembers the gifts of God, or contemplates His goodness and mercy in the present, or looks forward to the future fulfillment of His promises (cf. St. Bede).[626] Thanksgiving

625. Col. 785B, quoting I Tim. 2:1-2.
626. The reference may be to the famous scene of Bede on his deathbed, as related in the *Epistola Cuthberti de Obitu Bedae* by the monk Cuthbert, an eyewitness: "Nearly a fortnight before Easter (17th April, 734) he was seized by an extreme

is not merely a cold and formal acknowledgement of these good things, but a deep and ardent expression of love in which we pray *"per ineffabiles excessus."*[627] This kind of prayer tends by its very nature to soar beyond words and clear concepts. It is marked by great *purity* (of faith, hope, and love) by immense *joy*, and by a kind of *passivity* (*spiritus noster* instigatur . . .[628]). (Read c. 14).[629] They are prayers of *fire* (*preces ignitas*[630]) (785–86).

Chapter 15—Prayer of fire *from all four kinds. The four kinds of prayer* can be found alternately in one and the same person. Normally one of each type predominates in various degrees of the spiritual life. *Supplication* is more appropriate to the *beginner* who is not yet purged of his sins. *Prayers* are for the *progressives* who are advancing in virtue with confidence and faith. *Intercessions* are for the *perfect* who are able to pray for others with over-

_____

weakness, in consequence of his difficulty of breathing, but without great pain. He continued thus till the Ascension (26th May), always joyous and happy, giving thanks to God day and night, and even every hour of the night and day. He gave us our lessons daily, and employed the rest of his time in chanting psalms, and passed every night, after a short sleep, in joy and thanksgiving, but without closing his eyes. From the moment of awaking he resumed his prayers and praises to God, with his arms outstretched as a cross. O happy man! He sang sometimes texts from S. Paul and other scriptures, sometimes lines in our own language, for he was very able in English poetry, to this effect:—None is wiser than him needeth, ere his departure, than to ponder ere the soul flits, what good, what evil it hath wrought, and how after death it will be judged" (quoted in S. Baring-Gould, *The Lives of the Saints*, 16 vols. [Edinburgh: John Grant, 1914], 5:401-402).

627. Col. 785B: "through unspeakable ecstasies."
628. Col. 785C: "our spirit is impelled."
629. Col. 785BC: *"Quarto deinde loco gratiarum actiones ponuntur, quas mens, vel cum praeterita Dei recolit beneficia, vel cum praesentia contemplatur, seu cum in futurum quae et quanta praeparaverit Deus his qui diligunt eum prospicit, per ineffabiles excessus Deo refert. Qua etiam intentione nonnumquam preces ulteriores emitti solent, dum illa quae reposita sunt in futuro sanctorum praemia purissimis oculis intuendo, ineffabiles Deo gratias cum immenso gaudio spiritus noster instigatur effundere."* ("Finally, in the fourth place are put acts of thanksgiving, which the mind offers to God through unspeakable ecstasies, either when it recalls the past benefits of God, or when it reflects on present benefits, or when it looks forward into the future to so many benefits that God has prepared for those who love Him. With this intention also further prayers are sometimes accustomed to be offered while our spirit is impelled with immeasurable joy to pour forth inexpressible thanks to God, as we admire with purified eyes those future rewards which have been stored up for the saints.")
630. Col. 786A, which reads *"preces ignitasque."*

flowing charity. *Thanksgiving* is for the purified soul (of the mystic?). These souls "with most pure minds are carried away with most burning hearts into that prayer of fire which the tongue of man can neither express nor comprehend."[631] {Note the} originality of this doctrine: in any state or level man can sometimes offer pure and devout prayer—always a coalescence of all four (*WA* p. 221).[632] {There is} gradual progress (c. 16). Important (c. 18): *out of all four* comes the loftier state: contemplation of God alone; charity that burns like fire; *parrhesia* (*WA*, p. 222).[633]

Cassian goes on to remark however that in the contemplative's "prayer of fire" *all the kinds of prayer are likely to come together,* "in the form of an incomprehensible and most burning flame. . . ."[634] In this prayer the Holy Spirit prays in us with "unutterable groanings" and the soul with great *strength* rises up to God filled with innumerable intentions and thoughts all in one moment, which, when left to itself, the soul could not conceive in a long stretch of time! At the same time, he will tell us later that this is not pure contemplation. The prayer of fire is related rather to *Theoria Physica* than to the highest contemplation. Also, sometimes in the very lowest form of prayer (compunction), the soul is raised to these same heights of fire by the vision of the divine mercy.

To the higher degrees of prayer we must travel in a patient and orderly manner beginning at the bottom and working up (c. 16). *It is a great mistake to rush on ahead of grace in the spiritual life.* We may be able to convince ourselves for a while that we are getting somewhere, but in the end we will only have to go

631. Col. 786B.
632. The reference is to the translation of selections from Cassian in Owen Chadwick, ed. and trans., *Western Asceticism*, Library of Christian Classics, vol. 12 (Philadelphia: Westminster, 1958), 221: "So it happens that, whatever state of life a man has reached, he sometimes can offer pure and devout prayer. Even in the lowliest place where a man is repenting from fear of punishment and the judgement to come, his 'supplications' can enrich him with the same ardour of spirit as the man who has attained to purity of heart, gazes upon God's blessing, and is filled with an ineffable happiness" (c. 15; col. 786C).
633. *Western Asceticism*, 222: "Out of these four kinds of prayer rises the loftier state of prayer formed by the contemplation of God alone and by a charity that burns like fire. Here the mind throws itself into love for God and converses familiarly with him as with its own Father" (col. 788BC).
634. Col. 786B.

back and cover more laboriously and with greater difficulty the ground we had passed over too rapidly.

Chapter 17 shows how Jesus made use of all these forms of prayer—quotes from the New Testament are discussed as proofs of the fact (787).

After this, Cassian turns to an analysis of the Lord's Prayer— a standard requisite for any early treatise on prayer. Origen had commented on the Lord's Prayer in his own treatise *De Oratione*.[635] This is obvious because the *Pater* is the model of all Christian prayer. Let us never say it merely mechanically.

The Pater Noster

The opening words, says Cassian, are an indication that it is God's will that we seek the *parrhesia* (familiar speech, the liberty of sons) with God, lost by Adam—God is our Father, and He wills above all that we be united to Him in love and contemplation. Here Cassian sums up the constant tradition of the Fathers. Perfect contemplation is, he says, a state more sublime than anything included in the four kinds of prayer he has been discussing; this highest prayer has the following elements:

1. Contemplation and love of God alone. (It is the pure contemplation of the Trinity, not the *theoria* of God in creatures.)

2. The mind is taken out of itself, abandons itself, in pure love of God, and gives itself over to the most intimate and familiar union.

3. The soul then "converses" (not with words) with God with a very special kind of love (*peculiari pietate*) (c. 18; 788).

PATER NOSTER QUI ES IN COELIS:[636] When we call God our Father,

1. Freely and with full knowledge *we acknowledge His universal Fatherhood*. (These are basic patristic themes.)

2. Recognize that we are called by Him from a condition of servitude to creatures, to the liberty of sons of God. It is in a word

---

635. Chapters 18–30: see Origen, *Prayer, Exhortation to Martyrdom*, trans. John J. O'Meara, Ancient Christian Writers, vol. 19 (Westminster, MD: Newman, 1954), 65–129.

636. Col. 789A: "Our Father who art in heaven."

recognition of the great dignity of man, made in the image of God to live as His son (769).

3. We acknowledge that we are in *exile on this earth,* and far from our Father's house, and we deplore our exile, hastening as fast as we can to rejoin our Father in heaven with most ardent desire (*regio dissimilitudinis*).[637]

4. We *reject everything that hinders us in our journey homeward* to our Father and we refuse to become involved in anything which is not worthy of our divine sonship.

5. We implicitly promise to live as His sons, generously seeking not our own convenience and our own interests but His glory above all, "*Ut jam non pro nostris utilitatibus, sed pro nostri Patris gloria totum impendamus affectum*" (789–90)[638] (language of St. Thomas).[639]

This leads into the first petition: SANCTIFICETUR NOMEN TUUM:[640]

1. We protest that our whole desire and all our joy is found in His glory: ". . . *nostrum desiderium, nostrum gaudium, gloriam Patris nostri esse testantes*. . . ." (790).[641]

2. Thus we tend to imitate Jesus who "came to seek the glory of Him who sent me" (John 7).

3. This implies a *hunger for the salvation of souls,* as that of St. Paul who wished to be anathema in order that the Father might be glorified by the salvation of Israel. (Cassian comments on

---

637. "Land of unlikeness," a phrase particularly associated with St. Bernard: cf. Gilson, chapter 2 (33–59), which has this phrase as its title and considers the loss of likeness to God as the result of the Fall, and 224–25, n. 43, which discusses in detail the source and meaning of the phrase.

638. "so that now we might devote all our effort not for our own advantage but for the glory of our Father."

639. See II–II, Q. 83, art. 9 (ed. Gilby, 39:70/71): "*Finis autem noster Deus est, in quem noster affectus tendit dupliciter: uno quidem modo, prout volumus gloriam Dei; alio modo, secundum quod volumus frui gloria ejus; quorum primum pertinet ad dilectionem qua Deum in seipso diligimus; secundum vero pertinet ad dilectionem qua diligimus nos in Deo.*" ("Our goal is God, in whom our desires tend in two ways, first by willing the glory of God, and secondly by willing to enjoy his glory. The first desire pertains to the love whereby we love God in himself, while the second pertains to the love whereby we love ourselves in God.")

640. Col. 790A: "Hallowed be Thy name."

641. The text reads ". . . *nostri Patris* . . ." ("witnessing that our desire, our joy, is the glory of our Father").

Paul's desire to be anathema: "*Securus enim optat interire pro Christo, qui novit neminem posse mori pro vita*" [790].[642])

4. It implies *total self-forgetfulness in order* to think of the glory of God and the interests of immortal souls (791) (cf. Michaeas, Moses).[643]

5. It also implies *an ardent desire for the perfection of charity. Sanctificatio Dei nostra perfectio est*[644]—He is glorified in us by good works and true charity.

Cf. Tertullian: The *sanctus* of the angels; we are *angelorum candidati*.[645]

ADVENIAT REGNUM TUUM (c. 19).[646] ({Cf.} Tertullian: *Deus quando non regnat*[647] [note aggressivity].) This is the *secunda petitio mentis purissimae*.[648] (Note the *Pater* is the prayer of the Pure in Heart and the perfect—not merely of the beginner. Perfection in prayer does not mean passing on from the *Pater* to something else, but entering with the greatest purity and perfection into the full meaning of the prayer of Jesus Himself.)

1. The Kingdom of God means first of all *His reign in our souls by virtue*, and the victory over vice—evicting the kingdom of the devil.

2. It also means the *perfection of the Kingdom to be offered by Christ to the Father at the end of time*, when the elect enter into the glory of the Father (792).

3. It means the coming of Christ at the Last Judgement—therefore one must be pure in heart to utter this petition, otherwise we are inviting our own condemnation. (At least we must

642. The text reads ". . . *mori posse* . . ." ("He could safely wish to perish for Christ's sake, knowing that no one can be dead for the sake of life.") (The reference is to Romans 9:3.)

643. The reference to Moses is presumably to Ex. 32:32, when Moses asks to be struck from the book of life if the Lord does not forgive Israel. The reference to Michaeas is less clear; it probably refers not to the canonical prophet Micah of Moresheth but to Micaiah ben Imlah, the prophet who foretells disaster to King Ahab in I Kings (III Kings) 22 when all the other prophets are predicting victory.

644. Col. 791A: "The glorification of God is our perfection."

645. *De oratione* 3:1 (*PL* 1, col. 1156A): "future companions of the angels."

646. Col. 791B: "Thy Kingdom come."

647. *De oratione* 3:5 (*PL* 1, col. 1158B): "when does God not rule?"

648. Col. 791B: "The second petition of the purified mind."

have a firm hope that Jesus will forgive our sins and give us grace to amend our lives! And we must effectively strive to abandon ourselves entirely to His Providence and carry out in all things His holy will.)

FIAT VOLUNTAS TUA (supplicatio filiorum[649]*)* (c. 20):

1. We ask that His will be done on earth as it is in heaven. Cassian marvels at the loftiness of this petition. *Non potest esse major oratio, quam optare ut terrena mereantur coelestibus coaequari* (792).[650] It is to ask: *may men become the equal of the angels,* and fulfil His will as perfectly as the pure spirits. (The monk, called to an "angelic life" is therefore called to this kind of perfection of obedience.)

2. No one, says Cassian, can reasonably utter this petition unless he is *determined to see all things as coming from God*— whether pleasant or hard, and who believes that God is more solicitous for our best interests than we can be for ourselves (793).

3. Another meaning of this petition again bears on *the salvation of souls*—for "God wills all men to be saved"[651] and then the petition means: "Just as all the angels and saints in heaven are filled with the vision of God and His Truth, so *may everyone on earth be saved by coming to know God as their Father.*"[652] How beautiful and truly Catholic is Cassian's notion of prayer. Notice that always he sees things with the perspective of the whole Christ—at the same time, he sees clearly the importance of the monk's own individual salvation and sanctification, and he reconciles the two in such a way that there can be no conflict and no problem between the piety of the individual and the worship offered by the whole Body of Christ to the Father.

PANEM NOSTRUM QUOTIDIANUM (vel supersubstantialem) DA NOBIS HODIE (c. 21):[653] Like St. Cyprian and St. Ambrose,[654] Cassian

649. Col. 792B: "Thy will be done"; "the request of offspring."
650. "There can be no greater prayer than to ask that the earthly might be worthy to equal the heavenly."
651. Col. 793A–794A, a quotation from I Tim. 2:4.
652. Col. 793A–794A: an interpretive paraphrase, not a direct quotation.
653. Col. 794A: "Give us this day our daily (or supersubstantial) bread."
654. See Cyprian, *De Oratione Dominica*, c. 18 (*PL* 4, col. 531A–532A); Ambrose, *De Sacramentis*, 5:4 (*PL* 16, col. 452AC).

interprets this of the Holy Eucharist (another significant eucharistic text in Cassian!). There is no conflict between the two wordings of this petition—both mean the same thing and Cassian takes them *as completing one another*. The Bread we pray for is the Bread of Life, the "supersubstantial" Bread of the Word Incarnate, and it must be our *daily* Bread because the Holy Eucharist is to be received *every day* (in fact however the hermits only received Our Lord once a week). *NON EST DIES QUO NON OPUS SIT NOBIS HUJUS ESU AC PERCEPTIONE COR INTERIORIS HOMINIS NOSTRI* CONFIRMARE (795).[655] He adds that this same supersubstantial Bread (the vision of the Incarnate Word in heaven) will be our eternal life-giving food in heaven; we cannot come to the heavenly banquet unless we frequently receive the Body of the Savior sacramentally in this life.

DIMITTE NOBIS DEBITA NOSTRA (c. 22):[656] Like St. Benedict (cf. *Rule*),[657] Cassian sees in this petition *a way of determining in advance what will be God's judgement of us!* (796). We have in this petition not only a request which helps us to pull out by the roots every evil plant of *tristitia* and of *anger*, but also a sure way of providing for ourselves a favorable and clement judgement on the part of God Himself. He who does not forgive his brother from his heart cannot utter this petition without adding to the burden of his own sins! Cassian adds that in some Churches many members of the congregation would close their lips when this petition came along, lest they just make matters worse for themselves. Cassian says this is no excuse. *All must not only say the petition openly but strive to mean it*. This gives us something of the background of St. Benedict's prescription that the *Pater* be chanted aloud at Vespers and at Lauds.[658] The petition is a spe-

---

655. The text reads ". . . *nostri hominis* . . ." ("There is no day on which we do not need to strengthen the heart of our inner selves by eating and digesting this bread.")

656. Col. 796A: "Forgive us our debts."

657. See chapter 13: "For, being warned by the covenant which they make in that prayer, when they say *Forgive us as we forgive*, the brethren will cleanse their souls of such faults" (i.e., "those thorns of scandal, or mutual offense, which are wont to arise in communities") (McCann, 57).

658. See chapter 13: "Of course, the Office of Lauds and Vespers shall never be allowed to end without the superior finally reciting, in the hearing of all, the whole of the Lord's Prayer" (McCann, 57).

cial gift of God's mercy and an indication of His holy will that we act as His sons by forgiving others as He wills to forgive both them and ourselves.

ET NE NOS INDUCAS IN TENTATIONEM (c. 23):[659] This, says Cassian, raises a problem—for it is necessary that we be tempted in order that our virtue may be genuine and our love for God really solid and true. *Beatus vir qui suffert tentationem.*[660] Cassian therefore interprets this to mean: "*do not allow us to be overcome by temptation.*" (This interpretation is also given, with more details and qualifications and alternatives, by the Catechism of the Council of Trent.[661]) {According to} St. Augustine, Susanna was tempted but not *inducta in temptationem.*[662] Augustine ends with the idea of *unrecognized* temptation, when we think evil is good. {It} finally means—don't let things get too good.

SED LIBERA NOS A MALO:[663] Cassian explains this by quoting St. Paul: Do not permit us to be tempted beyond our strength but give us grace that we may bear the temptation (I Cor. 10).

Summary and conclusion of the Lord's Prayer (c. 24): Cassian now remarks drily that there is no mention in the Lord's Prayer of anything that would bring us riches or honors, no request for power and strength, not even a petition that our health and our temporal life may be protected. He says that we would offend God by asking Him for temporal things, but on this point the Church does not agree with him—his point is rather rhetorical and not to be taken too seriously. We can and indeed must pray for our temporal needs in so far as the aid of God in these matters is necessary to help us get to heaven.

659. Col. 798A: "And lead us not into temptation."
660. Col. 798B–799A: "Blessed is the one who endures temptation" (a quotation from James 1:12).
661. Cf. *Catechism of the Council of Trent for Parish Priests*, trans. John A. McHugh, OP and Charles Collins, OP (New York: F. Wagner, 1934), 565–76, esp. 572–73.
662. "[not] led into temptation": Augustine, "*De Sermone Domini in Monte,*" 2:9 (*PL* 34, col. 1283–84).
663. Col. 799A: "But deliver us from evil."

The Lord's Prayer leads to perfect contemplation. Like St. Teresa of Avila,[664] Cassian affirms that if we pray the *Pater* really well it can lead us to higher degrees of prayer, notably to that prayer of fire which he has already described. "This prayer [the *Pater*] leads those who practice it well to that higher state which we have described above, and brings them at last to that *prayer of fire* which is known and experienced by few and which is an inexpressibly high degree of prayer. . . ." (c. 25; col. 801). He recapitulates some of the characteristics of the "higher prayer":

1. It is beyond all man's senses and understanding.
2. It is made without the movement of the tongue or the pronunciation of words.
3. It is purely mental and indeed passive—made by the "mind illuminated by the infusion of heavenly light"[665]—not making use of human and limited forms of speech, but *with all the powers gathered together in unity* it pours itself forth copiously and cries out to God in a manner beyond expression, saying so much in that brief moment that the mind cannot relate it afterwards with ease or even go over it again after returning to itself.

This he says was the prayer of Jesus when He was alone on the mountain and even the agony in the Garden had this same character (col. 802). So in either case Jesus is the perfect model of prayer. There is no question that Cassian is here speaking of mystical prayer of a high degree and not of mere sensible consolations in ordinary prayer.

Fervor in Prayer (cc. 26 ff.): Cassian turns to the different sources of fervor in prayer which, he says, are innumerable and he calls them all "compunctions" (col. 802). These are sensible graces which aid us to be fervent in our prayer. It is for our part to remain disposed to receive these graces and to take advantage of them. We must not be ungrateful of the slightest chance to grow in prayer, and must not despise the humble and

---

664. See *The Way of Perfection*, chapter 25: "I tell you that it is very possible that while you are reciting the Our Father or some other vocal prayer, the Lord may raise you to perfect contemplation" (St. Teresa of Avila, *Collected Works*, 2:131).
665. Col. 801B.

ordinary opportunities offered us by God to do so. We must be ready for these special moments and touches of grace that awaken us from inertia. Here are some of them according to Cassian:

1. They can come with a *verse of a psalm,* which can provide an *occasionem orationis ignitae.*[666] The meaning of the psalms we sing are the primary and obvious source of light in choral prayer. Hence St. Benedict's advice—*mens concordat voci.*[667] (N.B. the Psalms' principle {is} to make them so much our own that we experience them as poems we ourselves have written [{*Conf.*} 10, c. 11]. This involves time, and patient rumination of texts, staying with one text until it is *fully absorbed.* This application *interiorly renews our spirit.*)

2. The fervor of our brethren in choir can excite us to greater compunction and attention in prayer—especially the distinctness and gravity with which they pronounce the psalms. (Cassian is thinking of the Egyptian office in which one monk chanted the psalm and the others listened.) With us the Gregorian melodies {would have a comparable effect}.

3. Spiritual conferences and exhortations given by the Fathers.

4. The death of someone dear to us—or especially of one of the brethren—can excite compunction and recollection and greatly aid our progress in prayer, reminding us of the last things and stirring us up to pray for or with the brother who has died and gone to his reward, sharing his victory in the Lord.

5. The remembrance of our own tepidity and negligence can excite in us salutary zeal for prayer.

In a word, Cassian declares that there are innumerable ways in which God stirs us up and awakens us out of our torpor, to keep us praying well (803).

Expressions of fervor (c. 27): Fervor is again equated with "compunction." (Note—see also St. Bernard, Serm. III Epiphany;[668]

---

666. Col. 802B: "an occasion for the prayer of fire."

667. *Rule,* c. 19: "*sic stemus ad psallendum ut mens nostra concordet voci nostrae*" ("so sing the psalms that mind and voice may be in harmony") (McCann, 68/69).

668. PL 183, col. 152CD: "*Hae sunt lacrymae devotionis, in quibus non indulgentia peccatorum, sed beneplacitum quaeritur Dei Patris, cum descendit in nos spiritus*

John Climacus Step 7.[669])

1. *Clamores intolerabilis gaudii*[670]—the holy hermits, possessed with "unbearable joy," shout and cry out in their cells and can be heard at a great distance! (not to be imitated by cenobites!) (col. 803).

2. At other times, the soul is overwhelmed by grace and reduced to total silence so that we cannot utter a word—*profound interior silence.*

It is well to examine the language in which he describes this grace. *Tanto silentio mens intra secretum profundae taciturnitatis absconditur.*[671] {He} redoubles words for "silence," hiddenness, and inwardness: *silentium, taciturnitas; secretum, absconditur; intra, profundae.* The *"mens,"* that which is most inward in man, is "hidden in the secret depths of silence"; *stupor subitae illuminationis*[672]—silences the sound of any word or the spirit may pour forth unutterable desires. Sometimes tears are the only outlet (cf. St. Benedict—*"compunctio lacrymarum"*[673]). He is talking of a simple form of contemplative prayer of beginners. Germanus readily admits he is familiar with this; however he thinks there is nothing more sublime—*"nihil sublimius."*[674] But {he} complains he cannot produce this at will. Is this possible?

In reply, Abbot Isaac describes different sources of "tears" with illustrations from the psalms, etc. (c. 29):

1. Some come from the memory of our sins (805).

---

adoptionis filiorum, testimonium perhibens spiritui nostro quod sumus filii Dei, ut mellifluum nobis vocem de coelo videamur audire, quia vere Deus Pater in nobis complaceat sibi." ("These are the tears of devotion, in which is sought not indulgence for sinners but the good pleasure of God the Father, when the Spirit of adoption as sons descends upon us, giving witness to our spirit that we are God's sons, as we seem to hear the sweet voice from heaven saying that God the Father is truly well pleased with us.")

669. Cf. *Ladder*, 7:9: "Keep a firm hold of the blessed joy-grief of holy compunction, and do not stop working at it until it raises you high above the things of this world and presents you pure to Christ" (114).

670. "Shouts of unbearable joy."

671. Col. 803B; translated by Merton below.

672. Col. 803B: "the amazement of a sudden enlightenment."

673. *Rule*, c. 20 (McCann, 68/69).

674. Col. 804A.

2. Some from the contemplation of our eternal reward, thirst for God and the desire of heaven (*"futurae claritatis"*[675]).

3. Some from fear of hell and of the Last Judgement.

4. The sins of others can be a source of tears for us, also.

5. Sorrow at the miseries of this present life (806).

Finally there are tears which are brought on by sheer force from "dry eyes." Cassian is willing to approve even these as being not without merit, but only in the case of the hardened sinner who has little or no knowledge of God. Those who have progressed a little in the spiritual life and have a taste for virtue are "by no means" to force themselves to weep as this would be very harmful, *for it would prevent them from ever arriving at the grace of spontaneous tears.* Climacus speaks of tears forced by vanity and self-will (Step 7) and manifested by pride and uncharitableness.[676]

Cassian here lays down an important principle: violence and strain are not only useless in the spiritual life, but they are harmful and prevent the true spiritual life from developing properly. *They kill spontaneity* which is absolutely necessary in our relations with God, and which is what we must try as far as possible to preserve, {and} may distract us from the humility which makes prayer fruitful. Note Cassian's respect for the natural makeup of man, and for his psychic mechanism.

St. Anthony on perfect prayer (c. 31): Abbot Isaac reverently brings in the name of Anthony the Great, the supreme model and doctor of prayer for the ancient Fathers. Anthony could pray whole nights *"in eodem excessu mentis"*[677]—carried out of himself with the same ecstasy. Anthony's description of perfect prayer is qualified by Isaac as a "heavenly statement which is beyond all that is human"—(in other words, inspired by God). NON EST PERFECTA ORATIO IN QUA SE MONACHUS, VEL HOC IPSUM QUOD ORAT,

---

675. Col. 805A: "future clearness."

676. Cf. *Ladder*, 7:44: "He who in his heart is proud of his tears, and secretly condemns those who do not weep, is like a man who asks the king for a weapon against his enemy, and then commits suicide with it" (119); cf. also 7:26, 30–35, 47 (117–19).

677. Col. 807B (which reads *"eodem in excessu mentis"*): "in the same ecstasy of spirit."

INTELLIGIT (col. 808).[678] In the opinion of Isaac, this is the last word on prayer, to which nothing further may be added. (The note added by Gazaeus lacks comprehension.[679])

When are our prayers heard? Are there indications by which we can know that God has heard our prayer?

1. Firm and unshakeable confidence in God is a sign that He has heard our prayer (cf. Mark 11: *Quaecumque orantes petitis, credite quia accipietis et fiet vobis*[680]).

2. "In the consent of two or more"[681]—in other words, in communal and public prayer.

3. Firm faith.

4. Assiduous perseverance.

5. Uniting almsgiving with our prayer.

6. Reform of our life and works of mercy (as opposed to fasting without charity—cf. Isaias 58).

7. The fact that we are overwhelmed by trials may be a sign that God has heard our prayer—(*Ad Dominum, cum tribularer, clamavi et exaudivit me. . .*[682]).

8. Finally, says Isaac, even though we may be poor sinners and lack all the above, our mere *importunity* in prayer will win us a hearing from God. For God urges us Himself to importune Him with constant prayers (811). Hence we should never give up merely because our prayers do not seem to be heard at first.

Cassian however adds that we should leave all our prayers up to the divine good pleasure and always conclude "not my will but thine be done" (816).

678. The text reads, "*Non est, inquit, perfecta . . .*" ("[He said,] 'It is not perfect prayer in which a monk is conscious of himself or of what he is praying.'")
679. Col. 807D: "Of course, with regard to this type and level of perfection: it does not pertain to any except the most holy and perfect, such as Anthony; by it one is elevated and caught up in spirit into God in prayer, so that one is aware of nothing else but God; it is certainly the most perfect way of praying, but let the one who is able to take it, take it."
680. Col. 809A (which reads ". . . *et veniet vobis*"): "Whatsoever you ask for while praying, believe that you will receive it and it will come to you" ("happen to you" in Merton's text).
681. Col. 809B, quoting Mt. 18:19.
682. Col. 810B: "I cried out to the Lord when I was in trouble, and he heard me" (Ps. 119 [120]:1).

Other qualities of prayer:

1. Secrecy and recollection—we must enter into the inner sanctuary of our own hearts and put aside cares and distractions to pray to our Father in secret.

2. Silence—we must "close the door"[683] of our babbling tongue.

3. We must present our petitions to God alone, without even an interior imagined audience—our prayer must not intrude upon our brethren by exterior sounds.

4. *FREQUENTER SED BREVITER ORANDUM EST*[684]—This is a true sacrifice and a salutary oblation—we get these prayers out before their purity can be tarnished by the enemy. This subject is continued in chapter 10 of *Conference* 10—"On perpetual prayer" (col. 831 ff.).

Constant Prayer (Conf. 10, c. 10; col. 831 ff.): Abbot Isaac gives what he calls a *"formula spiritualis theoriae"*[685]—a brief form of prayer which can be constantly repeated and meditated in the depths of the heart so that we return constantly to the presence of God and keep ourselves in a perpetual state of prayer. This repeated formula, constantly meditated, will fight off distractions and purify our hearts to contemplate Him. What is it? *DEUS IN ADJUTORIUM MEUM INTENDE* . . . etc.[686] It is a *perfectly universal* form of prayer applicable to all times, persons and states. It implicitly contains acts of all the virtues—humility, trust, confidence, faith. It infallibly brings the aid of God and overcomes the attacks of the devil. It is appropriate for all spiritual states—whether sadness or joy. We must make constant use of this ejaculation in the depths of our hearts, driving out all other thoughts with it in order to become truly poor in spirit, no longer trusting for a moment in ourselves but abandoning all care for ourselves into the hands of God. This *leads to contemplation* of the divine mysteries (col. 837). Evidently we must not misunderstand Cassian—it is not merely a question of mechanical repetition of the formula—not magic

683. Col. 817A.
684. Col. 817B: "One should pray often, but briefly."
685. Col. 852A, which reads *"spiritalis theoriae . . . formula"* ("a brief form for spiritual contemplation").
686. Col. 832B: "O God, come to my assistance . . ." (Ps. 69 [70]:2).

efficacy or hypnosis. The influence of Cassian was widespread on this point as on others. The practice of using the *Deus in adjutorium* at all times, especially at the beginning of each new action or observance, was universal in Western monasticism: cf. Warnefrid: *Consuetudo fuit et est monachorum ut in omnibus operibus, tam spiritualibus quam temporalibus, cum aliquid incipiunt, terna vice hunc versiculum dicere* (quoted in Symons, *Regularis Concordia*, p. 11[687]). It must be said not merely with the lips, but in the depths of our being, and with all sincerity, and desire.

Oriental monachism has always favored "short and fervent prayer" frequently repeated. The repetition may be rhythmical, and associated with rhythmic breathing, as in the case of the famous "prayer of Jesus" (in which Oriental monks repeat the Holy Name inwardly at each breath, with the desire of giving Jesus full possession of the very inmost source of life, as if imprinting His presence on their heart of hearts more deeply with each repetition).

Cassian intends that this prayer should be united with the practice of virtue. It should be used in every trial and temptation and should be as it were a springboard for virtuous reaction against the tempter. In particular, for example, against temptations to anger, it should be used in conjunction with meditation of the meekness of Jesus in His passion (col. 837). Use of this and other similar invocations from the Psalms brings us to the point where we recite the Psalms no longer as if they were the poems of another but as if they were composed by our own selves, so perfectly do they express our own inmost desires and affections (col. 838). This in turn leads to a deeper understanding of Scripture, in which we experience as it were the inner meaning by connaturality. Here again, says Cassian, we arrive eventually at the highest degree of prayer, *the prayer of fire* (see above). He describes it again, and this time adds one important

687. "It was and is the custom of monks to say this verse [*Deus in adiutorium meum intende*] three times in succession at the beginning of any work, whether spiritual or temporal" (*The Monastic Agreement of the Monks and Nuns of the English Nation*, translation by Thomas Symons, OSB of the *Regularis Concordia* [New York: Oxford University Press, 1953], 11, n. 4, quoted from *Pauli Warnefridi in Sanctam Regulam Commentarium* [Monte Cassino, 1880], 335); this same instruction is given in the *Regularis Concordia* itself in nn. 21 (17), 25 (20–21), and 55 (54). See also *Rule*, c. 35 (McCann, 89).

new note: it is not only devoid of all words and goes beyond all man's own powers, but it is also *a prayer without images* or concepts in the mind (839).

Conclusion: Such, in brief, is Cassian's doctrine on prayer as it is found in these two conferences. It is a doctrine drawn first of all from the Gospels and the other Sacred Scriptures, especially the Psalms, and inspired by the teachings and example first of Jesus then of the holiest of the Desert Fathers. *It is essentially very simple.* Yet it embodies in itself all that was best and most essential in the teachings of the great master of prayer Evagrius Ponticus. Evagrius, as an Origenist, was discredited and maligned and yet his doctrine has nevertheless survived and had a mighty influence both in the Eastern and Western Church:

1. through the survival of his book on *Prayer*, ascribed to St. Nilus;

2. through disciples like St. Maximus the Confessor;

3. through Cassian, who is the main disseminator of Evagrius' teaching on prayer in the West.

Note Cassian purifies the doctrine of Evagrius and removes controversial elements. It presupposes the whole Catholic theology of grace, the realization of our own nothingness and total dependence on the grace of God—it does not rely on elaborate techniques. On the other hand it is far from quietistic inertia. As long as God Himself does not bring the soul into a clearly passive condition, we must make serious efforts to pray, at the same time keeping our prayer down to the simplest elements—a brief ejaculation repeatedly meditated in the heart. Cassian's prayer is linked inseparably with the practice of all the virtues, especially faith, humility, poverty of spirit, purity of heart, patience, self-denial, obedience, abandonment to the divine will. The whole purpose of Cassian's prayer is to purify our hearts, to place them under the sway of divine grace, so that we may glorify God in our lives by unceasing praise.

Conferences—Parts II and III: The Later Conferences of Cassian

The first ten conferences form a coherent treatise on the spiritual life. They were written about 420. Before 426, Cassian produced a *second series of conferences*, going back over the same ground covered by the first series and filling in details, or clarifying where necessary. *Conferences* 11–17 form this second part: *Conference* 11 *on Perfection* is a supplement to *Conference* 1 on the aim of the monastic life; *Conference* 12 on Chastity completes *Conference* 4 on the desires of the Flesh and the Spirit, etc. Part II contains the famous thirteenth *Conference* on the Divine Protection which contains the technical errors on grace severely censored by St. Prosper of Aquitaine. We will consider in detail the sixteenth *Conference* on Friendship. Before 429 a *third series* of conferences (18–24), more particularly addressed to hermits, is written. (After finishing the *Conferences*, Cassian went on to write his *Treatise on the Incarnation* against Nestorius, at the request of his friend the future Pope St. Leo the Great. The *Treatise on the Incarnation* completes the *Conferences* by showing that because Christ is true God, the monk can attain to divinisation "in Him." Also he attacks Pelagianism as a consequence of the error that Christ is only man.)

Conference 16—On Friendship by Abba Joseph

Introduction—Abba Joseph, living in {the} Nile Delta, knows Greek and talks to them in that language. The other abbots spoke through interpreters (c. 1; col. 1011). Having asked if they are blood brothers and learned that they are not, but have been inseparably united since their monastic conversion, he embarks on a conference about friendship.

Chapter 2—The question: friendship is universal among all kinds of creatures, even basilisks and gryphons. However, friendship is usually based on a community of interests that can in one way or other admit of dissolution, with time or separation, or through a rupture, etc. Hence he will investigate the problem *whether there can be an indissoluble friendship.*

Chapter 3—Insolubilis amicitia[688]—can exist. It is possible for a friendship to be so deep that even death does not dissolve it.

---

688. Col. 1014B: "indissoluble friendship" (Cassian uses the phrase "*indissolubilis amicitia*" in the title of chapter 3, but then in the opening sentence of

Such friendship is based not on material interests only, but on *virtue. Haec est vera et indirupta dilectio, quae gemina amicorum perfectione ac virtute concrescit* (col. 1015).[689] A friendship that has its origin in virtue can grow as the friends progress in virtue, and is perfect when they are perfect. But the virtue must grow *pari passu*[690] on both sides; otherwise a divergence between the friends leads to separation. True spiritual friendship is then: *fida indissolubilisque conjunctio, quae sola virtutum parilitate foederatur. . . . in quibus* [*amicis*] *unum propositum ac voluntas, unum velle ac nolle consistit* (1017–1018).[691] This implies great selflessness and mortification—the rejection of self-will. The ideal is one of perfect friendship that is not disturbed by quarrels or disagreements, even concerning the means of perfection.

In order to see what he means by friendship (c. 14; col. 1028), {note that he} distinguishes: *agape*—general love for all, even enemies, {and} *diathesis*—a special superabundant love, including *agape*, but *going beyond it*—directed to those with whom we have most in common spiritually. Hence it is clear that Cassian does not speak of *exclusive* and selfish friendships, still less of carnal or sensuous relationships. The love of friends is a love of *superabundance* and a perfection of the universal love given to all. It is not possible without selflessness and purity, and it helps to perfect these and other virtues.

Chapter 6—Foundations of perfect spiritual friendship:

1. {There must be} complete renunciation of the world and of all possessions.

2. Each obeys the other, or yields to the advice of the other, even in personal and spiritual matters.

3. All other things, however good, are set aside for charity and peace.

---

this chapter, he says that "*unum genus est insolubile charitatis*" ["there is one kind of love that is indissoluble"] [1014B–1015A]).

689. "This is true and unbroken love, that which increases the perfection and virtue of friends in equal measure."

690. "in tandem; at an equal rate."

691. "a faithful and unbreakable union, which is created by likeness in virtues alone . . . in whom there exists a single purpose and attitude, a single willingness and unwillingness."

4. No just cause for anger is ever admitted.

5. {Each is committed} to resolve to try and cure the brother's anger as if it were one's own.

6. Both should live as if they were to die this very day. (This is the cure for all vice.)

In this way they will avoid all quarrels and all contentions even over abstract and speculative matters, will obey one another and will live in perfect peace. *This is a very high ideal of Christian friendship as the perfection of Christian charity and peace,* and hence is a proper and characteristic element in Christian sanctity. Those who live in this way are true disciples of Christ. *Important*: Not only to avoid anger oneself, but to heal by meekness all anger in the brother. One cannot remain unconcerned about the anger of another—contrast between Christian love and mere Stoicism.

Chapter 7—Sicut ergo nihil praeponendum est charitati, ita furori vel iracundiae nihil est econtrario postponendum (col. 1023).[692]

Chapters 8–9—Dissension arises among carnal men over carnal things. It arises among spiritual men over spiritual things. Humility is the remedy.

Chapter 10—Attachment to "lights" and opinions—{is} generated by {the} devil to produce discord.

Chapter 11—This attachment and consequent discord {is} unavoidable as long as monks trust in their own judgement—hence importance of submitting all one's ideas and thoughts to the judgement of a wise senior.

Chapter 12—Collatio—bringing together (ideas)—even the wise and brilliant need to "confer" with those less wise, who may be able to correct and guide them in certain matters.

Chapter 15—Important psychological observation, on humble reconciliation in differences: wrong attitude—when angry, to go off by oneself and try to allay anger by reciting psalms (n.b. psalms {are} traditionally supposed to do this); the right way—to humbly talk it out and come to an agreement. *Non vult nos*

---

692. "So just as nothing should be preferred to love, nothing should be shunned more than rage and anger."

Deus noster alterius despectui habere tristitiam (c. 16; col. 1030);[693] "Leave thy gift at the altar, . . . etc."

Chapter 17 and the following give examples of false virtue, or inadequate solutions to the problem of aggressivity and hostility among brethren. Some bear with injuries from seculars, but not from other monks (c. 17). {Others use} provocative silence: ". . . *ut eos magis ad iracundiam vultu tacito provocemus*"[694] (c. 18)—our duty is not only to avoid expressions of anger ourselves, but to help cure the anger of our brother. {Others show a} pertinacious refusal to eat, when angered with a brother (c. 19); this is a "diabolical" fast. {Still others are} provoking violence through hypocritically offering the "other cheek" (c. 20); the "right cheek" {is} interpreted as the depths of the soul—i.e., *interior* submission to exterior injustice and injury. Bearing the "infirmity" of the brother who is always mean and nasty and cannot bear anything himself {is required}. With such a one true friendship is not possible (c. 26).

The positive and negative aspects of the struggle against anger (c. 27): refusing to get even (*"date locum irae"*[695]); *omnia sustinere*;[696] positive charity {that} broadens and expands the heart and makes longanimity easy; humble efforts to submit and to allay the anger of the brother.

In conclusion, friendship depends on virtue. It can only truly and durably exist among the virtuous. A sworn pact of friendship is useless if not backed up by virtue.[697]

693. "Our God does not wish us to hold the sadness of another in contempt."

694. Col. 1032B: "so as to provoke them more deeply to anger by a silent countenance."

695. Col. 1040B: "give way to anger" (Rom. 12:19).

696. Col. 1041A, which reads *"omnia sustinet"* ("bears with all things" [I Cor. 13:7]).

697. Merton will return to Cassian in "Pre-Benedictine Monasticism," first series (16–33), with special emphasis on relation to Evagrius, on *Conference* 14, on *Conference* 3 (on the three renunciations), on purity of heart, and on contemplation.

APPENDIX A

Textual Notes

Readings adopted from I

166   "*Pecunia*" comes . . . Empire.] "cattle"? {*added on line in pencil*}
      Si ergo . . . cupitis,] *Si vere fratres divites esse quaeritis,*
217   (John 14:23)] (John 14:)

Readings adopted from II

1–2   Index of Contents] missing in copy text
10–11   "The heavens . . . lxi, 2).] copy "The heavens—etc. p. 50 *written in margin*
11   "Blessed . . . *Ad Martyr.*, 3).] READ Pourrat 52 bottom (quote from Tertullian) *typed; followed by written* (copy—Blessed martyrs etc.)
14   "We often . . . [*PG* 18:37]).] READ quote from Origen on virgins, Pourrat i, p. 45. and from St Methodius ibid. *(copy)*
14–15   Apocalypse 14:1-6: . . . blemish."] *typed* READ Apoc. *followed by written* 14:1-6 *(copy)*
20   establishment of] establish
      who for] for for
21   Read from *The Educator*] COPY from "The Educator"
22   Read Pourrat] Read (copy) Pourrat
34   who has] *preceded by* copy down to . . .
47   St. Basil emphasizes] emphasizes
94–96   3. *Spiritual . . . Apothegmata.*] *this page of text is missing in the original typescript, though the opposite-page insert for this page is here.*
99   *Saint.*] *Saint*–Feast
100   In chapter 73] b) In chapter 73
105   Cassian's error?] *followed by* (copy canons here)

107–108 Syria . . . birthplace.] Syria (improbable) *interlined below following* Romania,

127–28 Abbot Serenus is eminent] eminent

140 on February 29] on

145 this book] his book

162 He did . . . work] did no work *followed by interlined* did not know language could not

167 "For we . . . (I Tim. 6:7-11).] Copy I Tim 6:7-11.

171 not to attempt] to not attempt

174 "Let all . . . malice")] copy here

176 "You have . . . penny."] (copy) *following* not just monks.

227 Text . . . to it."] copy ch. 2 from Eng. Translation (Read)

228 The text . . . flesh."] copy ch. 5 from Eng. Translation (Read)

259 virtue.] *followed by additional handwritten page*: Conference XIV on Gnosis—Contemplative Knowledge *(De Spiritali Scientia)* by Abbot Nesteros. All arts & sciences have their rules & methods. In the "spiritual art" or the spiritual life there must also be methods & disciplines. This is

Readings adopted from "An Appendix to Cassian"

The Columbia University Rare Book and Manuscript Library has in its collection a shorter, earlier version of this material, three typed pages, dated "1958" in pen at the top right hand of the first page, and headed "An Appendix to Cassian. Evagrius Ponticus on Prayer." The text, sent to Sr. Thérèse Lentfoehr to be retyped, evidently served as source for the copy text version (presumably that typed by Lentfoehr) without its handwritten additions; it is virtually identical except for the following readings, which are clearly superior and original.

90 definitively] definitely

93 us to passion] me to passion

94 untainted] untained *in copy text; II reads* unstained

95 *Canticle,* 2:3.] *Canticle {in II—copy text page is missing}*

Additions and alterations included in I

97 **Lectures on Cassian**] *preceded by handwritten inserted page marked* (skip this page): *Cassian*—material for conferences / (1) importance of C. / St Benedict's favorite reading after Scripture. (Butler*) (Dom VH. p 2§) / St Thomas—loved C. & was influenced in his moral theology by him. / Dom VH laments neglect of Cassian in our monasteries. VH 2. / (2) Life of Cassian—360?-435—& his relations with Desert Fathers—cf

Christiani vol. 1.# / His fidelity to Des Fathers?—adapted to
Gaul? (VH.) / (3) His monastic works—*Their aim.*—complete?
exposition of the monastic life / Outline of Dom V.
Hermans
/ (I conf)—α)—In its externals Inst I–IV—see Inst 2.
col 97 / (I
conf)—β)—Active life—Inst. V-XII. / γ)—Contempl life—
Collationes / note—*not* a systematic or exhaustive treatment—rather—various *important aspects.* / Part I (I–X {*written
over* VIII}) 1) *Proximate end* of monk = contemplation / Last
end = God's Kingdom C. I / 2) *Discretion* = right use of
means. C. II / 3) *Triple renunciation* = the way. C. III / 4) *obstacles*—combat of flesh & spirit. C. IV / esp. the 8 capital
vices C. V / 5) *External agents in sanctification* C. VI—Trials /
VII–VIII. devil. / [omitted by VH!] IX–X on prayer!! / 6) *Various.* CC XI–XXIV. / [VH discusses these] (1 conf) Part II
(XI–XVII) / C XI. De perfectione / C XII. De castitate. / C
XIII. De Protectione Dei / C XIV. De Spiritali Scientia / C XV.
De Charismatibus / C XVI. De Amicitia. / C XVII. De
Definiendo. / (1 conf.) Part III / C. XVIII. The 4 kinds of
Monks. / C. XIX. Hermits & cenobites. / C XX. De Poeniten-
tiae fine. / C. XXI. De Remissione Quinquagesimae / C. XXII.
De Nocturnis Illusionibus / C XXIII. De Velle bonum et agere
malum / C XXIV. De Mortificatione.

　*{Cuthbert Butler, *Benedictine Monachism: Studies in Bene-
dictine Life and Rule* (London: Longmans, Green, 1919), 111.}
　§{Vincent Hermans, ocso, a monk of the Cistercian Abbey
of Westmalle, Belgium, was later Procurator General of the
Order in Rome and taught at the Collegio Sant' Anselmo;
Merton refers here to a series of Hermans' lecture notes on
Cassian, which included the comment on Benedict and
Cassian from Butler.}
　#{Léon Cristiani, *Jean Cassien, la spiritualité du désert*, 2 vols.
(Paris: Fontenelle, 1946).}

99　　　　He is . . . writer] *added on line*
　　　　　the source . . . West.] *added on line*
100–101　This is . . . soft.] *opposite page*
101　　　This gives . . . classic.] *opposite page* 3)] *added on line*
102　　　Gilson . . . tradition] *interlined*
104　　　*then God begins*] *then added in left margin before cancelled that*
108　　　Note: . . . Fathers] *interlined*
109　　　that of the Egyptians] that *altered from* the *followed by* of the
　　　　　added in right margin
　　　　　It is . . . Fathers.] *added on line*
　　　　　Abbot Chaeremon] *added in left margin*

114   *Abbot Nesteros*] *added in left margin*
115   Note: . . . *practice.*] *added in lower margin*
116   *Abbot Joseph*] *added in left margin*
       Abbot John; Abbot Piamon] *added in left margin*
       is a monastic city] *is interlined in pencil above cancelled* was
       lagoon] *preceded by cancelled* big
119   peace, for] *for added on line after cancelled* be- *and before*
       cancelled cause
       This gives . . . superiors.] *opposite page*
120   —even . . . involved.] *added on line*
121   anniversary of the death] death *written above cancelled* deposition
122   Panephysis.] *followed by cancelled* To this we shall return later
123   (*Conf.* 20)] *added in pencil in margin*
127   The "banquet" . . . guests.)] *opposite page*
130   The burden . . . sadness.] *opposite page*
131   Paul is saying] saying *interlined in pencil above cancelled*
       complaining
       in temptations, . . . sins.] *added on line*
132   for . . . monasticism.] *added on line*
       Origenism . . . errors.] *opposite page followed by cancelled* & his
       misuse of allegory
133   after . . . Evagrius,] *interlined with a caret*
       an Origenist . . . desert] *interlined with a caret*
       to please Origenist monks] *interlined with a caret*
134   He meets . . . Origen."] *added in lower margin*
135   deacon.] *added on line*
140   *Conferences* . . . 425-428.] *added in left margin*
       He died . . . semi-pelagian.] *interlined*
141   carried] *altered from* carry
       Sandals . . . the feet] *added on line*
146   The man . . . monk.] *added on line*
       (Note . . . child.)] *opposite page*
       (Note—this . . . novice-habit.)] *opposite page*
147   a rich . . . Incarnation.] *interlined*
149   Note . . . themselves.] *opposite page*
       The root . . . self-will.] *added on line*
150   "evil thoughts"] evil *interlined with a caret*
151   Note . . . rule.] *added on line* 14] *written over* 13
152   (between meals)] *interlined with a caret*
153   Summary of his points] *interlined*
156   though . . . systematic.] *interlined with a caret*
157   Note the. . . disaster.] *added on line*
157–58   respect . . . abilities.] *added on line*

158   But note . . . direction!] *opposite page; misplaced following* of
       the individual.
162   Again, . . . virtue.] *added on line*
166   in fact, cowardice.] *added on line in pencil*
       no courage.] *added on line in pencil*
       Si ergo, . . . Sexagesima)] Si vere fratres divites esse . . .
       Sexagesima *interlined in pencil*
173   Cassian's . . . anger.] *interlined*
       (as . . . vices)] *added on line*
174   Note . . . anthropomorphism.] *added on line*
179   and refusing . . . good.] *added on line*
       Above all, . . . spirituality.] *added on line*
180   *causes of our*] our *interlined with a caret*
181   work. . . . time.] *added on line*
183   We now . . . these two?] *added in lower margin* {*Tristitia* . . .
       *with God. appears to have been added at the same time but is not in-
       cluded in I*}
185   for an improvement.] *followed by cancelled* It is close to despair.
186   "Acedia" as a *passion*] "Acedia" *interlined above cancelled*
       "Taedium"
186–87 Presumably . . . cenobites.] *added on line*
188   and zealous . . . out] *added on line*
       It begets] *interlined with a caret*
       The monk] *added in left margin before cancelled* He
189   *for Acedia*] *added on line*
190   by vain] by *added after cancelled* with
192   need to] *interlined in pencil*
199   *Battle Against Carnal*] Carnal *interlined with a caret*
204   They show . . . perfection.] *interlined*
205   v.g. . . . God."] *interlined*
207   Applying . . . ends.] *opposite page*
       (freedom from passion)] *added in lower margin*
208   5] *added in left margin*
       6] *added in left margin*
209   7] *added in left margin*
210   Here Cassian . . . asceticism.] *interlined*
211   story here] here *interlined with a caret*
       (contemplation)] *added on line*
       Note . . . before God.] *opposite page;* and will . . . heaven.]
       added in left margin
212   Note . . . *individual.*] *added in lower margin*
213   He reproves . . . God.] *added in left margin*
       In this sense] *interlined with a caret after cancelled* However, the
       fact remains that

Anything . . . heart.] *added on line*
214 *Contemplation*] *preceded by cancelled The nature of*
of God] *interlined with a caret*
215 This implies . . . childlikeness.] *added in lower margin*
216 c. 18] *added on line*
217 Note . . . School of Alexandria] *opposite page*
218 *Summary*] *added in left margin*
2. To see . . . vanity] *interlined*
5] *altered from 2*
very important] *added on line*
6] *altered from 3*
7] *altered from 4*
Note . . . Médard.] *added in lower margin*
219 this time] *interlined with a caret*
were not distractions] were *interlined below cancelled* are
221 *Plan of the Conference*] *added in left margin*
The supernatural . . . Discretion.] *interlined*
232 chapter 2] 2 *altered from 1*
233 Prayer . . . virtue.] *added in left margin*
237–38 Naturally . . . alone.] *interlined*
238 Useless projects] *added in left margin before cancelled* They
240 deep and ardent] deep *interlined above cancelled* burning
241 At the same . . . contemplation.] *interlined*
242 Perfect] *added in left margin*
247 beyond our strength] beyond *interlined above cancelled* above
253 will fight] fight *added in left margin following cancelled* will keep
us in the presence of God *and before cancelled* and
and . . . Him.] *added on line*

Additions and alterations included in II:

5 certainly] *altered from* certain
9 tremendous.] *followed by typed cancelled* (next—deviations
13 cf. . . . below.] *added on line*
18 Origen . . . idea.] *added on line*
19 (an . . . it)] *interlined*
There is a . . . day.] *opposite page*
(enemy of Jesus)] *interlined*
"tomb" of the soul] *added in left margin*
universe . . . Ialdaboth.] *added on line*
20 Note . . . thought.] *opposite page*
In this . . . Jews.] *added on line*
At the same . . . devil.] *opposite page*

21 an apologia . . . Greeks.] *added on line*
   paths of Christianity.] *followed by typed cancelled* 3—Didaskalos
   —(Teacher of grown students) Christ forms the mature and
   perfect Christian
   Written . . . century.] *opposite page*

22 3—The *Stromata* . . . work] *added in lower margin*
   Stromata . . . gnosis.] *opposite page*
   In his . . . p. 70, par. 2] *opposite page*

23–24 Catechetical . . . theology.] *opposite page*

24 However, . . . error.] *interlined*

25 the first . . . exegete] *interlined with a caret*
   The greater . . . original.] *opposite page*

25–26 the oldest . . . sun).] *opposite page*

26 He sees . . . perfect.] *added on line*
   Origen's . . . Aristotle.] *interlined*
   1] *added in left margin*
   this . . . perfection.] *added on line*
   2] *added in left margin*
   Life-long . . . necessary.] *added on line*
   3] *added in left margin*

27 4. Origen . . . teaching.] *opposite page*
   1] *added in left margin*
   But . . . essential.] *added on line*
   2] *added in left margin*
   3] *added in left margin*

28 (see above)] *interlined with a caret*
   In the Oriental . . . God."] *added on line*
   4] *added in left margin*

29 5] *added in left margin*
   6] *added in left margin*
   7] *added in left margin*

30 It grew . . . that:] *added on line*
   Yet] *interlined above cancelled* However

32 Anthony . . . 251 A. D.] *added in upper margin*
   (270 A. D.)] *added on line*

33 (285–305)] *added on line*

36 Demonology] *interlined with a care*
   Special vices] *followed by* and demonology *interlined with a caret
   and cancelled*

38 (305–312)] *added on line*
   deeds] *interlined below cancelled* sins

42 Work . . . day.] *added in upper margin*

42–43 If one . . . subject.] *opposite page*

43	severe . . . store.] *added on line*
	severe . . . superiors.] *added in left margin*
	Nothing . . . God.] *interlined*
	twice . . . Praepositus] *added in left margin*
	The monks . . . at them.] *added on line*
	Great . . . admonished.] *opposite page*
44	Clerical . . . monks.] *opposite page*
	As part . . . becoming monks.] *opposite page*
45	called Annesi] *interlined with a caret*
	at Annesi] *interlined*
46	-93] *added on line*
	379 . . . Basil.] *added in lower margin*
	(See . . . Fathers.)] *interlined*
47	The second . . . p. 233.] *opposite page*
	and "unnatural."] *added in left margin*
	See . . . 239—Read.] *interlined*
	Then, like . . . love.] *opposite page*
48	Read . . . p. 314.] *added in left margin*
	Of very . . . 243.] *opposite page*
	ascetic] *added on line*
49	and self-custody . . . 488.)] *added on line*
49–50	N.B. St. Basil . . . 49).] *opposite page*
51	The other . . . friend.] *added on line*
	(not . . . prayer).] *added on line*
53	Note . . . Harvard.] *added on line*
	was seduced . . . He] *interlined with a caret*
	Gregory was . . . time (380 ff.)] *opposite page*
53–54	The Council . . . Gregory.] *interlined*
54	After . . . writing.] *opposite page*
55	*Contra Apollinarem* . . . Redemption.] *added in lower margin*
57	Exodus 19] 19 *added on line*
	Ascent . . . p. 70 ff.] *added on line*
61	(Note: . . . fasting.)] *interlined*
62	The *Laura* . . . p. 85).] *added in lower margin*
	In the lives . . . *contradiction.*] *interlined*
	(cf. Charles de Foucauld)] *added on line*
63	*St. Chariton* . . . full of "wonders."] *opposite page*
	St. Jerome] *interlined above cancelled* One of *followed by* The most famous monk *altered from* the most famous monks
	briefly.] *followed by cancelled* He wrote the life of St. Malchus.
64	(age 18)] *added on line*
65	important . . . *Aegypto.*] *interlined*
69	We should . . . call.] *added in lower margin*

temporarily] *interlined*
and finally . . . high] *added in left margin*
69–70   After {the} death . . . by bishops.] *opposite page*
71   (in *PL* 73)] *added on line*
written . . . 419–20.] *added on line followed by typed cancelled*
3—*Theodoret of Cyr*—part of the *Historia Religiosa* deals with
Syrian monks.
74   from . . . (Or)] *interlined*
75   must be seen . . . circumstances.] *added on line*
They became . . . Fathers.] *added on line*
76   In any . . . for us.] *interlined*
77   xxxviii] *added on line*
xlvi, lxi] *added on line*
xiii] *added on line*
xl, xlix, lxv] *added on line*
Silence . . . quiesce.] *added in lower margin*
80   *Amerimnia . . . Parrhesia] opposite page*
81   called . . . man."] *interlined*
(A third . . . two.)] *interlined*
are said to] *added in left margin*
belong] *preceded by cancelled* perhaps
The *Epistola*] The *interlined above cancelled* The most likely
genuine work of Macarius is his
81–82   was long . . . Ephrem.] *added in lower margin*
82   *The Epistola ad Monachos*—ascribed . . . virtues.] *opposite page*
to replace typed cancelled The Epistola ad Monachos or *ad
Filios Dei* is a kind of resume of the spiritual life according
to Macarius. Starts with the ideas of *conversion, compunction,* flight from the world. Followed by *active asceticism.*
Then the generous acceptance of *temptations and trials.* This
brings greater humility, increases compunction and self-
knowledge. As trials proceed, there is a twofold danger of
temptation—a) to vainglory when we think ourselves doing
well b) to discouragement when we feel we are getting
nowhere. The temptation of vainglory can lead to *indiscreet
asceticism* and a presumptuous opinion of our own powers. The temptation to discouragement leads to temptations
to *impurity,* which further shake resolves. The body begins
to clamor for satisfaction. (Note also that pride and indiscreet asceticism sometimes lead suddenly to discouragement and even a fall into sin.) When these temptations are
met with generous patient courage, there follows a period
of *peace and consolation.* Here God gives strength and re-

freshment. But this too is a temporary phase. It is followed by *greater and more interior trials* in which God seems to withdraw all help and deliver the soul to its enemies. Feeling of helplessness and futility, utter darkness and abandonment, like St. John of the Cross Dark Night of the Soul. The soul is "like a ship without a helm that runs hither and thither against the rocks." After this final purification, comes the perfection of the spiritual life when the soul is *directly and completely subjected to the Holy Ghost.* In complete poverty and purity, it lives with divine help and strength only. Here there are graces of *recognition of divine mercy,* and consequent *thanksgiving;* one lives in an atmosphere of praise and gratitude. Then a passage that suggests mystical union: "The Paraclete will begin to make a pact with his purity of heart and firmness of soul and holiness of body and with his spirit of humility and cause him to surpass all creatures and that his mouth may not speak the words of men, and that he may see right into the heart of things with his eyes . . . etc. . . . all these things He arranges in him duly and with discretion, not in turbulence but in tranquillity." However here great fidelity is required by the soul. It must remain pure and faithful to the pact with the Holy Spirit, otherwise punishment will follow by the return of trials. The faithful soul however will rejoice and be united to God as to the Fountain of Live. Here we find the three degrees of the spiritual life in a very early exposition. This material has become familiar to us after constant repetition but it is important to see it outlined in such an early document—a text of the desert.

grace.] *followed by cancelled* and with the *common life* of monks which is the way to the good.

way] *interlined above cancelled stages*

spiritual life,] *followed by cancelled* the various *trials* and *consolations* of prayer

especially] *followed by cancelled* with

omitted from this.] *followed by typed cancelled* Basically however we have to be familiar with this scheme.

82–83   So much . . . had to work.] *opposite page*

82   *in Migne PG*] *interlined*

        really the text] *preceded by cancelled* really by Macarius but that it is

        discovered.] *followed by cancelled* & published by W. Jaeger.

        full text] full *interlined above cancelled* true

83   letters ascribed to] *interlined above cancelled* genuine writings of
            For a . . . century.] *opposite page*
            Gregory of Nyssa,] *followed by cancelled* & not a heretic
            Macarian homilies] *followed by cancelled* although not by
            Macarius,
85–88   *Pseudo-Macarius* . . . spiritual theology.] *typed insert: separate
            page*
88   He came . . . cells."] *interlined*
88–90   In the earlier . . . based on Evagrius.] *typed insert: separate page*
90   The chief work of Evagrius] *added in left margin to replace can-
            celled* However, one of his chief works
            and again . . . 1959 ff.] *added in left margin*
91   purely spiritual] *followed by cancelled* always
92   exclusively intellectual] *followed by cancelled* still less is it purely
            speculation
            However . . . paradisiacal state.] *opposite page*
            The lower kind . . . image.] *interlined*
            The lower degrees . . . vice.] *added in lower margin*
93   After . . . themselves] *added in left margin*
            However . . . darkness.] *opposite page*
            he reaches] he *interlined above cancelled* we
            reaches] *altered from* reach
            the contemplative has] *interlined above cancelled* we have
            The true] The *altered from* the *preceded by cancelled* The first be-
            ginnings of
94   Note . . . God.] *opposite page*
            However . . . (*Or.* 62).] *added in lower margin*
95   In "Spiritual . . . explained.] *opposite page*
            In "Spiritual . . . (*gnosis*)] *interlined above cancelled* Here

97   **LECTURES ON CASSIAN**] *followed by typed cancelled* For
            Choir Novitiate. 1955–1956)
99   the Master . . . monks] *interlined with a caret*
            He is a *classic* . . . Fenelon, etc.] *opposite page*
100   It is due . . . *Collatio.*] *added on line*
            St. Benedict's] *interlined above cancelled* his
            (i.e. . . . Cassian)] *interlined*
101   that . . . reproach.] *added on line*
            Compare . . . respect.] *added in lower margin*
            (*Life of St. Dominic*)] *interlined*
102   the all-important] the *altered from* an
            especially St. Bernard.] *interlined*
104   (quoting Chaeremon)] *added on line*

105 adopts without . . . doctrine] *interlined above cancelled* clearly thinks

in Southern France] *interlined with a caret*

Denzinger—179] *interlined*

13, . . . 20] *interlined*

105–107 We here . . . *deficiamus in via.*] We here . . . error? (*copy canons here*) *added in lower margin*

108 or 365.] *added on line*

and in . . . Lehodey.] *interlined*

Notice . . . discussed!] *interlined*

Is . . . word?] *added in left margin*

(See . . . Cassian.")] *interlined*

109 Cassian is . . . old.] *interlined*

vow . . . Nativity.] *added on line*

They . . . seven] *added on line*

(Panephysis)] *interlined followed by cancelled* & Diolcos

At Panephysis.] *added in upper margin*

110–13 *Conference 11 . . .* next conference.] *added on inserted typed pages*

110 (servile attitude)] *interlined with a caret*

111 (Note . . . Son.)] *interlined*

c. 8] 8 *written over* 7

114 extremism.] *followed by cancelled* It is not the mind of the church that one should indulge in efforts explicitly directed to get rid of all first movements {*interlined above cancelled* motions} of concupiscence. Those who did this, which sincere and holy laid themselves open to errors.

This . . . humility.] *added on line*

116 Note the . . . *refusals.*] *opposite page*

Some think . . . 3.)] *opposite page*

118 Hermits . . . *Remoboth.*] *opposite page*

"to take . . . needs!"] *added in right margin*

119 They also . . . as monks.] *added on line*

121 Instead . . . solitude.] *added on line*

122 Pinufius first . . . points] *opposite page*

1) The beginning] *preceded by cancelled* The main points are:

123 Nitria was . . . Macarius.] *added in lower margin*

124 *Scete*] *added in margin*

124–25 Cassian spent . . . more.] *interlined*

125 The most . . . Scete.] *opposite page*

(see details above.)] *added on line*

of God.] *added on line*

also Pastor, Moses, etc.] *added on line*

living with] with *added in left margin to replace cancelled* by

126   Cassian refers . . . Scete.] *interlined; preceded by cancelled* He left some doctrinal writings.

        Paphnutius lived] Paphnutius *inserted in left margin before cancelled* He

127   They are invited . . . . c. 1)] *opposite page*

        consisted of] *interlined with a caret (opposite page)*

128   *Conference 7—. . . 16.)] opposite page*

129   3–4] *added on line*

        Note . . . relative.] *opposite page*

        It is . . . perfection] *added on line*

        Christ . . . believes] *added on line*

        (at None . . . generally)] *added on line*

130   A modern observer] *interlined above cancelled* One

        Those who . . . revenge.] *interlined*

        We *should . . . souls.] added on line*

        We are . . . frailty.] *added in lower margin, preceded by cancelled* including especially weakness of the flesh

131   This . . . Fathers.] *added in lower margin*

132   For Origen, . . . {23–29}.] *opposite page*

133   Bitter . . . Jerome] *added on line following cancelled* and a real fight began.

        (For . . . pages {88–96})] *added on line*; Evagrius—had been ordained lector by St. Basil and deacon by St. Gregory Nazianzen. Had been present at Council of Constantinople in 381—left the world because of temptation it offered—first settled on the Mount of Olives with Rufinus—then to Nitria for two years, then fourteen years in the desert of the Cells, greater solitude. *Regarded as the outstanding theologian of the Desert.* A leading Origenist. Died Epiphany, 399. *cancelled opposite page*

134   Was Cassian involved] Was *interlined*

        the Origenist conflict?] *interlined above cancelled* this?

        at this time] *interlined*

        The golden age] The *interlined above cancelled* Cassian left Egypt at the moment when the

        at the . . . century.] *added on line*

        Now . . . France.] *interlined*

135   no human . . . thinker.] *added on line*

        St. John . . . abuses] *opposite page*

136   (especially . . . Eudoxia)] *interlined with a caret*

        This party . . . Antioch.] *added in left margin*

        Chrysostom began] Chrysostom *added in lower margin to replace cancelled* he

        Chrysostom was exiled . . . God.] *opposite page*

136–37   Note . . . this time).] *added on line*
137   (On Provence . . . *Gaul*.)] *interlined*
137–38   *St. Martin* . . . huts.] *opposite page*
138–39   *Lérins*. . . . his Rule.] *opposite page*
140   Oriental . . . Roman.] *added in left margin*
          two . . . books.] *added on line*
          Part I—] *added in left margin*
          and Bk. 3] and *added on line following cancelled*—night office
          Bk. 3] *followed by cancelled day* hours
          (the . . . Mesopotamia)] ( ) *added*
141   The different . . . vesting)] *interlined*
          No symbolism?] *added in left margin*
          For outdoor use:] *interlined*
          This symbolized] *interlined with a caret*
          when on a journey.] *added on line*
141–42   *A final* . . . Byzantium.] *opposite page*
142   Read chapter 7.] *added in left margin*
          monk recites] monk *interlined with a caret*
143   Note . . . prayer!] *opposite page*
          (Read c. 10.)] *added on line*
144–45   *Book 3* . . . *Rule*, chapter 43.] *inserted page*
145   He also . . . long.] *added on line*
          This is . . . novice.] *opposite page*
          (Read this chapter.)] *added on line*
145–46   some . . . persevere.] *added on line*
146   even a small coin,] *added in right margin*
          It is important . . . etc.)] *opposite page*
          (Read)] *interlined with a caret*
147   In these . . . 10–13.] *opposite page*; postulant] *interlined above*
          cancelled novice
          Postulancy] *added in left margin*
148   (Read c. 8.)] *added on line*
          This . . . perfection."] *interlined*
          As regards . . . obedience.] *opposite page, misplaced before* What is
          Spiritual Father] *interlined below cancelled* superior
150   Also remark . . . understood.] *added in lower margin*
150–51   Cassian stresses . . . situation?] *opposite page*
151   the junior hastens] junior *interlined*; they *altered from* the *and*
          hastens *altered from* hasten
          The junior . . . attempts] junior *interlined*; they *altered from* the
          and attempts *altered from* attempt
          d) Clothing . . . (c. 11).] *opposite page*

e) Promptitude] *added in left margin before cancelled* d) They are prompt

Each monk . . . sleep on).] *opposite page*

Essence . . . *dominium.*] *interlined*

(c. 15)] *added on line*

152   The French monks] The *altered from* they; French monks *added in left margin*

Chapter 16] *added in left margin before cancelled* c. 1[4] *altered to* c. 16

Chapter 18] *added in left margin*

153   Read . . . perspective.] *interlined*

Chapters 30 and 31. . . . of all.] *opposite page*

154   It is . . . serious.] *added on line*

(*Read* chapter 34.)] *added in left margin*

But how . . . chapter 35.)] *interlined*

to the cares . . . family, etc.] *added in left margin*

155   When one . . . *signs.*] *interlined*

156   (chapter 41] *interlined with a caret*

it is . . . persevere] *added in left margin to replace cancelled* to last

he must . . . himself).] *interlined after cancelled* but only on his own patience

156–57   The knowledge . . . thought.] *opposite page*

157   Cassian begins . . . necessary] *opposite page*

159   let us return to] *interlined with a caret above cancelled* again

How are . . . appetite?] *interlined after cancelled* How are we to desire food and eat it?

better to have] have *interlined above cancelled* give

stuff] *interlined below cancelled* force him "stuffing"

(or course under *obedience*)] *added on line*

160   This . . . truth.] *added on line*

161   by a soul] *interlined above cancelled* in great measure by a sul {*sic*}

repeating . . . *Seniorum*] *added in left margin*

162   Chapter 25 . . . vocation is saved.] *cancelled by diagonal line in original typescript and omitted in I;* stet copy this as it stands *in upper left margin*

163   This book . . . *Fathers.*] *opposite page*

It is closely . . . connection.] *added on line*

combined . . . sense)] *interlined with a caret*

164   virtue of those] those *interlined above cancelled* one

resist] *altered from* resists

do not sin] do *altered from* does

Main . . . hell.] *added on line*; strength *preceded by cancelled* hope

and true . . . peace.] *added on line*

165   See . . . information.] *added on line*

The Fathers . . . one.] *added in lower margin*
166   Avarice] *pencilled addition on opposite page, not marked for insertion, cancelled in pen*: Distinction—between a vice that is *active & not felt* / we are content not to feel it / all have some of this / be ready to recognize when it come out / a vice that is *"felt" but inactive* / a vice that is *not felt & inactive* / a vice that is completely overcome—/ out of our system—/ don't feel it & don't have it.
(*Philargyria* . . . stronger.)] *interlined*
This . . . analysis.] *interlined*
Is our materialistic] Is *added in left margin*
society] *followed by cancelled* is
Perhaps . . . think.] *added on line*
and sold] *interlined*
167   See his . . . poverty.] *added on line followed by* COPY I Tim 6:7-11.
The early . . . temptations?] *opposite page*
168   After . . . turns to] *interlined above cancelled* Considers
This . . . saying.] *interlined*
so much . . . poverty.] *interlined above cancelled* in our context
169   deficient,] *interlined below cancelled* negligent,
(cf. *Rule* . . . 55).] *added on line*
170   giving himself] *preceded by cancelled* not {*perhaps* now *originally intended*}
in each . . . "lies] *interlined below cancelled* all this is lying
171   and especially Paul.] *added on line*
174   Ephesians 4:31] 31 *interlined followed by* copy here
175   READ: II Kings 16:4-12 . . . 19:18-23] *interlined below cancelled* (II Kings 19) 336.
4-12] 12 *interlined beneath cancelled* 11
they look] *interlined with a caret*
However . . . 36-46).] *opposite page*
Traditionally—(c. 10).] *added on line*
It "excludes . . . Spirit.] *interlined*
vice of anger] of anger *added in left margin*
176   and self-congratulation.] *added on line*
Read Matthew 5:21-26] *added on line following cancelled* (Matth 5.)
Very . . . monks.] *added on line followed by* (copy)
importance . . . Communion.] *interlined*
178   Read . . . at all.] *added in lower margin;* anger *followed by cancelled* against others
Note . . . from God.] *opposite page*
Cassian says] *added on line*
like . . . apple.] *added on line*

1] *added on line*
2] *added on line*
179   3] *added on line*
(Conversely . . . sadness.)] *added on line*
4] *added on line*
5] *added on line*
6] *added on line*
7] *added on line*
180   Yet . . . obligations.] *opposite page*
181   Note: today . . . sane.] *opposite page*
get along charitably] *interlined below cancelled* adapt {with *also erroneously cancelled*}
this . . . vocation.] *added on line*
182   Note . . . adjustment."] *interlined*
183   *Tristitia . . . with God.*] *added in lower margin*
183–84   *Other . . . Gregory.*] *added in lower margin*
184   *Boredom*] *interlined above cancelled* Sloth
Acedia . . . roughly] *interlined above cancelled* In the accompanying translation this is
should be read] *interlined below cancelled* It is translated
for . . . spirituality.] *added on line*
184–85   *Background: . . . psalmody.*] *opposite page*
184   says] seems to beg the question in saying *cancelled*; seems to *originally followed* by evade the issue
heaven."] *followed by cancelled* since that is one of the things the acediosus cannot do. The remedy seems to be not in abstract thoughts but in concrete activity, a return to healthy contacts with persons and environment. However, this ~~suggestion~~ remedy is traditional. All recommend it
185   death and] *interlined with a caret*
Definition of Acedia] *followed by cancelled* in Instituta X
some . . . salvation.] *interlined*
It certainly . . . indecision.] *added on line*
186   This would . . . acedia!] *interlined*
187   the cell] *preceded by cancelled* building of
as a physical building] *interlined with a caret*
187–88   Acedia is very . . . result.] *opposite page*
188   He applies . . . 5.] *opposite page*
189   (see . . . 4:11)] *added on line*
190   avoidance . . . things.] *added on line*
However . . . Christ.] *interlined*
see . . . 3:17-18)] *added on line*
191   and by . . . praised.] *added on line*

Indeed . . . there.] *added on line*
193 and culpably] *added in left margin*
194 Note: . . . desire.] *opposite page*
195 1—Spiritual] *Spiritual interlined with a caret*
200 *fundamenta . . . How?*] *opposite page*
Fear of God] *preceded by cancelled* What is this?
Humilitas . . . conquiri.] *added on line*
For the . . . 66).] *added on line*
in nullo . . . contristare.] *added on line*
This . . . Christ.] *added in left margin*
201 Notice . . . life.] *opposite page*
and seniors in the monastery] *added in left margin*
We must . . . (Martène).] *added in left margin*
202 Chapter 33 . . . comment.)] *added in lower margin before cancelled End of Cassian's Instituta. Gloria tibi Christe Rex.*
203 There are . . . solitude.] *inserted page;* This whole group is] *interlined with a caret*
Undoubtedly] *preceded by typed cancelled* IV The Conferences of Cassian. Having treated the Instituta in detail, we can look more summarily at the Conferences, dwelling at greater length on those which are really important, touching others in passing, and leaving the rest aside. *followed by handwritten cancelled* The Instituta describe the Cenobitic life—the "active" way. The conferences are above all for the hermits and contemplatives.
204 Hence . . . indifferent.] *interlined*
being an "art,"] *interlined with a caret following cancelled* like many trades and crafts
have . . . desert.] *interlined above cancelled* sustain labors in the monastery.
205 disinterested love] *added on line*
206 Note . . . gods.] *interlined*
207 He speaks . . . psalter.] *opposite page*
208 *Read* chapter 7.] *interlined*
to free it from passion] *interlined*
213 frightening] *preceded by cancelled* terrible and
fully] *interlined with a caret*
Hence we . . . become *skopos.*] *added on line*
is an . . . heart.] *added on line*
214 We may . . . devil.] *added on line*
Note . . . all."] *added in lower margin*
(*tenetur*)] *added on line*
215 Abbot Moses] Abbot *added in left margin*

215–16   manuscripts . . . semi-pelagianism?)] *added on line following cancelled* mss.
219   as if thoughts] as if *interlined*
221   But it . . . Counsel.] *added on line*
222   *omni intentione.*"] *added on line*
   Note . . . us."] *opposite page*
   (*anachoresis*)] *added on line*
   quid . . . Deum.] *added on line*
   Without . . . fruit.] *added on line*
   (*praetermittens utramque nimietatem*)] *interlined with a caret*
222–23   Discretion is . . . trial.] *opposite page*
223   Discretion in . . . *ad Deum* (528).] *interlined*
   following . . . well] *added on line*
   deluded after . . . flight] *added on line*
224   Father)]) *added followed by cancelled* director, superior)
   and submission . . . tradition.] *added on line*
   guidance of a Spiritual Father] Spiritual Father *interlined below cancelled* director
   The enemy . . . (col. 538).] *opposite page*
225   Conclusion: . . . Father.] *added on line*
   obviously proved] proved *interlined above cancelled* shown
226   instead . . . world"] *opposite page*
   also . . . Spirits."] *added on line*
226–30   *Conference 4 . . . ends here.*] *inserted handwritten pages*
231   They are . . . prayer.] *added on line*
   In an . . . norm of prayer."] *opposite page*
   passion.] *followed by cancelled* (Note—The other conferences of Cassian in so far as they are important for us, have been mentioned in passing and their contents have been noted briefly in the first part of the lectures on Cassian's relations with the monks in Scete and Lower Egypt. For instance Conference III on the Three Kinds of Renunciation, (see under Abbot Paphnutius) or Conference XXI on the Lack of Fasting during Paschal time, (see under Abbot Theonas) or XXIII De Velle Bonum et agere malum, (of the same).
232   All the virtues . . . themselves.] *added in lower margin*
233   *Ut eo . . . oratio:*] *interlined*
234   An interesting . . . peace.] *opposite page*
   De Mobilitate Animae] *added on line*
235   This implies . . . Cassian.] *interlined*
   He speaks . . . and grace.] *opposite page*
   (c. 5).] *added on line*
242   This is . . . mechanically.] *added in lower margin*

When . . . Father,] , *added followed by cancelled* we
we acknowledge] we *interlined with a caret*
249   With us the Gregorian melodies] *added on line*
254   The influence . . . p. 11).] *opposite page*
255   first of all] *interlined above cancelled* entirely
       Yet it . . . controversial elements.] *opposite page*
255–59 *Conferences—Parts II and III . . .* virtue.] *inserted handwritten pages*
257   In order . . . virtues.] *opposite page*

Additions and alterations not included in I or II:

41   cf. Cambridge—colleges] *interlined*
195   problem today] *added in left margin*
196   opposed to . . . is good] *added on line*
       (cf. St. Bernard)] *added on line*
198   Summary—. . . interior.] *interlined*
216   If prayer . . . etc.] *added on line*
228   cf. Plato] *added in left margin*
229   (cf. William of St. Thierry)] *added on line*
230   Letter)] *added on line*
232   constant prayer . . . virtues.] *opposite page*
233   Prayer climaxes . . . perfection.] *added on line*
       virtues—"strengths"] *opposite page*
234   *profundae . . . fundamenta]* added on line*
235   *Amor . . . meum.]* opposite page*
239   not . . . line!] *added in lower margin*
       cf. St. Bede] *added in left margin*
240   (Read c. 14)] *added in left margin*
       Chapter 15 . . . kinds.] *interlined*
241   originality . . . (c. 16).] *opposite page*
       charity . . . 222] *opposite page*
242   These . . . themes] *added in left margin*
243   *regio dissimilitudinis]* added in left margin*
       language of St. Thomas] *added in left margin*
244   Tertullian . . . aggressivity].] *opposite page*
246   cf. *Rule]* interlined with a caret*
247   St. Augustine . . . good.] *opposite page*
249   We must be . . . *voci.]* opposite page*
       N.B. the Psalms' . . . spirit.] *opposite page*
       2] *added on line before cancelled* 1
       3] *added on line before cancelled* 2
       4] *added on line before cancelled* 3

5] *added on line before cancelled* 4

249–50 Fervor . . . Step 7.] *added on line to replace cancelled* Here Cassian, somewhat after the fashion of Fr. Poulain,* lists some of the effects of mystical fervor:

*{A. Poulain, sj, *The Graces of Interior Prayer*, trans. L. Yorke Smith (London: Paul, Trench, Trübner, 1912): Part II, "Some General Ideas about the Mystic Union" (pp. 52–199) discusses twelve "characters" or qualities of mystical union.}

250 total silence] *followed by cancelled* and helplessness

It is well . . . possible?] *opposite page to replace* 3. Tears and lamentations are another expression of these graces, according to Cassian. The last point, about tears, excites the insatiable Germanus: he bursts out with another question, and wants to know how he can enjoy copious tears at will.

251 Climacus . . . uncharitableness.] *added on line*

may distract. . . . fruitful.] *added on line*

252 In the opinion . . . comprehension.)] *interlined*

253–54 not magic . . . hypnosis] *added on line*

APPENDIX B

Table of Correspondences:
Cassian and the Fathers—*Lectures and Taped Conferences*

Date	Page #	Opening Words	TMC CD #	Published Tape Title & #
4/28/62	226	*Conference 4*	1-2	*Cassian: Trials and Belief* A (Credence AA2067)
5/12/62	[231]		2-3	
5/14/62	231	*Conferences 9*	3-2	*Cassian: Trials and Belief* B (Credence AA2067)
5/19/62	232	*All the structure*	4-1	*Faith and Prayer* A (Credence AA2068)
5/26/62	234	b) Purify	7-1	*Cassian: Disposition for Prayer* A (Credence AA2069)
6/2/62	238	*The Different*	6-1	*Faith and Prayer* B (Credence AA2068)
6/9/62	239	*Intercessions*	8-1	*Cassian: Disposition for Prayer* B (Credence AA2069)
6/16/62	242	Here Cassian	8-3	*Our Father: Perfect Prayer* A (Credence AA2070) *The Our Father* 1A (EPB Series III)
6/23/62	243	3. This implies	9-3	*Spirituality of the Our Father* A (Credence AA2259) *The Our Father* 1B (EPB Series III)

Date	Page #	Opening Words	TMC CD #	Published Tape Title & #
7/7/62	245	1. We ask	11-1	*Spirituality of the Our Father* A (Credence AA2259) *The Our Father* 2A (EPB Series III)
7/14/62	246	*Dimitte nobis*	12-1	*Spirituality of the Our Father* B (Credence AA2259) *The Our Father* 2B (EPB Series III)
7/21/62	247	*Summary and*	12-4	*Our Father: Perfect Prayer* B (Credence AA2070)
7/28/62	252	*When are*	13-4	*Does God Hear Our Prayer* A (Credence AA2071)
8/4/62	253	4. *Frequenter*	14-4	*Does God Hear Our Prayer* B (Credence AA2071)

Notes on the Table of Correspondences

- Dates are in some cases conjectural: see Introduction, note 48.
- References are given by number to the recordings in the collection at the Thomas Merton Center at Bellarmine University, Louisville, KY, and by title and number to the published recordings released by Credence Communications, as well as those recordings previously released by Electronic Paperbacks.
- No tape exists for the conference (presumably given on 5/5/62) on material from page 228 (beginning "*Chapters 6–7*" through page 230 (up to "*Conferences 9 and 10*").
- The conference on 5/12/62 (TMC CD # 2-3), the only one of the series not commercially available, although intended to be a conference on Cassian, is completely taken up with discussion of the nuclear issue.
- Also commercially available is a tape entitled *Clement of Alexandria / Origen* (Credence AA2082) that corresponds to pages 20–26 of the present edition (beginning of "*The Christian Teachers of Alexandria*" section up to but not including "*Spiritual Doctrine of Origen*"), but was not part of a sequence of "Prologue to Cassian" lectures; the TMC CD #s are 18-4 and 20-3.
- TMC CD ## 55-1, 55-2, 55-3, 55-4, and 57-1, also focusing on Cassian, are taken from the *Pre-Benedictine Monasticism* conferences of 1963; these are also commercially available.

APPENDIX C

For Further Reading

I. Other Writings by Merton on Topics Treated in
Cassian and the Fathers

Ignatius of Antioch
"Church and Bishop in St. Ignatius of Antioch." *Seasons of Celebration.*
New York: Farrar, Straus and Giroux, 1965: 28–44.

Clement of Alexandria
Clement of Alexandria: Selections from the Protreptikos. New York: New
Directions, 1963.

Origen
"War in Origen and St. Augustine." Part 3 of "The Christian in World
Crisis: Reflections on the Moral Climate of the 1960s." *Seeds of Destruction.* New York: Farrar, Straus and Giroux, 1964: 134–51.

"Origen." *Collected Poems.* New York: New Directions, 1977: 640–41.

Gregory of Nyssa
"Vision and Illusion." Chapter 1 of *The Ascent to Truth.* New York: Harcourt, Brace, 1951: 21–29.

Jerome
"Virginity and Humanism in the Western Fathers." *Mystics and Zen
Masters.* New York: Farrar, Straus and Giroux, 1967: 113–27.

"Two Desert Fathers: I. St. Jerome; II. St. Paul the Hermit." *Collected
Poems.* New York: New Directions, 1977: 165–69.

Desert Fathers
The Wisdom of the Desert: Sayings from the Desert Fathers of the Fourth Century. New York: New Directions, 1960.

"Wisdom and Emptiness: A Dialogue by Daisetz T. Suzuki and Thomas
Merton." *Zen and the Birds of Appetite.* New York: New Directions,
1968: 99–138.

"The Cell." *Contemplation in a World of Action.* Garden City, NY: Doubleday, 1971: 252–59.

"The Spiritual Father in the Desert Tradition." *Contemplation in a World of Action*. Garden City, NY: Doubleday, 1971: 269–93.

"Macarius and the Pony." *Collected Poems*. New York: New Directions, 1977: 317–18.

"Macarius the Younger." *Collected Poems*. New York: New Directions, 1977: 319–21.

Cassian

"The Testimony of Tradition." Chapter 2 of *Bread in the Wilderness*. New York: New Directions, 1953: 16–24.

"Puritas Cordis [Purity of Heart]." Part 1, Chapter 1 of *The Silent Life*. New York: Farrar, Straus and Cudahy, 1957: 1–20.

"The Humanity of Christ in Monastic Prayer." *The Monastic Journey*, ed. Brother Patrick Hart. Kansas City: Sheed, Andrews and McMeel, 1977: 87–106, especially 90–94.

II. Significant Recent Writings by Other Authors on Topics Treated in Cassian and the Fathers

General Studies

Bouyer, Louis. *The Spirituality of the New Testament and the Fathers*. Trans. Mary P. Ryan. The History of Christian Spirituality, vol. 1. New York: Seabury, 1963.

Dunn, Marilyn. *The Emergence of Monasticism: From the Desert Fathers to the Early Middle Ages*. Oxford: Blackwell, 2000.

Jones, Cheslyn, Geoffrey Wainwright, and Edward Yarnold, eds. *The Study of Spirituality*. New York: Oxford University Press, 1986.

Kannengiesser, Charles. *Early Christian Spirituality*. Philadelphia: Fortress, 1986.

Louth, Andrew. *The Origins of the Christian Mystical Tradition from Plato to Denys*. Oxford: Oxford University Press, 1981.

Luckman, Harriet A., and Linda Kulzer, OSB, eds. *Purity of Heart in Early Ascetic and Monastic Literature*. Collegeville, MN: Liturgical Press, 1999.

McGinn, Bernard, John Meyendorff, and Jean Leclercq, eds. *Christian Spirituality: Origins to the Twelfth Century*. World Spirituality: An Encyclopedic History of the Religious Quest, vol. 16. New York: Crossroad, 1988.

McGinn, Bernard. *The Foundations of Mysticism: Origins to the Fifth Century.* The Presence of God: A History of Western Christian Mysticism, vol. 1. New York: Crossroad, 1992.

Spidlík, Tomás. *The Spirituality of the Christian East: A Systematic Handbook.* Trans. Anthony P. Gythiel. CS 79. Kalamazoo, MI: Cistercian Publications, 1986.

Williams, Rowan. *The Wound of Knowledge: Christian Spirituality from the New Testament to St. John of the Cross.* London: Darton, Longman and Todd, 1979.

Clement of Rome
First and Second Clement. Trans. Robert M. Grant and Holt H. Graham. The Apostolic Fathers: A New Translation and Commentary, vol. 2. New York: Nelson, 1965.

Didache
Barnabas and the Didache. Trans. Robert A. Kraft. The Apostolic Fathers: A New Translation and Commentary, vol. 3. New York: Nelson, 1965.

* * * * *

Niederwimmer, Kurt. *The Didache: A Commentary.* Minneapolis: Fortress, 1998.

Ignatius of Antioch
Ignatius of Antioch. Trans. Robert M. Grant. The Apostolic Fathers: A New Translation and Commentary, vol. 4. Camden, NJ: Nelson, 1966.

* * * * *

Corwin, Virginia. *St. Ignatius and Christianity in Antioch.* New Haven: Yale University Press, 1960.

Trevett, Christine. *A Study of Ignatius of Antioch in Syria and Asia.* Lewiston, NY: Mellen, 1992.

Montanism
Trevett, Christine. *Montanism: Gender, Authority and the New Prophecy.* Cambridge: Cambridge University Press, 1996.

Gnosticism
Robinson, James M., ed. *The Nag Hammadi Library in English.* San Francisco: Harper & Row, 1983.

* * * * *

Grant, Robert M. *Gnosticism and Early Christianity.* New York: Columbia University Press, 1961.

Jonas, Hans. *The Gnostic Religion: The Message of the Alien God and the Beginnings of Christianity*. Boston: Beacon, 1963.

Logan, Alastair. *Gnostic Truth and Christian Heresy: A Study of the History of Gnosticism*. Edinburgh: T. & T. Clark, 1996.

MacRae, George. *Studies in the New Testament and Gnosticism*. Wilmington, DE: Michael Glazier, 1987.

Perkins, Pheme. *The Gnostic Dialogue: The Early Church and the Crisis of Gnosticism*. New York: Paulist, 1980.

———. *Gnosticism and the New Testament*. Minneapolis: Fortress, 1993.

Neoplatonism

Blumenthal, H. J. *Neoplatonism and Early Christian Thought: Essays in Honour of A. H. Armstrong*. London: Variorum, 1981.

Wallis, R. T. *Neoplatonism*. London: Duckworth, 1972; Indianapolis: Hackett, 1995.

Merlan, Philip. *From Platonism to Neoplatonism*. The Hague: Nijhoff, 1960.

Clement of Alexandria

Ferguson, John. *Clement of Alexandria*. New York: Twayne, 1974.

Lilla, Salvatore. *Clement of Alexandria: A Study in Christian Platonism and Gnosticism*. Cambridge: Cambridge University Press, 1971.

Origen

An Exhortation to Martyrdom, Prayer, and Selected Works. Trans. Rowan A. Greer. Classics of Western Spirituality. New York: Paulist, 1979.

The Song of Songs. Commentary and Homilies. Trans. Robert P. Lawson. Ancient Christian Writers, vol. 26. Westminster, MD: Newman, 1957.

* * * * *

Clark, Elizabeth. *The Origenist Controversy: The Cultural Construction of an Early Christian Debate*. Princeton: Princeton University Press, 1992.

Crouzel, Henri. *Origen*. Trans. A. S. Worrall. San Francisco: Harper & Row, 1989.

Kannengiesser, Charles, and William L. Peterson, eds. *Origen of Alexandria: His World and His Legacy*. Notre Dame: University of Notre Dame Press, 1988.

Trigg, Joseph Wilson. *Origen: The Bible and Philosophy in the Third-century Church*. Atlanta: John Knox Press, 1983.

———. *Origen*. New York: Routledge, 1998.

Anthony

The Letters of St. Antony the Great. Trans. Derwas J. Chitty. Fairacres, Oxford: SLG Press, 1975.

Athanasius. *The Life of Antony and the Letter to Marcellinus.* Trans. Robert C. Gregg. Classics of Western Spirituality. New York: Paulist, 1980.

———. *The Life of Saint Antony.* Trans. Robert T. Meyer. Ancient Christian Writers, vol. 10. Westminster, MD: Newman, 1950.

* * * * *

Brakke, David. *Athanasius and the Politics of Asceticism.* Oxford: Clarendon Press, 1995.

Rubenson, Samuel. *The Letters of St. Antony: Monasticism and the Making of a Saint.* Minneapolis: Fortress, 1995.

Pachomius

Pachomian Koinonia: The Lives, Rules, and Other Writings of Saint Pachomius and His Disciples. I: The Life of Saint Pachomius and His Disciples; II: Rule; III: Other Writings. Trans. Armand Veilleux. CS 45–47. Kalamazoo, MI: Cistercian Publications, 1980–1982.

* * * * *

Rousseau, Philip. *Pachomius: The Making of a Community in Fourth-Century Egypt.* Berkeley: University of California Press, 1985.

Basil

The Fathers Speak: St. Basil the Great, St. Gregory of Nazianzus, St. Gregory of Nyssa: Selected Letters and Life-Records. Trans. Georges A. Barrois. Crestwood, NY: St. Vladimir's Seminary Press, 1986.

* * * * *

Fedwick, Paul J., ed. *Basil of Caesarea: Christian, Humanist, Ascetic.* 2 vols. Toronto: Pontifical Institute of Medieval Studies, 1981.

Meredith, Anthony. *The Cappadocians.* Crestwood, NY: St. Vladimir's Seminary Press, 1995.

Rousseau, Philip. *Basil of Caesarea.* Berkeley: University of California Press, 1994.

Gregory Nazianzen

Autobiographical Poems. Trans. Carolinne White. New York: Cambridge University Press, 1996.

On God and Christ: The Five Theological Orations and Two Letters to Cledonius. Trans. Frederick Williams, Lionel R. Wickham. Crestwood, NY: St. Vladimir's Seminary Press, 2002.

Selected Poems. Trans. J. A. McGuckin. Fairacres, Oxford: SLG Press, 1986.

Three Poems. Trans. Denis M. Meehan. Fathers of the Church, vol. 75. Washington, DC: Catholic University of America Press, 1987.

* * * * *

Ruether, Rosemary R. *Gregory of Nazianzus: Rhetor and Philosopher.* Oxford: Clarendon, 1969.

Gregory of Nyssa

Commentary on the Song of Songs. Trans. Casimir McCambley. Brookline, MA: Hellenic College Press, 1987.

From Glory to Glory: Texts from Gregory of Nyssa's Mystical Writings. Ed. Jean Daniélou and Herbert Musurillo. New York: Scribners, 1961.

The Life of Moses. Trans. Everett Ferguson and Abraham J. Malherbe. Classics of Western Spirituality. New York: Paulist, 1978.

The Lord's Prayer. The Beatitudes. Trans. Hilda C. Graef. Ancient Christian Writers, vol. 18. Westminster, MD: Newman, 1954.

* * * * *

Meredith, Anthony. *Gregory of Nyssa.* New York: Routledge, 1999.

Von Balthasar, Hans Urs. *Presence and Thought: Essay on the Religious Philosophy of Gregory of Nyssa.* Trans. Mark Sebanc. San Francisco: Ignatius, 1995.

Jerome

Kelly, J. N. D. *Jerome: His Life, Writings and Controversies.* New York: Harper & Row, 1975.

Syriac Monasticism

Brock, Sebastian. *The Syriac Fathers on Prayer and the Spiritual Life.* CS 101. Kalamazoo, MI: Cistercian Publications, 1987.

Vööbus, A. *A History of Asceticism in the Syrian Orient.* 3 vols. CSCO 184, 197, 500. Louvain: Secrétariat du Corpus SCO, 1958, 1960, 1988.

Historia Monachorum in Egypto

The Lives of the Desert Fathers. Trans. Norman Russell. Introduction by Benedicta Ward. CS 34. Kalamazoo, MI: Cistercian Publications, 1981.

Palladius

The Lausiac History. Trans. Robert Meyer. Ancient Christian Writers, vol. 34. Westminster, MD: Newman, 1965.

The Dialogue on St. John Chrysostom. Trans. Robert Meyer. Ancient Christian Writers, vol. 45. New York: Newman, 1985.

Pseudo-Macarius

The Fifty Spiritual Homilies and the Great Letter. Trans. George A. Maloney, SJ. Classics of Western Spirituality. New York: Paulist, 1992.

* * * * *

Stewart, Columba. *Working the Earth of the Heart: The Messalian Controversy in History, Texts and Language to AD 431.* Oxford: Clarendon Press, 1991.

Egyptian Monasticism

Ward, Benedicta, trans. *The Desert Fathers: Sayings of the Early Christian Monks.* (Translation of *Verba Seniorum,* Book V.) New York: Penguin, 2003.

———, trans. *The Wisdom of the Desert Fathers: Apophthegmata Patrum from the Anonymous Series.* Fairacres, Oxford: SLG Press, 1975.

———, trans. *The Sayings of the Desert Fathers: The Alphabetical Collection.* CS 59. Kalamazoo, MI: Cistercian Publications, 1975.

* * * * *

Burton-Christie, Douglas. *The Word in the Desert: Scripture and the Quest for Holiness in Early Christian Monasticism.* New York: Oxford University Press, 1993.

Chitty, Derwas. *The Desert a City: An Introduction to the Study of Egyptian and Palestinian Monasticism under the Christian Empire.* Oxford: Blackwell, 1966.

Harmless, William, SJ. *Desert Christians: An Introduction to the Literature of Early Monasticism.* New York: Oxford University Press, 2004.

Evagrius Ponticus

The Praktikos; Chapters on Prayer. Trans. John Eudes Bamberger. CS 4. Spencer, MA: Cistercian Publications, 1970.

Ad Monachos. Trans. Jeremy Driscoll. Ancient Christian Writers, vol. 59. New York: Paulist Press, 2003.

* * * * *

Driscoll, Jeremy. *The "Ad Monachos" of Evagrius Ponticus: Its Structure and a Select Commentary.* Studia Anselmiana, 104. Rome: Pontificio Ateneo S. Anselmo, 1991.

———. *The Mind's Long Journey to the Holy Trinity: The* Ad Monachos *of Evagrius Ponticus.* Collegeville, MN: Liturgical Press, 1993.

Cassian

The Conferences. Trans. Boniface Ramsey. Ancient Christian Writers, vol. 57. New York: Paulist, 1997.

Conferences. Trans. Colm Luibheid. Classics of Western Spirituality. New York: Paulist, 1985 (*Conferences* 1–3, 9–11, 14–15, 18).

The Institutes. Trans. Boniface Ramsey. Ancient Christian Writers, vol. 58. New York: Paulist, 2000.

The Monastic Institutes. Trans. Jerome Bertram. London: St. Austin Press, 1999.

* * * * *

Chadwick, Owen. *John Cassian: A Study in Primitive Monasticism*. Cambridge: Cambridge University Press, 1950; 2nd ed. 1968.

Funk, Mary Margaret. *Thoughts Matter: The Practice of the Spiritual Life*. New York: Continuum, 1997.

Rousseau, Philip. *Ascetics, Authority, and the Church in the Age of Jerome and Cassian*. Oxford: Oxford University Press, 1978.

Stewart, Columba. *Cassian the Monk*. New York: Oxford University Press, 1998.

ACKNOWLEDGEMENTS

Cistercian Publications gratefully acknowledges the inclusion of brief quotations from the following works:

The Fathers of the Church series.
The Apostolic Fathers, Fathers of the Church, 1. 1947.
St Basil: Ascetical Works. Fathers of the Church, 9. 1950.
Clement of Alexandria. Christ the Educator. Fathers of the Church, 12. 1954.
Early Christian Biographies, Fathers of the Church, 15. 1952.

The Rule of St Benedict in Latin and English. Translated Justin McCann. Burns and Oates, 1952.

Owen Chadwick, *John Cassian. A Study in Primitive Monasticism.* Cambridge University Press, 1950.

The Sources of Catholic Dogma. Translated Roy Deferrari. Herder, 1957.

Western Asceticism, Library of Christian Classics, 12. Westminster-John Knox Press; SCM Press, 1958.

The Merton Legacy Trust
Thomas Merton, *The Asian Journal.* New Directions, 1973.
Thomas Merton, *Contemplation in a World of Action.* Doubleday, 1971.
Thomas Merton, *The Hidden Ground of Love: Letters on Religious Experience and Social Concerns.* Farrar, Straus, Giroux, 1985.
Thomas Merton, *The Monastic Journey.* Sheed, Andrews McMeel, 1977.

Thomas Merton, *The School of Charity.* Farrar, Straus, Giroux, 1990.

Thomas Merton, *The Waters of Siloe.* Harcourt, Brace, 1949.

Thomas Merton, *The Wisdom of the Desert.* New Directions, 1960.

Thomas Merton, *Zen and the Birds of Appetite.* New Directions, 1968.

Pierre Pourrat, *Christian Spirituality,* 1. Translated W. H. Mitchell and S. P. Jacques. Newman Press, 1953.

Hans von Campenhausen, *The Fathers of the Greek Church.* Translated Stanley Godman. Pantheon Books, 1959.

Anne Fremantle, ed., *A Treasury of Early Christianity.* Viking Press, 1953.

INDEX

abandonment: 255

abbot: 50, 201

Abraham, Abbot: 116, 132–33

Accioly, Inácio, OSB: xvii

acedia: xxxix, 36, 116, 140, 183–90

Achab (Ahab), King: 223, 244

active life: 26, 99, 100, 114, 188, 207, 210–12

activism: 211, 235, 237–38

Adulius, St.: 62

Aelred of Rievaulx, St.: ix

agape: 257

Ahern, Barnabas, CP: xvii–xviii

Alaric the Goth: 136

Alcibiades of Lyons, St.: 17

Alexandria: 16, 18, 20, 23–24, 37, 45, 51, 60, 65, 133–34, 217

Alonius, Abbot: 79

Ambrose, St.: 16, 245

amerimnia: 80

Ammonas, Abbot: 79

Ammonius Saccas: 24

anachoresis: 79–80, 203, 222

Ananias and Sapphira: 118, 170, 173

Ananias of Damascus: 225

anastasis: 30

anchorites: 39, 45, 109, 117

angelic life: 15, 55, 245

angelism: 96, 188

anger: xliv, 36, 38, 91, 113, 115, 140, 149, 160, 163, 166, 168,

173–75, 177–78, 180, 183, 208, 234, 246, 254, 258–59

Anthony the Great, St.: ix, xxvi–xxviii, xxx–xxxi, xxxv–xxxvi, xxxix, 7, 31–39, 49, 60, 62, 74, 77, 80, 108, 118, 125–26, 157, 183, 222, 251–52

anthropology: 56

anthropomorphism: 133, 174, 231–32

Antiochus of Saint Sabas: 184

apatheia: 18–19, 22, 34, 66, 82, 85, 93–94, 207

Aphraat, St.: 69

apocatastasis: 24, 132

Apollinarism: 54–55

Apollo, Abbot: 225

apophaticism: 55, 57–58, 95–96

apostles, as models: 171–72

Archebius, Abbot: 162

Arianism: 45, 51–52, 54

Arles: 137–38

Arsenius, Abbot: 77, 125–26

ascetes: 13, 15, 29–32, 37, 157

asceticism: xxiii, xxxi, xxxiv, xxxvii, xl, 8, 17, 19, 24, 26–27, 30, 32–33, 35, 46, 62, 66, 69, 73, 78, 109, 115, 130, 138, 140, 156, 159, 166, 179, 185, 203, 210–11, 235

Assuerus (Ahasuerus): 217

Athanasius, St.: xxvi, xxx, 7, 31, 39, 45–46, 133, 183

Simeon, Abbot: 162
simplicity: lii, 73, 76, 200, 233
sin: 12, 25, 36, 42, 49, 59, 85, 107,
    123, 130–31, 149, 159, 173–75,
    178–79, 182–83, 186–87, 213,
    215, 250–51; original: 84, 103,
    105, 130
singularity: 194
Socrates: 20
solitude: xv–xvi, xxxvi, xliv,
    42–43, 60, 78, 121, 125, 163–64,
    177, 182, 187, 191–93, 204, 208,
    222, 234, 237
Solomon, King: 175
sorrow, spiritual: 182
Sortais, Dom Gabriel, ocso:
    xv–xvi
soul, goodness of: 35
Sozomen: 31
spiritual direction: xxviii, xl, 70,
    75–76, 189
spiritual father: 148, 150–51, 153,
    155–57, 197, 224–25
spiritual senses: 29, 188–89, 214
Staats, Reinhart: 82–83
stability: 58, 80, 112, 125, 132; of
    mind: 219
Stephen, St.: 33
Stewart, Columba, osb: 81, 83–87,
    136
Stoicism: 49, 258
Strothmann, Werner: 81
stylites: xxix, 69–70
suffering: 132
Sulpicius Severus: 65, 67, 73,
    137–38
superiors: 119–20, 142, 201
supplication: 92–93, 239–40
Susanna: 247
Suzuki, D. T.: xi, xxxv, 235
Symeon Stylites, St.: 69–70

Symeon the New Theologian, St.:
    85
Symeon the Younger, St.: 70
Symons, Thomas, osb: 254
Syncleticus: 172
synergy: 35

Tabenna: xl, 40, 121, 145, 153–56
tears, gift of: xxxv, 250–51
temptations: 32–33, 60, 91,
    131–32, 155, 159, 198, 203, 226,
    228, 247, 254
Teresa of Avila, St.: 57, 68, 248
Tertullian: 11, 13, 17, 20, 244
thanksgiving: 239–41
Thennesys: 109
Theodore, Abbot: xxxiv, 132, 162,
    203
Theodore of Lérins: 138
Theodore Studite, St.: 40
Theodoret of Cyrrhus: 69, 84
Theodosius I, Emperor: 52
Theodosius II, Emperor: 72, 126
theologia: 95–96
Theonas, Abbot: 128–31
Theophilus of Alexandria, Bp.:
    133–34
Theophilus of Antioch, Patriarch:
    136
theoria: 27, 57, 115, 130, 211, 242
theoria physike: xxxi, 94–95, 215, 241
Thesleff, Holger: 206
Thibodeau, Harold, ocso: xviii,
    xxv, xlix, lxv
Thomas Aquinas, St.: xxxv, 80,
    100–102, 184, 186, 210, 220, 243
Thomas Merton Center: xxiv, liv,
    lvii, lxv–lxvi
Timothy of Constantinople: 84
Tobin, Mary Luke, sl: xlviii
Tomlins, David, ocso: xxv

CISTERCIAN PUBLICATIONS
Texts and Studies in the Monastic Tradition

TEXTS IN ENGLISH TRANSLATION

THE CISTERCIAN MONASTIC TRADITION

Aelred of Rievaulx

- Dialogue on the Soul
- The Historical Works
- Liturgical Sermons, I
- The Lives of the Northern Saints
- Spiritual Friendship
- Treatises I: Jesus at the Age of Twelve; Rule for a Recluse; Pastoral Prayer
- Walter Daniel: The Life of Aelred of Rievaulx

Bernard of Clairvaux

- Apologia to Abbot William (Cistercians and Cluniacs)
- Five Books on Consideration: Advice to a Pope
- Homilies in Praise of the Blessed Virgin Mary
- In Praise of the New Knighthood
- Letters
- Life and Death of Saint Malachy the Irishman
- On Baptism and the Office of Bishops
- On Grace and Free Choice
- On Loving God
- Parables and Sentences
- Sermons for the Summer Season
- Sermons on Conversion
- Sermons on the Song of Songs, I-IV
- The Steps of Humility and Pride

Gertude the Great of Helfta

- Spiritual Exercises
- The Herald of God's Loving-Kindness, Books 1 and 2
- The Herald of God's Loving-Kindness, Book 3

William of Saint Thierry

- The Enigma of Faith
- Exposition on the Epistle to the Romans
- Exposition on the Song of Songs
- The Golden Epistle
- The Mirror of Faith
- The Nature and Dignity of Love
- On Contemplating God, Prayer, Meditations

Gilbert of Hoyland

- Sermons on the Song of Songs, I-III
- Treatises, Sermons, and Epistles

John of Ford

- Sermons on the Final Verses of the Song of Songs, I-VII

Other Cistercian Writers

- Adam of Perseigne, Letters, I
- Alan of Lille: The Art of Preaching
- Amadeus of Lausanne: Homilies in Praise of Blessed Mary
- Baldwin of Ford: Commendation of Faith
- Geoffrey of Auxerre: On the Apocalypse
- Guerric of Igny: Liturgical Sermones, I-II
- Helinand of Froidmont: Verses on Death
- Idung of Prüfening: Cistercians and Cluniacs. The Case of Cîteaux
- In The School of Love. An Anthology of Early Cistercian Texts
- Isaac of Stella: Sermons on the Christian Year, I-[II]
- The Letters of Armand-Jean de Rancé, Abbot of la Trappe
- The Life of Beatrice of Nazareth
- Mary Most Holy: Meditating with the Early Cistercians
- Ogier of Locedio: Homilies [on Mary and the Last Supper]
- Serlo of Wilton & Serlo of Savigny: Seven Unpublished Works (Latin-English)
- Sky-blue the Sapphire, Crimson the Rose: The Spirituality of John of Ford
- Stephen of Lexington: Letters from Ireland
- Stephen of Sawley: Treatises
- Three Treatises on Man: A Cistercian Anthropology / Bernard McGinn

EARLY AND EASTERN MONASTICISM

- Besa: The Life of Shenoute of Atripe
- Cyril of Scythopolis: The Lives of the Monks of Palestine
- Dorotheos of Gaza: Discourses and Sayings
- Evagrius Ponticus: Praktikos and Chapters on Prayer
- Handmaids of the Lord: Lives of Holy Women in Late Antiquity and the Early Middle Ages / Joan Petersen
- Harlots of the Desert. A Study of Repentance / Benedicta Ward
- Isaiah of Scete: Ascetic Discourses

- John Moschos: The Spiritual Meadow
- The Life of Antony (translated from Coptic and Greek)
- The Lives of the Desert Fathers. The *Historia monachorum in Aegypto*
- The Spiritually Beneficial Tales of Paul, Bishop of Monembasia
- Symeon the New Theologian: The Practical and Theological Chapters, and The Three Theological Discourses
- Theodoret of Cyrrhus: A History of the Monks of Syria
- Stewards of the Poor. [Three biographies from fifth-century Edessa]
- The Syriac Book of Steps *[Liber graduum]*
- The Syriac Fathers on Prayer and the Spiritual Life / Sebastian Brock

LATIN MONASTICISM

- Achard of Saint Victor: Works
- Anselm of Canterbury: Letters, I–III
- Bede the Venerable: Commentary on the Acts of the Apostles
- Bede the Venerable: Commentary on the Seven Catholic Epistles
- Bede the Venerable: Homilies on the Gospels, I–II
- Bede the Venerable: Excerpts from the Works of Saint Augustine on the Letters of the Blessed Apostle Paul
- The Celtic Monk [An Anthology]
- Gregory the Great: Forty Gospel Homilies
- Guigo II: The Ladder of Monks and Twelve Meditations / Colledge, Walsh edd.
- Halfway to Heaven
- The Life of the Jura Fathers
- The Maxims of Stephen of Muret
- Peter of Celle: Selected Works
- The Letters of Armand-Jean de Rancé, I–II
- The Rule of the Master
- The Rule of Saint Augustine
- Saint Mary of Egypt. Three Medieval Lives in Verse

STUDIES IN MONASTICISM / CISTERCIAN STUDIES

Cistercian Studies and Reflections

- Aelred of Rievaulx. A Study / Aelred Squire
- Athirst for God. Spiritual Desire in Bernard of Clairvaux's Sermons on the Song of Songs / Michael Casey
- Beatrice of Nazareth in her Context, I–II: Towards Unification with God / Roger DeGanck
- Bernard of Clairvaux. Man. Monk. Mystic / Michael Casey
- The Cistercian Way / André Louf
- Dom Gabriel Sortais. An Amazing Abbot in Turbulent Times / Guy Oury
- The Finances of the Cistercian Order in the Fourteenth Century / Peter King
- Fountains Abbey and Its Benefactors / Joan Wardrop
- A Gathering of Friends. Learning and Spirituality in John of Ford
- Hidden Springs: Cistercian Monastic Women, 2 volumes
- Image of Likeness. The Augustinian Spirituality of William of St Thierry / D. N. Bell
- Index of Authors and Works in Cistercian Libraries in Great Britain / D. N. Bell

- Index of Cistercian Authors and Works in Medieval Library catalogues in Great Britain / D. N. Bell
- The Mystical Theology of Saint Bernard / Etienne Gilson
- The New Monastery. Texts and Studies on the Earliest Cistercians
- Monastic Odyssey [Cistercian Nuns & the French Revolution]
- Nicolas Cotheret's Annals of Cîteaux / Louis J. Lekai
- Pater Bernhardus. Martin Luther and Bernard of Clairvaux / Franz Posset
- Rancé and the Trappist Legacy / A. J. Krailsheimer
- A Second Look at Saint Bernard / Jean Leclercq
- The Spiritual Teachings of St Bernard of Clairvaux / John R. Sommerfeldt
- Studies in Medieval Cistercian History
- Three Founders of Citeaux / Jean-Baptiste Van Damme
- Understanding Rancé. Spirituality of the Abbot of La Trappe in Context / D. N. Bell
- William, Abbot of Saint Thierry
- Women and Saint Bernard of Clairvaux / Jean Leclercq

Cistercian Art, Architecture, and Music

- Cistercian Abbeys of Britain [illustrated]
- Cistercian Europe / Terryl N. Kinder
- Cistercians in Medieval Art / James France
- SS. Vincenzo e Anastasio at Tre Fontane Near Rome / J. Barclay Lloyd
- Studies in Medieval Art and Architecture, II–VI / Meredith P. Lillich, ed.
- Treasures Old and New. Nine Centuries on Cistercian Music [CD, cassette]
- Cistercian Chants for the Feast of the Visitation [CD]

Monastic Heritage

- Community and Abbot in the Rule of St Benedict, I–II / Adalbert de Vogüé
- Distant Echoes: Medieval Religious Women, I / Shank, Nichols, edd.
- The Freedom of Obedience / A Carthusian
- Halfway to Heaven [The Carthusian Tradition] / Robin Lockhart
- The Hermit Monks of Grandmont / Carole A. Hutchison
- A Life Pleasing to God: Saint Basil's Monastic Rules / Augustine Holmes
- Manjava Skete [Ruthenian tradition] / Sophia Seynk
- Monastic Practices / Charles Cummings
- Peace Weavers. Medieval Religious Women, II / Shank, Nichols, edd.
- Reading Saint Benedict / Adalbert de Vogüé
- The Rule of St Benedict. A Doctrinal and Spiritual Commentary / Adalbert de Vogüé
- Stones Laid Before the Lord [Monastic Architecture] / Anselme Dimier
- What Nuns Read [Libraries of Medieval English Nunneries] / D. N. Bell

Monastic Liturgy

- From Advent to Pentecost / A Carthusian
- The Hymn Collection from the Abbey of the Paraclete, 2 volumes
- The Molesme Summer Season Breviary, 4 volumes
- The Old French Ordinary and Breviary of the Abbey of the Paraclete, 5 volumes
- The Paraclete Statutes: *Institutiones nostrae*
- The Twelfth Century Cistercian Hymnal, 2 volumes
- The Twelfth Century Cistercian Psalter [NYP]
- Two Early Cistercian *Libelli Missarum*

MODERN MONASTICISM

Thomas Merton

- Cassian and the Fathers: Initiation into the Monastic Tradition
- The Climate of Monastic Prayer
- The Legacy of Thomas Merton
- The Message of Thomas Merton
- The Monastic Journey of Thomas Merton
- Thomas Merton Monk
- Thomas Merton on Saint Bernard
- Thomas Merton: Prophet of Renewal / John Eudes Bamberger
- Toward An Integrated Humanity [Essays on Thomas Merton]

Contemporary Monastics

- Centered on Christ. A Guide to Monastic Profession / Augustine Roberts
- Inside the Psalms. Reflections for Novices / Maureen McCabe
- Passing from Self to God. A Cistercian Retreat / Robert Thomas
- Pathway of Peace. Cistercian Wisdom according to Saint Bernard / Charles Dumont
- Poor Therefore Rich / A Carthusian
- The Way of Silent Love / A Carthusian

CHRISTIAN SPIRITUALITY PAST AND PRESENT

Past

- A Cloud of Witnesses. The Development of Christian Doctrine [to 500] / D. N. Bell
- Eros and Allegory: Medieval Exegesis of the Song of Songs / Denys Turner
- High King of Heaven. Aspects of Early English Spirituality / Benedicta Ward
- In the Unity of the Holy Spirit. Conference on the Rule of Benedict
- The Life of St Mary Magdalene and of Her Sister St Martha [Magdalene legend]
- The Luminous Eye. The Spiritual World Vision of St Ephrem / Sebastian Brock
- Many Mansions. Medieval Theological Development East and West / D. N. Bell
- The Name of Jesus / Irénée Hausherr
- Penthos. The Doctrine of Compunction in the Christian East / Irénée Hausherr

CISTERCIAN PUBLICATIONS Titles Listing

EDITORIAL OFFICES

Cistercian Publications • WMU Station
1903 West Michigan Avenue
Kalamazoo, MI 49008-5415   USA
tel 269 387 8920   fax 269 387 8390
e-mail cistpub@wmich.edu

CUSTOMER SERVICE—NORTH AMERICA: USA AND CANADA

Cistercian Publications at Liturgical Press
Saint John's Abbey
Collegeville, MN 56321-7500 USA
tel 800 436 8431   fax 320 363 3299
e-mail sales@litpress.org

CUSTOMER SERVICE—EUROPE: UK, IRELAND, AND EUROPE

Cistercian Publications at Columba Book Service
55A Spruce Avenue
Stillorgan Industrial Park
Blackrock, Co. Dublin, Ireland
tel 353 1 294 2560   fax 353 1 294 2564
e-mail sales@columba.ie

WEBSITE

www.cistercianpublications.org

Cistercian Publications is a non-profit corporation.